D0743879

THERAPIST STORIES OF INSPIRATION, PASSION, AND RENEWAL

"*Therapist Stories of Inspiration, Passion and Renewal: What's Love Got To Do With It?* is a treasure trove of wisdom and experience. Each chapter is a gem, written by some of the century's leading clinicians. Treat yourself. You and your clients will be grateful."

—Scott D. Miller, Ph.D., Director of the International Center
for Excellence, co-author of *The Heroic Client*
and co-editor of *The Heart and Soul of Change*

"A wonderful book filled with charm, wisdom, and inspiration."

—Bill O'Hanlon, author of *The Change Your Life Book* and
Do One Thing Different and featured guest on *Oprah*

Why do you practice psychotherapy? In this exciting volume, some of the field's leading therapists tell true stories which evoke the pleasures, joys, and satisfactions that inspire passion for therapeutic work. Rather than focusing on the stresses and strains of being a clinician, these dramatic, poignant, wise, sometimes humorous and always soulful stories will help you gain (or regain) hope and excitement, and ultimately inspire a recommitment to a profession that, at its heart and soul, is about helping people.

Michael F. Hoyt, Ph.D. (Yale '76) is a senior staff psychologist at the Kaiser Permanente Medical Center in San Rafael, California. He is an expert clinician, an internationally respected teacher and lecturer, a well-known author and editor, and a recipient of the prestigious APF Cummings Psyche Prize for lifetime contributions to the primary role of psychologists in organized healthcare.

ALSO BY MICHAEL F. HOYT

Author:

Brief Therapy and Managed Care: Readings for Contemporary Practice (1995)

Some Stories Are Better than Others: Doing What Works in Brief Therapy and Managed Care (2000)

The Present is a Gift: Mo' Better Stories from the World of Brief Therapy (2004)

Brief Psychotherapies: Principles and Practices (2009)

Interviewer:

Interviews with Brief Therapy Experts (2001)

Editor:

The First Session in Brief Therapy (1992) (with Simon Budman and Steven Friedman)
Constructive Therapies, Volume One (1994)
Constructive Therapies, Volume Two (1996)
The Handbook of Constructive Therapies (1998)

THERAPIST STORIES OF INSPIRATION, PASSION, AND RENEWAL

What's Love Got To Do With It?

Edited by Michael F. Hoyt

Some reading for the sabbatical.

Happy Birthday!

David & Jeanie

Routledge
Taylor & Francis Group

NEW YORK AND LONDON

First published 2013
by Routledge
711 Third Avenue, New York, NY 10017

Simultaneously published in the UK
by Routledge
27 Church Road, Hove, East Sussex BN3 2FA

Routledge is an imprint of the Taylor & Francis Group, an informa business

© 2013 Taylor & Francis

The right of Michael F. Hoyt to be identified as the author of the editorial material, and of the authors for their individual chapters, has been asserted in accordance with sections 77 and 78 of the Copyright, Designs and Patents Act 1988.

All rights reserved. No part of this book may be reprinted or reproduced or utilised in any form or by any electronic, mechanical, or other means, now known or hereafter invented, including photocopying and recording, or in any information storage or retrieval system, without permission in writing from the publishers.

Trademark notice: Product or corporate names may be trademarks or registered trademarks, and are used only for identification and explanation without intent to infringe.

Library of Congress Cataloging in Publication Data
Therapist stories of inspiration, passion, and renewal : what's love got to do with it? / edited by Michael F. Hoyt.
    p. cm.
    Includes bibliographical references and index.
    ISBN 978-0-415-50083-8 (hardback : alk. paper) — ISBN 978-0-415-50084-5 (pbk. : alk. paper)
    1. Psychotherapy—Miscellanea. 2. Counseling. 3. Psychotherapist and patient. I. Hoyt, Michael F.

    RC480.5.T5194 2012
    616.89'14—dc23

    2012008351

ISBN: 978-0-415-50083-8 (hbk)
ISBN: 978-0-415-50084-5 (pbk)
ISBN: 978-0-203-10247-3 (ebk)

Typeset in Bembo and Stone Sans
by EvS Communication Networx, Inc.

Namaste

No one wants to die. Even people who want to go to heaven don't want to die to get there. And yet death is the destination we all share. No one has ever escaped it. And that is as it should be, because death is very likely the single best invention of life. It's life's change agent; it clears out the old to make way for the new. Right now, the new is you. But someday, not so long from now, you will gradually become the old and be cleared away. Sorry to be so dramatic, but it's quite true. Your time is limited, so don't waste it living someone else's life. Don't be trapped by dogma, which is living with the results of other people's thinking. Don't let the noise of others' opinions drown out your own inner voice, heart and intuition. They somehow already know what you truly want to become.

—Steve Jobs (2005), Stanford University Commencement Address

My benefactor's question has meaning now. Does this path have a heart? If it does, the path is good; if it doesn't, it is of no use.

—Carlos Castaneda (1968), *The Teachings of Don Juan:*
A Yaqui Way of Knowledge

We must try to contribute joy to the world. I didn't always know this and am happy I lived long enough to find it out.

—Roger Ebert (2011), *Life Itself: A Memoir*

To live now as we think human beings should live, in defiance of all that is bad around us, is itself a marvelous victory.

—Howard Zinn (2002), *You Can't Be Neutral on a Moving Train:*
A Personal History of Our Time

No matter when I died there would be places left to visit and beauty still to enjoy. I cannot imagine a better life than I have had. Many thanks and much love to all of you.

—Mary Goulding (December 2009), farewell/deathbed letter

Right from the moment of our birth, we are under the care and kindness of our parents, and then later on in our life when we are oppressed by sickness and become old, we are again dependent on the kindness of others. Since at the beginning and end of our lives we are so dependent on others' kindness, how can it be in the middle that we would neglect kindness toward others?

—The Dalai Lama (quoted in *The Sun*, January 2012)

I think here especially of the teeming number of therapists whose practices are nourished by the discourse of spirit, love, and God, and yet who are unable to gain legitimacy in speaking of these matters. These therapists represent rich and significant traditions within the culture, and if constructive therapies do indeed emphasize the value of co-construction, then room must be made for constructive dialogue.

—Kenneth J. Gergen (1998), Foreword, *The Handbook of Constructive Therapies*

CONTENTS

FOREWORD

Stephen G. Gilligan

At every moment a new species arises in the chest —
Now a demon, now an angel, now a wild animal.

There are also those in this amazing jungle
who can absorb you into their own surrender.
If you have to stalk and steal something,
steal from them.

— Rumi, "A Goat Kneels"

I took my first Psychology course in the early '70s, while a student at UC Santa Cruz. As I recall, there were five assigned books for the course: Freud's *Interpretation of Dreams*, Carl Roger's *On Becoming a Person*, Abraham Maslow's *Toward a Psychology of Being*, Joseph Campbell's *Hero with a Thousand Faces*, and Alan Watt's *The Book: On the Taboo Against Knowing Who You Are*. Each book was like fireworks on Independence Day, bursting open places within me that I didn't know existed. The ideas were inspiring, astonishing, resonant, and fascinating. They spoke to human life in terms of its depth, dignity, and potentials. I committed to a Psychology major and never looked back, enjoying the unfolding of an amazing professional journey over the past 35 years.

The light of this field has dimmed noticeably in recent years. Psychotherapy has become all too industrialized, medicalized, dehumanized, and limiting. Human beings are reduced to pathologized categories of biochemical imbalances that need to be drugged by expensive psychiatric medications. Human connection, whether in the therapeutic relationship or in a person's social fields, is paid lip service if not ignored completely, despite clear evidence that the therapeutic relationship is the most significant factor in therapy outcomes (Duncan,

Miller, Wampold, & Hubble, 2009). This fundamentalistic movement proceeds with scanty evidence supporting its core premises and long-term outcome claims (see Kirsch, 2010; Whitaker, 2010). Is it any wonder that therapists have lost connections to their roots as healers?

Therapist Stories of Inspiration, Passion, and Renewal: What's Love Got To Do With It? is an exceptional call to return to our humanistic roots, where therapists see clients as having strengths, resources, and the infinite capacity to change their lives. Just as important, the writers share intimate stories of their own struggles and development as therapists in ways that invite readers to allow themselves the same learning journeys. As I read each chapter, I felt like that young university student inspired by a beautiful array of creative thinking and acting. Simultaneously, I could feel the slightly discouraged older therapist in me cheering and happily resonating to the highest therapist values and practices touched upon in the book. Much credit goes to Michael Hoyt, who came up with the idea and then gathered some of the best therapists of our day to speak to it.

One of the strengths of the book is how it deeply gives primary focus to "life beyond the problem." Rather than reducing people to their perceived pathologies, the book contributors emphasize therapy as a relationship in which therapists open to their clients and appreciate their unique resources and challenges before clinically acting. In such a view, presenting problems and symptoms are of course relevant, but no more so than a person's resources and capacities to grow and change (see Gilligan, 1997).

This profoundly positive orientation avoids what Joseph Chilton Pearce (1981) has called "the error correction error." Pearce points out that in any significant learning challenge there is a primary goal and then many subgoals by which to realize it. For example, each baby carries an innate biological injunction to "learn to walk." As cursory observation reveals, this primary learning is realized via sub-processes such as *stand, balance, imbalance*, and the old family favorite, *fall*. When a toddler inevitably falls, attention doesn't stay long on the fall, but rather incorporates that feedback into the next round of learning to walk. Comes a time, Pearce says, that we fall and develop "neuromuscular lock" onto the "error." This reorganizes the system from the primary positive orientation—whether it be *walk*, or *live*, or *create*, or *grow*—to a secondary "negative" process, resulting in what Pearce poetically calls the "fall from grace."

Psychotherapy can either affirm this problem-defined identity or encourage a solution-focused self, capable of both transforming problems and creating a life "beyond problems." The chapters in this book present multiple ways to skillfully accomplish the latter. It includes the blood, sweat, and tears of some of the best therapeutic healers in contemporary psychotherapy. I hope that you enjoy and benefit from it as much as I have.

References

Duncan, B. L., Miller, S. D., Wampold, B. E., & Hubble, M. A. (Eds.). (2009). *The Heart and Soul of Change: Delivering "What Works" (2nd ed.).* Washington, D.C.: APA Press.

Gilligan, S. G. (1997). *The Courage to Love: Principles and Practices of Self Relations Psychotherapy.* New York: Norton.

Kirsch, I. (2010). *The Emperor's New Drugs: Exploding the Antidepressant Myth.* New York: Basic Books.

Pearce, J. C. (1981). *The Bond of Power.* New York: Dutton.

Whitaker, R. (2010). *Anatomy of an Epidemic: Magic Bullets, Psychiatric Drugs, and the Astonishing Rise of Mental Illness in America.* New York: Broadway/Random House.

ACKNOWLEDGMENTS

First of all, a gigantic *THANK YOU* to all of the chapter authors! Rubin, Art, Laura, Jon, Lillian, Nick, Carol, John, Joe, Eric, Ken, Tobey, Chris, Sue, Jack, Murray, Jeffrey, Judy, Don, Bob, Ram Dass, Shakti, Shellie, Teresa, Karin, Dan, Terry, and Michael: WOW! BIG MAHALO!!

And to Stephen Gilligan, another big *THANK YOU* for the excellent Foreword.

Thank you also to Routledge Publishers (Taylor & Francis Group). George Zimmar, Editor-in-Chief, thank you; Marta Moldvai, Senior Editorial Assistant, thank you; Lynn Goeller, Project Manager at EvS Communications, thank you; and thank you to all the people—the paper makers and printers and designers and office workers and delivery drivers and bookstore people—whose labor made the book that you, dear reader, are holding.

I also appreciate the authors and publishers that granted permission for use of copyrighted material.

Additional thanks to the American Psychological Foundation and the Nicholas and Dorothy Cummings Foundation for the generosity of the APF Cummings Psyche Prize.

As always, kudos to the Kaiser/San Rafael Medical Library and the Mill Valley Public Library.

During the production of this book, the psychotherapy world lost three more giants: Albert Ellis, Dick Fisch and James Hillman. I knew them, and others that I have known—Insoo Kim Berg, Steve de Shazer, Erik Erikson, Bob and Mary Goulding, Jay Haley, Paul Watzlawick, John Weakland, Carl Whitaker, and Michael White, and Lewis Walberg—are also gone. As my friend Moshe Talmon said, "Fear no death. We are going to join a very good group of people!"

Various friends and colleagues have provided help and inspiration in different ways. In addition to those who contributed chapters: Henry Abramovitch, Mauro Amador, Steve Andreas, Carol Shaw Austad, Ellyn Bader, Simon Budman, (the late) Richard Centers, Peter Chinnici, Jack Covington and Karen Solov, Lance Davidson, Yvonne Dolan, (the late) Dennis Farrell, Steven Friedman, Evan Garelle, Mitchell Ginsberg, Richard Greenberg, Rob Guerette, Alan Gurman, Jim Gustafson, Riley Guy, Don Hidalgo, Mardi Horowitz, Judy Hoyt and Bill Schultz, Bob Humphries and Sally Robinson, Michele Levasseur, Shari Kirkland, The Lillard Family, Linda Manzi, Scott Miller, Ali Navarro, Bill O'Hanlon, (the late) Jeffry Ordover, (the late) James Palmer, Clem Papazian, Dan Patterson, Jean Price, Harvey Ratner, Bob Rosenbaum, Harry and Orsolya (and Andrew) Salzberg, Gerson Schreiber and Barbara Kaplan, Rich Simon, Jerome Singer, Tyson Underwood, Norm Weinstein, Stephen Xenakis, Michael Yapko, Jeff Zeig, Phillip Ziegler. My late parents, Bernard and Ruth Hoyt; my grandparents, Ben and Libby Bernstein; and my brother Bill are in there, too. Thanks, y'all!

Some of my client/patients—whose names necessarily will remain anonymous—have also especially stoked my fires. Thank you for your trust, your courage, your creativity, your resilience. I love you all.

To my wife Jennifer and my son Alex—you are my inspiration, passion, and renewal!

ABOUT THE EDITOR AND CONTRIBUTORS

Michael F. Hoyt, Ph.D. (Yale 1976) is a senior staff psychologist at the Kaiser Permanente Medical Center in San Rafael, California. An expert clinician and internationally respected teacher and lecturer, Dr. Hoyt is the author of *Brief Therapy and Managed Care*, *Some Stories are Better than Others*, *Interviews with Brief Therapy Experts*, *The Present is a Gift*, and *Brief Psychotherapies: Principles and Practices*; as well as the editor of several volumes. He is a Woodrow Wilson Fellow and has been honored as a Continuing Education Distinguished Speaker by both the American Psychological Association and the International Association of Marriage and Family Counselors, as a Contributor of Note by the Milton II. Erickson Foundation, and is a recipient of the prestigious APF Cummings Psyche Prize for lifetime contributions to the role of psychologists in organized healthcare. Contact: DrMHoyt@comcast.net.

Contributors

Rubin Battino, M.S. (Mental Health Counseling), **Ph.D.** (Chemistry), is a Licensed Professional Clinical Counselor in Yellow Springs, Ohio, and a Professor Emeritus of Chemistry at Wright State University. He is the author of eight books in the field of psychotherapy, including *Metaphoria: Metaphor and Guided Imagery for Psychotherapy and Healing*, *Expectation: The Very Brief Therapy Book*, *Ericksonian Approaches: A Comprehensive Manual*, *Healing Language*, and *Howie and Ruby: Conversations 2000–2007*. Contact: rubin.battino@wright.edu

Arthur C. Bohart, Ph.D. is Professor Emeritus of Psychology at California State University in Dominguez Hills. He is also affiliated with Saybrook Graduate School and Research Center. His books include *How Clients Make Therapy*

Work: The Process of Active Self-Healing, Empathy Reconsidered: New Directions in Psychotherapy, Constructive and Destructive Behavior, Foundations of Clinical and Counseling Psychology, and *Humanity's Dark Side*. Contact: abohart@csudh.edu

Laura S. Brown, Ph.D. is a clinical and forensic psychologist in independent practice in Seattle, Washington; and the founder and director of the Fremont Community Therapy Project, a low-fee training clinic. Her many books include *Feminist Therapy; Cultural Competence in Trauma Therapy: Beyond the Flashback; Recovered Memories of Abuse: Assessment, Therapy, Forensics; Subversive Dialogues: Theory in Feminist Therapy*; and *Rethinking Mental Health and Disorder: Feminist Perspectives*. Contact: laurabrownphd@gmail.com

Jon Carlson, Psy.D., Ed.D. is Distinguished Professor in the Division of Psychology and Counseling at Governors State University, Illinois; and a psychologist at the Lake Geneva Wellness Clinic, Wisconsin. He was named one of five "Living Legends in Counseling" by the American Counseling Association, and has also received the American Psychological Association Award for Distinguished Career Contributions to Education and Training in Psychology. He is the producer of hundreds of professional therapy training videos. Among his many books are *Adlerian Psychotherapy: Theory and Practice, Culturally Inclusive Empathy Skills, Couples Therapy, Moved by the Spirit, Brief Therapy with Individuals and Couples, Family Therapy Techniques, Their Finest Hour, Time for a Better Marriage*, and *Never Be Lonely Again*. Contact: jcarlson@genevaonline.com

Lillian Comas-Díaz, Ph.D. is a psychologist based in Washington, D.C., where she maintains an active private practice and is affiliated with the Institute for Transcultural Mental Health and the George Washington University of School of Medicine. Her books include *WomanSoul: The Inner Life of Women's Spirituality, Women of Color: Integrating Ethnic and Gender Identities in Psychotherapy, Clinical Guidelines in Cross-Cultural Mental Health, Multicultural Care: A Clinician's Guide to Cultural Competence*, and *Women Psychotherapists: Journeys in Healing*. Contact: lilliancomasdiaz@gmail.com

Nicholas A. Cummings, Ph.D., Sc.D. is Distinguished Professor Emeritus at the University of Nevada, Reno; Distinguished Founding Professor, Nicholas A. Cummings Doctor of Behavioral Health Program, Arizona State University; and President of the Cummings Foundation for Behavioral Health. A recipient of psychology's Gold Medal for lifetime contributions to practice, his many activities include past president of the American Psychological Association, past director of the Mental Research Institute, a founder of the California School of Professional Psychology, founder of American Biodyne (the leading practitioner-directed behavioral healthcare company), and one of the original "Dirty Dozen" who achieved professional status for the field of psychology. His

48 books include *Focused Psychotherapy*, *The Essence of Psychotherapy*, *The Practice of Psychology: The Battle for Professionalism*, *The First Session with Substance Abusers: A Step-by-Step Guide*, *Eleven Blunders that Cripple Psychotherapy in America*, *Surviving the Demise of Solo Practice*, *Behavioral Health in Primary Care*, *The Collected Papers of Nicholas A. Cummings (Volumes 1 and 2)*, and *Understanding the Healthcare Crisis*. Contact: CummFound@aol.com

Carol A. Erickson, M.S.W. is a licensed marriage and family therapist as well as a licensed clinical social worker based in Northern California. The oldest daughter of Milton H. Erickson, M.D., she has taught therapy and hypnosis workshops worldwide. She has also produced (with Thomas Condon) a series of multi-evocation™ audio programs, including *Natural Self Confidence*, *Self Hypnosis*, *Rapid Pain Control*, *Quick Stress Busters*, *Easy Enhanced Learning*, and *Deep Sleep & Sweet Dreams*. Contact: The Erickson Institute, P.O. Box 739, Berkeley, CA 94701.

John H. Frykman, Ph.D., M.Div. is a San Francisco-based marriage and family therapist, founder of the Cypress Institute, an ordained Lutheran minister, and organizer of the Drug Treatment Program at the Haight-Ashbury Free Clinic. His books include *A New Connection: An Approach to Persons Involved in Compulsive Drug Use*, *The New Hassle Handbook: A Guide to Surviving the Teenage Years*, and *Making the Impossible Difficult: Tools for Getting Unstuck*. Contact: JohnFrykman@comcast.net

Elizabeth "Shakti" Gawain, B.A. is a pioneer in the field of personal development. An internationally renowned teacher of consciousness, her books— which include *The Dolphin's Gift*, *Creative Visualization*, *Living in the Light*, *The Path of Transformation*, *Four Levels of Healing*, *Creating True Prosperity*, and *Developing Intuition*—have sold more than 10 million copies and have been translated into more than 30 languages. Contact: P.O. Box 377, Mill Valley, CA 94942.

Stephen G. Gilligan, Ph.D. is a psychologist based in Encinitas, California. He was a major student of Milton Erickson and is a recipient of the rarely given Lifetime Achievement Award from the Milton H. Erickson Foundation for his many contributions. He is the developer of Self-Relations Psychotherapy and known throughout the world for his inspirational teaching. His numerous books include *Therapeutic Trances*; *Brief Therapy: Myths, Methods and Metaphors*; *The Courage to Love*; *The Legacy of Erickson*; *Walking in Two Worlds*; and *The Hero's Journey*. Contact: StGilligan@aol.com

Joseph A. Goldfield, M.S.W. is a licensed clinical social worker based in New York City. Before getting his graduate degree from UC Berkeley, he was a professional travelling actor, musician, and pantomimist. He is the coeditor of

Mental Wellness in Aging: Strengths-Based Approaches as well as the author of several professional articles. Contact: joegoldfieldcswr@aol.com

Eric Greenleaf, Ph.D. directs the Milton H. Erickson Institute of the Bay Area and practices in Albany, California. He teaches hypnotherapy worldwide, studies trace healing in Bali, and wrote *The Problem of Evil: Ancient Dilemmas and Modern Therapy*. Milton Erickson chose Eric to receive the first M.H. Erickson Award of Scientific Excellence for Writing in Hypnosis. Contact: ericgreenleaf@me.com

Kenneth V. Hardy, Ph.D. is Professor of Family Therapy at Drexel University in Philadelphia, Pennsylvania, and Director of the Eikenberg Institute for Relationships in New York City. His books include *Teens Who Hurt: Clinical Interventions for Breaking the Cycle of Violence, Minorities and Family Therapy*, and *Revisioning Family Therapy: Race, Class, and Gender*. Contact: kvh24@drexel.edu

Tobey Hiller, M.A. is a Marriage and Family Therapist based in San Rafael, California. She is also a Certified Psychodramatist and has led groups in hospital and university settings, provided training and consultation in group process and organizational development to various healthcare organizations, and led relationship-enhancement workshops for couples. In addition to her book, *Recreating Partnership: A Solution-Oriented Collaborative Approach to Couples Therapy* (with her husband, Phillip Ziegler), she is the author of the novel *Charlie's Exit* and three volumes of poetry (*Crossings, Certain Weathers,* and *Aqueduct*). Contact: tobey@igc.org

Chris Iveson, B.Sc. is the cofounder of BRIEF (formerly known as the Brief Therapy Practice), the premier group offering solution-focused therapy and training in London. His books include *Whose Life? Community Care for Older People and Their Families; Problem to Solution: Brief Therapy with Individuals and Families; BRIEFER: A Solution-Focused Manual; Brief Coaching: A Solution-Focused Approach;* and *Solution-Focused Brief Therapy: 100 Key Points and Techniques*. Contact: ChrisIveson@brief.org.uk

Susan M. Johnson, Ed.D. is Professor of Clinical Psychology at the University of Ottawa in Canada and Distinguished Professor in the Marital and Family Program at Alliant University in San Diego, California. She is the co-developer of Emotionally Focused Couples Therapy and the Director of the International Center for Excellence in Emotionally Focused Therapy. Her books include *The Practice of Emotionally Focused Couple Therapy, Emotionally Focused Therapy for Couples,* and *Hold Me Tight: Seven Conversations for a Lifetime of Love*. Contact: www.iceeft.com

Jack Kornfield, Ph.D. is an internationally renowned meditation teacher and one of the leaders in introducing Buddhist practice and psychology to the West. He is a cofounder of the Insight Meditation Society in Barre, Massachusetts, and of the Spirit Rock Meditation Center in Woodacre, California. His books include *A Path with Heart*; *After the Ecstasy, the Laundry*; *The Art of Forgiveness, Lovingkindness, and Peace*; and *The Wise Heart: A Guide to the Universal Teachings of Buddhist Psychology*. Contact: www.jackkornfield.org

Murray Korngold, Ph.D. is a San Francisco-based licensed psychologist, acupuncturist, and practitioner of traditional Chinese medicine. The author of *First Draft: A Life to Talk About,* he has also been a labor organizer and political activist, a Hollywood screenwriter and playwright, one of the original LSD researchers in the 1950s, and a founder of the Los Angeles Free Clinic. Contact: MurrayKorngold@comcast.net

Jeffrey A. Kottler, Ph.D. is Professor of Counseling at California State University, Fullerton; and co-founder of the Empower Nepali Girls Foundation. He is the author of over 80 books, including *On Being a Therapist, The Client Who Changed Me, Creative Breakthroughs in Therapy*, and *The Assassin and the Therapist: An Exploration of Truth in Psychotherapy and in Life*. Contact: jkottler@Exchange.Fullerton.edu

Judith Mazza, Ph.D. is a psychologist based in Bethesda, Maryland. She specializes in short-term problem-solving therapy for couples, families, and adult individuals. Known as a "therapist's therapist," she formerly was Clinic Director of the Family Therapy Institute of Washington, D.C., where she taught and supervised for many years. Currently she is on the faculty of the Walter Reed National Military Center where she continues to teach and train therapists. She is an invited presenter at various conferences in the United States and abroad. Contact: jmazza@familytherapy.com

Donald Meichenbaum, Ph.D. is Distinguished Professor Emeritus, University of Waterloo, Ontario, Canada; Research Director of the Melissa Institute for Violence Prevention, Miami; and Distinguished Visiting Professor, University of Miami. He is one of the founders of Cognitive Behavior Therapy, and was identified in an *American Psychologist* survey of North American clinicians as "one of the 10 most influential psychotherapists of the 20th century." His books include *Cognitive Behavior Modification, Facilitating Treatment Adherence: A Practitioner's Guidebook, A Clinical Handbook/Practical Therapist Manual for Assessing and Treating Adults with Post-Traumatic Stress Disorder (PTSD), Treatment of Individuals with Anger-Control Problems and Aggressive Behaviors: A Clinical Handbook*, and most recently, *Roadmap to Resilience*. Contact: dhmeich@aol.com

Robert A. Neimeyer, Ph.D., is Professor of Psychology at the University of Memphis (Tennessee), where he also maintains an active clinical practice. His many books include *Techniques of Grief Therapy*, *Grief and Bereavement in Contemporary Society*, *Constructivism in Psychotherapy*, *Lessons of Loss*, and *Meaning Reconstruction and the Experience of Loss*; as well as two volumes of poetry, *Rainbow in the Stone* and *The Art of Longing*. Contact: neimeyer@memphis.edu

Ram Dass (formerly known as Richard Alpert, Ph.D.) is an American contemporary spiritual teacher. Founder of Seva Foundation, Hanuman Foundation, and the Love Serve Remember Foundation, his many books include *Be Here Now*; *The Only Dance There Is*; *Grist for the Mill*; *Miracle of Love*; *How Can I Help? Stories and Reflections on Service*, *Compassion in Action*; *Still Here: Embracing Aging, Changing and Dying*; *Paths to Love: Living the Bhagavad Gita*; and *Be Love Now*. He is also the subject of the documentary film, *Ram Dass: Fierce Grace*. Contact: www.ramdass.org

Michele Ritterman, Ph.D. is a psychologist based in Berkeley, California. Her books include *Using Hypnosis in Family Therapy*, *Hope Under Siege: Terror and Family Support in Chile*, and *The Tao of a Woman*; her book in progress is *From Trance to Stance*. Recognized as the mother of the integration of hypnosis and family therapy and one of Milton Erickson's leading students, she originated the concept of the symptom as a trance state that is suggested by people and social structures. From this basic concept, she framed therapy as the production of counter-inductions, hypnotic sequences that impact the symptom trance. She has trained thousands of therapists around the globe in her approach to working with couples and families. Contact: mritter732@sbc.global

Teresa Robles, Ph.D. is President of the Board of the Centro Ericksoniano de Mexico in Mexico City. She recently received the Lifetime Achievement Award from the Milton H. Erickson Foundation. Dr. Robles teaches worldwide. Her books (which have been translated into many languages) include *A Concert for Four Hemispheres in Psychotherapy*. Contact: tere@grupocem.edu.mx

Karin Schlanger, M.S. is a Senior Research Fellow at the Mental Research Institute in Palo Alto, California; and is Supervising Associate Professor at the Hospital de la Santa Creu y San Pau in Barcelona, Spain. She also has been Adjunct Clinical Instructor, Psychiatry and Behavioral Sciences, Stanford University; and is the Director of the Grupo Palo Alto in California. A marriage and family therapist, her publications include *Focused Problem Resolution: Selected Papers of the MRI Brief Therapy Center* and *Brief Therapy with Intimidating Cases: Changing the Unchangeable*, as well as many articles and chapters both in English and in Spanish. Contact: kschlanger@igc.org

Dan Short, Ph.D. is a psychologist in private practice in Scottsdale, Arizona. Long affiliated with the Milton H. Erickson Foundation, and a member of the graduate faculty of Argosy University (in Phoenix), his books include *Hope and Resilience: Understanding the Psychotherapeutic Strategies of Milton H. Erickson* and *Transformational Relationships: Deciphering the Social Matrix in Psychotherapy.* Contact: hope@iamdrshort.com

Terry Soo-Hoo, Ph.D. is Professor of Educational Psychology, California State University East Bay, Hayward. In addition to teaching and supervision, he provides culturally sensitive therapy to adults, families, couples, and adolescents. He also conducts training and consultation to organizations and mental health agencies. He has published numerous articles and chapters in the professional literature on topics of multicultural counseling, family therapy, couples therapy and consultation. Contact: terry.soohoo@csueastbay.edu

Michael White, B.S. (deceased) was the cofounder (with David Epston) of the Narrative Therapy approach to psychotherapy. His books include *Narrative Means to Therapeutic Ends*; *Experience, Contradiction, Narrative, and Imagination*; *Re-Authoring Lives: Interviews and Essays*; *Narratives of Therapists' Lives*; and *Reflections on Narrative Practice: Essays and Interviews.* He was affiliated with the Dulwich Centre, Adelaide, Australia.

1

THE JOY OF THERAPY

Editor's Invitation and Preview

Michael F. Hoyt

The book you have in hand, dear reader, is a full-length volume of stories by therapists about the pleasures, joys, and satisfactions that help to inspire and renew the therapists' passion for their work. In essence, we are in the business of going into small rooms with unhappy people and trying to talk them out of it. It can be very fulfilling, but the work is not easy. As Hippocrates (c. 460–377 BCE) advised long ago:

> Life is short, the art long, opportunity fleeting, experience treacherous, judgment difficult. The physician must be ready, not only to do his [*sic*] duty himself, but also to secure the cooperation of the patient, of the attendants, and of externals.

A number of writers (e.g., Baker, 2003; Kottler, 1999; Norcross & Guy, 2007; Skovholt & Trotter-Mathison, 2010; Weiss, 2004) have commented on the stresses and strains of being a psychotherapist, and have provided useful guidebooks to help therapists better manage their self-care. There are also books called *The Joy of Sex*, *The Joy of Music*, *The Joy of Feeling*, *The Joy of Cooking*, and *The Joy of Parenting*—but so far, no *The Joy of Therapy*. (I checked: there is also no *Chicken Soup for the Therapist/Counselor's Soul*.)

A number of authors, of course, have commented on the personal satisfactions they obtain from being therapists. As Dlugos and Friedlander (2001, p. 298) note in their study of passionately committed psychotherapists, "In spite of experiencing the same pressures, demands, and conflicts that confront all psychotherapists, some have managed not only to survive, but also to thrive, experiencing a joy, love, and passion in their work that enhance rather than detract from their passion for other important life commitments." As one of my early mentors, Carl Whitaker (1982), wrote: "I became more and more convinced that psychotherapy was something I did for myself and the patient merely participated [p. 32].... Thus, technique plus personal involvement makes for continuing growth: not technical, not professional, but personal. There is no steady state. One must either grow or shrivel!" (p. 286). (Whitaker's *Midnight Musings of a Family Therapist* [1989] is one of my favorite therapy books.) In another fine book, *The Gift of Therapy*, Irvin Yalom (2002) provides numerous clinical "tips" and in the last chapter ("Cherish the Occupational Privileges," p. 258) he extols the work that therapists do: "Not only does our work provide us the opportunity to transcend ourselves, to evolve and grow, and to be blessed by a clarity of vision into the true and tragic knowledge of the human condition, but we are offered even more. We watch our patients let go of old self-defeating patterns, detach from ancient grievances, develop zest for living, learn to love us, and, through that act, turn lovingly to others. It is a joy to see others open the taps of their own founts of wisdom."

In their book, *The Client Who Changed Me: Stories of Personal Transformation*, Jeffrey Kottler and Jon Carlson (2005) present 23 leading clinicians each telling how an encounter with a client caused the therapist to grow, to become more personal and present, to change their approach, etc. Some of the narratives describe how the therapist was inspired by his or her client, although the overall emphasis is not on how the encounter has served to keep the therapist energized in the face of difficult challenges with other clients. In two other excellent books, Kottler and Carlson (2008, 2009)—both of whom contribute fine chapters of their own to the present volume—report episodes of various master therapists doing masterful therapy. The stories describe highly skilled and creative work, often with especially difficult clients.

Why This Book? And Why Now?

Why have a book of therapist stories of inspiration, passion, and renewal? This book picks up the theme of "better stories" from my earlier book, *Some Stories Are Better than Others* (Hoyt, 2000, pp. 19-22):

> What makes some stories better than others? Ultimately, of course, the answer must come from each individual freely, lest we impose our own values or beliefs. In general terms, stories involve a plot in which characters have experiences and employ imagination to resolve problems over time.... From this perspective, therapy can be understood as the purposeful development of a more functional story; "better" stories are those that bring more of what is desired and less of what is not desired....
>
> Aesthetics, effects, and ethics are all important. We like stories that are well told; that are vivid and eloquent; that involve the generation and resolution of some tension; that see the protagonist(s) emerge successfully, perhaps even triumphantly. A "good" story does more than merely relate "facts"; a "good story" invigorates.

Good stories are well-crafted and involve plots that capture the imagination (Booker, 2004; McKee, 1997). In the present volume the stories are "better" because they are true—not fictional—and because they move the therapist (and hopefully the reader!) as well as the client/patient.[1] An inspiring story would be good to hear almost any time. Lately, however, things have gotten especially tough, both in the larger world of economic downturn and in its impact on the world of psychotherapy practice. As my friends John Sharry, Brendan Madden, and Melissa Darmody (2001, pp. 106–107)[2] at the Brief Therapy Practice in Dublin have written:

> It is one thing to be respectful, optimistic, curious and flexible in a well-resourced agency with clients who are largely at the customer level of motivation. It is quite another thing to maintain a respectful constructive stance in a context where clients are largely at a visitor or complainant level of motivation, in a very under-resourced agency where you feel undervalued and unsupported; or worse still where there are high levels of conflict (either within the agency or outside). In these instances it is easy to become "burnt out" or pessimistic…. If this happens therapists do not have the optimism and energy to take on difficult cases. It is therefore crucial for therapists to take steps to monitor and maintain their own mental health and resourcefulness, to ensure that they stay as customers to their work.

In addition to enjoying editing and writing and looking for my next publishing "project," I also have more personal reasons for wanting to produce this book.

---

1   The terms *client* and *patient* will be used back and forth throughout this volume, following the preference of particular authors. As I have written elsewhere (Hoyt, 1995, 1996, 2009), each term may carry certain implications about the nature of the therapeutic relationship and the very reason for professional contact. *Client* may emphasize the egalitarian and minimize the implication of pathology, whereas *patient* may connote both a medical model (sickness and doctor-patient hierarchy) and the idea of the problem having to do with the alleviation of suffering. What one calls the participants and the process (*therapy? treatment? intervention? facilitation? consultation?*) helps to establish a meaning context (roles, power relations, ideas about how change occurs) and thus influences their work together.

2   In *Narratives of Therapists' Lives*, Michael White (1997a, pp. v-vi) similarly wrote: "I believe that most readers would be familiar with the extent to which experiences of demoralisation, fatigue and exhaustion are commonly expressed in the culture of psychotherapy. Here, I am referring to the experiences not of persons who consult therapists, but of therapists themselves. Many therapists speak openly about their sense of despair, and a considerable number 'drop out,' suffering from what is often called burnout. Yet others all too frequently find themselves struggling with a painful sense of lack of direction in their work, often feeling that, despite their best efforts, they are only marking time, and just managing to keep their head above water while they do so…. Many different explanations are offered for this phenomenon. Some of these refer to the nature of the work itself—that it is demanding and at times quite overwhelming. Others problematise the self of individual workers: they are 'not cut out for it', they have 'unresolved issues', they are 'co-dependent', and so on. Yet other explanations refer

Moving through my fourth decade of fulltime clinical practice, I sometimes feel tired and need my own inspiration. As my wife and I approach our financial "retirement" goals, I find myself challenged by the thought, "I don't really need to work just to make money—so why keep doing what I do?" I want to hear others' answers to help me find (or remember) my own.[3] Additionally, I am aware of issues of "legacy" and the desire to engage in what Erik Erikson (1959) called *generativity*, the healthy later-in-life activity of nurturing younger generations. I also just love good stories and know colleagues that can tell them—especially stories that are now professionally and existentially pertinent to me.

Don't worry—I'm not saying that I'm burned out or "done." I've found inspiration recently watching the wonderful documentary movies *Buck* about the real "Horse Whisperer," who overcame his abusive childhood and uses his sensitivities to work with horses who have people problems; and *Sing Your Song*, about the life and work of the extraordinary entertainer-social activist, Harry Belafonte. I enjoyed Kay Redfield Jamison's (2004) *Exuberance* and loved Keith Richard's (2010) *Life*. Reading Father Gregory Boyle's (2010) *Tattoos on the Heart: The Power of Boundless Compassion* about his work with gangs in East Los Angeles, and Laura Hillenbrand's (2010) *Unbroken: A World War II Story of Survival, Resilience, and Redemption* are also heartening. I get thrills and a rush listening to Billy Joe Shaver (2005) sing "Live Forever" and advise us not to let our children feel forsaken, and Warren Zevon (2003) saying goodbye as he asks us to "Keep Me in Your Heart." My family, friends, dogs and cats, art, and Nature nurture me; my teachers abide (see Hoyt, 2004).[4] Some of my colleagues are helpful, and it is a joy to help patient/clients and see them make improvements and grow. I cherish a painting an artist-patient gave me with the inscription, "With deepest gratitude for all the support of my art and creativity and for saving my life!" (I told her that while I take my salary to the bank, I would take her message and what it meant to my heart.) Recently, another

---

to the institutional structures that provide a context for this work—to the fact that these structures are non-supportive and demoralizing to staff—and to developments in service delivery that are being increasingly dictated by the economics of the 'free' market place, not by what might be in the best interests of persons according to criteria that are important to them."

3   Some years ago a colleague of mine once remarked, "I see what you're doing with your editing, Michael. When you get interested in a topic, you ask a bunch of the experts in the area to each write a chapter for you, kind of a personal tutorial. You put them all together and publish a book." I think she was on to something—and I'll share my experts with you!

4   The great architect Frank Lloyd Wright (1957/1992, p. 396, emphasis in original) wrote: "I guess I use the word *nature*, as I always have, in rather a confusing way because I always put a capital 'N' on the word, and why? Because we write the word God with a capital 'G' don't we? Now *Nature* is all the body of God we are ever going to see! As you study it, instead of looking *at* it, look *into* *Nature*. The reason is the *why* of this or that and by way of such interior *Nature* study, increase your knowledge of what constitutes *truth*. Do this concerning anything and you will soon find that its Nature is the *beauty* of it."

woman who has struggled made a big, positive change. We enjoyed her "victory" in my office. When the session finished, I opened the door. She walked out and turned one way, toward the door to the street; I turned the other, took a few steps around the corner and down the corridor, then pumped my fist and said aloud "Yes!" I looked up and saw one of my colleagues, in her office, her door open, looking at me. She smiled. See what I mean?

I hope the same is true of you and that this book will add to your energy as well as provide ideas about ways to be helpful. "There is a story in this book that can inspire and strengthen you, wherever you may be on your journey" (Lesser, 2005, p. xix). My intention here is to inspire joy, hope, excitement, recommitment, and love. As Kathleen Kemarre Wallace (2009, flycover) has written, "I hope you listen deeply and let these stories in. They ... are for all time, for the old days, to help remember the old people, but also for the future and for young people now."

How This Book Came to Be: Process and Invitation

I first had the idea to be the moderator for a panel on "Therapist Inspiration and Renewal" at the Eleventh International Congress on Ericksonian Approaches to Hypnosis and Psychotherapy, held in Phoenix from December 8-11, 2011. I approached three colleague-friends (John Frykman, Eric Greenleaf, Michele Ritterman)—they all readily agreed to participate as speakers, and the conference organizer (Jeff Zeig) kindly accepted the proposal. (Their chapters, based partially on their panel presentations, are contained herein.) The idea then began to grow in my mind. After some initial communication with George Zimmar, the editor-in-chief at Routledge Publishers (who had published two of my earlier books: Hoyt, 2000, 2001), I sent the following invitation to a number of leading figures in the psychotherapy field (including many who are not particularly affiliated with Ericksonian ideas):

> I am writing to invite you to contribute a chapter to an exciting new book: *THERAPIST STORIES OF INSPIRATION, PASSION, AND RENEWAL: WHAT'S LOVE GOT TO DO WITH IT?*
>
> I would hope that each author, in his or her own words, would discuss the heart and soul of their work, what makes it worth doing, the love and poetics of helping people change, how you renew your hope and energy, etc. Comments about whatever inspires you and keeps you going strong—family, friends, clients/patients, inspiring teachers, spiritual/religious matters, politics and social justice, 'giving back,' etc.—will be relevant. I'm sure that readers will be moved and encouraged by everyone's words.
>
> Personal stories are welcome in which you, in your own way, tell a revealing tale or recount a compelling incident—more 'Chicken Soup' than scholarly exegesis, so to speak. Why do you do this work? The

stories can be dramatic, poignant, humorous, soulful—and touching! Please describe a time in which you were inspired and re-energized in your therapy work, perhaps by something your client/patient said or did, perhaps by some mentor's recalled "words of wisdom," perhaps by something else. How were you moved and rejuvenated? What's love got to do with it? Please include what happened, how you reacted, what sense you make of the experience, how it impacted your work, and what lessons it may have for readers.

As editor, I will write an introductory chapter and a concluding chapter extracting themes and lessons. At a time when many therapists are frustrated by developments in the therapy world (managed care, heavy caseloads and diminished incomes, narrowly defined methodologies replacing broader humanistic conceptions; plus the usual problems of countertransference, burn out, and possible vicarious traumatization), a volume that inspires and brings out the best in us will be a welcome boon and an almost sure winner.... I expect this book will be a volume we will all be glad to be a part of, well received and much read.

The response was extraordinary. Many accepted with great enthusiasm, and a couple of authors actually wrote and sent in their chapters within a couple of weeks! I regretted that there were a number of potential excellent authors—including some friends, please forgive me—who I could not invite because of page limitations.

Everyone in the List of Contributors is an accomplished author; some are amazingly prolific. This made my job as editor relatively easy, occasionally massaging some punctuation but mostly applauding and shouting "More, more!" and "Louder, louder!" As you will see in the chapters that follow, dear reader, descriptors like *beautiful, touching, funny, brilliant, amazing, erudite, tender, wise, passionate,* and *inspiring* all truly apply. Before introducing the specific chapters, a few words about terminology are in order.

Stories? Inspiration? Passion? Renewal? Love?

Story. From the Latin *historia* (its Greek root is *istor,* meaning "learning by inquiry"). We humans make sense of our experience, conceiving our subjective realities by assigning meaning to what happens: "[A] story can be defined as a unit of meaning that provides a frame for lived experience. It is through these stories that lived experience is interpreted. We enter into stories, we are entered into stories by others, and we live our lives through these stories" (White, 1992, p. 80). As we search for meaning (Frankl, 1963; Yalom, 1980), we weave narratives or stories. These stories, in turn, conceive us—that is, they shape our awareness and guide our actions, around and around. Stories are usually told in words—prose, poetry, and song—but they are also experienced somatically and emotionally. "Stories are the vehicle that moves metaphor and image into experience.... Stories invite a kind of vision that gives shape and form even to the invisible, making the images move, clothing the metaphors, throwing color into the shadows. Of all the devices available to us, stories are the surest way of touching the human spirit" (Kurtz & Ketcham, 1992, p. 17).

Inspiration. From the Latin *inspirare* (its Greek equivalent is *enthusiasm),* meaning "to breath into," implying an infusion of divine power that enlivens or enlightens. A related term, *influence,* came from the Latin *influent* ("in-flowing") and referred originally to the astrological idea of an ethereal fluid thought to flow from the stars and to affect the actions of humans—an emanation or transmission. As Freud (1915/1961, p. 17; also see de Shazer, 1994) wrote: "Words were originally magic and to this day have retained much of their ancient magical power. By words one person can make another blissfully happy or drive him to despair.... Words provoke affects and are in general the means of mutual influence among men." Covey (2010, p. ix) elaborates: "There is a language of success and a language of distress. There is a language of progress and a language of regress. Words sell, and words repel. Words lead, and words impede. Words heal, and words kill.... When words are used properly, they sing out to the human heart." As Albert Schweitzer said, "In everyone's life, at some time, our inner fire goes out. It is then burst into flame by an encounter with another human being" (quoted in Hall, 2010, p. 126).[5]

Passion. From the Latin *passio,* meaning originally "to suffer," but now more generally meaning "intense emotion compelling action." Indeed, it is our passions—our strong emotions—that provide our lives with meaning (Damasio, 2000; Solomon, 1976). *Compassion* ("with passion") refers to "sorrow or pity excited by the distress or misfortunes of another"; *sympathy* ("the same"), *tenderness, resonance,* and *responsiveness* are synonyms. *Empathy* (from the Greek *empatheia, en* = in + *pathos* = suffering), meaning "imaginative projection of one's own consciousness into another being," is closely related. Stories that evoke strong feelings—joy, wonder, gratitude, fear, sadness, pain—are recalled and move us.

Renewal. From the Anglo-Saxon root *niwe,* meaning "having existed or been made but a short time" (opposite of "old"), combined with the root *re-,* meaning "again": hence, "to make new again, to restore freshness or vigor" (the synonym *restore* means "to return to an original state after depletion" and the synonym *rejuvenate* means "to restore to youthful vigor or power"). An inspiring story can "recharge our batteries," "refresh our supplies," and "re-encourage us" (from the Latin *cor,* meaning "heart").

Love. From the Anglo-Saxon *lufu,* meaning "A feeling of strong personal attachment induced by sympathetic understanding, or by ties of kinship; ardent affection." The Greeks contrasted *eros* and *agape,* the former term referring to

---

5   In his *Autobiographies,* William Butler Yeats (1935/1999) wrote: "Education is not about filling buckets. It is about starting fires."

sexual-erotic attachment, while the later referred to unconditional or familial affection (Fromm, 1956; Seguin, 1965). In Hebrew, *ahava* can be translated as "love"; the word is a verb ("to give"), emphasizing the action involved. The King James Bible tells us, "There is no fear in love; but perfect love casts out fear, because fear hath torment" (1 John 4:18). Buddhists use the Pali term *metta* to refer to the sublime state of "loving-kindness." The Arabic words for "love," *hubb* and *mawadda*, appear repeatedly in the Qur'an. The term *Namaste* (which is the salutation that opens this book instead of a traditional dedication) comes from the Indian subcontinent. It is derived from the Sanskrit and Persian root *nams*, meaning "to bow" or "salute divinity" and can be translated as both "Greetings" and "The spirit in me respects the spirit in you."

As the philosopher-psychotherapist-poet Mitchell Ginsberg (2012, p. 273) has expressed it:

Love[6]

Love
is caring, good-will, warmth, gentleness.

Love
is active, not passive. It is what we do, not what happens to us.

Love
is coming to know the other, and it
is respecting the other's yearnings and needs and personality.

Love
is attentive, appreciative, and caring.

Love
looks outward to the other and sees
another individual,
not a mirror image of ourselves.

Love
looks inward and sees
the delicate intimacy of our connection with the other,
a combination of separateness and closeness.

Love
calls us
to reach out, to seek understanding,
to seek being understood, to find harmony and respect.

---

6   From M. Ginsberg (2012), *Calm, Clear, and Loving: Soothing the Distressed Mind, Healing the Wounded Heart* (2nd edition, p. 273). San Diego, CA: Wisdom Moor Publishing. ©Mitchell Ginsberg, 2012. Used with permission.

Love
is patient, enduring, persevering.

Love
is deeply engaged with heart-felt commitment
when disharmonies reign,
and it flows gently and effortlessly,
when relationships are relaxed and easy,
letting closeness blossom.

Love
is soulful intensity, and, as well, passionate appreciation.

One colleague, whose excellent chapter is contained in the pages that follow, wrote to me expressing concern about the book's subtitle: *What's Love Got
to Do with It?* He was worried that potential readers might think it was about
relationship problems or sexual disorders. Not to worry.[7]

Therapist Stories of Inspiration, Passion, and Renewal: What's Love Got to Do with It?

In the chapters that follow, the authors open their—and our—hearts and minds,
over and over. You may want to turn to a particular section, but I also suggest
reading through, from front to back. The chapters are arranged alphabetically,
by the authors' last name. More information about the authors is available in the
List of Contributors that precedes this introductory chapter. Please allow me to
make a brief introductory comment about each chapter.

In Chapter 2, Rubin Battino starts us off nicely, asking "What is Really
Important in Life?" His answers—formed in the crucible of working with Hospice patients—have to do with finding bliss, meaning, and one's own song. He

---

7 Another invitee, a Northern European, chose to decline writing a chapter. In his letter he
explained, "I work very little as a clinician these days." He went on to comment: "I was at
the Networker conference [in Washington, D.C.] this year and realized that this topic is very
popular. Lots of seminars about how to enjoy your work and how to renew yourself. There
might be something specific to America because I have never seen the topic on the list in
any European conference. I have not seen therapists looking for chicken soup in Europe. Is
there a cultural difference here? It would be interesting to understand what it is all about.
For me the work is just work and it is interesting like any other work by the mere fact that it
is an interesting challenge. We love our work, I think, by seeing the daily problems to solve
as exciting challenges or conundrums to decipher. And what could be better than solving
challenging and interesting problems for a living?" Maybe there are some cultural nuances
here, but maybe his lack of interest in the topic is also why my correspondent is working very
little as a clinician these days. I'll bet that most European therapists—as well as most therapists
from Asia, South America, Africa, Australia, and everywhere else—want inspiration, passion,
and renewal.

also beautifully highlights the importance of acceptance, careful listening, and the encouraging use of what he calls "healing language."

In Chapter 3, "Helping Clients Heal Broken Hearts," Arthur Bohart challenges the idea that psychological problems come primarily from attempts to avoid pain. He eloquently describes the courage and creativity of his clients as they face their many difficulties.

In Chapter 4, "Not Quitting My Day Job: How Being a Therapist Heals Me," Laura Brown explains how, when she came to a point of serious personal and professional burn out, teaching the fundamentals of psychotherapy to trainees (which helped to remind herself about the magic of assisting others), engaging in the practice of aikido, and opening her heart as she worked with her clients restored her joy and compassion.

In Chapter 5, "Turning the Mind into an Ally," Jon Carlson writes with extraordinary feeling and immediacy about appreciating the support of caring others and the importance of recognizing choice as he faces unexpected life-threatening heart disease and cancer. Remarkably, he wrote and sent me his paper the day before he underwent quadruple-bypass surgery; three days later he wrote again to say he was feeling better; two days later, another email: "Tubes were just removed—I'm a new man."

In Chapter 6, "Duende: Evocation, Quest, and Soul," Lillian Comas-Díaz introduces the soulful Spanish term *duende* into the conversation (borrowing it from the great poet, Federico Garcia Lorca) and helps us understand aspects of her own journey of self-reclamation and renewal as well as some the cultural nuances of her clinical work.

In Chapter 7, "Psychotherapy's Soothsayer," Nick Cummings explains how his Greek grandmother, Frieda Fromm-Reichmann, Erik Erikson, Ted Kennedy, and others helped him become a clinical innovator, a visionary and highly successful entrepreneur, and a president of the American Psychological Association.

In Chapter 8, "It Warms My Heart," Carol Erickson describes how as a little girl she sat on the knee of her father, Dr. Milton Erickson, and learned how to observe and solve problems. She also provides some interesting case examples to give us a sense of what she does with her clients.

In Chapter 9, "Love's Got Everything to Do with It!" John Frykman takes a highly personal autobiographical approach, describing incidents from his life that have taught him the importance of love and relationships.

In Chapter 10, "Off the Couch and Outside the Box," Joe Goldfield discusses how he learned that clinical helping and being creative could fit together. He gives numerous examples of ways he organically combines the utilization approach of Milton Erickson with solution-focused therapy concepts and techniques, noting that the trust clients place in him catalyzes his desire to bring all that he can to their service.

In Chapter 11, "Life is with People," Eric Greenleaf describes how he has helped some of his clients cope with illness and adversity and how they, subsequently, have helped him cope with his own life challenges. He notes that he truly finds himself, not via intrapsychic examination, but in and through personal relationships.

In Chapter 12, "On Being Black in White Places: A Therapist's Journey from Margin to Center," Ken Hardy describes the multilayered impact of growing up being marginalized as a minority and how it has informed his awareness that therapy and healing involves both psychological solutions and the essential need to address and redress sociopolitical and cultural oppression with clients and in the world at large.

In Chapter 13, "Up the Hurry Stairs," Tobey Hiller turns on her literary talent to take us inside several encounters she had with a client. Penetrating intelligence rings throughout. The writing is sharp and the insights are plentiful and humane.

In Chapter 14, "Road Trip," I recount an adventure I had with my father. We often get unstuck from life's calamities by letting go, changing attitudes, thinking outside the box, shifting perspectives and accessing our overlooked personal resources. Sometimes that's not enough, however, as I learned once in the middle of the night.

In Chapter 15, "Blue on Blue: A Love Story," Chris Iveson tells about a series of meetings with an elderly couple that took place in London. Tipping his hat to his main mentor, Steve de Shazer, Chris lets us see how asking the right questions, ones that focus on clients' strengths, can make all the difference.

In Chapter 16, "Exhilarating Couple Therapy: Singing to My Soul—Holding Steady to My Science—Filling Up My Heart," Sue Johnson, the co-developer of Emotionally Focused Therapy, describes the importance of working with attachment and emotions—the basis of our humanity—to help both clients and therapists feel more connected and alive.

In Chapter 17, "The Bodhisattva: Tending the World," Jack Kornfield tells us how his personal search for happiness led him to Thailand and to Buddhist teachers and teachings. He notes that every wisdom tradition tells us that meaning and happiness cannot be found in isolation but through generosity, caring, love, and understanding. He invites us to consider taking the vows of a *bodhisattva*, the Sanskrit word for a being who is devoted to awakening and to acting for the benefit of all that lives.

In Chapter 18, "Herman's Wager," Murray Korngold takes us on a charming magical mystery tour that forced him to open his mind and consider the implications of so-called "anomalous experiences." He, too, invites us into an expanded sense of "self."

In Chapter 19, "Love is a Four-Letter Word in Therapy," Jeffrey Kottler goes to the heart of the matter. His surprising encounter with one of the giants of the psychotherapy world reveals something vital not usually associated with that particular giant's reputation.

In Chapter 20, "The Journey of a Lifetime: Or, the Adventures of Being a Therapist," Judy Mazza describes some of her early interests in matters psychological, the importance of key figures (including B.F. Skinner and Jay Haley) in her development, and the rejuvenating satisfactions she gets from both practicing as a therapist and being a supervisor and mentor.

In Chapter 21, "At My Mother's Kitchen Table: Who Are We, But the Stories We Tell?" Don Meichenbaum, one of the founders of Cognitive Behavioral Therapy, describes both the roots of his Constructive Narrative Perspective as well as the core psychotherapeutic skills required to help clients. He is, as always, both witty and very wise.

In Chapter 22, "The Poetics of Practice: Becoming 'Well Versed' in Loss and Grief," Bob Neimeyer begins by telling about a tragedy in his own life that informed his interest in therapy and the experience of loss, and then gives us a very sensitive look into his work with two grieving clients. A published poet, he provides two very moving poems to further deepen our understanding.

Chapter 23, "Natural Compassion," is a collaboration between Ram Dass and Shakti Gawain. When I read this true story back in 1985 in the first pages of *How Can I Help? Stories and Reflections on Service* (Ram Dass & Gorman, 1985) I was thrilled—and have kept it on my bookshelf all these years. I am grateful for their permission to reprint it here.

Chapter 24, "The Tao of a Woman," is by Michele Ritterman. A longtime student of both Salvador Minuchin and Jay Haley and Milton Erickson, she describes how she came to conceive of symptoms as trance states suggested by couples, families, and social systems. She gives several clinical examples of how her therapy approach is thus the production of counter-inductions. Also a published poet, she generously provides us with several poems to enrich our appreciation of the ideas she describes.

Chapter 25, "Creating Paths with Heart," is by Teresa Robles. Quoting the famous advice of Carlos Castenada's (1968) Don Juan to "follow a path with heart," she beautifully describes how she learned this in her own life, as well as how she helps clients work with Universal Themes and Universal Wisdom.

Chapter 26, "Get Off Your High Horse: Reflections of a Problem Solver in Palo Alto," is by Karin Schlanger. Now the Director of the Brief Therapy Center at the Mental Research Institute where she was once a student, she recounts her experiences learning to meet people nonjudgmentally where they are at—both because it allows for more effective and respectful therapy and because it is a more positive way of looking at the world.

Chapter 27, "Finding Humanity in Darkness," is by Dan Short. He beautifully describes creative ways to see through the darkness to find health and humanity. He also provides ways for therapists to help protect their own psyches as they work with disturbing material. If Colonel Kurtz in Joseph Conrad's *Heart of Darkness* (1899/2007, p. 86) had read this chapter, he might have thought "The hope! The hope!" after muttering his famous cry, "The horror! The horror!"

Chapter 28, "In Search of the Spirit: A Therapist's Journey," is by Terry Soo-Hoo. He describes both his personal evolution as a therapist as well as gives several fascinating examples of the approach he has developed, which he calls Strength-Based Multicultural Integrative Therapy. We get to see how he connects with clients, appreciates their particular resources (including cultural context), and helps them move forward in their lives.

Chapter 29, "Conscious Purpose and Commitment Exercise," is by Michael White, the much-respected Australian social worker and family therapist who died in 2008. Drawn from an interview we did together (Hoyt & Combs, 1996) and consistent with the motto ("The person is not the problem; the problem is the problem") of the Narrative Therapy approach he co-founded, White eloquently expresses his view that opposes the undermining of therapists' motives and provides an exercise for readers to use to help them reclaim and reinforce their positive sense of purpose. To use two metaphors from his writing (White, 1989, 1997b), it is a pleasure to "say hullo again" and to "re-member" Michael, who was brilliant, life-affirming, and a friend taken from us much too soon.

Chapter 30, "Themes and Lessons: The Invitation Revisited," provides my editor's review and discussion of some of the ideas to be gleaned from the various chapters, as well as an invitation to the reader to consider his or her own sources of inspiration, passion, and renewal.

Enjoy Yourself!

The whole is greater than the sum of the parts. There is a lot to ponder. As Walt Whitman (1855/1996) wrote in *Leaves of Grass*:

> I celebrate myself,
> And what I assume you shall assume,
> For every atom belonging to me as good belongs to you. (1996, p. 27)
>
> [...]
> Do you see O my brothers and sisters?
> It is not chaos or death ... it is form and union and plan
> ...it is eternal life.... it is happiness.
>
> The past and present wilt ... I have filled them and
> emptied them,
> And proceed to fill my next fold of the future. (1996, p. 87)

Herman Hesse (1951, pp. 137-138) also wrote, in *Siddhartha*:

> Siddhartha listened. He was now listening intently, completely absorbed, quite empty, taking in everything. He felt that he had now completely learned the art of listening. He had often heard all this before, all these numerous voices in the river, but today they sounded different.... They were all intertwined and interlocked, entwined in a thousand ways. And

all the voices, all the goals, all the yearnings, all the sorrows, all the pleasures, all the good and evil, all of them together was the world. All of them together was the stream of events, the music of life. When Siddhartha listened attentively to this river, to this song of a thousand voices; when he did not listen to the sorrow or the laughter, when he did not bind his soul to any one particular voice and absorb it in his Self, but heard them all, the whole, the unity; then the great song of a thousand voices consisted of one word: Om—perfection.

I hope you will find in this collection, dear reader, inspiration for your passion and renewal for your spirit and that it will help you help those you work with to get to where they want to go. May peace be upon you.

References

Baker, E.K. (2003). *Caring for Ourselves: A Therapist's Guide to Personal and Professional Well-Being.* Washington, DC: American Psychological Association.

Booker, C. (2004). *The Seven Basic Plots: Why We Tell Stories.* New York: Continuum.

Boyle, G. (2011). *Tattoos on the Heart: The Power of Boundless Compassion.* New York: Free Press/ Simon & Schuster.

Castaneda, C. (1968). *The Teachings of Don Juan: A Yaqui Way of Knowledge.* New York: Ballantine.

Conrad, J. (2007). *Heart of Darkness.* New York: Penguin Classics. (work originally published 1899)

Covey, S. (2010). ForeWord. In *Aspire: Discovering Your Purpose through the Power of Words* (K. Hall, Ed.; pp. ix-xiv). New York: William Morrow/HarperCollins.

Damasio, A. (2000). *The Feeling of What Happens: Body, Emotion and the Making of Consciousness.* New York: Vintage/Random House.

de Shazer, S. (1994). *Words Were Originally Magic.* New York: Norton.

Dlugos, R.F., & Friedlander, M.L. (2001). Passionately committed psychotherapists: A qualitative study of their experiences. *Professional Psychology: Research and Practice, 32*(3), 298–304.

Erikson, E.H. (1959). *Identity and the Life Cycle.* New York: Norton.

Frankl, V.E. (1963). *Man's Search for Meaning: An Introduction to Logotherapy.* New York: Washington Square Books.

Freud, S. (1961). Introductory lectures on psycho-analysis. In *The Standard Edition of the Complete Psychological Works of Sigmund Freud* (Vols. 15-16, pp. 3–463; J. Strachey, Ed.). London: Hogarth Press. (work originally published 1915)

Fromm, E. (1956). *The Art of Loving.* New York: Harper & Row.

Ginsberg, M.D. (2012). *Calm, Clear, and Loving: Soothing the Distressed Mind, Healing the Wounded Heart* (2nd ed.). San Diego, CA: Wisdom Moon Publishing.

Hall, K. (2010). *Aspire: Discovering Your Purpose through the Power of Words.* New York: William Morrow/HarperCollins.

Hesse, H. (1951). *Siddhartha.* New York: New Directions.

Hillenbrand, L. (2010). *Unbroken: A World War II Story of Survival, Resilience, and Redemption.* New York: Random House.

Hoyt, M.F. (1995). *Brief Therapy and Managed Care: Readings for Contemporary Practice.* San Francisco: Jossey-Bass.

Hoyt, M.F. (Ed.) (1996). *Constructive Therapies (Vol. 2).* New York: Guilford Press.

Hoyt, M.F. (2000). *Some Stories Are Better than Others: Doing What Works in Brief Therapy and Managed Care.* Philadelphia: Brunner/Mazel.

Hoyt, M.F. (2001). *Interviews with Brief Therapy Experts.* New York: Brunner-Routledge.

Hoyt, M.F. (2004). *The Present is a Gift: Mo' Better Stories from the World of Brief Therapy*. New York: IUniverse.

Hoyt, M.F. (2009). *Brief Psychotherapies: Principles and Practices*. Phoenix, AZ: Zeig, Tucker & Theisen.

Hoyt, M.F., & Combs, G. (1996). On ethics and the spiritualities of the surface: A conversation with Michael White. In M.F. Hoyt (Ed.), *Constructive Therapies* (Vol. 2, pp. 33–59). New York: Guilford Press. Reprinted in M.F. Hoyt, *Interviews with Brief Therapy Experts* (pp. 71–96). New York: Brunner-Routledge, 2001.

Jamison, K.R. (2004). *Exuberance: The Passion for Life*. New York: Vintage/Random House.

Kottler, J.A. (1999). *The Therapist's Workbook: Self-Assessment, Self-Care, and Self-Improvement Exercises for Mental Health Professionals*. San Francisco: Jossey-Bass.

Kottler, J.A., & Carlson, J. (Eds.) (2005). *The Client Who Changed Me: Stories of Therapist Personal Transformation*. New York: Routledge.

Kottler, J.A., & Carlson, J. (2008). *Their Finest Hour: Master Therapists Share Their Greatest Success Stories*. Bethel, CT: Crown House Publishing.

Kottler, J.A., & Carlson, J. (2009). *Creative Breakthroughs in Therapy: Tales of Transformation and Astonishment*. New York: Wiley.

Kurtz, E., & Ketcham, K. (1992). *The Spirituality of Imperfection: Storytelling and the Search for Meaning*. New York: Bantam/Random House.

Lesser, E. (2005). *Broken Open: How Difficult Times Can Help Us Grow*. New York: Villard Books/Random House.

McKee, R. (1997). *Story: Substance, Structure, Style, and the Principles of Screenwriting*. New York: ReganBooks/HarperCollins.

Norcross, J.C., & Guy, J.D., Jr. (2007). *Leaving It at the Office: A Guide to Psychotherapist Self-Care*. New York: Guilford Press.

Ram Dass, & Gorman, P. (1985). *How Can I Help? Stories and Reflections on Service*. New York: Knopf.

Richards, K. (2010). *Life*. New York: Little, Brown.

Seguin, C.A. (1965). *Love and Psychotherapy*. New York: Libra Publishers.

Sharry, J., Madden, B., & Darmody, M. (2001). *Becoming a Solution Detective: A Strengths-Based Guide to Brief Therapy*. London: BT Press.

Shaver, B.J. (2005). "Live Forever." Song on *The Real Deal*. Houston, TX: Compadre Records.

Skovholt, T.M., & Trotter-Mathison, M.J. (2010). *The Resilient Practitioner: Burnout Prevention and Self-Care Strategies for Counselors, Therapists, Teachers, and Health Professionals* (2nd ed.). Needham Heights, MA: Allyn & Bacon.

Solomon, R.C. (1976). *The Passions: The Myth and Nature of Human Emotion*. Garden City, NY: Doubleday/Anchor Press.

Wallace, K.K. (2009). *Listen Deeply, Let These Stories In* (with J. Lovell). Alice Springs, Australia: IAD Press.

Weiss, L. (2004). *Therapist's Guide to Self-Care*. New York: Routledge.

Whitaker, C.A. (1982). *From Psyche to System: The Evolving Therapy of Carl Whitaker* (J.R. Neill & D.P. Kniskern, Eds.). New York: Guilford Press.

Whitaker, C.A. (1989). *Midnight Musings of a Family Therapist* (M.O. Ryan, Ed.). New York: Norton.

White, M. (1992). Family therapy training and supervision in a world of experience and narrative. In *Experience, Contradiction, Narrative and Imagination: Selected Papers of David Epston and Michael White 1989–1991* (D. Epston & M. White; Eds., pp. 75–95). Adelaide, Australia: Dulwich Centre Publications.

White, M. (1989). Saying hullo again: The incorporation of the lost relationship in the resolution of grief. In *Selected Papers* (pp. 29–36). Adelaide, Australia: Dulwich Centre Publications.

White, M. (1997a). *Narratives of Therapists' Lives*. Adelaide, Australia: Dulwich Centre Publications.

White, M. (1997b). Re-membering. In *Narratives of Therapists' Lives* (pp. 22–52). Adelaide, Australia: Dulwich Centre Publications.

Whitman, W. (1996). *Poetry and Prose*. New York: Library of America College Editions. (*Leaves of Grass* first published 1855)

Wright, F.L. (1992). Building for local government: The Marin County Civic Center. In *Truth Against the World: Frank Lloyd Wright Speaks for an Organic Architecture* (pp. 381–411; P. J. Meehan, Ed.). Washington, DC: The Preservation Press/National Trust for Historic Preservation. (speech originally given 31 July 1957)

Yalom, I. D. (1980). *Existential Psychotherapy*. New York: Basic Books.

Yalom, I. D. (2002). *The Gift of Therapy: An Open Letter to a New Generation of Therapists and Their Patients*. New York: HarperCollins.

Yeats, W.B. (1999). *Autobiographies*. (W.H. O'Donnell & D.N. Archibald, Eds.) New York: Scribner/Simon & Schuster. (work originally published 1935)

Zevon, W. (2003). "Keep Me in Your Heart." Song on *The Wind*. New York: Artemis Records.

2

WHAT IS REALLY IMPORTANT IN LIFE?

Rubin Battino

What is *really* important in life? The great religions and philosophers have all had a go at this, and there are some commonalities. Three of my favorite authors came up with the following:

- Joseph Campbell (2004)—to find your bliss
- Viktor Frankl (1959)—to find meaning
- Lawrence LeShan (1989)—to sing your own unique song

These all speak to me in different ways. The answers I have come from my score of years of being a facilitator for support groups for people who have life-challenging diseases and their caregivers. A while back I read Bernie Siegel's book, *Love, Medicine and Miracles* (1990). It had a profound effect on me, and I asked myself, "Rubin, you have skills that can be used to help people who have serious diseases, why aren't you using them?" Here was a surgeon who broadened his interaction with patients to become emotionally and passionately involved with these suffering people in a compassionate, caring, and loving way. He converted himself from being a mechanic to being a healer. Bernie reached my conscience and humanity. There was an Exceptional Cancer Patient support group (based on Bernie's book and principles) in Dayton, Ohio, that let me join them. We met twice each month at Hospice of Dayton. At the end of a meeting, about two years after I had joined, two of the members came up to me separately and said effectively the same thing, "Rubin, you know I like you now." This was both shocking and rewarding. What they were saying is that it had taken the group that long to convert me from an observing intellectual to a feeling human being, a real member of the group. At one point I even had the temerity to rewrite the Serenity Prayer, with which we ended every meeting, because my linguistic analysis found it faulty! I was a very slow learner, and they finally won me over. (I eventually became a co-facilitator of the group, and then its facilitator. The group continues to meet at the Senior Center in Yellow Springs, near Dayton.)

The essential healing aspect of this group is that everyone has the opportunity to speak while the rest of us listen attentively, and do not interrupt or make comments. To really be *heard* is rarer than you might imagine. We became the most intimate of family and friends to each other because we actually *listened* to whatever each member said. In fact, the central skill in being a good therapist (or a good person) is to listen without an agenda or thinking about an intervention—just to be there for that person. When someone is seriously ill or at the end of their life they do not want to listen to you and your stories and your advice.

A number of years ago on one of my visits to New Zealand, I worked with a cancer support group in Christchurch. One member of the group who had prostate cancer, Keith, said to me one day, "You know, Rubin, having this cancer has been a blessing. I have been married for 25 years and I never knew what love was until this happened." Being diagnosed with a life-challenging disease (I prefer this phrase over the scary and limiting "life-threatening"—my sensitivity to the effects of language led me to write a book on healing language; see Battino, 2011) is having an opportunity forced on you to consider what is really important in your life. At one time or another everyone in our groups has used the word "blessing" with respect to this trial in their life. They all come up with variants of the same two things: relationships and Nature. Before discussing them, I want to share with you something Keith told me on a subsequent visit when I asked him how he was doing. He said me that the cancer was in abeyance, and that he talked to it every day, saying, "I don't mind you being there, and I don't mind you taking sustenance from me. I just want you to know that if you decide to grow that you will kill us both." Keith lived for a long time *with* his cancer.

Over the years I have done a number of presentations on the subject of the title of this paper. After some introductory material and telling a few stories, I ask the group to break up into smaller groups of no more than four people. They are to share what is really important to them and can write this down. After a few minutes they are asked to share what is *really really* important in their lives. Finally, they are asked to think about what is *really really really* important. (Jean Houston, heard on an NPR broadcast, has found that there are deeper layers when you go to really really really.) At this point those who are willing to share can tell the larger group what it is that they found, and this is written down so that all can see it. In my presentations I end with a group meditation which weaves in what was listed, and also gives everyone the opportunity to think about their choices, what was written, and any actions they may take based on what they have learned. Typically, I ask people to hold hands (I join them) for the meditation so that they are not alone.

The two themes mentioned above—relationships and Nature—are the core. Many years ago I read a book by Zborowski and Herzog (1952) about life in the Jewish *shtetls* (small villages) in Eastern Europe that was entitled *Life is With People*. That title has stuck in my mind for 60 years, and it has become the *leit-motif* of the closing meditation. *Life is with people*. Keith discovered what love was. The diagnosis forced him to face the finiteness of life—what was he going to do with the time that remained to him? Do you/I/we need a diagnosis of cancer to make this discovery? (The motto of the support group is, "You may have to believe the diagnosis, but you do not have to believe the prognosis." The former is based on the interpretation of medical tests, the latter is an educated *guess*.) Life is with people and what are you doing *now* to connect with and enhance the significant relationships in your life? Do you need to mend fences with relatives and friends? Do you need to get in touch with them and arrange time together? Will you do this? You are not alone—remember that one hand washes the other, you cannot touch without being touched, and you cannot love without experiencing love.

If you are nearing the end of your life, it is important to share the following with significant others (based on Ira Byock's [2004] work):

- I love you.
- Please forgive me.
- I forgive you.
- I forgive myself.
- Thank you.
- Goodbye.

The three statements involving forgiveness are central to taking care of unfinished business and attaining closure. (Note: the one about forgiving yourself is my addition.)

George Burns (1998) has written an important book entitled *Nature Guided Therapy* that discusses the incorporation of nature into psychotherapy. This is generally overlooked or not even thought about. Yet, for people who are re-evaluating what is important in their lives, nature becomes quite significant. There is just something inherent and even primal in human beings about being in contact with nature. Our roots connect us to the earth, and our imaginations connect us to the sky. This cloud—that blade of grass—a raindrop—a star—the sound of running water—the wind in the treetops—a snowflake—thunder—insect sounds—birdsong—a purring cat—an ocean breeze—waves rolling up a beach—a hawk soaring—the smell of new mown grass—a colored leaf lazily falling. How often have you heard, "Take the time to smell a flower"? Contact with nature is essential to being alive. All of the patient rooms in Hospice of Dayton look out on a bird-feeder, and grass and growing things. Geese and ducks wander the grounds, and there are visiting dogs and cats.

The psychologist Lawrence LeShan (1989) spent many years working with "terminal" cancer patients. (They were the only ones that the medical doctors would let him work with since it was thought that since they were "terminal" he could do them no harm with psychotherapy!) He found that the one thing that brought them back to life and hope and contact was eliciting their unfulfilled hopes and dreams. What was it they had always wanted to do that the imagined and real constraints on their lives prevented them from doing or experiencing? When I was young I wanted to be an opera singer. To be able to let my voice soar and fill a room with arias was a dream. Somehow music was not part of my growing up or early life. When I was 45 I started studying piano, and when I was 48 I started taking voice lessons. Unfortunately, none of my teachers recognized that I needed to first really learn about the basic things in music like distinguishing notes and tempos and note values. So, I learned piano mechanically and was never aware of what note (vocal or instrumental) was higher or lower than another—I just got no training in those basic skills. My voice teacher was excellent and she eventually got me to the point where I could actually belt out arias and fill a room with my voice. But, I was never sure I was singing the right notes in the right key or range. In a way, I achieved my dream of singing opera to my satisfaction.

The other dream I had was of being a writer. There has certainly been success in this area in my career as a professor of chemistry with four books and over 150 publications. Although there is a certain amount of creativity in scientific writing, the dream was to be a *creative writer*. That dream has been achieved in writing 17 plays, publishing poetry, and in the 8 books I have written in psychotherapy. Two of my plays are biographies of Viktor Frankl (2002) and Milton H. Erickson (2008), an interesting combination of creativity and professional writing. There are more dreams out there, too, to be worked on. Find out what your clients' dreams and hopes and daydreams are since they are the key to their essence. Frankl would add that finding *meaning* is a big part of that essence.

A number of years ago I had the supporting role of Boraccio in Shakespeare's *Much Ado About Nothing*. Over the years I have been involved in community theater as an actor, director, and set builder. (Only once did I direct one of my own plays for a professional theater group.) I am a competent actor, but in the brush-up rehearsal for *Much Ado* something occurred that was extraordinary. In studying my lines a magic thing happened in that I finally understood Shakespeare's lines and the phrasing and delivery so that they made innate organic sense. I had one major speech, and that brush-up night I delivered it in a kind of out-of-body experience where I observed myself being Boraccio. When I finished the speech all of those present burst out into spontaneous applause! For a moment or two I was completely befuddled. Who were they applauding? It was as if I was possessed and transformed into another person who gave that speech in an utterly congruent and believable way. Please note that for the rest of the performances I did my usual competent acting, but never got back to that transcendent delivery. I have asked professional actors about this phenomenon and been told that they, too, have experienced it as isolated random occurrences. That is, it was not reproducible. Can this also occur in other areas?

There have been a number of times in a given session with a client when there was a sense of the "Force" (in *Star Wars* terms) being with me. That is, as consciously aware as I am during sessions, there was a feeling that I was saying and doing things that were well beyond my normal skills. The sessions went remarkably smoothly and well—I could tell from the end- of-session interaction with the client and subsequent follow-up that something extraordinary had occurred. I could wax mystical and state that it was something transcendental, something above and beyond and not explainable by experiment or observation or scientific method. I just know that this has happened several times, and I wonder if others in the field have ever experienced this same phenomenon. These exceptional sessions may be the result of training, or may be random. Can it be said that some of the therapists whom we regard with awe like Milton Erickson, Virginia Satir, Fritz Perls, and, in recent times, Ernest Rossi, had a direct link to the "Force"? We do know that these therapists were astute observers with lifetimes of conscious practice. This is something to wonder about ...

In thinking back over my life, I sometimes speculate on how I managed to survive to the age of 80. There were no traumatic or dramatic events that I could point to. My family expected me to become a medical doctor instead of a professor of chemistry and a therapist. There was a familial expectation of going beyond the small family businesses in the garment industry in New York City. It is true that I had the advantages of attending the Bronx High School of Science, the City College of New York, and Duke University. On the other hand, I was sufficiently troubled as a teen-ager, youth, and young adult to have considered suicide at various times. I got help of a sort when I lived in Chicago by being in psychoanalysis on and off for seven years. That appeared to be the only game in town then, although Carl Rogers was doing some revolutionary things in the field in Chicago at the time. Still, almost everyone I knew was "in analysis." It wasn't until my body faked a heart attack when I was living in the Dayton area that I received really useful help from a Gestalt therapist, Howard H. Fink, Ph.D. We recently (Fink & Battino, 2011) published an oral history based on seven years of conversations. I still recall the magic of being in a 24-hour marathon group. (Do they do that anymore?) After completing therapy I was invited to join a Gestalt Therapy training group rather than get some more group therapy. I was the only lay person in that training group, and it led me to the mid-life addition of a degree in mental health counseling, and a second career. This was in the heady days of encounter groups, and I attended many of them. In looking back I wonder how we got from the touchy-feely days of encounter to evidence-based approaches. It is my opinion that much has been lost in these changes. For example, when I do training workshops in various approaches I am always amazed at how little the attendees know about the history and development of psychotherapy. In a recent workshop only one student knew anything at all about NLP (Neurolinguistic Programming) or Gestalt Therapy.

Although I have been trained in and have learned many approaches to psychotherapy (I primarily operate out of an Ericksonian mode of hypnosis and psychotherapy now), I have evolved to my own style of very brief therapy (typically only one or two sessions; see Battino, 2006). I call this way of working "chatting." Much has been written about the therapeutic alliance, a way of being with a client where the client has the sense that you are both existing in the world in similar ways. So, I have chats with my clients. This necessarily involves more self-disclosure than most therapists would find comfortable. The self-disclosures, of course, are relevant to what the client has told me about his/her life, and what is troubling them. (I prefer linguistically to have clients have troubles or concerns rather than problems.) They know that I use hypnosis if it makes sense to do so. Sessions typically end with hypnosis that is built around what has arisen during the chat. Various ideas are thrown out and reinforced. Since I work for myself these sessions are always open-ended—I do marvel at how others actually work by the clock!

Every once in a while when someone learns about my volunteer work with people who have life-challenging diseases they ask me, "Isn't that hard to do? Most of them die, don't they?" It is true that I have been to many funerals and memorial services. In the course of my work I have met and spent time with many exceptional people I would not have otherwise known. We shared pain and sorrow and joy. The intimate time spent with them recognizing the finiteness of their lives (and ours!) was worth the sadness of their deaths. Without this involvement my life would have been relatively shallow and meaningless. Let me give you an example.

About 18 months ago a friend called and asked me if I would visit someone I knew casually in town who had cancer, and who wanted hypnosis. This began an intensive three-month experience with Lionora. She had colon cancer which had metastasized and was no longer treatable. Lionora had trained as a shaman and was adept at shamanic practices and healing. She was also a musician, singer, composer, artist, writer, and playwright. I knew that she wanted hypnosis for pain control since medication was contrary to her belief system. So, we discussed this and many other areas, such as the slew of practical matters that are there at the end of life. At one point I convinced Lionora that it was okay to join a hospice program and take pain meds so that she could be as sentient as possible as long as possible. Early on I videotaped Lionora talking about her life in two one-hour sessions. The DVDs were for her family and friends. I even got her to sing on one of the tapes.

Together with Lionora and her family we designed a memorial service and hand-out. I agreed to organize the service and officiate. After her death we had a full house of friends and family and shamanic clients. Several close people gave formal remarks, and then we had a group sharing celebration in which people stood and told stories, many of them humorous. (It is usual that meetings of the support group I facilitate include humor and laughter.) Yes, it was sad that Lionora had died at the age of 60. In those three months I had the opportunity to really really really know and love someone I otherwise would have just known casually. Life is with people, and we are not alone.

Thanks for letting me share with you some of what makes doing therapy blissful, meaningful, and an inspiring song for me.

References

Battino, R. (2002). *Meaning: A Play Based on the Life of Viktor E. Frankl.* Carmarthen, UK: Crown House Publishing Ltd.

Battino, R. (2006). *Expectation. The Very Brief Therapy Book.* Carmarthen, UK: Crown House Publishing Ltd.

Battino, R. (2008). *That's Right, is it Not? A Play about the Life of Milton H. Erickson, M.D.* Phoenix, AZ: The Milton H. Erickson Foundation Press.

Battino, R. (2011). *Healing Language: A Guide for Physicians, Dentists, Nurses, Psychologists, Social Workers, and Counselors.* www.Lulu.com

Burns, G.W. (1998). *Nature-Guided Therapy.* New York: Brunner/Mazel.

Byock, I. (2004). *The Four Things that Matter Most.* New York: Free Press.

Campbell, J. (2004). *Pathways to Bliss: Mythology and Personal Transformation* (D. Kudner, Ed.). Novato, CA: New World Library.

Fink, H.H., & Battino, R. (2011). *Howie and Ruby: Conversations 2000–2007.* www.Lulu.com.

Frankl, V.E. (1959). *Man's Search for Meaning.* Boston: Beacon.

LeShan, L. (1989). *Cancer as a Turning Point: A Handbook for People with Cancer, Their Families, and Health Professionals.* New York: Penguin Putnam.

Siegel, B. (1990). *Love, Medicine, and Miracles.* New York: HarperPerennial.

Zborowski, M., & Herzog, E. (1952). *Life is with People: The Culture of the Shtetl.* New York: International Universities Press.

3

HELPING CLIENTS HEAL BROKEN HEARTS

Arthur C. Bohart

We are supposed to discuss what inspires us, renews us, what is the heart and soul of our work, what are the poetics of helping people change. My answer to all of this is simple: *The courage and creativity of the people I've worked with to overcome their broken hearts.*

Avoidance and Courage

My view is largely in contrast to our field's dominant belief that clients' problems lie in avoidance. To the contrary, I believe in their courage. From the perspective of many current theories, clients have problems because they are denying into awareness various experiences and thoughts; they are avoiding facing up to behaviors, feelings, memories and motives discrepant with their self-images; they are adopting pathological behaviors to avoid feelings; and in general they are defending against facing up to things that are painful. They prefer the safety of their pathology to the uncertainty inherent in taking the risk to change. So instead of emphasizing their courage, these theories emphasize their avoidance. The goal of therapy then becomes to get them to "face up," although it may not be framed quite so bluntly.

On the surface, it would seem contradictory to say that clients avoid pain. Clients come to therapy because they often are experiencing a great deal of pain. Their lives aren't working. They experience painful contradictions. They see themselves as failures. They are depressed or anxious. They are drinking too much. They are cutting themselves, they have symptoms of post-traumatic stress disorder, they have obsessive rituals, and so on. These things bring them pain. Yet they are continuing to strive to find a way of functioning. It seems odd to accuse them of avoiding pain. The way theorists get around this is to argue that clients prefer the pain of their symptoms to the deeper pain they would experience if they were to face up to themselves. Clients become the equivalent of the self-flagellants of the Middle Ages: they prefer to hurt themselves instead of take the chance of facing up to deeper pain.

I do not deny that clients' avoidance plays some role in some problems. However, I do not believe that avoidance generally lies at the root of psychopathology. I do not believe, for instance, that alcoholics primarily drink in order to avoid feelings. For me, theories that focus on client avoidance have a moralistic quality to them. In essence, they say that people have psychological problems because they are failing to be courageous. They don't overtly accuse them of that—at least most don't (but see Wile, 1984, 1992 on accusatory ideas in psychotherapy). To the contrary, most therapists are sympathetic. As human beings themselves, they can "understand" why people would want to avoid awful truths, repressed memories, unpleasant feelings, and upsetting memories. Yet they know that clients must face up to free themselves from the shackles that are binding them.

There is some truth in the idea that accessing and experiencing painful emotions and memories helps. I take it as an empirical fact that when clients do let themselves experience feelings they may have not previously experienced, and look at thoughts or memories they had not previously examined, they frequently get better. Clients themselves will sometimes say that they found it useful to discover they had been avoiding and that the helpful thing about therapy was that they were finally able to face up. The fact that accessing painful affects and memories helps does not mean, however, that avoidance of the feelings, etc., is what caused the dysfunctionality, any more than the fact that aspirin helps headaches means that an absence (avoidance?) of aspirin causes headaches.

The idea that avoidance is the primary factor at the root of client problems does not match up to my experience of my clients. In my experience, what looks like their avoidance is usually a side effect of other things going on. Furthermore, when clients do access feelings and experiences they presumably have been avoiding, I see that as a result of important changes that have already happened rather than the cause of change itself.

In my experience, clients usually feel embattled. They are feeling threatened. They are feeling unsure about their ability to manage their lives. They feel threatened from outside: perceiving their external worlds as dangerous, unaccepting, unforgiving. Or they feel threatened from inside. They are dismayed with themselves—perceiving themselves as damaged, wrong, bad, dysfunctional. They are scrambling to find a place in this world. They are doing the best they can to keep themselves together. Sure, they avoid, but not because they are afraid of the pain. They avoid because they don't have the time, the luxury, the safety, or the space to "face up." They are too busy preserving enough self-organization and interpersonal organization to function. (This is even an implication of the Alcoholics Anonymous Serenity Prayer: Don't try to control the things you cannot control.) Yes, that self-organization and/or interpersonal organization may not work very well. It may be "pathological," but it is the best they can do under the circumstances. The threat of the pain or feeling is not the threat of the pain per se, but the fear that if they pay attention to it, it will overwhelm their ability to cope and their worlds will dissolve. In other words, what they are afraid of is not being able to cope. And so they "avoid" (don't pay attention to) in order to keep a foothold, in order to keep a place on the planet.

I am always impressed by the amount of pain my clients are willing to face up to and yet keep on going. Almost like people who have terrible wounds but keep on going in war, they keep on keeping on as best they can. They may deny that they drink too much, but that is not because they cannot face up but because they are trying to preserve some sense of control, of dignity, in order to keep on going. Courageously they invent some way to live in a world that seems difficult or unlivable from their perspective, perhaps because they blame themselves (and secretly or not so secretly do not believe they measure up, or do not deserve to be on the planet). Yet, "broken leg" or not, they keep moving. What they do to survive is not always pretty. Often it contains self-destructive elements. That is why they come to therapy. But they do the best they can, even knowing that they are being self-destructive sometimes, making of their lives what they can out of what they have available to them. If they are avoiding, it is because they are too busy acting to "face up," or they do not see the use in it, or they do not believe they can face up without dissolving or disintegrating.

I think of my client who was depressed because she felt the burden of caring for her aged father, who had Alzheimer's Disease. Her family "rule" was that the oldest child was supposed to care for the parents. Her siblings assumed it was her responsibility and that she would do it. The thought of putting him in a "home" was not acceptable in her family. Yet having the father move in with her had terrorized her life. She had to spend all her time tending to the father, who had a penchant for wandering out in the street, sometimes unclothed. He demanded constant attention. This was ruining her relationship with her husband. Basically it had ended their sex life, because who knew when he might wander in. She was worried her husband was going to get fed up and look elsewhere. When I saw her she met *DSM-IV* criteria for "Major Depressive Disorder." Yet she had been "keeping on keeping on" for months, despite her serious depression, doing the best she could to keep her life stitched together.

You could look at her through the "avoidance" lens. From our modern Western perspective the answer was obvious: put the father in a home. She had a right to a life. She had obligations to others besides the father, most notably her husband. Her siblings did not have the right to demand that she be the one to bear this burden all by herself. So what kind of dysfunctional cognitions, avoided feelings, or unresolved childhood memories were keeping her stuck? Perhaps she would have to "face up" to the deep pain, guilt, and shame she would experience were she actually to confront the possibility of her putting him in a home and violating her family rules. You might even wonder if her adherence to these rigid *shoulds*, and subsequent depression, masked even deeper feelings she was avoiding, perhaps pains and shames from early childhood. In any case the job of the therapist would be to get her to face up to and examine these rigid beliefs and her rigid loyalty to them, and in so doing, face the pain of her siblings' disapproval, her disloyalty to the tradition of her family, and so on.

I did not try to get her to face up. Nor did I challenge her dysfunctional cognitions. Rather, I marveled at her strength, her courage. I marveled at how she kept going under such pain, with so many threats, how she was trying to deal with the cards that she saw herself as having been dealt, trying to live in an almost unlivable situation. I didn't gush over her. Mostly I just did my Rogerian thing and empathically reflected. But I like to imagine that she picked up my admiration in the tone of my responses.

It turned out that on top of everything else she was criticizing herself. She either criticized herself for thinking about putting herself and her marriage first over her father and family, or she criticized herself for not being more independent of her family and for not putting her marriage first. In either case she was criticizing herself for being a coward, for not taking her life in her hands and "facing up." To the contrary of avoiding pain, she was inflicting it on herself. Why? She was trying to "whip herself into shape"—except she didn't know which shape it was. She was trying to do the "best thing." Note that part of her problem was that she was criticizing herself for the very thing we therapists often criticize such clients for (in our heads or at conferences when we analyze such cases).

I don't know if it was because she could tell I was on her side and I wasn't criticizing her, but through our relationship she was able to take a deep breath, stop, and reflect. Her "mental space" opened up and she was able to look at what was going on. Her self-organizing wisdom emerged (Bohart, 2013) and she was able to evaluate and balance all the priorities in her life. Did she then spontaneously "face up" and confront and work through rigid *'shoulds'* and subsequent guilt and shame? Actually, not so much. What she did was focus more on the future than on the present or the past. She moved into a kind of "wise person" place, from which she could observe herself, her siblings, her family history, and her marriage, and figure out what was the wisest thing for the future for all concerned. That, she decided, was to put the father in a home. There was one nearby. She would be able to regularly visit and so meet, symbolically at least, the charge of her family. I don't particularly recall her working through guilt or shame as part of this decision. To the extent that she did, that happened *after* she had accessed that wise place and had made her decision, in a kind of follow-up. What I do know is that a week later the "Major Depression" was gone.

I am dumbfounded when we are told by psychologists that we have a ubiquitous tendency to avoid pain. Of course we don't want to hurt, but I am amazed at how much humans do *not* avoid pain. I think of little children learning to walk. Over and over they fall down, bruise their knees, get up, cry a little, but keep trying. Another example: People staying in bad relationships, hoping somehow that their partner will treat them better. If anything, sometimes we are too courageous.

People face up to pain all the time and live with a great deal of it. Despite the current positive psychology movement, life has been described as full of suffering. As William Butler Yeats (1889/1989, p. 18) says, "the world's more full of weeping that you can understand." Still, I am in agreement with James Hillman (1996) when he writes: "Because the 'traumatic' view of early years so controls psychological theory of personality and its development, the focus of our remembering and the language of our personal storytelling have already been infiltrated by the toxins of those theories [p. 4].... A theory so degrading to inspiration deserves the derision I am giving it. Compensation theory kills the spirit, by robbing extraordinary persons and acts of their sui generis authenticity" [p. 25]." If humans weren't reasonably adept at facing up to pain, I doubt our species would have survived. We face up to pain (a)when it is necessary, (b) when we can see some gain from facing up, and (c) when we believe we are able to face up to it and master it.

Psychopathology and Broken Hearts

So where do broken hearts come in? I agree with Jerome and Julia Frank (1993) that most people who come to therapy come because they are demoralized. They have been fighting a losing battle. Whatever they are confronting has them down for the count. They want to find a place on the planet. They want to be productive, to have good relationships, to be connected, but they are failing. If they can't get what they want, at least they'd like to get what they need (Jagger & Richards, 1969). But they aren't, and so they are demoralized, suffering from a broken heart. Their heart is broken because they do not know how to find a workable place on the planet.

This may be because they view themselves as damaged, or because they don't see themselves fitting into the world. I believe what we call *psychopathology* arises from an interaction of person and situation. It is not something "in" people. Usually, it arises when people encounter situations that they cannot master, where they feel unsafe, vulnerable, unappreciated, or actively rejected. Feeling unable to cope, they develop symptoms designed to help them stay alive—and then the symptoms themselves become a further obstacle that breaks their heart.

Part of it is the situation. Life often is not particularly kind or supportive. It is a cliché that many therapists teach their clients that "life is not fair." And life really can be, at least experientially, unfair. I don't have a count of how many of my clients have encountered unfair situations in their lives: bosses that mistreat them, jobs that do not use their talents, parents and families that make unfair demands on them (such as my depressed client above with the father with Alzheimer's Disease), economic situations that make it hard for them to get a job, mismatches in romantic relationships, living in dysfunctional social environments, poverty, racism, homophobia, and on and on.

However, clients' characteristics also contribute to making a situation difficult. This can have to do with people's vulnerabilities from childhood. You could say that some situations "prey on" our weaknesses, or differences, magnifying and exacerbating them. If we lack self-confidence, we can suffer in a culture which prizes it. If we are shy, we can suffer in a culture that emphasizes extroversion (there is no "Social Outgoing Disorder" but there is a "Social Anxiety Disorder"). If we have been abused and feel particularly vulnerable, we may be particularly susceptible to exploitative individuals, or panic easily when we lose support.

But it may not be our vulnerabilities per se. It may be our differences that make it difficult for us to fit in and be accepted. I know of a client who is highly creative. He works, however, in a job where being a drone is prized. It is a well-paying job. He does not want to give it up in the current economy, but he is actively put down when he comes up with a creative idea. He feels frustrated and depressed. Yet he has a family. To leave that job now and strike out on his own is unthinkable. There are also plenty of children, sometimes called names like "Attention Deficit Hyperactivity Disorder," who simply do not do well in the typically 25–40 student classrooms in American schools, where all students sit in orderly rows and obey the teacher. Yet these same children may do very well in schools with alternative structures (see Nylund, 2000).

I even believe this is true, at least to some extent, with disorders like schizophrenia. I wonder how much some people diagnosed with schizophrenia deteriorate because of how we treat them: we see them as pathological; they see themselves as pathological; a frightening altered state of consciousness becomes more frightening, and they break down. What if they were given safe guides to help them navigate the experience, instead of being told they have a horrible pathological illness and being pumped full of drugs? We know the answer to this, at least for many, if not all, people with this diagnosis. We know that recovery rates in industrialized countries like the United States are far lower than they are in so-called less-developed countries (Leff, 1992; Whitaker, 2010) where "treatment" is more support-based than medication-based. And we know that a program that helps people having psychotic breaks by giving them a safe place to have the experience can lead to better recovery rates than through conventional treatment (Mosher, Hendrix, & Fort, 2004). And we now know that many individuals who are able to affirm their identities while hearing voices do not necessarily deteriorate (see, for instance, the Hearing Voices Network, www.hearing-voices.org).

So psychopathology comes from a broken heart. The person is confronted with a situation where they cannot get their needs met, where they do not get support, where their talents and strivings are not recognized, where they simply cannot get an "edge," where their vulnerabilities and liabilities really get in the way. They react at first by trying, but when things go wrong, they give up, lose hope, and get demoralized. Then they find other, more dysfunctional ways of staying on the planet, trying to mend their broken hearts. It is these things that we call "symptoms." Symptoms come from trying to live in difficult or unlivable situations, and then trying to cope with the situation in a genuine, honest, and well-meant way, but a way which paradoxically often backfires and makes things worse.

I think the worst environmental situation that creates psychopathology is the fact that as a species we are not very good at embracing difference. At best we *tolerate* difference. We rarely *appreciate* it. The biggest block that many of my clients have run into is a lack of understanding, appreciation, or acceptance by others. This often feeds back into a lack of self-acceptance. That is, they experience others not understanding, appreciating, and accepting them. Worse, it is often that the others negatively judge them. They then "internalize" this. Why? Because they are trying to be honest with themselves and to listen to others. They are trying to do right by themselves, even if, in so trying, they injure themselves.

Carl Rogers (1961) held that "conditions of worth" (i.e., lack of unconditional acceptance and positive regard) in childhood caused problems. But conditions of worth are not merely found in childhood. They are omnipresent. I don't think I've worked with anyone who has not been denigrated by people or who has not denigrated themselves because of a mismatch in their here-and-now environments, not just in childhood. I don't recall working with anyone who has not run into adult situations where they were not appreciated for who they were.

Recently, I read an article by Bartlett (2009), who made points very similar to the ones I'm making: that it is often being *different* per se that "creates" psychopathology, as people who are different are judged, isolated, and treated differently (read: disparagingly) by society. He gives the example of Emily Dickenson, who basically was a complete loner. As far as anyone knows, she preferred to be by herself. There is no evidence that she was a loner because she had "Social Anxiety Disorder." Yet, according to Bartlett, psychologists have apparently judged her as "disturbed." Apparently she has even been seen as psychotic. It is not hard to imagine other labels she might have gotten, such as "Schizoid" or "Avoidant Personality Disorder."

Imagine Emily Dickenson being alive now. Even if someone didn't drag her to a therapist, where she would all-too-likely have been diagnosed something or other, she might have made the mistake of watching television, where she would have learned from talk shows or commercials that there was something wrong with her. Imagine her beginning to view herself with alarm. Had she not been socially anxious before, she could easily have become so as she fought against her tendencies to be herself. She might have run out and gotten some Zoloft.

Unfortunately, I am not convinced our profession is much better at genuinely appreciating difference than is society in general. I was a sex therapist for a number of years. I worked with a number of people who did not enjoy sex. Some of them were bothered by their disinterest or lack of enjoyment; others were not bothered by it except that they thought they should be bothered by it because society told them there was something wrong. There is now a term for it: "Disorder of Desire." The result is that they felt deformed and damaged. Yes, some of them had been abused as children and that was undoubtedly why they didn't enjoy sex. But I was far more concerned with their self-denigration than that they didn't enjoy sex. They didn't even give themselves a chance to figure out if they wanted to enjoy sex or not because they were so beaten down by what society—and the mental health professions—had to say about them. Because they thought there was something wrong with them they had striven to enjoy sex, had failed, and felt even worse about themselves. Another example is someone who does not value or cherish close relationships. They would rather be by themselves. They are told they have a fear of intimacy, or that they are schizoid.

What if we lived in a society where "different" people were really prized, treated as dignified individuals, and listened to? Sabat (2001) has shown how professionals often do not listen to Alzheimer's patients because they believe that the difficult things the patients say reflect the disease. Yet, as Sabat demonstrates, if you really listen to them as people, you hear them trying to communicate through their disease, and as you do this they can become more sensible.

So I believe that clients suffer from broken hearts. They are usually trying their best as best they can from their point of view, based on their experiences in life, the places they have been in, and the places they are now in. But they are broken-hearted because they are not managing to make it work. And so they come to psychotherapy.

Psychotherapy

This brings us full circle to the question of this book: What inspires us, renews us, what is the heart and soul of our work, what are the poetics of helping people change? My answer to all of this: *My clients' courage and creativity.* I hope I have clarified what I mean by my clients' courage. I haven't talked much about creativity. I believe that clients show a lot of creativity in their symptoms, which are attempts to find livable ways of being on the planet. Typically, they have tried many things that have not worked. Yes, more of the same, perhaps repeating patterns, but usually ringing creative variations on the patterns, trying to make them fit, not realizing perhaps that no matter how creatively you improvise on the same melody it is the same old melody and that you are just not going to create something new that way. But the point is that they are being creative. Nothing is ever repeated the exact same way twice. Look closely and you will see creativity.

So the task of psychotherapy is to provide a space, a place, a relationship, some tools, whatever, that helps the client mobilize that same courage and creativity into more productive directions towards the future. For me, that means psychotherapy is a process of hearing, listening, and appreciating another person (there are other ways to facilitate this from other points of view—see Bohart & Tallman, 1999). It is hearing the unique person inside them, that person struggling to make sense out of the world, to thrive and cope. And as I hear them, they come into focus more. And as they come into focus more, they "fall into place" more, and as that happens they become centered in themselves more. And as that happens, they begin to trust their judgment more. And as that happens, they begin to take risks more spontaneously, not just because some therapist told them to. And as that happens, their judgment improves. And as that happens, as they now see themselves as being able to preserve personal organization while facing up to neglected experience, they may do that if necessary. Neglected emotions and experiences from childhood may emerge if, as part of this process of them coming home to themselves, that is necessary. As I have said, my experience is that facing up to feelings is often a *consequence* of change that has already happened, a marker of change rather than itself a cause. That is not to say that it may not also be useful to learn from those neglected experiences, but it may not be necessary. Sometimes my clients have moved on without doing that. Sometimes what is healing is the exploration of the future, not the past.

I could give many client examples but I will give only one. Some years ago, Cindy came to see me. She was 21, pregnant, depressed, and suicidal. She had gotten herself into a dysfunctional marriage with someone who had gotten her pregnant and had now abandoned her. She had moved back home to live with her mother, who constantly denigrated her; previously for how she had lived her life, now for being "so stupid" as to get pregnant.

Cindy was overweight and had been teased throughout her adolescent years. Because of her weight she was not attractive by conventional California high-school standards, and, more to the point, did not feel attractive. She had tried to carve a place for herself by hanging out with a group of teenagers who were rebels: not good students who engaged in drug-taking and promiscuous sex. In that group she had taken drugs and engaged in promiscuous sex with some of the boys, who were clearly using her. She knew they were using her, at some level at least, but had chosen not to direct a lot of personal attention to it (you could say she had "avoided" it) because it was better to get love and touching somehow than to have none at all. She had gotten married after having sex with one guy one drunken night. He had subsequently left. She was alone, pregnant, with no visible means of support, so had gone back to live with her mother, who returned to criticizing her.

I would call this an "unlivable situation"—she had no money, no job, no skills, was pregnant, and was living with a critical mother. In the past her mother had constantly undermined her. Whenever she wanted to lose weight, the mother would just "happen" to go out to the store and stock up on potato chips, cookies, and ice cream. After she had graduated from high school, she had tried to go to a community college. Her plan was to become a teacher. Whenever she would get a good grade in some class, her mother would tell her that it didn't mean anything because the class was easy. After awhile she had dropped out. She had held a few menial jobs, but had given them up as she had gotten involved with her rebellious friends. However, at another level, she had never given up. She had gone to another therapist who had told her that she needed to take responsibility for herself. She described his manner as punitive and discouraging and she had quit. When she told him she was going to quit he told her she was "avoiding." Recently she had finally found a job as a barista in a coffee shop. However, between being pregnant and depressed, she could barely get herself up every morning to go.

I think you could say she was broken-hearted. Yet she was persisting. I admired that. I was in my radical Rogerian days. I did nothing but listen, get to know her, and appreciate her. I admired her courage and intelligence. I just listened and she found her own way. She got the idea to go to church. They had a support group for unwed mothers. She joined it. Suddenly she had some peer support. They liked her at the church. She helped around the church, then started helping with the church school classes for the children. She found she was a natural-born teacher. Her self-esteem started to improve.

Even though she was living at home with her undermining mother, as she got her "sea legs," so to speak, she found ways of handling her mother better. She made subtle adjustments in how she stood up to her, things I could not even identify. Yet their relationship changed. The mother became less punitive and more supportive. After the baby was born, the mother seemed to soften even more. Cindy was able to go back to school. This time she did not let her mother undermine her. After about a year, she was no longer depressed and suicidal.

We saw each other for another year at which point she was doing well. She decided she didn't need to come to therapy anymore. Subsequently, for another few years I would see her every now and then for a booster session. And then we lost touch. This was back in the 1980s. I heard from her recently. She somehow had found my email address, even though I had moved from Southern to Northern California. She is now in her late 40s, had become a licensed teacher, and works at an elementary school. She thanked me. She told me that what had helped was that I cared and that I had believed in her. But I think it was her tenacity, her courage, and her determination. What I did was to appreciate and support that.

Conclusion

I want to make it clear that I what I am saying here has nothing to do with the fact that I am a Rogerian therapist, albeit an integrative Rogerian therapist who will use whatever helps if necessary. In fact, it is because my clients are courageous that I am able to get away with being a pure Rogerian therapist much of the time. But different clients want different things, and I am happy to provide them if I am able to. In the long run, I have come to rely on my clients' creativity and courage to make therapy work, no matter whether facilitated by my simple empathic presence, cognitive behavioral techniques, psychodynamic exploration, or strategic techniques. No matter what techniques and procedures are used it is my clients discovering that they can get up off the mat and use their own creativity to find ways of creating new meaning in their lives that helps them heal broken hearts. Deep down, I think what has been most helpful from me is that I have had faith in them. Somehow that situates them more on the planet, helps them find their own center of gravity, helps them feel remoralized, helps them feel recognized, and helps them keep going.

I'd like to conclude with a quote from William Faulkner's (1949/1969) Nobel Prize speech: "I believe that man will not merely endure: he will prevail. He is immortal, not because he alone among the creatures has an inexhaustible voice, but because he has a soul, a spirit capable of compassion and sacrifice and endurance. The poet's, the writer's, duty is to write about these things. It is his privilege to help man endure by lifting his heart, by reminding him of the courage and honor and hope and pride and compassion and pity and sacrifice which have been the glory of his past. The poet's voice need not merely be the record of man, it can be one of the props, the pillars to help him endure and prevail." I like to think that the role of the therapist is to be like that of the writer, and that it is my clients' capacities to not only endure but prevail that makes therapy work.

References

Bartlett, S.J. (2009). From the artist's perspective: The psychopathology of the normal world. *The Humanistic Psychologist, 37*(3), 235–256.

Bohart, A.C. (2013). Darth Vader, Carl Rogers, and self-organizing wisdom. In A.C. Bohart, B.S. Held, E. Mendelowitz, & K.J. Schneider (Eds.), *Humanity's Dark Side: Evil, Destructive Experience, and Psychotherapy* (pp. 57–76). Washington, DC: American Psychological Association.

Bohart, A.C., & Tallman, K. (1999). *How Clients Make Therapy Work: The Process of Active Self-Healing.* Washington, D.C.: American Psychological Association.

Faulkner, W. (1949/1969). Banquet speech. In H. Frenz (Ed.), *Nobel Lectures, Literature 1901–1967.* Amsterdam: Elsevier Publishing Company. Retrieved November 8, 2011, from http://www.nobelprize.org/nobelprizes/literature/laureates/1949/faulkner-speech.html,.

Frank, J.D., & Frank, J.B. (1993). *Persuasion and Healing.* Baltimore, MD: Johns Hopkins University Press.

Hillman, J. (1996). *The Soul's Code: In Search of Character and Calling.* New York: Random House.

Jagger, M., & Richards, K. (1969). "You Can't Always Get What You Want." Song on record album, *Let It Bleed*. New York: Decca Records.

Leff, J. (1992). The International Pilot Study of Schizophrenia: Five-year follow-up findings. *Psychological Medicine, 22*, 131–145.

Mosher, L. R., Hendrix, V., & Fort, D. C. (2004). *Soteria: Through Madness to Deliverance.* Bloomington, IN: Xlibris.

Nylund, D. (2000). *Treating Huck Finn: A New Narrative Approach to Working with Kids Diagnosed ADD/ADHD.* San Francisco: Jossey-Bass.

Rogers, C. (1961). *On Becoming a Person.* Boston: Houghton Mifflin.

Sabat, S.R. (2001). *The Experience of Alzheimer's Disease.* Oxford, UK: Blackwell.

Whitaker, R. (2010). *Mad in America* (2nd ed.). New York: Basic Books.

Wile, D.B. (1992). *Couples Therapy.* New York: Wiley.

Wile, D.B. (1984). Kohut, Kernberg, and accusatory interpretations. *Psychotherapy, 21*(3), 353–364.

Yeats, W.B. (1989). "The Stolen Child." In R.J. Finneran (Ed.), *The Collected Poems of W.B. Yeats: A New Edition* (pp. 18–19). New York: Collier Books/MacMillan. (work originally published 1889)

4

NOT QUITTING MY DAY JOB

How Being a Therapist Heals Me

Laura S. Brown

The first time I was paid to do something officially psychotherapeutic, I was 18, and working in a summer job after my second year of undergraduate school. I was a recreation therapy assistant at the local state psychiatric hospital. It was the realization of a dream that had begun when I was nine, the year that my own encounters with a school psychologist created in me the desire to become one of those people. He had listened well to my distress, and I had asked him what you called what he did. "I'm a psychologist," said Mr. Skipper—and thus I decided half a century ago that I, too, would be one of these people who listened for a living.

I had prepared long and hard for that first day on the job. I had read Freud's (1900/1953) *The Interpretation of Dreams* in high school and Rogers' (1961) *On Becoming a Person* during my first year at college. I had been the good listening ear to my peers through my adolescence, and participated in encounter groups. I was raring to go. In the way that some girls (or so I am told) dream about their weddings, I had dreamed about my first chance to conduct a therapy session.

I was not disappointed, although I was enlightened and perhaps given warnings of life to come, in those two months at Fairhill Psychiatric Hospital. I learned about timing—the patient with her slashed wrists newly sewn back up who spilled all to me one lonely Saturday morning because I was the only staffer around who had the time and patience to listen to her wanted nothing to do with me come Monday, having spilled too soon for her own comfort. Lesson learned; one can listen too well. I learned about compassion—our patients were the sickest and the poorest, and had lives that this privileged middle-class adolescent could barely begin to fathom. They taught me about realities that I had never imagined. I began to realize that summer that the people who honored me by sharing their pain would always be my best and most effective teachers; I learned more in those three months than I did from all of my coursework. I had my first inkling of what it meant for a psychologist to get published when one of the staff psychologists came into team meeting crowing about having had an article accepted to *Psychotherapy* (a journal of whose editorial board I have gone on to become a member of); I recall thinking, "Hmm, I want to do that, too," not having any idea at all of what it meant—or that my life would be marked by hours and hours in front of computers, preparing manuscripts.

Most importantly, that summer let me know myself to be right about my career dream. I loved being a therapist, even in the restricted and truncated form taken by the role of recreation therapy assistant (for which I would have been even better prepared had I ever learned how to play a sport). My summer at Fairhill Psychiatric saw me through a year of rejection by every graduate school to which I applied in my last year of college, fueled my desire to try again, and taught me that my long wished-for desire to become a psychotherapist was worth pursuing.

Pursue it I did. I finished graduate school too young, started a practice, stumbled through the accidents of the unconscious into working with survivors of trauma (see Brown, 2006, 2008; Kottler & Carlson, 2008). I wrote about my work; I became visible in my field. I was working to heal the world—*tikkun olam*, as we say in Hebrew (Brown, 1997). I began to be invited to travel and teach, to give keynote speeches at conferences. I was living my dream.

Oops!

Fast forward to 1999. My life was in a very bad place indeed. A relationship of 20 years was imploding at the speed of light. I was under attack from another professional who had decided to find ways to take me down when I refused, after years of acquiescence, to give in to her threats one more time. I was depressed and anxious and overwhelmed. I was, in my own opinion, not being a particularly good therapist. I recall the sensation of my heart becoming encrusted and hard, my soul numbing and deadened. My work, once so energizing and joyful, had become a source of dread. On the nights that I did sleep, I hated to get up in the morning and go into the office. On the much more frequent nights that I did not sleep, I tossed and turned in the feelings of being trapped in a vortex that had no exit.

I found an escape. I took most of the subsequent year off. It's not usual for a private practice psychotherapist to take a "sabbatical," which is what I was calling this flight from the painful place that my work had become. We don't get paid vacations in private practice; if no money is coming in because we're not working, then we have nothing on which to fall back. This is especially true if you are a person who has never had another adult sharing expenses who might temporarily shoulder the load of bills, nor a supportive family of origin on which to fall back. In March, 2000 when I stopped working I had some

savings, a mortgage, and a belief that I might never go back to work as a psychotherapist because my heart had hardened so badly in the two previous years.
I told clients I would be back in six months, and did not return to the office for
nine. But on the day that I started my sabbatical, I was seriously considering
never going back to work in the only job I had ever really had. Like someone
terribly betrayed by their first and only true love, I was thinking about breaking
up with psychotherapy and quitting my day job.

I spent those nine months with one toe in the water of psychology and the
other foot and then some dangling over a precipice. I did some consultation to
bring in money, since consulting didn't require an open heart, responded to the
occasional emergency from a client who would not call the therapists to whom
I referred her, and spent two months out of the country working as the on-site
psychologist for a reality TV program—definitely not like anything I had been
doing in my practice, and work that did not require an open heart, but rather
the willingness to co-exist with a large collection of biting insects. Like my
first job in recreation therapy, I would have been better prepared for that job if
I had learned to hike and camp than by having been a psychologist for 20 years.

During my time off I engaged in a desultory exploration of other activities
for making a living. I took some coaching workshops, thinking that perhaps,
given that my skills were transferable, I could move out of the fraught field
of trauma treatment and work with folks who had high-quality problems. I
looked into going to law school, but the idea of sitting in a classroom again,
but this time on the wrong side of the lectern, left me cold. None of what I
considered excited me. I wrote a very bad mystery novel and published it under
a pseudonym, exorcising some of the demons of my recent breakup (as my current partner says, "Do not piss Laura off too much, or she'll kill you off in a
novel"). I saw my therapist weekly, likely boring her to tears with my case of
chronic fearful stuckness. I met someone new, although for the first year and
a half of that relationship I was as ambivalent about her as I was about being a
psychotherapist. I could feel passion for very little.

January of 2001 found me back in my office, slowly rebuilding my practice.
I wasn't really ready to be there; I simply had come up with no better solution
to the problem of paying the mortgage. My life was slightly more settled than
it had been, but my passion for psychotherapy had not returned. In some ways
this probably helped me; I set tighter boundaries on my availability, transferred
care of some clients who I knew I could no longer work with because of that
diminished capacity to be on-call and, more important, the diminished capacity to be emotionally open to the people across the room from me. I began to
treat my work as a job, not a vocation; it was what I did because it was what
I knew how to do, and people were still willing to pay me to do it. On not-
quite-autopilot I could do it well enough to get by.

At the end of that summer, I accepted an offer to teach at a local professional
school, feeling relieved that this would allow me to cut back to a day a week as

a psychotherapist. It was significantly less money than I had earned in years, but that mattered less than that teaching felt like a safer haven; I could use skills that were developed, and that did not require me to have an open heart.

After I wrote that last paragraph, I opened up my old calendar program on my computer and looked at 2002 and 2003. My recollections of my work during that time—cautious, reserved psychotherapy practice with clients who I had carefully screened to not be likely to ask much of me emotionally—were confirmed by those calendar entries. In May of 2002 I began to work with a consultant; I recall telling her how burned I felt by what had happened at the end of the 1990s, and how uncertain I was about using the tools that had made me capable as a therapist—my intuition, my willingness to trust my clients, my love and compassion for them. The other professional who had gone after me had used a client who had been very dear to me as a weapon with which to harm me; I had become fearful. I did very little therapy for several years, not only because of my teaching schedule; I was still trying to find my way back to feeling at home in my work, and still uncertain that I ever would. I continued to consider whether to quit my day job.

What Happened?

So what changed things? Because today I am once again a full-time psycho-therapist. I run a training clinic (the Fremont Community Therapy Project in Seattle, Washington), one that I founded in 2006 as I left the employment of the professional school. I started it in large part because I wanted to share my enthusiasm and passion for social-justice-infused psychotherapy with the rising generation of psychologists. Today, my work happens with an open heart. Even in the times like these in the winter of 2011, when people with whom I practice are suffering and teetering on the edge of life's abysses, I find my work once more deeply gratifying and empowering. I am healed, and I think I am more connected than ever to my dream job.

Three things happened that healed me. The first was that I had to teach the basic therapy skills class at the professional school. Being given the task of designing and then teaching the first class to all of the incoming students pushed me back into my own initial encounters with the art and science of psy-chotherapy. I had to dredge up the readings that had inspired me. I had to dig into my experiential data base to find those moments with my clients that had humbled me, moved me, shaken me, stretched me, to share with my students. I had to talk to two or three sections of that class every week for four years about what was sacred about the act of listening. "You have to listen for listening's sake, listen as if your life depended on it, because it does," I told class after class of would-be clinical psychologists.

I was, it turns out, also telling myself these stories. I was disrupting the terrible numbed-self, fearful, deadened-heart narrative that I had constructed around my work in the second half of the 1990s. I was reminding myself of who I had been, and of how magical it could be to be present during the process of transformation that is psychotherapy. I had the responsibility of inspiring my students to take on this work. To do that, I had to re-inspire myself. My students offered me the opportunity to do that by inspiring me with their own dreams and determination.

Many of my students were as I had been, in life-long pursuit of the dream of becoming a psychotherapist. Most of them had not had my social class advantages, or the fortune of growing up in a neighborhood chock full of people whose work one might read in graduate training; my students' paths had been longer and more circuitous than my own. More than half of them were the first members of their families to attend college; one, sitting weeping in my office after the first week of classes, certain that she did not belong there, had dropped out of high school at age 16 to support her family. Another, also tearful, approached me after our first class meeting, during which I had casually dropped mention of "my partner, she," to ask if it were really okay to be a lesbian in psychology, since it had been anything but okay where she had come from. Some of my students were immigrants who had built successful first careers in more culturally approved fields before finally following their hearts into a healing practice.

My students got me to wake up from my professional vegetative state. In warming to them and their stories, and in becoming their mentor, I had to resurrect the warm and compassionate heart of a therapist within myself. I discovered myself being incrementally less tentative with my partner, with my colleagues, and ever so gradually, with my clients as well.

One of the ways in which I had become hyper-cautious and closed in my 21st century practice was my avoidance of all things self-disclosing. This was an about-face from how I had always worked and from what I had passionately believed to be core to the theory that guided me. Feminist therapy, a field that I helped to develop, had centered the use of self-disclosure within its framework of empowering, egalitarian relationships (Brown, 2009; Brown & Root, 1990; Brown & Walker, 1990, Feminist Therapy Institute—see Ballou, Hill, & West, 2008). I had particularly been guided by the work of Clara Hill and her co-authors (Hill & Knox, 2002) about the power of in-the-moment disclosures in the relational context of therapy; letting the client know how I was feeling about what was happening between us and thus allowing a heightened degree of transparency and personal vulnerability on my own part had been normal in my work—in the time before my heart had closed up.

In drawing on self-disclosure with my students, and particularly in being transparent about my own therapeutic errors, struggles, and failures, which I have come to believe are the very best teaching moments that any experienced psychotherapist can offer to a novice, I did exposure therapy on myself for my fear of being transparent and vulnerable with clients. I found in the classroom, as I had once known in the therapy office, that the most powerful and effective messages of change and transformation are those in which I am both, as the musician Cris Williamson (1975) wrote, *The Changer and the Changed*. As a teacher, I was forced to look in the mirror of my work as a psychotherapist and see how it had wounded me almost fatally, and then transform that wound into what I was passing along to my students. My heart, which had been broken in my office, healed in my classrooms as I told my students my stories of being inspired and terrified alike by the amazing profession into which they were entering.

One of the stories that I eventually was able to tell my students was the in-progress version of this one. There is clearly no more effective way to teach the centrality of self-care than to illustrate, with one's own life, the consequences of inadequately attending to it. So I talked, at first a little, and later, as I taught ethics classes, more and more, about how much I had put myself at risk by allowing myself to get exhausted and numb. One of the transformative aspects of teaching, and one that had continued to heal me, has been mentoring my students, and now my clinic trainees, in the practice of good self-care. Because I owed it to this younger generation of colleagues, I became more caring of and compassionate with myself.

So I found my way back, in the classroom, to an open heart and a willingness to once again have my clients see me for the wounded healer who I am. That was the first step of being returned to myself, and given my life's trajectory, a not altogether unpredictable one. Although I had fled into teaching as a refuge from the rigors of the open-hearted work of psychotherapy, I had always known that the best teaching is also a fully open-hearted practice. Once safely in the classroom I could embrace that knowledge, and in so doing, shake the scales and scar tissue off my heart.

The second step of the path back to myself has been deeply unexpected. Background to this: I was the kid picked last after last for every sports team in school. My family did not participate in athletic endeavors (one could get hurt, which in my family you would think was in the Torah as a commandment, "Thou shalt not get injured doing physical activity"); I could swim and ride a bicycle, and by my late 40s was as fearful moving about in the world as I was then fearful moving about in the murky waters of psychotherapy.

Three months after I turned 50, I tripped and fell on a dry flat street on a sunny day while out walking my dog. My phobias of going down things (hills, stairs, anything with a downward slope) began to increase exponentially; add dampness, which is ubiquitous in Seattle in March, and I was nearly paralyzed out of doors. My partner was at first patient, then emphatic that I needed to get over whatever was going on. I, too, knew that my phobia of going down things, which had first emerged while trying to walk down from the top of a mesa in Israel in 1970, was expanding from occasionally annoying to seriously problematic. I went on-line, Googled "Aikido in Seattle," found a *dojo* that was offering a beginning series a week off, signed up on-line and went to my first martial arts class.

Why aikido? I had read George Leonard's (1972) *The Transformation* when in graduate school, and been drawn to his descriptions of the principles of this relatively newer martial art. Leonard, one of the first of the Euro American aikido *sensei*, wrote about the notion that the warrior was powerful not because of using greater force with an opponent, but rather by blending with the aggressive energy, stepping to one side, softening vision, and connecting open-heartedly with the opponent. All of this had seemed compatible with the ideas of how to construct egalitarian relationship in psychotherapy that I was then struggling to develop. I also knew, from reading Leonard, that aikido involved a lot of falling down. I would go to an aikido class to learn how to fall again, I told myself; this was intentional exposure therapy for my fear of falling as I went down things.

That was nine years ago. As I related in a presentation at the APA Convention a few years back (Brown, 2007), I spent the first year on the mat crying during class, after class, and about class. My fearful, constricted physical self, which at the time was matched entirely by a fearful constricted professional self, had no idea how to operate in an environment where I was asked to watch an instructor and replicate the actions. Finding my center? "What center?" I kept asking myself. I had lost whatever center I had ever had when my heart closed up. But the ghost of the pretty good therapist I had once been kept whispering to me, "Stay here. This is good for you. Have the courage to do what you ask your clients to do. Do something hard; how else can you have the moral authority to ask them to do anything hard?"

I have stayed, and in staying have had further healing of my therapist's heart. Nine years into my practice of aikido I still wear the blue belt of an advanced beginner; injuries have slowed my progress, which was already glacial, and I seem to tear a rotator cuff every time I get serious about my next belt test. Nonetheless, I show up on the mat three times a week, and I show up filled with joy. Aikido has been a locus of deep transformation and healing for me. Because I am not a physically gifted athlete, not supple or quick, my practice of this art required me to dip into the art I already knew— psychotherapy. It turned out that the only way I could compensate for being older, slower, and more physically remedial than every other person in the *dojo* was to utilize my knowledge of how to open-heartedly regard another person with compassion, no matter how frightening they might be. In other words, I had to be in my therapist self with my heart open when I stood opposite my training partners on the mat. If I wanted not to render myself powerless in aikido, I had to remember how to powerfully connect in the energy of relational space.

Thus aikido became the second step in my recovery of self. Aikido also gave me something that my own psychotherapy never did, the ability to inhabit my body. I had left my body from the vocal chords on down from the time I was very young; in graduate school I had clipped out a Jules Feiffer cartoon from a magazine in which a disembodied head floated above a body saying, "This is my body. If I didn't need it to carry me around I'd get rid of it." That cartoon expressed my sentiments perfectly; the non-brain-non-voice parts of my embodied self were a foreign and problematic territory to me. It took aikido to bring me back to my body, where I learned to attend to and love what it was telling me.

Some of the wisdom of the body was painful; I learned at long last how I had "accidentally" become a trauma therapist as I became more able to tell myself some truths about my own earlier life, and learned, too, how I had hidden from the wounds that had ripped open in my psyche in the late 1990's. While the specifics of these awarenesses are those I intend to keep private forever, let me just say that I finally understood myself and my trajectory through relationships clearly. More of that wisdom was empowering and liberating, though; as I became more sure-footed in my physical movement through the world, so I became more metaphorically sure-footed in my work in the therapy office. I could trust myself on the mat to keep safe when large young men were attacking me. I particularly have come to enjoy a training practice called *randori*, in which I get to be attacked simultaneously by three people and am tasked with keeping all of us safe and well. The woman who smiles her way through a *randori*, greeting each attacker with a loving open heart and the thought, "Oh there you are, dear one," as she throws them out of her way, that's me; the little short round creature in white training uniform on the mat has come to inhabit the therapist self to whom I have returned. Aikido gave me back my courage.

Finally, my clients have healed me. I have had the utmost honor and privilege to sit in the presence of brave human beings who bring me their pain and struggles and allow me to be their partner in healing. When I was suffering from a closed and crusted heart, I could not allow these amazing people to heal me; I could not sense their power, could not resonate with their pain. I could only push myself from the depths of my zealous self-discipline to do the best job for them that I could; I could be responsible, but not responsive. I could feel for them; I could not feel *with* them, which is what the word "compassion" means when translated back to the root. Because I was not able to trust myself, I did not trust them.

Because my teaching and my aikido practice did the work of restoring me to much of myself, I became able again to be with my clients as I had been when I first fell in love with psychotherapy practice. When I returned to my own sense of personal power I could feel theirs. My open heart could fill with compassion; I could see my clients clearly, and allow them to see me. Thus when a client is suffering terribly in my presence I can allow that person to see how much this pains me, to disclose how this person's pain is reminiscent of my own experiences—and thus, to also share my knowledge that there is a path out of despair. When I am in this relationship with another human who is healing, I am privy to their wisdom. In creating the emotionally safer places in which they can walk over the canyons of their pain and fear I must myself cross those deep and narrow defiles as they exist inside of myself so that I can truly invite them to also cross over. I must be willing to be transparent in my caring for them rather than hide behind formality as I did when I started back to work a decade ago.

Healing Myself, Healing the World

To do all of this I must tend to my own well-being. I cannot hold hope in the face of despair, which is in the imaginary list of skills in the imaginary description of my day job, if I am deep in the trance of despair myself. I cannot believe in the possibility of love in the lives of others when I do not grant that gift to myself. When out of my own center, I cannot hold center for someone who is teetering. Because life perforce re-opens old wounds and creates new ones continuously, my open-hearted work with my clients creates both the opportunity and necessity to attend to and heal those wounds. My relationships with the people who have entrusted me with their own wounded hearts keeps me healing my own, daily.

I have not quit my day job. In almost losing my first true love, I have discovered new depths in her. I make my bows in the direction of the evidence base for psychotherapy (and utter the secular version of prayers of thanks to John Norcross (2011; Norcross, Beutler, & Levant 2005; Norcross, Hogan, & Koocher, 2008) and Bruce Wampold (2001) and my other psychotherapy process research friends for having compiled the evidence for the power of the open heart in therapy); ultimately, I know today from my own trip back from the brink that it is my willingness to sit mindfully, compassionately, and in relationship with others that constitutes the power of this work. As, today, I enter the first day of my sixth decade on the planet, knowing that what is before me will be shorter than that which lies behind, I experience profound gratitude for having been able to nearly lose and then regain my joy in practicing psychotherapy, and to have that joy be a component of this half of life. I would not cherish this love nearly so much had I not almost broken up with her; in confronting the existential chasm of her loss, I found myself, and did so better, more clearly, and with more intention of purpose.

The great poet of the broken heart, Leonard Cohen (1993, p. 373, emphasis in original), writes (in "Anthem"):

> *Ring the bells that still can ring.*
> *Forget your perfect offering.*
> *There is a crack in everything.*
> *That's how the light gets in.*[1]

---

1 Excerpted from *Stranger Music* by Leonard Cohen. Copyright ©1993 Leonard Cohen. Reprinted by permission of McClelland & Stewart.

The crack in my life in 1999 was a deep and wide one—and the light has come back in, bright and clear.

References

Ballou, M.B., Hill, M., & West, C.M. (Eds.). (2008). *Feminist Therapy Theory and Practice: A Contemporary Perspective*. New York: Springer.

Brown, L.S. (1997). The private practice of subversion: Psychology as *tikkun olam*. *American Psychologist, 52*, 449–462.

Brown, L.S. (2006). *Relational Perspectives on Trauma Treatment*. New York: Haworth Press.

Brown, L.S. (2007, August). Finding my center: Martial arts on the way to Tikkun Olam. In J.C. Norcross (Chair) *Psychotherapist Self-Care: Leaving It at the Office*. Symposium presented at the 115th Annual Convention of the American Psychological Association, San Francisco, CA.

Brown, L.S. (2008). *Cultural Competency in Trauma Therapy: Beyond the Flashback*. Washington, D.C.: APA Books.

Brown, L.S. (2009) *Feminist Therapy*. Washington, DC: APA Books.

Brown, L.S., & Root, P.P. (Eds.). (1990). *Diversity and Complexity in Feminist Therapy*. Binghampton, NY: Haworth Press.

Brown, L.S., & Walker, L.E.A. (1990). Feminist therapy perspectives on self-disclosure. In G. Stricker and M. Fisher (Eds.), *Self-Disclosure in the Therapeutic Relationship* (pp. 135–156). New York: Plenum.

Cohen, L. (1993). "Anthem." In *Stranger Music: Selected Poems and Songs* (pp. 373–374). New York: Vintage/Random House.

Freud, S. (1953). The interpretation of dreams. In J. Strachey (Ed.), *The Complete Psychological Works of Sigmund Freud* (Vols. 4 & 5, pp. ix–62). London: Hogarth Press. (work originally published 1900)

Hill, C.E., & Knox, S. (2002). Self-disclosure. In J.C. Norcross (Ed.), *Psychotherapy Relationships that Work* (pp. 255–265). New York: Oxford University Press.

Kottler, J., & Carlson, J. (Eds.). (2008). Recovery from therapy abuse: A case from Laura Brown. In *Their Finest Hour: Master Therapists Share Their Greatest Success Stories* (pp. 135–147). Bethel, CT: Crown House Publishing.

Leonard, G. (1972). *The Transformation: A Guide to the Inevitable Changes in Mankind*. New York: Delacorte Press.

Norcross, J.C. (2011). *Psychotherapy Relationships that Work: Evidence-Based Responsiveness* (2nd ed.). New York: Oxford University Press.

Norcross, J.C., Beutler, L.E., & Levant, R.F. (Eds.). (2005). *Evidence-Based Practices in Mental Health: Debate and Dialogue on the Fundamental Questions*. Washington, DC: APA Books.

Norcross, J.C., Hogan, T.P., & Koocher, G.P. (2008). *Clinician's Guide to Evidence Based Practices: Mental Health and the Addictions*. New York: Oxford University Press.

Rogers, C. (1961). *On Becoming a Person*. New York: Houghton Mifflin.

Wampold, B.E. (2001). *The Great Psychotherapy Debate: Models, Methods, and Findings*. Mahwah, NJ: Erlbaum.

Williamson, C. (1975). *The Changer and the Changed*. Record album. Los Angeles: Olivia Records (30th anniversary enhanced edition now available from Wolf Moon Records).

5

TURNING THE MIND INTO AN ALLY

Jon Carlson

There is no shortage of good days; it's good lives that are hard to come by.

—Annie Dillard (1974, *Pilgrim at Tinker Creek*)

Along with Jeffrey Kottler, a series of books (Kottler & Carlson, 2002, 2005a, b, 2007, 2008, 2009, 2010; Kottler, Carlson, & Englar-Carlson, 2012; Kottler, Carlson, & Keeney, 2004) were completed that called for a new level of honesty and self-disclosure regarding therapy. We looked at creativity, spirituality, alternative healing methods, success, lies, failure, strange events, and even how clients change the therapist. In completing the book on lies, deception, and psychotherapy entitled *Duped*, I stated (Carlson, 2010, p. 19, emphasis added), *"I do what I do because of who I am, not because of what someone does to me."* I realize that it was not always like this with me. I spent much of my life reacting and over-reacting to what others did or what they thought I should do. I am not even sure how I ended up in college, married, and professionally productive. I was for so many years living on automatic pilot. I was oblivious to the many voices that dictated my life. Fortunately, they must have been good voices guiding my path.

My internal voices were positive because I have been blessed in so many ways. I was raised in an intact family and supported by a large extended family and friendship network that now circles the globe. I have discovered that my life, once centered in achievement and acquisition, seems to have shifted to helping and social service. I have realized the pleasure I receive from simple acts of good will and generosity to others. It might be something as simple as starting conversations with people I do not know or commenting on pleasant qualities that others possess such as cheerfulness or a smiling demeanor. The Buddhists call this process "loving-kindness" or *metta*.

I learned about *metta* from my friends in Thailand, where I have consulted for over a decade. The process involves meditating on yourself, then those close to you, those in your world, and finally those people who trouble you. The process simply involves focusing on wishing each person, beginning with yourself and then moving on to others, wishing them positive blessings like "may you be happy, safe, peaceful and free." I am sure that after years of practicing this deceptively simple process my reality has been altered.

In the mid-1970s I became acquainted with TM or Transcendental Meditation and realized that I have control over the many thoughts that travel through my brain each moment of the day. After TM, I learned many other Eastern wisdom practices including *mindfulness* and *vipassana meditation*. As I developed these disciplines, I became more and more aware of thoughts and my choices. I learned to create a life of action rather than reaction. Today, in addition to *metta* practice, daily meditation for me involves doing *passage meditation*. This process involves memorizing passages from spiritual writings and meditating on them. I also read from a variety of sacred texts each morning. Throughout my day I remind myself to be mindful in whatever I do and practice *metta* with those I have contact.

Six months ago I was diagnosed with an aggressive form of cancer. Now I have a new challenge: I'm dying. I remember reading an Aldous Huxley biography where he took drugs to help him to become fully aware and alive when he was diagnosed with cancer. His mind seemed to remain as good as ever. The drugs that I seem to be taking are the ones that take away my experience. I want to appreciate what could be the final stage of life, but the pain is intense and my mind does not seem to respond as it was trained. When I try to practice Buddhist *lojong meditation* and focus on the pain, it is hard to change my relationship to this pain and disease. I know I still have work to do.

I keep reminding myself that cancer has done a lot to my body (e.g., no hair, 70 pounds lighter) over which I have little or no control, yet I still control my mind. It is up to me how I let cancer affect me. I am living with cancer and not dying from it. I have been doing what I like and liking what I do. I still can make choices. Even my reaction to the ever present pain is my choice. I would not expect pain to disappear at this time in life. My choice is to accept the pain just like I have accepted a lifetime of personal and professional happiness. Pain is not my enemy, nor my friend—it just is what it is.

As I write this chapter, I am laying on the bed of our summer home in northern Wisconsin. The 100+ year-old log cabin has a modern house attached. My wife Laura, our children, their spouses, and our grandchildren are all in the next room playing board games. I think right now it is *Scrabble*. Everyone enjoys one another and all are concerned about my health and this new life stage. I am no longer the physically strong one, I seem to need more sleep, and

I'm not allowed to take part in the work around the cabin nor the nightly beer samplings. What I can do is to be present. I concentrate on being mindful and aware of each moment. I need to remain aware of what I do have and not focus on what is missing. I have realized that my mind is like a radio and I control the channel that is being played. When I listen to the channels that focus on the missing elements and what has been lost to the disease they become cravings and desires and keep me from being present. I have become aware of the sudden rainstorms, the over-tired grandchildren, the confused dogs, and the adults who are thinking about their life without their husband, father, or grandfather. I am able to ask for and receive help and to be honest with whatever is happening inside my body. There are no secrets.

I still do what I do because of who I am and although I try not to react, much of what I do is dictated by the disease, such as the many appointments with doctors or for lab tests. The important thing is how I go about these things: showing cheer, smiles and humor are among the positive behaviors that I attempt to showcase. I don't need the stress of self-pity, anger or sadness to burden me, although many people have asked, "Don't you get mad or aren't you angry? You have always been so healthy and never sick, it doesn't seem fair." It is as if they believe I am supposed to be this unhappy, complaining person.

I have had to allow others to take care of me. My cardinal life principal has been to not do things for someone that they can do for themselves. I now have to let people help me do so many things as body has weakened, my endurance has significantly decreased, and my awareness challenged. The responsibility for carrying groceries, driving the car, paying bills and responding to emails have all been taken on by various family members.

During my life I have received so much gratification/satisfaction from doing things for our five children and family. All have gone to college, three have multiple graduate degrees, all five have traveled the world and enjoyed their childhoods and youth. I have purchased their cars, paid for their college, and provided support as it was needed. This was what I saw as a parent's job. Now my job appears to be grateful as I let them take care of me. My wife of 44 years has depended on me for many things she now does for us. She has accepted the challenge and does it in a quiet and matter-of-fact manner. She has put her life on hold as I learn how to get out of bed, walk, shower, and basically start over from ground zero. The family does what they do out of genuine love and concern. Giving is so much easier for me than receiving! This makes the process even more of a challenge.

As I think of this chapter, I imagine what I might have written about if cancer would not have occurred. It probably would have been something that would have been interesting but not so deeply felt. It would have been words not feelings. It would have been written to add another line to my vitae. This piece has been to talk about dealing with life in the manner that many of our clients face as we coach them back to health.

The most important message from all of this is that caring people who go the extra step makes a huge difference. The four or more cards, letters, emails and gifts that arrive daily have truly moved me. Clients, colleagues, friends have all taken the time to share how their lives have been touched by mine. I know that I should know this but it has been a big surprise. I have done what I have done because of who I am. I have not pursued the awards and recognition that come with a long career. I have done what I enjoyed and believe that I have pursued happiness and not self-importance.

This illness helps me to appreciate the importance of choice as I deal with this life challenge. I am not sure what the outcome will be. The cancer appears to be in remission, and I now wait for a stem cell transplant that will help to cure the cancer. The physicians have now discovered a major heart problem that will require a quadruple by-pass in the next week. The heart problem seems to be the result of the chemotherapy and heredity. My friends and family want to know how much more can I take? Again everyone says, "It is OK to be angry, you have worked out your entire life, ate well, etc." It again seems to be a new round of learning and growth for me.

As the Buddha says, "With our thoughts we make the world." I have just become aware of the t-shirt that I am wearing: *"Do what you like, like what you do. Life is good."* I think this will be my new mantra.

References

Carlson, J. (2010). Why I do what I do. In J. Kottler & J. Carlson (Eds.), *Duped: Lies and Deception in Psychotherapy* (pp. 15–19). New York: Routledge.

Dillard, A. (1974). *Pilgrim at Tinker Creek*. New York: HarperCollins.

Kottler, J., & Carlson, J. (2002). *Bad Therapy: Master Therapists Share Their Worst Failures*. New York: Routledge.

Kottler, J., & Carlson, J. (2005a). *The Mummy at the Dining Room Table: Eminent Therapists Reveal Their Most Unusual Cases and What They Teach Us About Human Behavior*. San Francisco: Jossey Bass.

Kottler, J., & Carlson, J. (2005b). *The Client Who Changed Me: Stories of Therapist Personal Transformation*. New York: Routledge.

Kottler, J., & Carlson, J. (2007). *Moved By the Spirit: Discovery and Transformation in the Lives of Leaders*. Atascadero, CA: Impact Publishers.

Kottler, J., & Carlson, J. (2008). *Their Finest Hour: Master Therapists Share Their Greatest Success Stories*. Bethel, CT: Crown House Publishers.

Kottler, J., & Carlson, J. (2009). *Creative Breakthroughs: Tales of Transformation and Astonishment*. New York: Wiley.

Kottler, J., & Carlson, J. (2010). *Duped: Lies and Deception in Psychotherapy*. New York: Routledge.

Kottler, J., Carlson, J., & Englar-Carlson, M. (2012). *Beyond the Fifty Minute Hour*. New York: Routledge.

Kottler, J., Carlson, J., & Keeney, B. (2004). *The American Shaman: An Odyssey of Global Healing Traditions*. New York: Routledge.

6

DUENDE

Evocation, Quest, and Soul

Lillian Comas-Díaz

I've often lost myself, in order to find the burn that keeps everything awake.

—Federico García Lorca (1993)

The first time I remembered the force, I was feeling powerless. I had migrated from Puerto Rico, the island of enchantment, to the land of opportunity. The transition was challenging. When I arrived at my destination, I felt a palpable sense of culture shock. Searching for fulfillment, I encountered disappointment. Instead of freedom, I found oppression. To my dismay, xenophobia, racism, and sexism welcomed me to a New England town. In response, I lost myself in a sea of nostalgia.

I did not burn my cultural ship upon arrival to unwelcoming shores. Instead, I buried my ancestry and forgot where. To cope with pain, I became disconnected from myself. Deep in mourning, I struggled with the loneliness of an outsider. I felt as if my soul had abandoned me. Consequently, *saudade* invaded my life. The Portuguese word for profound nostalgia, *saudade* became a yearning for my soul.

Adrift, I embarked on a psychic quest. Out of nowhere, I found my family album. I dreamt of a safe haven as I turned its pages. Unexpectedly, a picture of a girl in a flamenco dress interrupted my reverie. I stopped breathing. The girl emanated a dark and light aura. The photograph awakened me from my stupor. Curious, I took the picture out of the album and placed it on my trembling hands. I barely recognized the girl in the flamenco dress as myself. Like a prism, the photo reflected a forgotten part of myself.

Waves of memory reminded me of how much I used to love flamenco. Suddenly, I became overwhelmed by a mysterious energy. I connected with the strange and familiar force that possessed the girl in the flamenco dress. This elusive power was *duende*.

Duende: A Mysterious Power

I will always be on the side of those who have nothing, of those to whom the peace of nothingness is denied.

—Federico García Lorca (1933)

The Merriam-Webster dictionary defines *duende* as "the power to attract through personal magnetism and charm" (http://www.merriam-webster.com/dictionary/duende). This definition can be misleading, however, since, as García Lorca (1933) wrote, *duende* is "the mysterious power that everyone feels and no philosopher has explained." Nonetheless, artists have attempted to define it by associating *duende* with inspiration, evil, spirit, soul, magic, danger, mystery, passion, blood, and fire, among others.

Federico García Lorca's (1933) definition of *duende* seems to best capture the fullness of this concept. In his famous lecture, "The Theory and Play of the Duende," García Lorca (1933) described *duende* as a mysterious power, a struggle born out of an ancient culture. According to him, "all that has dark tones has duende." He wrote: "The duende, then, is a power, not a work. It is a struggle, not a thought. I have heard an old maestro of the guitar say, 'The duende is not in the throat; the duende climbs up inside you, from the soles of the feet.' Meaning this: it is not a question of ability, but of true, living style, of blood, of the most ancient culture, of spontaneous creation." Indeed, duende "has to be roused from the furthest habitations of the blood."

In my experience, *duende* is felt rather than described. I seem to have a genetic link to *duende*. I grew up with my maternal Puerto Rican grandparents. Their Andalusian heritage was more shown than told. "*Tiene duende,*" my grandmother used to shout as we watched flamenco movies with dancers engulfed in fire. "What is *tener duende*?" I asked my grandmother. "To have a thirst that can only be quenched through death," she replied with a strange smile. Early in my life, I learned that *duende* dances at the edge of life and death. A bearer of death (Lopez-Pedraza, 1990), *duende* affirms and intensifies life. Along these lines, *duende* signals a radical change and portends a new life.

After a reconnection with my Andalusian core, I decided to follow my grandparents' traditions. I resolved to exorcize my *saudade* with *duende*. Preparing for the ritual, I received an ancient insight: "You do not posses duende, instead, duende possesses you."

How do you rouse *el duende*? Fortunately, I found the answer in a dream: A young girl in a flamenco dress smiled at me as she danced at the edge of a precipice. My dream interpretation revealed what I already knew; but had long forgotten: *Duende* has to be incited. To accomplish this task, I needed to retrieve my soul.

Foolishly, I thought that I knew how to call my soul back. I felt confident after consulting shamans, *curanderas* (healers) and *espiritistas* (mediums). I did not expect what happened during the moment of reclaiming myself. Without notice, *duende* declared war. Suddenly, I realized that the arrival of *duende* signaled a struggle with myself. To defend against cultural oppression, I had repressed my ethnic pride. Simply put, my cultural amnesia fiercely battled against my cultural memory. In pain, I became aware of such contradiction, and allowed myself to release my amnesia.

Surprisingly, the struggle evolved into a dance of mystery, contemplation, and awakening. I became mesmerized by the dance. In this condition, I remembered my grandmother's voice: "Dance is a way to connect with our indigenous wisdom." As I danced with *duende*, I soothed my *saudade*, found redemption, and reconnected with my soul.

Towards the culmination of the struggle-dance I felt branded by *duende*. In this feverish state I embarked into another psychic quest. However, this time around I found my destination in liberation and healing. Indeed, reaching deep into my soul was liberating. Reconnecting with blood, both ancestral and contemporary, was exhilarating. Since *duende* ignited a rage for living, I translated this passion into a thirst for social justice. In this process, I remembered García Lorca's mandate of "being at the side of those who have nothing" (quoted in Cobbs, 1992, p. 115). Simply put, I committed to becoming a liberation psychologist in order to side with the oppressed and to promote personal and collective change.

My healing-liberation journey uncovered "the burn that keeps everything awake." In this context, I affirmed my pledge to multiculturalism. As a synchronistic note, Federico García Lorca, who lived in Andalusia—a place with a multicultural history of Jewish, Muslim, and Christian conviviality—was committed to "the Gypsy, the Negro (Black), the Jew, the Moor which all Granadinos (people from Granada) carry inside them" (quoted in Cobbs, 1992, p. 118).

A passion for justice inhabited the space emptied by my *saudade*. With my renewed zest for life, I co-founded the Puerto Rican Psychological Association of Connecticut with several colleagues. Under the aegis of social justice, we became cultural warriors, ambassadors, and healers. Besides nurturing our minds and hearts, we feed our bodies with Puerto Rican food, toned our muscles dancing *salsa*, and practiced familism through our solidarity to each other (Comas-Díaz, 2012).

Duende continued to battle me. This struggle-dance led me to reconnect with my healing legacy. Like other vital aspects of myself, I had forgotten my folk-healing lineage (Comas-Díaz, 2011). After reclaiming this legacy, I merged healing into my psychologist identity. Notably, my *duende* struggle-dance led me to merge ethno-indigenous healing with mainstream psychotherapy. More-over, it helped me to envision a *duende* psychotherapy.

Duende Psychotherapy: A Dance of Pain, Passion, and Power

Dance is the hidden language of the soul of the body.

—Martha Graham

How to summon *duende* in a psychotherapy practice? Similar to the pain of childbirth, the arrival of *duende* brings a new life. Therefore, like a surgeon who wounds in order to heal, *duende* plays with Thanatos to ignite a passion for life. It is after our struggle-dance with *duende* when we become most alive.

Consistent with this notion, I believe that the presence of *duende* in psy-chotherapy can promote power and healing. In his discussion of *duende*, Elkins (2009, p. 124) observed that good psychotherapy is similar to *duende* because both entail "something vital, but almost ineffable." Moreover, Elkins stated that *duende* is the energy that opens clients' hearts and infuses them with new passion and power.

Notwithstanding its common elements with mainstream psychotherapy, *duende* favors archetypical psychotherapy. It is in this form that *duende* dances with Shadow. Within this framework, depression corresponds to *duende* sad-ness; anxiety to a fear of *duende*; mania to a drunken *duende*; and anomie to a melancholic *duende*. In my experience, however, *duende* psychotherapy special-izes in the dance of soul-making. In other words, *duende* enhances the commu-nion of body and soul. To illustrate, *duende* comes during the dark night of the soul. Conceived by John of the Cross, the concept of the dark night of the soul represents the journey of the soul into a union with the divinity (http://www.ccel.org/ccel/john_cross/dark_night.toc.html).

Following this analysis, sufferers develop wisdom as they endure pain during their soul journey. Such path culminates in the temple of mystical love. *Duende* moves sufferers through a different developmental path from John of the Cross' soul journey. Instead of asking for the purification of the body, *duende* embla-zons sufferers with a passionate fire. In this way, the mysterious power anchors individuals into their physical senses, and demands them to commune with their wound.

I am familiar with this process as I see a significant number of wounded individuals in my clinical practice. Indeed, the legions of the wounded are increasing exponentially. Working with this population requires healing the wound that never closes. Since *duende* loves the pain, a *duende* psychotherapy aids by infusing meaning into the wound. In this meaning-making process, *duende* facilitates soul retrieval. Let me offer an example.

As a psychologist, I have seen clients suffering from *susto* (fright), a culture-bound syndrome denoting the loss of the soul after a painful and ter-rifying experience. As a result, healing *susto* requires the recovery of the soul via the reconnection with the body. Given that dis-ease results from a cultural disconnection, healing within this model involves a reclaiming of ancestral roots. As a healer, *duende* arrives to help us connect with our selves. In this way, *duende* infuses us with a power to call back our soul. Such a healing power entails embracing the struggle-dance, impregnating the body with passion, and creating a renewed sense of life. Consider the following clinical vignette.

Carlos, a Salvadoran American gay man, was referred to me for treatment of depression. Grieving a romantic breakup, Carlos began to abuse alcohol and to engage in what he called "meaningless and empty" sex. I used an interper-sonal psychotherapy (Klerman, Weissman, Rounsanville, & Chevron, 1984) approach with some success in treating Carlos' depression. However, he still complained of experiencing anomie (*duende* melancholia). While assessing his cultural strengths, Carlos reported that as a child he loved flamenco dancing. Subsequently, I suggested a reconnection with Carlos' childhood passion. Ini-tially, my client rejected the idea. Carlos struggled with the suggestion, stating that "it was too painful to go back."

Instead, I proposed a desensitization technique with a gradual and successive approximation schedule. To illustrate, first, Carlos was to listen to flamenco music; then, he was to watch flamenco movies/videos. Afterwards, Carlos was to attend a flamenco dancing function. At this point, and on his own volition, Carlos joined a flamenco troupe. Finally, he began to dance professionally. Needless to say, Carlos awakened his *duende* and regained his passion for life.

Along these lines, Federico García Lorca (1933) argued for the need to dif-ferentiate *duende* from angel and muse. He observed that while both angel and muse come from outside, *duende* needs to be awakened from within. In other words, since everyone has *duende* within, everyone has the potential to awaken *duende*. Therefore, as a psychotherapist, I aim to summon *duende* in the life of my wounded clients. John's clinical vignette, like that of Carlos', illustrates the awakening of *duende* in psychotherapy.

John, a 35-year-old African American married man, came to see me after his employer recommended mental-health treatment. John reported having a strong support system at home with his wife, his 12-year-old daughter, and his family of origin. John worked as a staffer in a congressman's office. He described his work as being extremely stressful. His level of irritability resulted in strained relationships with his coworkers, especially, with White men. John believed that he was victim of aversive racism—a discrimination involving dis-sociation between implicit and explicit stereotyping. Indeed, empirical studies showed that individuals who in self-report measures seem to be non-prejudiced, have generally negative attitudes toward African Americans (Dovidio & Gaert-ner, 1986). Succinctly put, researchers have found that aversive racism entails the expression of complex, implicit, and or subconscious racism (Dovidio &

Gaertner, 1998). Moreover, John's experience at work was aggravated by his exposure to racial microaggressions—the intentional or unintentional assaults that occur on a regular basis solely due to individuals' race (Pierce, 1995). Since microaggressions entail demeaning and subtle insults against minorities, the exposure to microaggressions affects victims' sense of trust, competence, normality, and visibility (Sue et al., 2007). Therefore, John could not openly confront his White co-workers, given the subtle nature of their aversive racism. Nonetheless, he decided to remain at his job. John identified the structural racism against African American men in the work force, and the ensuing difficulty in finding employment, as reasons for not resigning from his job.

Overall, John opted to work on stress and anger management. In particular, he worked on coping with aversive racism. Subsequently, John learned relaxation techniques and joined a yoga group. Albeit a significant amount of clinical progress was made, John continued to feel, in his words, "like a trapped warrior." During a psychotherapy session, John asked me if I knew about *capoeira*. He had attended a *capoeira* demonstration, invited by a man from his yoga class. I responded that practicing this Afro Brazilian blend of martial arts and dance proved to be therapeutic for some individuals. Moreover, I encouraged John to try *capoeria*. As a result, John began to practice *capoeira*. Several months later, he reported that he was no longer feeling trapped. In particular, John enjoyed *capoeria* because it helped him to survive in a hostile work environment. Also known as the dance of war, *capoeira* was developed by the descendants of African slaves who disguised their military exercises as a dance. By dancing *capoeira*, the slaves did not elicit their owners' suspicion. As a survivalist mechanism, *capoeira* helped the slaves to train themselves in order to fight the colonial oppression.

Through his practice of *capoeira*, John seemed to channel his *duende* energy into a warrior identity. He expressed feeling free from his oppressive situation at work. John stated: "When I practice *capoiera*, I feel possessed by a force that infuses me with power and love."

Conclusion: What's Love Got to Do with It?

Love is a battle, love is a war; love is a growing up.

—James A. Baldwin

As a wounded healer, I relate to my clients' woundedness. In this way, I honor their quest, witness their darkness, and support their soul making. When appropriate, my woundedness teaches me to assist others in the awakening of their *duende*. Likewise, psychotherapists can assist wounded individuals to infuse themselves with *duende* passion and power.

In this task, I gently encourage my clients to awaken their *duende*. When *duende* declares war, I encourage my clients to engage in the struggle-dance. I conceive the *duende* process as an act of love. Indeed, the struggle with *duende* mirrors the enthusiastic process of awakening the god within. As an attendant of my clients' soul, I, too, am infused with such enthusiasm—one that leaves me feeling renewed, connected, and complete.

In a similar vein, García Lorca (1933) affirmed that the arrival of *duende* generates an almost religious enthusiasm. He observed that when Andalusians witness the presence of *duende*, they invoke the divinity with cries of *"Viva Dios!"* Moreover, Garcia Lorca asserted that Andalusians reclaim their Muslim roots when they exclaim *"Olé, Olé!"*—a cry so close to *"Allah, Allah!"*

A healer-warrior, *duende* alchemizes suffering into love. For instance, Nick Cave (1999), a musician and writer, asserted that *duende* gives birth to creativity, and in turn, creativity is moved by love. According to Cave, the writer who refuses to explore the darkness of the heart will never be able to write convincingly of the wonder, the magic, and the joy of love. Certainly, Cave equates the journey of the soul with the ultimate attainment of love.

Following a similar line of reasoning, a psychotherapist that does not explore darkness cannot help her clients aspire to experience the wonders of love. As a psychotherapist, I strive to facilitate my clients' soul-making process. Indeed, when we struggle, or even better, when we dance with *duende*, we experience the fullness of life.

The girl in the flamenco dress continues to dance to the music of life. As a middle-aged woman, I greet *duende* whenever it arrives. Moreover, I embrace *duende* as I welcome the struggle. I have learned that at the end of the dance, *duende* rewards us by renewing our capacity to live and to love.

References

Cave, N. (1999, September 25). *Nick Cave's Love Song Lecture*. Retrieved from http://www.everything2.com/index.pl?node_id=800055

Cobbs, N. (1992). *Archetypal Imagination: Glimpses of the Gods in Life and Art*. Hudson, NY: Lindisfarne Press.

Comas-Díaz, L. (2012). *Multicultural Care: A Clinician's Guide to Cultural Competence*. Washington, DC : American Psychological Association.

Comas-Díaz, L. (2011). Transcultural woman: Healing in a strange land. In L. Comas-Diaz & M.B. Weiner (Eds.), *Women Psychotherapists: Journeys in Healing* (pp. 81–95). New York: Jason Aronson.

Dovidio, J.F., & Gaertner, S.L. (1986). *Prejudice, Discrimination, and Racism*. San Diego, CA: Academic Press.

Dovidio, J.F., & Gaertner, S.L. (1998). On the nature of contemporary prejudice: The causes, consequences and challenges of aversive racism. In J.L. Eberhardt & S.T. Fiske (Eds.), *Confronting Racism: The Problem and the Response* (pp. 3–32). Thousand Oaks, CA: Sage.

Elkins, D. (2009). *Humanistic Psychology: A Clinical Manifesto: A Critique of Clinical Psychology and the Need for Progressive Alternatives*. Colorado Springs, CO: University of the Rockies Press.

García Lorca, F. (1933). *Teoría y juego del duende* [Theory and play of the duende] (A.S. Kline,

Trans.). Retrieved from http://www.poetryintranslation.com/PITBR/Spanish/LorcaDuende.htm In Spanish:http://homepage.mac.com/eeskenazi/duende.htm

Klerman, G. L., Weissman, M.M.., Rounsanville, B., & Chevron, E. (1984). *Interpersonal Psychotherapy of Depression*. New York: Basic Books.

Lopez-Pedraza, R. (1990). Reflections on the duende. In *Cultural Anxiety* (pp. 55–78). Einsiedeln, Switzerland: Daimon Verlag.

Pierce, C. M. (1995). Stress analogs of racism and sexism: Terrorism, torture and disaster. In C.V. Willie, P.P. Reiker, & B.S. Brown (Eds.). *Mental Health, Racism and Sexism* (pp. 277–293). Pittsburgh, PA: University of Pittsburgh Press.

Sue, D.W., Capodilupo, C.M., Torino, G.C., Bucceri, J.M., Holder, A.M.B., Nadal, K.L., & Esquilin, M. (2007). Racial microaggressions in everyday life: Implications for clinical practice. *American Psychologist, 62*(4), 271–286.

7

PSYCHOTHERAPY'S SOOTHSAYER

Nicholas A. Cummings

In 2001 *The Psychotherapy Networker* (Simon, 2001) published a feature article titled "Psychotherapy's Soothsayer" in which they extolled the fact that I had been predicting accurately the course of psychology and psychotherapy for half a century. As I read the article it sunk in that I had, indeed, predicted everything from brief, intermittent psychotherapy as the modal practice, changes in education permitting clinicians to hold faculty positions, the displacement of psychotherapy by psychotropic medications, the medicalization of psychiatry with its abandonment of psychotherapy, the growth and over-taking of psychology by pre-doctoral psychotherapists performing most of psychotherapy, and most importantly, the industrialization of healthcare and the usurping of mental health delivery by managed care. There were many more discussed in the article, but my reaction was, "What's the big deal? Anyone should have seen these 'train wrecks' bearing down on us."

In the late 1970s when I began predicting the industrialization of healthcare, and especially mental healthcare, the leadership at the American Psychological Association actually said I was "paranoid." It was argued, "How could something like psychotherapy be industrialized, as it is the epitome of the doctor-patient relationship?" To me the question was the opposite: What has taken so long for a sector that encompasses one-fifth of the gross domestic product (GDP) to industrialize? Manufacturing industrialized in the early 1900s, mining in the 1930s, and retailing in the 1970s. By the 1980s even agriculture industrialized with huge corporate farms rapidly squeezing out the family farms. Looking way back, transportation and communication industrialized in the late 1800s with thousands of miles of railroad tracks and telegraph lines spanning the continent. The time for the industrialization of mental healthcare was overdue. I lamented what I saw coming, and since the term "managed care" had not yet been invented, in my 1986 *American Psychologist* article (Cummings, 1986) I called it a "locust" that would sweep over our practices. Why couldn't my colleagues see it coming?

In frustration, in 1985 I founded American Biodyne, a totally psychology-driven company to demonstrate that we could pre-empt the "locust" and usurp what was to become managed care. I stated that I would limit the company to half a million enrollees, and I invited my colleagues to come and spend as much time as needed to learn how to go out and form the next 50 such companies. We would pre-empt managed care by doing it right. The APA now scoffed that "Nick had added grandiosity to his paranoia. Where is he going to find 500,000 enrollees for such a crazy scheme?" Well, I found them in three months, launched the company, and waited. No one came except Wall Street. So after three years I took my foot off the brake, and American Biodyne grew to 25 million enrollees in the next seven years.

As the locust, now officially called "managed care," rapidly spread over the land, the APA frantically went into high gear opposing this disruption. It was as effective as had been the telegraph industry, which had dismissed the telephone as "a gadget with no future," trying to stop being replaced after the fact. The APA lost the battle; almost all Americans now receive their healthcare and mental healthcare from some form of industrialized delivery. From its exalted position of having been accepting millions of dollars from the special assessment levied on licensed psychologists, the now-chagrined APA Practice Directorate played a disingenuous game of "CYA" (which doesn't mean Cover Your Assets). It accused me for over a decade of having invented managed care, a classic case of blaming the messenger (see N.A. Cummings, 2000, 2002).

Why couldn't my colleagues see what was coming? Even more, I wondered, why was I the lone prescient? I looked back to my formative years for an answer.

Looking Back

I had just finished pre-med (a three-year curriculum at the time) in two years and had an acceptance to medical school when I asked myself, "Do I really want to be a surgeon?" I wrote the medical school and asked if my acceptance would be good for next year. I never received a reply, but I did receive a letter from President Roosevelt telling me that a committee of my fellow citizens had selected me for military service. World War II was raging, and I was drafted. Ignoring all my schooling, the Army sent me to Texas where I underwent infantry training which included frequently recurring 35-mile forced marches while carrying a full field pack, grenades, rifle, and helmet. After losing count on the number of these, I walked into my company's area one evening and saw an announcement that a new form of combat troops to be called "paratroopers" was being formed. All would be volunteers between ages 18 and 22, in top physical condition, and to begin immediately. I thought jumping out of airplanes has to be a lot easier than marching 35 miles and I volunteered. At Fort Benning, Georgia, I soon learned this was a huge mistake: I jumped out of airplanes and then marched 35 miles! But here it was that as a combat paratrooper I learned about psychology.

I rose rapidly in rank, mostly because those above me in rank were killed or badly wounded, and soon was battlefield commissioned as a combat officer. The 82nd Airborne Division was suffering about 40% of its casualties to "jump door fever." A superstition among paratroopers was based on a misunderstanding of the law of averages. Since the average was three combat jumps before being killed or wounded on the fourth jump (two and three, respectively, for an officer), paratroopers would fearlessly make three combat jumps because "It is not my time." But then there came the fourth jump, and frequently a trooper would freeze at the jump door. The jump sergeant would count to 10 and, if the trooper did not jump, he was pushed out by the sergeant's boot in the small of the trooper's back. A certain cadence has to be maintained: too soon and the men would run into each other in mid-air, too slow would result in overshooting the jump target. After being pushed, the trooper would all-too-often hit the ground in severe panic, forget all of his training, and be killed by the enemy. What could be done to prevent jump door fever?

The military, through General William Menninger, brother of Karl and co-founder of the famous Menninger Clinic, had established the School of Military Neuropsychiatry in Long Island, New York. I was chosen to attend a two-week crash course taught by Dr. Frieda Fromm-Reichmann, a world-renowned psychoanalyst, on how to talk the terrified trooper willingly out the jump door in ten seconds. She taught us that although love is the strongest emotion, it is slow in evolving. Rage is immediate and compelling. She taught me and a select group of my fellow combat officers how to mobilize rage in the interest of health, insulting the trooper so that he jumped out the door in defiant rage—thus saving his life. For example, I remember one fellow, let's call him Antonelli. When he froze in the doorway, I said—deliberately using a scurrilous anti-Italian slur—"Are all you d—s cowards, or just you?" He snarled, "F—k you, Captain!" and jumped. Later, when we met on the ground, we embraced as comrades.

I never lost another trooper to jump door fever after that brief training. And there was never a time I used this intervention that later the trooper, who realized what I had done, did not thank me for it. The trooper was soon aware and grateful, usually by the time he hit the ground. Even though I was known for my later advancement of brief psychotherapy (e.g., see Cummings & Sayama, 1995), in retrospect this is by far the briefest psychotherapy I have ever done.

I reasoned that if psychology could do that with a 10-second intervention, I wanted to be a psychologist. (Parachuting into Buchenwald near the end of WWII to help liberate the concentration camp and seeing the unfathomable cruelty and carnage that some humans had perpetrated on others also stimulated my interest in psychology—but that's another story for another time: see Austad, in preparation). Dr. Fromm-Reichmann encouraged me, and took me with her on her rounds. In that World War II era, long before medications, fecal smearing by schizophrenics was common. When confronted by such a patient, doctors would walk away, instructing a psychiatric attendant to clean up the mess. Not so Fromm-Reichmann. In one pocket of her smock she carried sets of surgical gloves and the other she filled with candy bars. When seeing a patient smearing feces she would sit on the floor, put on a pair of gloves, and begin smearing with the patient. After a few minutes she would discard the soiled gloves and hand the patient a candy bar, saying, "Here, you may like this candy bar better than feces. I'll come by here again tomorrow morning about this time. If you are not smearing your feces I'll know you prefer a candy bar and I will have another one for you." I never once saw this intervention to fail. She taught me that just because a schizophrenic talks to us does not mean that the patient has really let us into his or her world. One gains entrance by joining the patient's delusion. She taught me how to do this in a variety of ways depending on the delusion, and I used it throughout my career, almost never having to rely on medication.

Once again a civilian and graduate student, now in psychology, I found that the profession was (and alas, still is) not known for innovation. I complained about this to my psychoanalyst, Erik Erikson, who was himself such a forward thinking practitioner that at the time he was highly criticized by his fellow psychoanalysts. He was my analyst long before his eventually being claimed by all schools of psychotherapy, which in my disdain for intellectual fortresses I long ago labeled "psycho-religions." In the tenth month of my four-times-a-week psychoanalysis he told me we would be terminating in two months. I protested, "Am I doing something wrong?" "No, you are doing very well, but if we continue you will become a very successful, stodgy and even insufferable psychoanalyst. But if we stop now, you will spend the rest of your life innovating." For the one and only time I jumped up from the couch and faced him, an act that in that era was tantamount to giving God the finger. He calmly told me face-to-face in response to my shouting that I could get another analyst, "but the blood will not be on my head." We spent the last two months of my analysis with me insisting we would not quit and he insisting we would. He won, and I have been innovating ever since, having formed 23 organizations such as the four campuses of the California School of Professional Psychology (CSPP), thus launching the professional school movement. All of these 23 organizations were to help my myopic colleagues to hopefully see the future in progress. Alas, more often than not I experienced disappointment.

How did Erikson know this? Perhaps it was the discovery in my analysis of my experience in the first grade, which I began not knowing a word of English. My grandmother, who lived with us, came late to America and never learned English, so we spoke Greek at home. I had many cousins in our large extended family who all spoke Greek, so I had no shortage of playmates with whom I could communicate. Once in school I was terrified by an environment speaking nothing that I could understand. Bewildered, I was speechless. In response my teacher was angry, demanding I speak up, and accusing me of being stubborn and defiant. I was so terrified that I became mute, and was sent to a sadistic principal who would have me remove my shoes and socks and then she would beat me on the bottoms of my feet with a stinging ruler until the bottoms of my feet were red. I did not show these to my mother as I thought I was doing something wrong to bring this on. This was my life day after day, a terrified mute, who was after three weeks subjected to psychological testing by one of Lewis Terman's students who came to Salinas, California (where my family lived) from Stanford at the Lincoln School's request. I recall only one of several tests she administered. It consisted of a series of blocks whose size did not coincide with their weight (i.e., a small block might weigh more than a larger block). She apparently instructed me to arrange them according to weight, but not understanding this, I logically did what a five-year-old would intuitively do: I arranged them in an obvious fashion from small to large. A few days later a social worker came to our home with papers for my grieving mother to sign. My father had recently died of a ruptured appendix in the then pre-antibiotic world, and my mother was so distraught that she was in no condition to question. Without understanding what she was about to do, she began to sign the papers thinking they were perfunctory to my school. Just then my Uncle Mitchell came to look in on his widowed sister-in-law, and read the papers. I was being committed to the Sonoma State Hospital for Mentally Retarded Children! He tore the papers up, chased the social worker out of the house, drove to the school, and confronted the teacher and the principal, "Don't you realize this boy cannot speak English?" In retrospect, this was monumental ignorance on the part of the school authorities, as it was in the 1920s, the height of European immigration to the United States. Our country was full of foreigners who could not speak English. He made arrangements for my cousin Ted, who was in another first grade and who spoke English, to be transferred to my class and act as my interpreter. I learned English fluently within two months, and years later was scoring in the genius range on now much more refined intelligence tests.

Erik Erikson's comment upon my recollecting this saga was to point out that I had almost been destroyed by a student of one of psychology's "greats," Lewis Terman himself. "You are bound to never, as a psychologist, be plagued by the herd instinct. You will question so-called authority and you will innovate." He was not one to mince words, and although his bluntness would put-off the very proper psychoanalysts of that era, his style was really complimentary and even encouraging.

Erikson also knew of another of my change-making bouts with erroneous authority, a history of which we fully explored in my sessions with him. At age nine I had contracted polio, and was left paralyzed from the waist down. My parents were told I would never walk again, and I was encouraged by my doctors to take heart and succeed in life as had then-President Franklin Roosevelt who was also paralyzed by poliomyelitis, or "infantile paralysis" as it was then known. "You see," I was told, "You can even become president even though you cannot walk," which was small comfort to a previously athletic nine year old. My grandmother heard of and believed Sister Kenny, a nurse who insisted that even with passive exercise a person young enough could regain leg innervation. The medical community scoffed, and attacked her as being a charlatan. In spite of this, my grandmother insisted that there was nothing to lose by trying what Sister Kenny was admonishing. She insisted I try riding my bike, which I had previously loved so much. Like Fromm-Reichmann she used rage, yelling in Greek, "Do you want to be a hopeless cripple the rest of your life? You are only nine, so why not try. The doctors don't know everything. I'll help you get your scared fanny on that bike." At first I was able to go only a few yards before I fell and lay helpless, but soon it was city blocks and then miles. Within one year I was doing 50 mile trips and I began soon walking again, haltingly at first, but in no time with no detectable difficulty. I'll never forget my grandmother disdainfully and purposely using the awful word "cripple" instead of milder terms such as "impaired" or "handicapped." Erikson commented, she knew how to invoke rage in the interest of health even before Dr. Fromm-Reichmann. She had to defy my mother who tearfully would plead with me not to get my hopes up and then have them dashed to the ground.

Before my analysis, I met and within three months married Dorothy Mills, who has been my partner for 64 years, and who has always encouraged me in my innovations which more often than not necessitated a brash defiance of existing authority. Erikson commented: "Most men marry women like their mothers. You married the reincarnation of your Grandmother Mary." How true!

As a veteran on the G.I. Bill I began graduate studies in psychology at the University of California, Berkeley, where I had no patience with the absence of clinical practice and training in the new clinical psychology program hurriedly stitched together right after World War II by the university whose sole intent seemed to be to grab hold of the monies now offered by the V.A. and NIMH for clinical training. I even defiantly told the renowned Professor Edward Tolman that I had no intention of being a rat runner. In his incredibly delightful cynicism he suggested I transfer to a Skinnerian doctoral program where I could become a pigeon pecker. I entered the University of Southern California (USC) program and soon left. I tried the Claremont Graduate School where I obtained a masters degree in a combined Greek classics and graduate psychology program and then left there, too. With Dot's help we finally found a truly innovative clinical program, founded by Gordon Derner at Adelphi University in New York. There I learned to be a clinician, and was able to repay Gordon years later when, after I founded the free-standing California School of Professional Psychology, I helped him make the Adelphi program the first professional school on a university campus. It saddens me that after Gordon's death his program, renamed the Derner Institute, steadily became an outdated long-term psychoanalytical program, and seemingly remains so to this day.

After graduation my first employments involved innovation. I became Chief Psychologist for California's newly enacted sexual deviant program, an alternative treatment setting in lieu of prison that eventually became Atascadero State Hospital. Then, I participated in the deinstitutionalization of two California state hospitals, first Mendocino and then Modesto. Dorothy saw an ad for chief psychologist at Northern California's Kaiser Permanente hospitals and clinics, and she encouraged me to apply, which I did half-heartedly along with some 50 other applicants. When interviewed by founder Dr. Sidney Garfield and co-founder Dr. Morris Collen, I was told that if hired I would have to agree that anytime in the first six months I could be fired without further explanation. This was like waving a red flag in front of a bull. I determined then and there I would get the job and would succeed in it. At the time I did not know the reason this was said, but I later learned that my predecessor had been Timothy Leary who subsequently became known as the high priest of LSD. This was before his LSD days, but he had apparently greatly under-achieved in his role at Kaiser Permanente, making his employers wary of psychologists. Why did Sid Garfield persist in wanting a psychologist in that role? I learned only after my employment that he believed psychiatrists were ultimately physicians and would fall back on being physicians rather than psychotherapists who would understand and treat somatizing patients psychologically instead of medically.

Being Chief Psychologist at Kaiser was the epitome of my innovative learning. Garfield was a genius who invented capitated prepaid healthcare and made it work when no one else could. Morrie Collen, my immediate boss, not only encouraged me to innovate, but pushed me to do so. Taking hold, I ran with the dictum, sometimes going farther than my mentors anticipated. I got to know the great industrialist Henry J. Kaiser who would urge us to "find a need and fill it." I often over-stepped my authority, making Morrie nervous at times. This was especially true in my representing Kaiser Permanente in Washington where the Kennedy administration was enamored of my discovery of medical cost offset. I often spoke and published without prior authorization, not because I was being defiant, but because my presence in Washington, including the 18 times I testified before the Congress, required immediate answers. I was fired and rehired within hours three times for speaking and committing without pre-authorization. The last was by Sid Garfield and Morrie Collen, after which I would tell anyone who even thought of having me fired that since I had been fired and rehired by the founders themselves, I was invulnerable. It had also become apparent after each violation that what I had said or committed was for the best.

At Kaiser Permanente I wrote the nation's first prepaid psychotherapy coverage in 1959 and made it work (Cummings, 2002b). Before that, psychotherapy had been a written exclusion on all of the nation's health insurance policies. Soon all policies began to include psychotherapy, not for psychotherapy's sake, but because it reduced *medical and surgical* costs (see Cummings & VandenBos, 1981). Much to Sid and Morrie's surprise, I priced the first monthly capitation rate at under $1 and emerged with a real cost of only half that. I was very proud when in dedicating a large new Kaiser facility in Walnut Creek, California, Sid Garfield said it was paid for by the savings realized in medical cost offset resulting from our new psychotherapy coverage.

And so, when the need came to show psychology how it could assume the leadership and usurp Wall Street in the impending industrialization of mental healthcare, I knew how to do it by effective, efficient psychotherapy, never resorting to session limits, precertification, and all the other bean-counter techniques universally employed by managed care companies. American Biodyne was psychology driven and spent 15% of all psychotherapists' time in quality assurance. When rival companies tried this, they almost went broke and had to quickly go back to bean-counter techniques. Also, all decision-makers were psychologists, not MBAs or psychiatrists, who designed staff-model Biodyne Centers of six psychologists and social workers for each 30,000 enrollees, replicating this for each additional 30,000. Each center was thus very manageable, and encouraged to innovate in accordance with the needs of the community it was serving. Our motto was that "healthcare is a local issue," with needs varying often dramatically from locale to locale. For example, the need in Detroit was to treat substance abuse, while only a few miles away in the Detroit suburbs it was mostly domestic problems. American Biodyne eventually grew to 25 million covered lives served by 10,000 psychotherapists covering all fifty states.

When after 10 years I left the company, it abandoned the staff model in favor of networks. It then began to lose control, experienced its first lawsuits, and soon found itself resorting to bean-counter techniques. Within a year or two it was swallowed up by the swirl of consolidation of managed behavioral health companies in which no one knew how to do it right.

Toward the Future

In my own life I continue to innovate, the latest being the unprecedented success of the Nicholas A. Cummings Doctor of Behavioral Health Program at Arizona State University. I continue to innovate because I was fortunate in having and finding innovative mentors: Grandmother Mary, Dr. Frieda Fromm-Reichmann, my wife Dorothy, my analyst Erik Erikson, Dr. Gordon Derner, then finally physicians Drs. Sidney Garfield and Morris Collen. And there were others, like Senator Edward (Ted) Kennedy for whose Senate Health Committee I was an adviser while he taught me the ins and outs of government in Washington. I continue to innovate at age 88, and am pleased to see the first project in 1963 in which I co-located psychologists as behavioral care providers (BCPs) in primary care settings, practicing side-by-side with primary care physicians (PCPs), become APA policy in 2009 (Bray, 2011). Happily, I have lived long enough to see the association of which I am a past-president go from scoffing at co-located psychological care for 46 years to finally adopting it officially.

My daughter, Janet Cummings (2002, p. xxxviii), herself a fine psychologist, says tongue-in-cheek that my continued passionate involvement in the healthcare of our nation and our world means that I have "flunked retirement."

References

Austad, C.S. (in preparation). *The Life and Times of Nicholas A. Cummings: A Biography.*

Bray, J.H. (2011). Reforms in treating children and families. In N.A. Cummings & W.T. O'Donohue (Eds.), *Understanding the Behavioral Healthcare Crisis: The Promise of Integrated Care and Diagnostic Reform* (pp. 343–366). New York: Routledge.

Cummings, J.L. (2002). A personal note: A brief biography of Nicholas Cummings. In *The Collected Papers of Nicholas A. Cummings, Vol. 2: The Entrepreneur in Psychology* (pp. xxii–xxxviii). Phoenix, AZ: Zeig, Tucker & Theisen.

Cummings, N.A. (1986). The dismantling of our health system: Strategies for the survival of psychological practice. *American Psychologist, 41,* 426–431.

Cummings, N.A. (2000, 2002a). *The Collected Papers of Nicholas A. Cummings, Vols. 1-2.* Phoenix, AZ: Zeig, Tucker & Theisen.

Cummings, N.A. (2002b). The founding of the Kaiser Permanente mental health system: How the first comprehensive psychotherapy benefit was written. In *The Collected Papers of N.A. Cummings* (Vol. 2, pp. 1–18). Phoenix, AZ: Zeig, Tucker & Theisen.

Cummings, N.A., & Sayama, M. (1995). *Focused Psychotherapy: A Casebook of Brief, Intermittent Psychotherapy Throughout the Life Cycle.* Philadelphia: Brunner/Mazel.

Cummings, N.A., & VandenBos, G.R. (1981). The twenty years Kaiser Permanente experience with psychotherapy and medical utilization: Implications for national health policy and national health insurance. *Health Policy Quarterly, 1*(2), 159–175. Reprinted in N.A. Cummings, *The Collected Papers of N.A. Cummings* (Vol. 1, pp. 126–142). Phoenix, AZ: Zeig, Tucker & Theisen.

Simon, R. (2001, July/August). Psychotherapy soothsayer: Nick Cummings foretells your future. *Psychotherapy Networker, 25*(4), 34–39, 62.

8

IT WARMS MY HEART

Carol A. Erickson

Growing up for me was unusual, as I grew up in a mental hospital not realizing that it was a very different world than what most children experience. My playground was the hospital grounds and some of my special friends were mental patients. I played with the other doctors' and staff members' children, yet my favorites were some of the adult patients who had "grounds parole." We also had our "maids" who came into our apartment to clean or do the dishes, trying for a higher level of "parole" on their way to being discharged.

I talked to my "special people" and shared my secrets with them and appreciated our mutually caring relationship. My psychiatrist father, who I called "Dad" and the staff and patients called "Dr. Erickson," had given some basic rules for these relationships, such as I could not give them gifts nor could I talk about the family. However, they could and did talk to me and they gave me small gifts. I did not understand at that time why they had to be locked up and "shepherded" or monitored so much of the time. I thought they were nice people. I liked them and I deeply appreciated that they cared about me.

When, in my younger years, I asked my father why they had to be locked up, he told me that sometimes they were dangerous. I do remember "Rose," who was one of my special people because of our interactions and because she would sing to me. Then one day she was crying and sobbing in the day porch (a locked setting). I called to her, asking what was the matter. She said they had taken away her new pretty dress with the sparkling mirror buttons because she had cut herself with the buttons. She was so sad and so unhappy. I also remember Emma H., who was a lovely, sweet grandmotherly person to me. She gave me whiffs of perfume and pretty hankies and hugs and she would talk about her family and how she missed them. I would hug her and she would hug me and we really cared about each other—and then she was gone.

Dad's Knee

Some of the particular memories of that growing up time had to do with my Dad, Milton H. Erickson. He was studying hypnosis, and I began learning pain control for myself as a very young child under his coaching. One of the activities that we did together was very intriguing to me. In the evening, he would hold me on his lap and tell me stories about a particular group of characters. In these stories, one of them would encounter a serious problem. Then, my Dad would say to me, "What should _____ do?" And I would think about the situation and offer up a possible solution. Then, my Dad would tell me that the solution would not work because of Complication X or Complication Y. So I would think carefully, taking these complications into consideration and proffer a different solution. Then Dad would say to me, "Oh, that's very good, Carol, but that won't work because of Complication Z." So I would again consider all the complications or factors, ask questions about the situations, and come up with an adjusted version of the solution. And again, we would often do a third round. He would always compliment me on my young problem-solving skills, and sometimes I would come up with a very good solution. And, when the problems were solved and later the story finished, I would get down and go to bed. When I grew up, I realized that my father was teaching me to listen, think, and problem-solve very early in my life.

When my father would take me on ward rounds with him, he would explain some things to me that I didn't understand. One lady laughed and laughed and laughed, and I didn't see anything funny. My father said she was a hebephrenic, she had a kind of illness, a form of schizophrenia.

Out of these adventures with many different people I came to have a wide tolerance of different ways of being in the world. Also, in some ways I wanted to help these people who were so sad and/or locked up. However, I knew, without a doubt, that I did not want to be a teacher. As I grew up, I was a very good student and thought of maybe becoming a psychiatrist. However, the costs of medical school put me off, so I married young and had six children in six years. My days and nights were filled with the needs of all of these little people and it was an incredible training ground for listening, observing, anticipating, predicting, recognizing and solving situations and problems. I loved being a mother and sharing, relieving, explaining, teaching and resolving the multiplicity of problems that needed solutions. It was a challenge, an adventure, a wonder ride into imagination, thinking, creating, and developing a variety of answers and solutions that would enrich each of the children and myself so we could all win.

I started college classes after having two children. My first class was called "The Theory of Emotions" and it called on me to learn many new things and gave me fresh understandings as well as knowledge and questions and beliefs. The second class was "Basic Psychology." The professor was teaching his last class before retiring. I disagreed with many of his statements, and at that point I decided to become a psychotherapist. Partly, I did this because the professor was so rigid and his answers so limited and inflexible that it seemed to my young mind that according to his view, life would not be enjoyable and it would become a tedious daily task with a thousand limitations.

My picture of "life" was quite different. As I looked around, it seemed to me that the world was a glorious place, and the challenge in living was to take on the various problems, situations and tasks with an open mind, creativity, adaptability, and flexibility, all the while keeping a sense of humor, having fun, appreciating the "touches of joy" and developing satisfaction for the achievements both within myself and within others. In looking back, I can truly see how some of the values that I took into my being as a child, as a person growing up, as a student and as a mother developed out of my years growing up with patients in the three separate state hospitals in which I had lived.

Perhaps one of the benefits of being a therapist is the necessity of seeing problems, dilemmas, situations, and attitudes from so many different points of view; with that comes the understanding and blessings of the gift of flexibility. To hear or comprehend a set of difficulties belonging to a person or client who feels totally locked in or locked out and then to help them work through their difficulties in a respectful and sometimes delicate, or humorous or challenging way or ways until the client feels free to make clear and/or appropriate choices as they continue their life journey is a soul-satisfying gift. To be part of life on this planet with all of its beauty and wonders and possibilities for change is both an incredible challenge and a joy.

Hypnosis

Hypnosis was a special, almost magical "thing" when I was a child. I knew my father used "it" on people. And I remember him using it on me as a young child when I was hurt and had to have stitches. I learned to use it for myself, in particular for pain control after I was in a bad car accident. Later on I began using it for a number of tasks to help improve my own performance in a variety of ways.

Then, of course, it seemed so natural to use hypnosis in my private practice. I attended a couple of hypnosis workshops with the idea of broadening my own perspectives, and I realized that I was already using light trance states on a regular basis on both myself and others. With that in mind, I believe that hypnosis to some degree is almost implicit in my work with clients. It may be a very light relaxed trance state or a deeper working trance or a somewhere in-between trance state. I always discuss it with clients ahead so that there are no objections and we become a working team.

Sometimes the trance state is just a relaxing time-out, and very often it is a light-to-medium trance state where we can explore new perspectives in a comfortable way. I use and utilize gentle hypnotic suggestions and sometimes gentle embedded commands to assist the client towards building new or more positive behaviors and goals. I also sometimes give post-hypnotic suggestions to my clients. I believe that I use hypnosis every day in my own life and I believe it is always present to some degree with most if not all of my clients. And lately, in various workshops, I have begun teaching both therapists and clients how to have their very own personal working trances.

I have experienced very deep trance. However, I rarely do deep trance work and I don't believe it is needed. Also, I do give myself lots of post-hypnotic suggestions and smile when I perform as requested. Then, I thank my wise unconscious self. I can't imagine my life without hypnosis in various forms. It truly helps my heart to sing.

A Few Examples

Speaking of change, I recollect a client we will call "Edward." He was very conscientious and meticulous in his planning so that he would do no wrong. Always careful and thoughtful and thinking ahead how the task in his life at that moment should be handled, he could not complete his doctoral dissertation because it might be incorrect. As his deadline to complete it was only 6 months away and he had only completed two out of five chapters, he had basically given up and was most discouraged. He was very clear that he could not do it "wrong." He was desperate and dutiful, though, so I first secured his agreement that he would engage in a series of "homework" assignments, even if they at first didn't seem right or make sense to him. He promised. I then directed him to go to a large parking lot and to park his car, not between the lines, but sideways across three spaces. He protested, and I responded "No matter, you guaranteed me that you'd do your homework—just do it." He complied and told me about it at the next session. He stated that he had felt very uncomfortable. Also, he was confused and did not understand why. Then, I instructed him to park at an expired meter and wait for the meter-maid. He was to tell her that the meter was expired. He protested, saying "But, I will get a ticket." Again, I reminded him of his promise to do his homework and I explained that at some point he would understand. Again, he did the homework—and got a ticket, which he paid. (Later, we discussed how "serious" a problem it was that he had violated the meter rule.) A third exercise involved paying too much to a cashier in a grocery store. Finally, after a couple of weeks of these exercises, I advised:

"If you don't finish another chapter by our next appointment, you have to pay me $400."

"But that's not right!"

"Maybe, but we have to do what we have to do."

When he came to the next appointment, I asked "How'd it go?"

"I've got another chapter done—you're not going to get any extra money!"

Through discussion and this series of strategic "homework" exercises, he developed new understandings and awarenesses and finally felt free to complete the dissertation on time—even if it was "wrong." (No, I would not really have taken his $400—astute readers may detect some combination of "desensitization" and "ordeal therapy.") He received his Ph.D. and is now on a university faculty and is a well-known consultant, as well as being happily married—no longer locked in by "perfectionism."

Another person comes to mind when I think of change. We will call her "Virginia." She was 55 years old when we met, never married, living alone in her deceased parents' home and working in a big company doing paperwork all day. She also had had a complete hysterectomy. Asked what she would like from therapy, she was very clear and adamant that she wanted the therapist to do therapy and hypnosis so that she would have a baby. (I thought to myself, "Hmmm—OK, hypnotherapist, 55 and had a hysterectomy; let's see how you get a baby out of this!") I never directly questioned the possibility of pregnancy. Instead, I discussed various possibilities with her. She was of normal intelligence, hard-working, and yet quite sad and lonely. She told me that her mother, her father, and her brother had all lived in her home and that all three had died of cancer. We talked about whether she was ready for what she thought she wanted. We came to an agreement that she needed to prepare herself and get ready for a big change.

As with many of my clients, I used hypnosis to help her build a foundation and develop her resources (ego strengthening). I taught her a simple way of going into trance, utilizing her interest in her health by explaining that a relaxation trance would be good for her body and help her to take better care of the animals (dogs and cats) with whom she lived. I complimented her on her "industry," for being such a hard worker. To prepare her, I modeled how I can close my eyes and go into a trance. I carefully observed her responses and calibrated instructions similar to these for her to say aloud, so that her unconscious, body, and conscious could all hear it:

> Wise Unconscious,
>
> Please assist me to do this in the wisest way, to use my resources, to help my body. I don't know how you do it, but I know that you know what I need to know.... [etc.]

It was clear that she had no social life. We enumerated a number of things that needed to happen before she would be ready, and her therapy homework was to work on these various tasks. Because she was interested in babies and children, one of the tasks was to go to at least six different churches to find one that was compatible for her. She was to volunteer to work in the Sunday school, taking care of the babies, after she had been attending awhile. She found one and started attending their social hour after the services. She told me that she made wonderful cookies and wanted to contribute them to the "Tea and Cookies" social hour. Then, she told me that she had volunteered for the nursery. Later on, she said that she had realized that she didn't really want to care for the little ones in the nursery, so we agreed that she would volunteer to assist the 8-year-olds in their Sunday school class, as well as baking the cookies and participating in the social hour. She had made some friends there, and everybody loved her cookies.

Then one day, she came and told me that the people at church wanted her to go with them in the summer for a month's tour of Europe. She said that she hoped I would understand, that she didn't have time to take care of a baby or even an 8-year-old as she had to get ready for the trip in 3 months. So we discussed what she might want to do to get ready to go. She got ready and then went and had a wonderful time. She told me at that last visit that she didn't want a baby or an 8-year-old because she already had "a new family."

Another changer, I believe, was "Evan." He was very prominent in his field. He called for an appointment. When we had just begun his session, he began to sob deeply and intensely, and only said a very few words over our two-hour meetings. This behavior was repeated each time he came. I sat with him attentively, sometimes gently putting my hand upon his knee so that he would know I was there and he was not alone. Near the end of a session, I would provide some tea and crackers or cookies. He got to choose. We would spend the last portion of the session sipping tea and nibbling the cookies or crackers and gently talking about his childhood. We met for about five two-hour sessions. Each time, he would cry heavily, and then we would have refreshments. Finally, he told me that he did not need to come back and he thanked me. A couple of years later, he wrote a note thanking me and included some artistic drawings as a gift.

I am not sure what "strategy" occurred. However, he was in deep, old grief and pain. I sat there being with him, listening and caring, and we shared eating and drinking together. Perhaps being able to safely relive, release and relieve some very early, old pain and grief with a caring person provided him with new perspectives that enabled him to pursue a second successful career as an artist.

"Donald," a 64-year-old man, was referred to me by his employer. He told me that he was desperate. He said that he was within 6 months of retiring and receiving a pension, but he was tired of working and irritable and would sometimes blow-up and tell off other employees and/or customers. It has gotten so bad that his employer was close to firing him and Don would lose his pension.

He told me that he was in good health and that he was so weary of the stupidity and incompetence that he saw at work. We discussed this and both agreed that there was much stupidity and incompetence in the world. I asked him if he wanted to contribute to the "S & I," as we called it. He was horrified and said, "Absolutely not!"

Then, we discussed what he wanted to do when he retired. He had many possibilities of different things in mind. As it turned out, he would need his pension to do these activities. I asked him to figure out about how many years he thought he would receive the pension. He estimated 25 years. I asked him to multiply the monthly allowance by 12 and then to multiple the total yearly allowance by 25. He did so and arrived at a very large sum. I asked him as homework to make five 8½ × 11 signs with the amount on each. He did, and we discussed how much a temper tantrum was worth as he looked at one of the signs. He got the point. So he worked out places to post these signs at his work to remind him of his chosen goal. One was taped to his desk, one was on the door of his office, etc. I am happy to say that Don completed his last 6 months and very happily retired.

Talking about change also brings to mind "Phyllis." A young woman, she came in to see me and managed for almost two hours to tell me how much she was victimized by her parents, her siblings, her friends and her co-employees. When I finally interrupted, she told me there was more. I assured her that I understood that, and I said that I could help her if she would guarantee me that she would do her homework. She absolutely promised that she would do it ALL, no matter what, if I could help her. I explained that she had to get a one-hour cassette tape and record each side completely with all her victimization stories until it was full. Then, I explained the absolute necessity of her listening to the tape before she came to her next appointment. I said that it was for her to check and make sure that she did not leave out anything important. My hidden agenda, of course, was for her to hear herself and how she sounded.

When she came to the second appointment, she told me that she was shocked and ashamed at how she sounded when she listened to the cassette. We discussed victimization and whether she wanted to "buy into it" or become more aware and healthily selfish. She choose the latter, so her next homework was to read the paperback book *When I Say No, I Feel Guilty* by Manuel Smith (1975). She plunged into learning more listening, evaluating, and asserting skills and truly changed her life. She still calls me once a year to share selected vignettes of the year just ending.

Connection

As I think of the many dear individuals I have met through therapy who struggled and wrestled with their own limited ideas and horizons to build for themselves and their families better ways of being, I am pleased and grateful that I could contribute in some way to their growth, explorations, and learnings in their individual and shared journeys through life. Sometimes I feel like I'm doing the work I first learned sitting on my father's knee, solving problems.

As I live each day, I sometimes encounter an object, or an idea, or a habit (good or bad) or some experience that reminds me of a former client(s), and it can influence my actions at that point. For example, once in a great while

I am on the edge of losing my temper and yelling at "my hapless victims," I then remember the cost of doing so and I usually either regroup and say all my sentences starting with "I" and have these sentences be about me; or, I shut my mouth and take time and space to ascertain what I really want and need before I talk with "them" again.

I make an effort to do my best at least 90% of the time, never demanding perfection. I love and share many happenings—sad, bad, and glad—with my own true family as well as all my chosen family members. To me, it feels like I have an enormous extended family out in the world and that there are mutual sharings and carings and warm feelings between us. It warms my heart. I hope that I have paid my rent on the planet, in part, by helping others even as they have helped and/or educated me.

Reference

Smith, M.J. (1975). *When I Say No, I Feel Guilty.* New York: Dial Press/Bantam Books.

9

LOVE'S GOT EVERYTHING TO DO WITH IT!

John H. Frykman

For as long as I can remember, I have loved people. My Swedish immigrant grandmother, Sophia, loved me, and I loved her deeply. She taught me how to churn butter, make sausage, bake bread, pick up chicken eggs, and weave rugs on a loom (*vävstol*). Whenever other family members would criticize me ("He's spoiled, he doesn't behave," etc.), she would answer:

> *Han ska bli bättre nästa år.*
> (He will be better next year.)

She lived to 86, and nary a hair on her head ever turned gray!

My grandfather, Per August Kindberg, had been a shoemaker and tenant farmer in Sweden. Immigrating to America, he saved enough to buy a small farm (pigs, cows, chickens, a horse for plowing), and to bring the whole family of 10 to the United States. He was also a circuit-riding preacher, and I was forced to listen to his sermons, not allowed to raise questions. In time, he was ordained a Lutheran minister, and for me he was a model of passion, determination, and faithfulness. On the other hand, I also had a mischievous side to me, and sometimes would taunt my grandfather. He would chase after me with his cane but couldn't catch me.

My father, on the other hand, was a kind, quiet, gentle man, not given to rhetoric, but down-to-earth, patiently dealing with everyday problems. At about age four, I asked him: "Pappa, I don't understand Grandpa and his preaching. How do I know that he's right about God? Why do we have so much trouble if God cares for us? It doesn't make any sense to me."

"Mm-hmm," he nodded. "Let me show you something. Come around to the back porch." The porch was about four feet off the ground. Pappa had me stand on the porch, while he was on the ground. "Let's play a game. You jump, I'll catch you. It'll be fun." I jumped, he caught me. It was fun. Over and over again.

Then he said, "This time, before you jump, close your eyes. I know it'll be scary, but you know I'll be here, and I'll catch you."

I was scared. But I trusted my father. He was dependable and kind. I got up my courage, closed my eyes, and jumped. My father caught me. *"That's what God is like. You can't see him or hear him or talk to him in person, but when you need him, he's there to help you."* What a big lesson to learn at age four! I could believe what my father taught me about love, dependability, faithfulness, and security—the big ideas, because I knew that he lived his life that way, and that he loved me.

The only time Pappa ever disciplined me physically was when I tried to ride our huge, black, gentle Newfoundland dog, Bruno. Suddenly, I started to slip off, panicked, and grabbed his ear to hang on. Bruno yelped. Pappa took me by the hand, gave me a quick swat on the behind, and said, "Don't hurt Bruno. He's our friend."

My mother was just about the opposite personality of my father. Lively, playful, passionate, explosive, always wanting to entertain. She came to the United States at age 11 and was soon working as a maid on the North Shore near Boston. When she was put into school, it was in the first grade, because she didn't speak English. She continued only through the second grade.

Out of many stories I could share about her, I'll tell just one. At age 12, I began Confirmation Class at our church. It was a two-year intensive course, meeting once a week for three hours with the pastor, required attendance at Sunday Worship (we had to take notes on the sermon), read assignments from the pastor (the first I remember was Harry Emerson Fosdick's *On Being a Real Person*), and to memorize the whole of Martin Luther's *Small Catechism*. The culmination of it all was a "trial" (an oral exam given in front of the whole congregation), and finally Confirmation on Pentecost Sunday. I never would have made it without my mother's help. Every day, when I got home from school, she would spend an hour or more with me: "What is the meaning of the third article of the Creed?" Then she would ask questions about Holy Communion, Baptism, The Lord's Prayer. At the exam before the assembled congregation, we had to answer with rote memorizations every question the pastor asked us. I was the only one who didn't miss a single one. My mother could have passed the test easily as well. She cared so deeply for me--not just hugs and kisses, but always wanting me to succeed. She was the embodiment of "Love's got everything to do with it."

When she became "*Mucka*" (grandmother) to my three children, she had the same overflowing love for them.

All of our early family conversations were in Swedish (*Svenska*), because we didn't speak English at home until I started school in a one-room schoolhouse,

Steven's Corner School, Rehoboth, Massachusetts. We had six grades, about 40 pupils, and one teacher, Miss Waite. All the children were Roman Catholic except three of us—Jimmy Withers, Jerry Fine, and me. I could tell so many stories from those years—with what was a second family. Talk about love. When I was 17 and in high school, Miss Waite sold me her 1930 Model A Ford Roadster—only 21,000 miles on it—for $50.00. (I wish I still had it, rumble seat and all.)

I was learning that people help us figure out meaning and values in life. Love makes the difference. Throughout my life, relationships have influenced the choices I've made, the opportunities I've had.

At the tender age of eight, I walked into a significant life-changing "opportunity," one that still affects me deeply, even to this day. On a windy afternoon in April, 1940, I was strolling down a country road toward a meeting place with my parents. I'd been playing make-believe with friends and was costumed as a prince, with a red cloth sash tied diagonally across my chest. I could see my father down the road, waiting in our gray, 1937 Chevrolet sedan, smoking his King Edward cigar. The road bordered a cornfield belonging to Bliss Brothers Dairy, and now was rough stubble having been mowed for silage. Five German shepherd dogs were playing there, chasing in circles and drawing closer to me with each one. Suddenly, I was surrounded, a target, and they were growling, biting me, tearing my flesh, tossing me about as if I were a rag doll—but actually prey. (Later, I learned that they were male dogs, chasing a female in heat.) As they were biting and the stubble was cutting my head, arms, and legs, I felt no pain because I was in shock. But a heroic woman, who lived in a nearby house, Grandma Salley, had grabbed a red-hot poker, and chased and whacked them until they ran away. Then she'd carried me to her house and called for an ambulance (another miracle in those days—a home with a telephone).

At the hospital, I could hear the nurses in the corridor: "He'll never walk again," and "It's a wonder he's still alive." The story was front-page news, including a large photo of my mauled, bandaged face. Later, more dramas: local constables had shot the dogs, whose owners were of German descent, during this time of war in Europe.

My hospital visitors included our Congressman and representatives of the Boston Red Sox, bearing a fully autographed baseball. One night, with no fanfare at all, Ted Williams himself came to visit me and promised: "When you can walk again, come to a game and sit with me in the dugout." Great timing— I had been discouraged and lonely, but Ted's visit excited me, and eventually, I sat in the dugout at Fenway Park.

Throughout school days, so many people inspired me with care, love and affection:

In fourth grade, a new teacher, Miss Holt, would drop by my house after school and give me confiscated comic books. She knew that we couldn't afford such things but that they helped me read better and better. I didn't know then the term "teacher's pet," but I knew she cared about me, and I worked harder and harder to please her.

In seventh grade, a Catholic nun, Miss Lemieux (on leave to care for her ill mother), taught me Latin. In ninth grade, *the terrible and ferocious* Miss Beckwith, Principal and math teacher, pushed me to "get things right." At the regional high school for 10th grade, we were motivated by having one of Fordham University's original "Seven Blocks of Granite," Leo Demarco, as our football coach. With seven minutes to go in our first game, we were behind 6–0. I was a rookie fullback and hadn't played one minute, when Coach Demarco called me over, put his hand on my shoulder, and said, "Frykman, you are going in. You will get the ball directly from the center, and you will score." By the time I got to the end zone, my helmet was gone, my jersey was torn off and my shoulder pads almost off, but I was in the end zone and had scored. With the extra point, we won the game. I played every game from then on. Throughout high school, our team piled up championships with the skills and motivation of Coach Demarco leading us.

In college years, I learned that even bad luck can be manipulated into good luck. Coach Demarco arranged a football scholarship for me at the University of Massachusetts, Amherst with a condition to do janitorial work at the U.S. Agricultural Center on campus. A fellow team member shared the job with me. One night, while cleaning, we ran across a tape-recorder (a new invention then), which we could not resist playing with—e.g., telling dirty jokes and playing them back. We didn't know that the tape was the Farm Bureau Report for the following morning, ready to be broadcast to area farmers. On schedule, the radio technician came in to work, put the tape on, and went out for breakfast. Needless to say, the program was not what the farmers expected, and we were called on the Dean's carpet and suspended for one semester. I managed to turn the punishment into a reward that changed my life. Not wanting to waste months in idleness, I applied to Wentworth Technical Institute (where my father had graduated many years before) and began studies for a Certificate in Architectural Construction.

During my second year at Wentworth, while the Korean "Conflict" occupied the country, I was drafted into the Army. Again, mini-miracles based on relationships just "happened." Our young commanding officer for basic training turned out to be a former fraternity mate from UMass. Of course, I was in no position to ask for special favors (nor would I have wanted to) but he was in a good position to accelerate my basic training regimen, so that we'd have more time to enjoy each other's company.

Soon we received orders for Korea. After a grueling troop train journey from the East to the West Coast, we endured a typhoon-tossed voyage to Sasebo, Japan (last stop before Korea). Disembarking from the troop ship, I couldn't believe my ears at a similar freaky coincidence of good luck. While being herded through the monsoon rains to soaked squad tents, I recognized the voice giving orders: my Drill Instructor from ROTC at UMass! I couldn't believe it, but I called out to him, and within 10 minutes he had put a buddy and me in a taxi to a downtown hotel. "When it's time for you to go to Korea, I'll come get you, give you your uniforms and weapons, and take you to the dock." Again and again, I was learning that good relationships seem to open doors.

In Korea, more doors opened. I can see now that I was being shown a way that eventually revealed my interests in psychotherapy and ministry.

Although my time in Korea was only shortly before the truce, we still had to carry our M-1 carbines wherever we went, be back at night for curfew, and report at assembly in the morning. One day on free time, I went to the nearby town and was visiting with a very poor Korean family (they lived in a mud hut with mats on a dirt floor). Engrossed in struggling to communicate, I suddenly realized, "It's already after curfew!" and that it would be dangerous for me to try to get back to the battery.

The gracious Korean family understood and invited me to stay the night with them in their home. I awoke early and wanted to get back before assembly and roll call, but the Koreans insisted on feeding me eggs. I managed to eat the eggs (of unknown origin), fried in fish oil. Thanking them profusely, I began my run back to the battery, hoping to arrive before roll call where I could be "Present and accounted for, sir!"

Just then I noticed a parked jeep—and saw one of our top officers selling alcohol to Koreans out of the back of the vehicle. My soldier regimentation clicked in: I came to attention, saluted, said "Good Morning, Sir" and ran for my life back to the unit.

As the daily routines progressed, I fearfully awaited the consequences. About 15.00 hours came the order: "The man wants to see you." I went in, saluted, then said, "Private Frykman reporting as ordered, sir."

The captain looked me up and down. "John, have a seat. I've been thinking. You are one of the only soldiers in our battery that has much education. We need to have a Troop Information and Education NCO. Would you consider taking that assignment? I would promote you to corporal. We would put a squad tent frame on a foundation, constructing a building where you could have a classroom and library, your quarters," etc. etc. etc. "You'll also need access to a Jeep, so you can get materials, take people for appointments ..." I was a bit stunned, but quickly responded: "Yes, Sir—sounds good to me, Sir!"

Again, love opened doors. The company chaplain asked, "Could I conduct Sunday Services in your classroom?" He was a Southern Baptist, but not like my sweet-talking stereotype—he was for real. I'd be lying in my bed during his services, listening, and a glimmer of faith began to be rekindled in me. He was a non-judgmental preacher who was open, striving to serve in a difficult situation. He provided a window to new spirituality for me, and I will be forever grateful.

Returning to the States from Korea, I completed my training in Architectural Construction at Boston's Wentworth Technical Institute and, during this culminating period, received a very special gift of "Love's got everything to do with it." After the Army, I had been struggling with my own identity, what life was all about, what I really wanted to do, etc. Meanwhile, I was again living in small-town Rehoboth and commuting daily to Boston. I was drawn to the new young pastor at our Lutheran church and his Danish wife. I started going to their home every evening, seeking their counsel and advice. I'm sure I was a chronic pain in the ass, but they accepted me and my turmoil. *Never once did they criticize me or close the door on me.* It was a lesson I have never forgotten to this day. While my grandfather had played a significant role, my decision to go to seminary and become a Lutheran minister was inspired by the love of these good people.

Ever since then, I've never been traditional, or made much money, but I've been successful in terms of my own values, my own willingness to learn from "those who made a difference to me." My ministerial education and early career centered on inner-city and social change areas, which naturally led to counseling and professional training/work in psychotherapy.

Throughout my adult life, I've alternated working as a full-time Lutheran minister or a full-time psychotherapist, always doing some of the "other" while doing mostly the task at hand.

For example, work in inner-city ministries on both East and West coasts in the 1960's naturally involved civil rights, community organization, and drug abuse. I was fortunate to be "on the ground" with pioneers, learning first-hand from such as Martin Luther King, Jr., and Saul Alinsky. When injustices needed to be challenged, my parish in East Oakland was able to provide meeting space for the young Black Panthers. Years later, my San Francisco parish was ejected from the denomination for ordaining Gay and Lesbian clergy. We challenged the institution born of love to live it.

At a career juncture, I was asked to establish a Drug Treatment Program for the Haight-Ashbury Free Clinic. Up and running with funding, medical support (from the Clinic and the nearby University of California Medical Center), plus a crew of volunteer paraprofessional counselors, I sought advice from Jay Haley at Palo Alto's Mental Research Institute. I learned that Jay had recently moved to Philadelphia's Child Guidance Center, but that the Brief Therapy Center was just getting underway at MRI. Dick Fisch, John Weakland, Paul Watzlawick, and Art Bodin welcomed me as an observer and in short order, invited me to join the team in their new research-model treatment program.

A few years later, the burgeoning drug abuse problem brought me a job offer from a very different social scene. The Carmel, California, school district asked me to develop a new position called Community Counselor. I recruited and trained peer counselors at the high school, and I travelled to Philadelphia to learn from Jay Haley's program at the Child Guidance Center. Before long, the other Monterey Peninsula school districts had their own Community Counselors and we all co-operated as a team.

Truly, "love's got everything to do with it" when teenagers care for each other and save each others' lives.

During this time of historic, global social change, institutions were seeking outside experts as consultants. They knew that they could not solve their own systemic problems. I did a lot of consulting work with agencies as far-flung as the U.S. Army and Air Force in Europe; Oslo, Norway's Youth Office; many states' drug treatment programs; the federally-funded Drug Abuse Training Center; and Finland's programs for child welfare, family therapy, etc. I made liberal use of media aids, assistants, varied teaching techniques, and the arts--knowing that people learn better through such variety. For a time, as a family therapy trainer for California's Community Mental Health Centers, I recruited my good friend and "speaking poet," Ric Masten to do half-hour sessions of his poetry around a given theme. Poetry is not meant to have a set meaning, but here is one of Ric's poems that I think speaks especially to therapists. As Ric would say, "My poems make a corral around an idea—you have to make of it what you will."

Who's Wavin'?[1]

I ain't wavin' babe, I'm drownin'.
Goin' down in a cold lonely sea.
I ain't waving babe, I'm drownin'.
So babe quit wavin' at me.

I ain't laughin' babe, I'm cryin'.
I'm cryin', oh why can't you see?
I ain't foolin' babe, I ain't foolin',
So babe quit foolin' with me.

I'm screamin' that I'm gonna drown.
And you're smiling babe, and you're wavin',
I ain't wavin' babe, I'm drownin'.
Goin' down right here in front of you.
And you're wavin' babe, you keep wavin',
Hey babe, are you drownin' too?

Oh.

---

1   From R. Masten (1980), *Stark Naked*. Carmel, CA: Sunflower Ink, p. 29. © Ric Masten, 1980.
    Used with permission.

Learning from Some Remarkable Mentors

Over the years a few of my mentors and teachers have included Jay Haley; Madeline Hunter; Dick Fisch, M.D.; Paul Watzlawick; John Weakland; Milton H. Erickson, M.D.; William Glasser, M.D.; Gregory Bateson; and Irwin Shapiro, M.D. There are so many more people and specific thanks to give that I cannot pretend that the list is complete. However, with confidence, I can say that my mentors are the essence of "Love's Got Everything to Do with It."

Saul David Alinsky (1971), the great political organizer and non-violent activist, was also a major influence. I went to Chicago to learn from him—he understood systems and worked with them all the time. Once, on his way to Hawaii, he had a layover at Oakland Airport. We were organizing poor people in the public housing projects of Oakland, and the City Council had passed a resolution that Alinsky was not to be allowed within the City borders. We arranged a press conference at the airport for his layover, during which he said that he'd brought a "present" for Mayor Houlihan. I asked, "What's in the package?" He replied, "It's diapers. When Houlihan learns I've been in Oakland, he's sure to shit!"

I also learned about the importance of strategy and tactics from Jay Haley (e.g., 1963, 1969, 1977, 1984), who had been Erickson's prime student (Haley, 1973, 1985). My introduction to Jay was his book *Strategies of Psychotherapy* (1963), brought to me by a volunteer at the Drug Treatment Program in the Haight-Ashbury. The book blew me away so powerfully that I contacted Jay and arranged to visit him at the Philadelphia Child Guidance Center ASAP. Just as quickly, Jay and I became friends and colleagues. When I prepared to visit Milton Erickson for the first time, Jay advised that I take the bold (and risky) step of addressing him only by his first name. Milton had no problem with this communication. From then on, whenever I prepared to visit Milton, I would ring Jay, tell him what I wanted to learn from Milton, and get advice on effective communication.

In 1972, when a group of us organized Cypress Institute, our first public offering was a two-day workshop with Jay. The day before the workshop, he agreed to review with me some videos of clients I was working with at the time. I was terrified, but knew it was an opportunity I couldn't pass up. He had many suggestions, insights, etc. At the end, he gave me one of the most reinforcing and beautiful compliments I could never have imagined it: "John, I know you will find this hard to believe, but you act more like Milton (Erickson) in a session than anyone else I have seen." Talk about, "Love is what it's all about"! I've never forgotten it. He charged me nothing for any of that time spent viewing the videos.

Jay remains the clearest presenter of ideas and strategies—in both speaking and writing—whom I have ever known. I owe him so much for the tremendous influence he has had on my professional thinking and skills.

When I met Milton Erickson for the first time, I had been on an intellectual and emotional journey for years. (I had a consulting job in Phoenix and
recruited John Weakland to work with me so that he could introduce me to
Milton. When we came into Milton's living room, he said to John, "Would you
go over and sit in that chair and go into a trance while I talk to John.") John
(W.) complied. Later, Milton asked me to do two things before returning to
learn from him: "1. Take a beginning course in Anatomy. 2. Practice observing people in restaurants, etc. Ask yourself, what does their behavior mean, not
why are they doing it."

That, for me, is essentially what therapy is all about: Taking what the family,
couple, or individual bring to you, then using it to help them solve the presenting problem. Love and respect and the willingness to be vulnerable are essential
to the process.

When I got to know Gregory Bateson, he told me: "Don't be afraid to let
your mind go to places it doesn't even understand. Trust the observations it
brings to you." Interestingly, when he gave a workshop for us at Cypress Institute, he started by saying: "Ladies and Gentlemen, what you are looking at is a
dinosaur, getting ready to return to being coal." He lectured at a level that was
hard to reach, but powerful and compelling.

Some help from Paul Watzlawick: Working with a middle-aged woman
who was plagued with a chronic "issue of blood." I called Paul and asked him if
he would be willing to work with her, using hypnosis. Conventional medicine
had already determined that there seemed to be no cause for the bleeding. She
described it to me as "a showing that won't stop." We arrived at MRI (Mental
Research Institute, Palo Alto, California) and Paul was waiting in his office for
us. After asking a few clarifying questions, Paul guided her into a trance, and
in a very animated way, moving his hands way up and down, and raising and
lowering his head, said, "You don't know, but your body knows, how to stop
this 'issue of blood.' You can allow your body to take charge and end this issue
of blood. And, you won't need to explain it, you will only need to accept it. "

We had driven quite a distance to get to MRI. On the way home, we
stopped at a roadside place to get a snack, and take a little break. She went in to
use the "conveniences" and when she returned, she said: "John, the bleeding
has stopped!! It's amazing!" It never started again.

No story about Dick Fisch moves me more than his discovery, accidentally,
of Brief Therapy. He was a classically-trained psychiatrist, but had gotten into
having discussions with Jay (Haley) on a fairly regular basis about strategies for
change. He didn't put much credence in Jay's answers, but he enjoyed listening
to them. At a hospital outpatient clinic where he was working in San Francisco,
he was presented with a patient who had "urinary urgency," using the toilet
30 or 40 times a day. She worked in one of the sweat shops of the time, sewing
dresses. She also was a Russian immigrant and had difficulty communicating
in English. Dick didn't know what to do, but remembered a man Jay had talked

about, who wet the bed every night. Instead of his usual pattern, Jay had asked him to change his behavior when awakened by wetting the bed. "Get out of bed, put on running clothes, and run for a mile. It will be good for you. When you get back, put the wet pajamas back on, get into the wet bed, and sleep the rest of the night." It was not long before the bedwetting was over.

Dick thought that perhaps he could do something akin to that with his patient. He asked his patient (who worked the afternoon shift from 12:00 noon–9:00 p.m.), "If you could choose, how many times would be acceptable to use the toilet in the morning?" She said, "Three." "So, just as an experiment, every morning you may use the toilet three times. If you are going to use it more, go into the bathroom, climb into the bathtub, and wet yourself. Then you can go clean yourself and go on with the rest of your day." As you might imagine, she never had to "wet herself," and a reasonable period was extended to cover her time working, then again when she would travel by bus to visit her daughter and grandchildren, etc. In a very real way, Brief Therapy was born. I have a video of Dick telling this story and sharing his surprise and glee at the outcome.

John Weakland and I travelled many places doing workshops together. One of my favorite memories was of a workshop we were doing at a hospital in Seattle. Neither of us liked "role plays" and always asked if we could demonstrate brief therapy with someone having a genuine problem, not someone role playing. Often, very difficult cases were presented for us to work with. At the Seattle hospital, we were introduced to a psychiatric ward patient who was catatonic. John Weakland volunteered to interview him. John introduced himself to the patient, told a little about what we were doing, and then asked an opening question. The patient did not answer. "I'm sorry, but I couldn't tell if you heard my question. Would you be willing to give me a signal that you have heard what I have asked?" John asked another question, again got no verbal response and then said, "Thank you, I'm glad you are hearing what I am saying." He continued to ask more questions, each time affirming the response. Finally, after a question, the man burst out with, "What do you mean, 'Thank You?! I didn't give you any response to acknowledge your questions." The door had been opened and a "normal" interview ensued.

A few examples of my use of strategies growing out of MRI (see Fisch, Weakland, & Segal, 1982; Watzlawick, Weakland, & Fisch, 1974), Erickson, Haley, Alinsky, that relate directly to *Love's Got Everything to Do With It*:

Working with a woman and her early adolescent son who is having trouble in relationships with peers, school work, no father or father figure, and to almost every question the same answer, "I don't know."

"Is there anything at all that gives you pleasure, a feeling of satisfaction?"

"I like doing puzzles, but even then, I can never finish them."

"This is a really difficult problem. I need to think about this before making any suggestions. In fact, I probably need to consult with some of my therapist friends for advice on how to proceed. Between now and when I see you next week, I'd like you both to keep track of how difficult everything is. Just write it down on a 3 × 5 card and bring them to me next week. Would you be willing to do that? Even if it is very difficult?" (I didn't want either of them to think that I was minimizing the problem.)

In the intervening week, I purchased a puzzle that I knew was easier than puzzles he had done. At the next meeting, mom brought five cards, he brought seven. The content of the cards was not important. However, the fact that they had followed through was important; also, that he had made more cards than his mother. To them I said, "I did some homework, too. I bought this puzzle and brought it along today. Do you think, Bobbie, that you are able to do it?"

"No problem. (Not, "I don't know.") It won't take but a couple of minutes. May I do it now?"

He completed it quickly. He had already demonstrated that he could complete things, and that he had more to say than "I don't know." The rest was easy. It was no longer a story of misbehavior, schoolwork, any of the rest, but the clear knowledge that he and his mother could complete things and not be stuck in the repetitive trap of "I don't know."

Working with a couple who had sexual problems, everything seemed wrong, nothing seemed right. They seemed to care for each other, wanted to be together; but there was never time for sex or intimacy. I suggested some desensitization exercises *á la* Masters and Johnson (1966), communications skills *á la* Mace and Mace (1989), and more. Nothing seemed to help.

"There's something missing here, would you mind if we had our next session at your home?"

They were happy to oblige. When I arrived I asked for a tour of the house. When we finally got to their bedroom, it was like walking into an office. There were files, a fax machine, computers, papers strewn about, books on the bed, etc. We went into the living room and I started to tell a story: "A bedroom should be a place to rest, a place for sensuality, a place of peace. Would it be O.K. with you if we went in there right now and took everything out that does not support those kind of sentiments?"

At first silence, but then, some laughter, more joshing about, and a tentative challenge: "What kind of a therapist are you, anyway?"

At our next session, they brought a bouquet of flowers and a box of chocolates, and gave them to me. There was no need for any further sessions.

Love's Got Everything To Do With It!

My wife, Cheryl Arnold, and my three children—all adults now, Kristin Linnea, Lars Andrew, and Erik John—are why I can speak of love with such confidence.

References

Alinsky, S.D. (1971). *Rules for Radicals: A Pragmatic Primer for Realistic Radicals.* New York: Vintage/Random House.

Fisch, R., Weakland, J.H., & Segal, L. (1982) *The Tactics of Change: Doing Therapy Briefly.* San Francisco: Jossey-Bass.

Haley, J. (1963). *Strategies of Psychotherapy.* New York: Grune & Stratton.

Haley, J. (1969). *The Power Tactics of Jesus Christ and Other Essays.* New York: Avon.

Haley, J. (1973). *Uncommon Therapy: The Psychiatric Techniques of Milton H. Erickson. M.D.* New York: Norton.

Haley, J. (1977). *Problem-Solving Therapy.* San Francisco: Jossey-Bass.

Haley, J. (1984). *Ordeal Therapy: Unusual Ways to Change Behavior.* San Francisco: Jossey-Bass.

Haley, J. (Ed.). (1985). *Conversations with Milton H. Erickson, M.D.* (vols. 1-3). New York: Triangle Press.

Mace, D., & Mace, V. (1989). *How to Have a Happy Marriage* (2nd ed.) Nashville, TN: Abingdon.

Masten, R. (1980). "Who's Wavin?" In *Stark Naked* (p. 29). Carmel, CA: Sunflower Ink.

Masters, W., & Johnson, V. (1966). *Human Sexual Response.* New York: Little, Brown.

Watzlawick, P., Weakland, J.H., & Fisch, R. (1974) *Change: Principles of Problem Formation and Problem Resolution.* New York: Norton.

10

OFF THE COUCH AND OUTSIDE THE BOX

Joseph A. Goldfield

I had always been involved in creative endeavors. As a young child growing up in a rough neighborhood in the Bronx, I drew constantly, and went to a high school for Arts and Music. My mother was a poet and an artist. I began college as a theater major, but left to become a professional mime. During this period I performed at a few nursing homes, and, after seeing the loneliness of the residents, I began to develop an interest in entering the helping professions. Chronic knee problems curtailed my mime career, and I went back to college in Psychology. During this time I taught mime at a school for deaf children. I decided to get a Master's degree in Social Work, assuming I would become an advocate for either disabled individuals or in gerontology (see Ronch & Goldfield, 2003). When studying for the GREs, I became interested in word roots, multiple meanings of words, and the nuances of language. Later, when I was working as a clinical social worker in a group home in Oakland, California, I would incorporate creating rap songs into the therapy sessions. Some of the teenagers expressed themselves in rap a lot, so I started to rap back. Many of our therapy sessions were totally in rap.

In graduate school, my vision of my future career was forever changed when I took a family therapy course and saw videos of extremely creative therapists—Salvador Minuchin, Jay Haley, Cloé Madanes. I saw that clinical helping and being creative could fit together. This inspired me to get a post-graduate fellowship in family therapy under the tutelage of a gifted therapist, Rodney Shapiro, Ph.D., and I went for sporadic trainings in strategic therapy with Haley and Madanes. These therapists continually referred to their mentor, Milton Erickson, M.D., and the more I learned about how he practiced therapy, the more inspired I became.

Milton Erickson's Utilization

Milton Erickson did not have a psychological model for why people had certain difficulties or how to promote change, but rather based his work on a perspective he called "utilization." He believed that the client's abilities, preferences, and unconscious tendencies could be assessed and put into play to help the client. Erickson was a keen observer and developed an extraordinary understanding of human nature. He saw what motivated people to act in certain ways, saw that when a person's perception of a situation shifted the person responded very differently to events than they had previously. He saw how a little change could "snowball" and become a major positive influence in a person's life.

Erickson believed that the client's unconscious mind was a separate, unperceived ally of the conscious mind, that it was always listening and that it could be spoken to either in a trance state (he had a myriad of techniques for inducing a trance) or in normal conversation. He developed a sophisticated way of conversing with his clients in order to make suggestions to the unconscious mind, which he believed responded best to indirect suggestions rather than authoritative instructions. Erickson was famous for his skills of communicating in ways that evoked the capacities of his clients, and was well known for his teaching stories about the innovative interventions he performed (Haley, 1973; Rosen, 1982). I was impressed by his profound humanity and artistry—he brought all of himself to the service of his clients: his intelligence, his insight, his creativity, his compassion, and even occasionally his backyard!

Having this high standard as my guidepost continues to motivate me as a therapist. It keeps me curious about my clients and different approaches to therapy I might incorporate into my practice; it encourages me to bring my experiences both as a therapist and as a human being into the sessions with my clients. The goal of utilizing my client's abilities to help them create positive changes in ways that are organic to them shapes everything I do. I interact with and observe my clients to learn how they make sense out of their world. I look to discover their strengths and the ways they approach different aspects of their lives. I strive to develop a relationship of mutual respect that will allow me to best support them as they work toward their goals. The process of communicating to my clients in ways that speak to them on both conscious and unconscious levels fascinates me, and requires a combination of analytic reasoning, intuition and creativity that I find both challenging and rewarding.

Erickson's observational powers were legendary—he had the extraordinary ability to accurately read the client's slightest change in posture or vocal intonation, which would inform him how to steer the conversation to discover capacities and strengths. He used hypnosis to communicate therapeutic ideas with the client's unconscious, and was known to be able to transition between conversation and trance-induced states with a patient in a seamless way.

For myself, I have found the model of Solution-Focused Therapy to be extremely helpful in uncovering client strengths, and I find the technique of progressive relaxation with embedded hypnotic suggestion a good way for me to communicate with my client's unconscious mind in a normalized context. For this reason, I'd like to cover these topics next.

Solution-Focused Therapy

Steve de Shazer (1985, 1988) and Insoo Berg (1994) co-created the model of Solution-Focused Therapy. They believed that people became so overwhelmed by their problems that they lost their ability to access parts of themselves that could improve their situation. Their model de-emphasized the need to solve the problem directly, but instead focused on the client's ability to move beyond the problem. Their model uses a constellation of questions designed to take the client out of their problem-biased state as well as to uncover the skills and strengths the client possesses that could help them transcend their problem.

One type of questioning involves what is referred to as *scaling*: the clinician would ask the client to quantify, using a numerical scale from 0 to 10, how they are doing in terms of how their problems are effecting their life, their motivation to create change, their confidence in sustaining progress. Not only does this give the therapist a good way to track how the client is doing, it also inherently moves the client toward perceiving their problem as existing within a spectrum of good and bad, shifting the client toward being able to perceive nuanced shifts in their situation rather than having a black-and-white view in which they could only see black.

Scaling questions about how the client was *coping* were used if the client gave low numbers on scaling questions or conveyed that they were struggling. This often led to the client seeing that despite their apparently insurmountable difficulties they were not powerless: they were already using effective tools to keep things from getting worse—tools that if used more might shift things to the better. On other occasions a discussion of possible coping strategies might get started, with the therapist helping the client become cognizant of their internal strengths as well as external resources they had available to help them stabilize themselves in the face of their problem.

Another series of questions took advantage of the fact that there are always *exceptions* to any situation—and getting the client to see how these were not random, uncontrollable acts of nature, but rather were caused by a constellation of factors that the client had the power to reproduce. This would shift the client toward being able to see that they already had the ability to experience moments in life that were not dominated by their problem, and that the work that was needed was for them to shift the balance more toward these positive times.

A third type of questioning ("*The Miracle Question*") was based on getting the client to envision what their future life might look like if their problem wasn't there. By shifting the client's mental state out from under the burden of their problem, this would allow the client to rediscover parts of themselves they had lost touch with, and become aware of the aspects of life that they enjoyed.

In addition to questioning the client and discussing the insights yielded from their responses, the therapist would provide the client with *solution-oriented tasks* to be performed between sessions—often assignments either to make exceptions happen more, or to begin doing something that they had identified would be occurring if their problem did not exist.

At the end of a session the therapist often would incorporate compliments to the client on skills and strengths the client had mentioned that were likely to be significant in helping them to be victorious over their problem.

In a classic solution-focused therapy session, the therapist adheres to the above approach as the sole method of intervention. As determined by the client's responses, the therapist moves from one avenue of inquiry to another, until scaling, coping, exceptions, or the hypothetical solution yield the information needed to get the client shifted away from their problem-induced stasis. I appreciate the usefulness of this approach—sometimes it is all that is needed—but mostly in my practice I tend to use the questions not as a complete-unto-itself system, but instead as valuable tools in my utilization toolbox. I see the solution-focused interventions harnessing the behavioral aspects of the client in a way that is unique to the client—very much in line with what Erickson proposed.

Progressive Relaxation with Embedded Hypnotic Suggestions

Progressive relaxation was initially developed by physician and psychiatrist Edmund Jacobson (1938) in the 1920s. In this technique the client is taught to recognize the sensation of muscle tension in their body, and then to tell their muscles to relax—this is done starting at one part of the body and then progresses until the significant muscles of the arms, legs, trunk, and face have been relaxed. Jacobson found that this approach was very valuable for people with anxiety and other nervous disorders, and it has become a standard stress management tool for clinicians. I was introduced to a guided form of progressive relaxation in the 1970's when I was studying mime—the teacher would finish class with us lying on the floor and tell us to relax the various muscles in our body in a progressive sequence.

When I began working with individual clients, many of them showed signs of stress—either they had significant external stressors in their lives, or their inability to get past the psychological difficulties they were having was causing them stress, or both. I began incorporating guided progressive relaxation into their sessions, usually at the end so they would be able to return to the outside world in a better state. If clients found this helpful, I would give them the option of bringing in a recording device so they could have something to use when they weren't with me.

When I was attending a workshop on Ericksonian Hypnosis given by Dorothy Larkin, a past president and faculty member of the New York Milton H. Erickson Society for Psychotherapy and Hypnosis, she mentioned that therapeutic suggestions could be embedded into progressive relaxation techniques. This added an intriguing dimension to my practice. I have always been fascinated by the intricate workings of the human body, and I will use this knowledge to discuss some aspect of function of the muscle group being focused on, or a physiologic mechanism of the body, to create a metaphor for a therapeutic suggestion or idea. I find that this is also an outlet for me to explore the nuances of meaning that can be developed by creative choices in wording.

Having trust in the craft of therapy allows me to be curious as to how things will unfold in beneficial ways for my client, even when I find the client's initial presentation daunting. I'd like to share with you some cases from my practice that have been memorable for me. I hope that you will enjoy them, and that they will convey some sense of what has kept me going after 25 years as a therapist.

A Potpourri of Cases

Ellen. Early in my clinical career I worked with Ellen, a 40-year-old woman, helping her adjust to her recent divorce. The divorce had been initiated by her "ex" a few months before, after one year of marriage. The clinical tools that seemed to be most useful came from the solution- focused model, specifically coping, exceptions, and hypothetical solution questions. She was making a good adjustment, was regaining her emotional equilibrium, and was proactively making plans regarding her future. Suddenly, she called in crisis and asked for an immediate appointment. She came in the next day with a thick official document from her ex's lawyer. The document consisted of many pages alleging emotionally abusive acts that Ellen had supposedly perpetrated on her ex—acts that she did not recall happening. For example, the first page stated that on a certain date she had made an anti-Semitic comment. She told me that she remembered the date, and said they had had a nice picnic. She said she was really confused, she had no clue of what he was referring to. Seeing the papers made her doubtful of her own memories of the past.

The papers had her frozen like a deer in headlights. Erickson once stated that often the mechanism of the problem contains the mechanism of the solution—this gave me an idea. I asked her permission to make a copy of the pages of the document for my purposes. I came back, gave her the originals. I stated I agreed that she was confused, and that she seemed to not know whether she could trust her own memory of what had happened or the accounts given on the pages. I asked if we should settle this right now, to which she agreed. I held up page 1, and began to make a paper airplane out of the page, stating "If there's validity to this, it should fly." I let the plane go, and it quickly crashed (I'm very bad with paper airplanes). "Now, as for the second page ..." Within minutes, there were crashed paper airplanes all over the room. Soon the absurdity of the situation became apparent and she let out a big laugh. She said she would send a copy of the documents to her lawyer. Surprised and frightened by the "legal" nature of the documents, she regained her perspective when she watched them come to their comical and ultimate demise—like the lights coming on after a movie. I suspect having the experience of seeing something that had completely thrown her for a loop converted into something to laugh at served her well in her future legal dealings.

Don. An 89-year-old gentleman had originally come in due to depression related to caregiving for his two older sisters, one who was blind and the other who suffered from dementia. The sisters lived together in a different borough of New York. His wife, with whom he lived, also had medical problems. Don had been a famous comedian on a popular TV sit-com in the 50s, and his successful stand-up comedy career was still in place. His physician put him on a mild antidepressant, and recommended that he have someone to talk to about his caregiver stresses. Don told me that he needed to be upbeat for his wife and sisters, so he wanted support to be able to discuss how depressing it was to see his sisters and wife decline. We met every couple of weeks as he continued to adjust to his sisters' deterioration. Ultimately, the demented sister died, and the blind sister developed mild dementia and was placed in as assisted living facility. When there was a crisis, Don's wife would tell him "go see Goldfield," and he would schedule an extra session.

The support that was most salient to him consisted of solution-focused coping tools and focusing on exceptions. He would come in and unload about the frustrations he was having or the distressing circumstance he was having to dealing with. I would empathize and validate his experience. He would often talk about a gig that was coming up, or some colleague he had met who had complimented him on his work. When we discussed things that helped him cope, he identified the theme of his ongoing stand-up jobs as being the most helpful to him, not only during the time of the show, but before the show getting his material together, practicing his material with his wife, as well as the accolades he would get for a time after the show—when he saw other professionals later they would tell him how much they had enjoyed it. Recognizing that his work provided him with the social interaction, mental stimulation, and respect from younger generations that promotes successful aging (Ronch & Goldfield, 2003), I encouraged him to find as many opportunities as possible. The session with me would often end with him telling me a few quick one-liners that made me laugh, and I could see his pride at his mastery of his art form—he would leave smiling and upbeat. I believe this was his way of re-asserting his own sense of self-efficacy and reducing any sense of dependence on me that he might have felt during the session.

A few months after it had seemed that he had re-established his equilibrium and his situation had stabilized, he called urgently to set up an appointment. He sounded quite anxious, so I got him in right away. He explained that he was suddenly having memory problems. His physician had ruled out any neurological disorders. He had an important stand-up performance coming up in two weeks. As his type of humor was typically rapid one- to two-line jokes, filling a 45-minute performance required an immense amount of material. He explained that at his level in his profession having material written on some form of crib sheet to help with his memory was considered extremely amateurish. He clarified what he wanted was a session to practice and test his memory, like a dress rehearsal, to which I agreed.

As he started telling jokes, I saw him transition from being anxious about his craft and unsure of his memory into being the accomplished comedian he was. The next half hour was spent by him telling me really funny jokes—the more he got into his rhythm the more his memory was flawless. His timing became masterful. At one point I was laughing so hard I had to ask him to let me catch my breath between jokes. I could clearly see his confidence returning. When he began to write me a check for the session, I told him I could not accept the full fee. I explained that I could not do this because he had provided me with so much hilarity and laughter that I had gotten something personal out of the session. He tried to insist, but I also insisted, until we agreed to split it up the middle. As he was leaving, he said he would continue to mentally prepare in ways he always had before. I asked if I could call him to find out how the gig went. I could see that my being doubled up in laughter, combined with my insistence on not getting the full fee, had given him strong reassurance that his mind was working fine.

Two weeks later I called—his wife told me that he was away but that he had told her to expect my call and to tell me that the gig was a huge success. A few months later he called and said his career continued on track.

Sharon. I was working for an employee assistance program (EAP) where the clients would come for a few sessions primarily for assessment and referral and/or crisis counseling. Sharon was in her early 40s, reported being overwhelmed and under tremendous stress. She was a single mother of two girls, age 11 and 9. Their father was extremely unreliable and only minimally involved in their lives. He was not providing child support. Sharon worked fulltime as an executive assistant with a very demanding boss. Despite all the personal and professional stressors, she endeavored to give her daughters an enriched quality of life, ferrying them to play dates and classes and after school church activities. She mentioned she was a very religious Catholic. She was sobbing as she told me of her plight. She also reported that she was not sleeping well. As we discussed her situation, I brought up some basic stress management points. She stated that she did not have time to do anything for herself, that her needs would have to be on the backburner at least until her daughters grew up. But she also stated that she could not continue on as things were.

At that point I realized that making a referral for ongoing services would be useless unless I could find a way to help her believe she had a right to have some personal "down" time. At first the paradigm of caregiver stress came to mind: I thought about educating her regarding the need for caregivers to take care of themselves lest they become burnt out and unable to remain effective in helping others. I thought about how I could present this to her, and realized I didn't have enough credibility in her eyes for her to be able to hear what I was saying. Then, I remembered that she had told me she was a religious Catholic—and I realized that this was a case that needed divine intervention. I mentioned that my understanding of the Bible was limited and acknowledged I hadn't been keeping up lately, but went on to say that my understanding was that God had worked for six days and then rested on the seventh. Therefore, His work-to-rest ratio was 6 to 1. She suddenly stopped crying. I asked her if she believed that we were made in God's image as the Bible stated. She said "Yes." Therefore, I continued, we too must need to rest at a 6-to-1 ratio of work to rest. I proceeded to build up the idea of rest: was it passive, just sleeping? Was it doing relaxing, enjoyable things? Or do different types of rest depend on one's needs? She stated that she had never thought of it that way but it made sense to her.

Asked about a follow-up appointment, she said she would like to think about it. A follow-up call two weeks later revealed that she was sleeping more and had made arrangements so that her mother could help with the daughters a bit more. She asked me about the EAP's referral to legal services to look again at getting child support from her ex. She also mentioned she was taking her full lunch hours and occasionally taking long walks on her lunch hour. She felt that she really didn't need further psychological counseling. Having utilized her deepest beliefs to motivate her to do what she needed to do, I had no doubt that she would be successful in gaining a balanced life.

Ajani. An African immigrant, he had been referred to me for severe depression by his attorney, who was extremely worried about his weight loss and depressed demeanor. His American wife had abruptly left him after a short marriage. His description of the marriage sounded as if he had been a victim of emotional and financial abuse. He reported that she frequently put down his manhood and sexual prowess when they were out with her friends. She also prevented him from sending any money to his poor family in Africa. One day she left without a trace, and he was notified she was divorcing him. He was able to go to work, where he kept to himself, and then would go home, where he was alone—he was living a very isolated life. He was in an extremely vulnerable position, and I saw that discussing his situation with me was very difficult for him. Social isolation, depression, negative self-esteem, and trauma were all variables operating in a vicious cycle. Although he had a brother who lived in the same state, he was not in contact with him, as he was ashamed about himself and his situation. I realized it would be better to communicate with him indirectly.

We agreed that he was under a lot of stress. I mentioned how people who study stressors rate the stress of a divorce after a bad marriage very high, almost as high as being incarcerated. This was meant to normalize his reactions and also to allow me to offer teaching him progressive muscle relaxation. When I got to the upper arms, I mentioned how the biceps and triceps are always in subtle communication, and had developed this ability long ago, below the level of awareness. Later, when I got to the upper legs, I added how the quadriceps and hamstrings work together in ways to help each other with the demands of walking on level ground and especially when going over rough terrain. In this way I communicated to him the importance of communication and connection and mutual support, anticipating that this would help him get beyond his discomfort regarding talking to his brother. Afterwards, he stated that he felt very relaxed and refreshed. We agreed that he would bring in a recording device so we could do the technique again and record it so he would have it for future use.

The following week he reported that he had called his brother and, in fact, had arranged to visit his brother, sister-in-law and their children. Over the next month he continued to see his brother, went through the divorce process, began to spend more time with his brother, even began to go out to clubs and friends' houses with his brother and sister-in-law's circle of friends. During that time he was able to accept a recommendation from me to see a physician to be sure that his weight would be looked after—a sure sign that he was getting more on track.

Greg. Greg was a CPA working at a small, low-level firm. His girlfriend had been nudging him about getting engaged. They were a compatible couple wanting to get married and have children. The problem going forward was that Greg didn't think he could move out of the job he had, a move which would be needed if they were to have a family. The stumbling block was that Greg had a severe, chronic stuttering problem, for which he had had treatment his whole life. He came to me looking for help, stated he had no idea how I could help him but he was extremely distressed. He explained that for a stutterer, job interviews—the first step in moving up—not only were torture, but were by their nature biased against him, as he believed that any interviewer would consciously or unconsciously react negatively to his stuttering. Greg was highly intelligent, and I had no reason to doubt him. I asked if there was any connection between tension and stuttering, and if so, I could teach him a relaxation technique. He said that through years of speech therapy he had been taught relaxation techniques and that these helped in the office but would be of no help when he was being interviewed or in another highly tense situation. He felt that at least having someone to talk to was important.

I didn't know how I could help him, but I knew I could offer support, and maybe in time would be able to give him something more. Over a few sessions I discovered that he had a wonderful sense of humor. Often our sessions would include humorous exchanges on various topics. We developed a nice rapport. I knew that he felt trapped and I knew I had no idea what I could do to help him, but as Milton Erickson had said, not knowing is the calling card of the unconscious. I thought it out: first, Greg was certain that his speaking would ruin any interview; second, he had no control over how he said things; third, probably a performance anxiety dynamic was involved; fourth, the interview situation would make him very tense; fifth, to tell Greg to leave it to chance and hope that a recruiter would not be negatively affected by his stuttering would not be helpful to him.

At the next meeting, I told I had been thinking a lot about his dilemma. I encouraged him to get a few interviews with some of the larger, higher paying firms. I told him that once he got to the interview, he should quickly and thoroughly size up the interviewer and keep his focus on them, and based on his sizing them up to think of something he could say that would suddenly and immediately terminate the interview—something he and I could have a really good laugh about. He called me two weeks later, having gotten a new job.

Greg was convinced that his stuttering took away any possibility of him being able to control what happened in the interview. This impeded his ability to get to the future he desired, as no doubt it had ruined things in the past. But I knew first-hand that Greg had a strong command over what he had to say. I thought I could shift his attention to that instead of to how he spoke. Also, since he was convinced his speech would be a total turn-off, and end the possibilities that the interview could yield a job, I wanted to put that process under his control. Since we had a good rapport and he felt I was someone who understood his plight, by giving him a secret mission associated with me, along with a vision of talking to me about it afterwards, I provided a way to feel supported and not isolated during the interview. Having his secret mission be humorous was likely to create a relaxing shift for him whenever he thought of it, helping with his tension both real and anticipated associated with the interview.

Hal. Hal was originally referred to me by his psychiatrist. He had been in treatment for ongoing depression for years, and this had become more unmanageable when his wife was diagnosed with a severe brain tumor. They had two children, a four-year-old girl and an eight-year-old boy. At this time much of our focus was about eliciting coping strategies and brainstorming regarding logistics of care, including coordinating medical opinions and treatments of various doctors in various states. Hal spent enormous energy taking care of his wife, visiting her in the hospital every night until she fell asleep, being there for his children, and working. He was able to utilize family members to be at home with the children when he was unable to be at home. Eventually, his wife passed away. Hal did everything to keep continuity in his children's lives, including after-school hobbies as well as getting them into counseling. I complimented Hal regarding how he was keeping his children's lives as stable as possible given the family tragedy.

After a few years, due to cuts related to job outsourcing, Hal lost his position in human resources and returned in crisis. He was very depressed, his self-esteem was low, and he was very down on himself. Even though as a human resources person he knew that most decisions regarding downsizing were not based on a problem with the employee that was being let go, he had a lot of self-doubt, feeling that he had somehow caused his loss of employment and that he had let down his kids. He told me that he thought he might have lost his job because he cared too much about people, that he should have been more mechanical, more efficient in his work. He worried about the disruptive changes to his children's world that might result. I conveyed my confidence in his resilience, pointing out the many difficulties he had overcome to success-fully keep his children's world stable and predictable in previous difficult times. He responded well to this and became energized. He subsequently created his own business that he could do at home, which allowed him to continue to provide continuity for his children.

The third episode occurred during the recent economic recession. His home business was no longer able to provide enough income to sustain himself and his family; he had already filed for bankruptcy. He was having trouble getting a job, which he believed was in part due to the bankruptcy, and he was having trouble finding a cheaper apartment in New York City. Some sessions of brain-storming led him to develop a plan of moving upstate closer to his extended family where he and his children could afford to live. His son had just begun college and so would not be disrupted by the move. Hal discussed the move with his daughter and did some preliminary research about her new school, which helped her to look forward to the move as well. I suggested that Hal and his daughter both discuss the move with the daughter's therapist so it would be the least disruptive.

He decided to move, but as the deadline came closer he didn't think that he would be able to pack and move on time. I reminded him that he had never had problems in a crisis regarding his energy. A month later he moved, and two weeks afterwards he got a job. He called to tell me, saying I was one of the few people who would appreciate this news. I congratulated him, and said it had always been very moving to me how he had continually succeeded in providing stability in his children's lives despite the various stressors he was faced with and his tendency toward being depressed and down on himself. I asked him what in our work had been most useful to him, and he stated that he had had always left feeling more encouraged and able to be proactive. I was able to have this effect on him because I had seen repeatedly how his caring for those he loved energized him to conquer extraordinary obstacles, both external and internal. I was able to give voice to the evidence, conveying my genuine respect and con-fidence in his abilities, and this allowed him to transcend the negative thoughts that tended to get in his way.

Word!

I once made a rap song about family therapy for a course I was teaching at the University of Illinois. I thought it would be a nice learning tool for the students in preparing for their final exam. Insoo Berg heard about it, and commissioned me to write and perform one in honor of John Weakland at a conference held in New Orleans (Goldfield, 1993). She then commissioned me to do songs about Steve de Shazer (Goldfield, 1998a) and Michael White (Goldfield, 1998b) for a conference they did together in Milwaukee (White & de Shazer, 1996). Here is part of the one about de Shazer, highlighting the Brief Family Therapy Center (BFTC), their emphasis on brevity/efficiency, the types of questions they ask, and making allusions to de Shazer's (1985, 1988) *Keys* and *Clues* books. I chose to use vernacular language both as a tip of the hat to de Shazer, whose clinical population mostly lived in the inner city, and for the artistic impact as I knew many in the audience were not expecting to hear such language at a therapy conference.

The Master of Faster[1]

Suppose while you're sitting there a miracle happens,
You hear some funky syncopated lyrical rappin.'
What will you notice, what will the signs be,
That you're hanging with the Homeys of the B.F.T.C.?

We don't pack no guns 'cause we carry Occam's razor,
Word up to Insoo Berg and Steve de Shazer.
They are our captains, they are heavy and have fame,
Don't mess with us, termination is our frame!

[....]

You wanna join us now, you are ready to bang,
You're gonna say "Wow" when you comprehend our slang:
Six useful questions, perseverance and persistence,
Deconstructs and disses on that bad boy, Resistance.
It ain't our business if a client is deranged,
We only want to know about their pre-session change.
We take exception to problem talk,
Scale that mutha up and down, until it takes a walk.
If there's been trauma, don't be a dope,
Your client's in crisis, find out how they cope.
To position your client for their miracle blastoff,
Validate and normalize and compliment your ass off!

---

1   From J.A. Goldfield (1998), "The Master of Faster." In M.F. Hoyt (Ed.), *The Handbook of Constructive Therapies* (pp. 243–245). San Fransisco: Jossey-Bass. Copyright © Joseph A. Goldfield, 1998. Used with permission.

[....]

You've all freaked the funk, now you're word to the max,
Jammin' with your client's goals is the hip-hop task,
'Cause if you wannabe a master of faster like me,
I've given you some clues, but your clients hold the keys.

Conclusion

Being a therapist for the past 25 years has allowed me the privilege of having relationships with many people I would not otherwise have known. As I work with them, witnessing their vulnerability and helping them apply their strengths to improve their situation, I gain an appreciation and respect for who they are as people, beyond the scope of their problem. Their trust in me to make some positive difference in their life catalyzes for me the desire to bring all that I am to their service.

References

Berg, I.K. (1994). *Family-Based Services: A Solution-Focused Approach*. New York: Norton.

de Shazer, S. (1985). *Keys to Solution in Brief Therapy*. New York: Norton.

de Shazer, S. (1988). *Clues: Investigating Solutions in Brief Therapy*. New York: Norton.

Goldfield, J.A. (1993). "Rapnotic Induction No. 1." *Journal of Systemic Therapies, 12*(2), 89–91. Reprinted in M.F. Hoyt (Ed.), *Constructive Therapies* (Vol. 2, pp. 370–371). New York: Guilford Press.

Goldfield, J.A. (1998a). "The Master of Faster." In M.F. Hoyt (Ed.), *The Handbook of Constructive Therapies* (pp. 243–245). San Francisco: Jossey-Bass.

Goldfield, J.A. (1998b). "The Problem Talks Back." In M.F. Hoyt (Ed.), *The Handbook of Constructive Therapies* (pp. 245–248). San Francisco: Jossey-Bass.

Haley, J. (1973). *Uncommon Therapy: The Psychiatric Techniques of Milton H. Erickson, M.D.* New York: Norton.

Jacobson, E. (1938). *Progressive Relaxation*. Chicago: University of Chicago Press.

Ronch, J.L., & J.A. Goldfield (Eds.). (2003). *Mental Wellness in Aging: Strengths-Based Approaches*. Baltimore, MD: Health Professions Press.

Rosen, S. (1982). *My Voice Will Go with You: The Teaching Tales of Milton H. Erickson*. New York: Norton.

White, M., & de Shazer, S. (1996, October). *Narrative Solutions/Solution Narratives*. Conference sponsored by Brief Family Therapy Center, Milwaukee, WI.

11

LIFE IS WITH PEOPLE

Eric Greenleaf

The seven years 1999–2006 were ones of almost biblical difficulty for my life. I had endocarditis, emergency surgery on my femoral artery, a severe ileosecal infection. Then, I was diagnosed with prostate cancer. On completing radiation treatment I was told to prepare for open heart surgery a few months later. In this same time period both my parents died. And, in an ironic twist to the various scales of stressors, we redid our house completely.

Looking back on this time, I thought to write as a therapist about how one deals with such complex miseries. Having already survived being hit by a car going 55 miles per hour while a pedestrian, I knew first hand the meaning of Milton Erickson's phrase "unconscious resources," and the unselfconscious value of the stories others tell us about their own successful responses to illness, injury and loss (Greenleaf, 1994).

Dr. Erickson's approaches to any individual were widely varied. They included utilization of every expression of the person, from symptoms to cultural norms to actions and habits, to styles and tastes. Importantly, he always situated his response in both the relationship he had with the patient and in the wider relational world of the patient; and he always promoted action by the patient to help them resolve their own dilemmas. I set out, unselfconsciously, to do things that way, too. And, thinking like a hypnotist, I found myself treating my dilemmas as I hoped to treat my own patients' troubles.

Some years ago I read a book called *Remarkable Recovery: What Extraordinary Healings Tell Us about Getting Well and Staying Well* (Hirshberg & Barasch, 1999), which is a series of narratives about people who have had desperate diseases and circumstances and how they recovered against the statistical odds and even their own expectations. What I took from the book were two things: (1) Everyone recovered in his or her own way. Some people took a completely allopathic, conventional medicine approach to their illnesses, some people threw all of that overboard and did only alternative treatments, some people threw all treatments out and changed their lives and went to the South Pacific, other people changed their lives alongside the medical treatment. One thing that seemed to me true was that the people who did well decided on their own path, and that could be with the chief physician at Stanford University or with a faith healer in Guadalajara; and (2) It struck me that each person that did well and survived in these circumstances had one person who did not give up on them no matter what or whether they gave up on themselves—it could be a sister, a wife, a husband, a friend, a physician, a hospice worker.

I looked back in my records for the period and saw that for the first and only time in my 35 years of practice, I was seeing seven cancer patients, aged late 40s to 80. Granted I'm older and my patients are older. I started to learn about this illness very directly from them. So I want to write first about two cases of people who saw me and then about my own treatment. This is just to demonstrate that the individual guides the treatment in her own way.

One woman, Karen, I had worked with for 25 years. She was blinded by a tumor of the brain that regrew and had to be removed every 15 years or so. She had a couple of surgeries. The first one rendered her blind in her 20s. Her great success in life I believe was because she has always been herself very emphatically, and when I worked with her hypnotically it was through her great abilities as an athlete. She came in 5th at the Paralympics in Women's Downhill Skiing at 35, and also learned to fly on the trapeze in her 40s. She started a business and had a long, good marriage. Together we worked on many kinds of recoveries from many kinds of injuries—emotional, physical, and interpersonal—and many medical procedures over time.

In November 2004, an oncologist told her, and this is typical of these stories, "You have stage four metastatic lung cancer. There is nothing we can do." Her husband remembers the oncologist saying, "She will be dead by June 2005." She survived twice as long as he said, and until the last few months, when she had hospice care, it looked like she might actually manage to beat this thing.

The first thing she said to the oncologist when he delivered this terrible news to her was *"You've never met anyone like me."* Her blood work was normal by March 2005. She said, "Since I'm living, I feel placid." And she was working hypnotically every day. She was taking Tarcera and other medicines. She said, "I feel more immediate, I'm here right now. I feel normal." She had a good scan in September 2005; some of the lesions had died off and no new ones had grown. In November she held a dinner which was called "Kick the Crap Out of Cancer." She and her husband hosted a big, wonderful dinner, and we went and met everyone who loved her. She was very widely loved in her community. November 2005, a year after her diagnosis, her lungs were stable, but she had a brain metastasis. She then had three brain surgeries in three months, one with a gamma knife and two to reduce swelling. And then it was decided that she would stop treatment except for palliative treatment with pain killers.

I visited her at home each week during that time, and the last time I saw her she had a great deal of pain medicine and so her husband had to wake her. She said, "Oh Eric, I have so much to tell you." I do know that the last thing she told me unprompted was about a week before that, when she suddenly sat up and said, "My goal is to take one step unaided."

The second patient with cancer, Judy, tells her own story of hypnotic treatment in an unpublished memoir, *My House on Stilts*. She writes:

"What does this mean?" I asked the oncologist, a kind man with terrible burdens; he had hundreds of tragedies in his bailiwick. "I'm hoping—hoping—for two years for you," was what he said.

I closed my notebook and went to bed.

A few days later, it was time for the appointment with the therapist, Eric Greenleaf. His room had rough wooden walls that reminded me of the cabins at summer camp, deep chairs, and shelves painted a rich red that were filled with tiny, colorful figurines. When I rested my eyes on these as I talked, I realized that some were costly carved ivories, some were delicately hand-painted wooden figures, and some were Happy Meal toys or the small dolls from play sets my children had had when they were younger. They lived together in the red shelves in a harmonious silence.

"The thing is, everyone says I have to have a positive attitude, that it's all a matter of attitude. But it's not in my nature. Don't misunderstand me. I mean, I hope to survive this, I plan on fighting it tooth and nail until someone tells me there's no more point. But I'm not stupid. I know the statistics."

"What are they, just for information's sake?"

"I don't even want to repeat what my doctor said. It can't be right, it's unacceptable, I'm trying to get it to quit crashing around in my head." Tears, again. "Damn, damn, damn. My little daughter is only nine."

He passed me some Kleenex.

"So everyone keeps telling me, 'think positive.' As if they know what this is like. 'Positively,' I assume they mean. They tell me I have to 'live for the moment.' I've got this boyfriend, he's English—that's a whole separate thing. I was about ready to get rid of him when everything hit the fan, and I chickened out. Him, too, it's even worse, he's got that British thing where everything always has to be lovely, everything is always 'for the best.' But if I die, how can it be 'for the best' for my daughters, I asked him? And do you know what he said? He said, 'Well, but then you'd be dead, so you wouldn't care.' Do you believe that? He's going for the live-for-the-moment Olympics."

"There's no one who, taking a walk, can resist looking down the road for as far as she can see, as well as appreciating the little twigs and leaves and flowers that are directly in her path. No one should be telling you to live some other way, just because you're sick right now," Eric said.

"They all want me to think 'positive.' They say it will cure me. Everyone's always telling me about some aunt of theirs, or someone, who cured herself of breast cancer by having a positive attitude. Supposedly, I'm doing this wrong. But damn it, it's not my fault that I have this, and it's not going to be my fault if I die from it. The way everyone thinks I'm supposed to do this, it's not my way. I'm not that kind of a person. I'm a pessimist. I'm a lawyer, a litigator. You get your case ready, you work it up as well as you can, but you have to know your odds of winning, or losing. You can't lose sight of the worst-case scenario—or the best-case either, for that matter. You have to settle if your case is shit."

"You don't get to settle here, do you?"

"No, so I have to be ready for the worst. And I have no idea how to do that." This is what Eric said: "No one knows what will happen. And so you have to prepare for life. And you have to prepare for death.

"To prepare for death, you have to get your affairs in order. You have to complete projects. You have to make memories for your children, and the others you love. You have to keep being their mom. You have to tell them you know they're sad and mad and scared, that you're sad and mad and scared, too, but that you intend to survive this, that you love them, and then you have to yell at them to pick up their laundry. You have to celebrate what needs celebrating. You have to keep doing whatever art it is you do. You have to prune the unnecessary things and people, the deadwood, so you can grow. You have to say what you need to say. You have to keep living while you're living.

"To prepare for life, you have to get your affairs in order. You have to complete projects. You have to make memories for your children, and the others you love. You have to keep being their mom. You have to tell them you know they're sad and mad and scared, that you're sad and mad and scared, too, but that you intend to survive this, that you love them, and then you have to yell at them to pick up their laundry. You have to celebrate what needs celebrating. You have to keep doing whatever art it is you do. You have to prune the unnecessary things and people, the deadwood, so you can grow. You have to say what you need to say. You have to keep living while you're living."

"During the next few weeks, before the chemo started to hit me too hard, I dug out my living will and advance directive and told my sister where to find them. I finished a quilt I'd started years earlier from the remnants of dresses and Halloween costumes I'd made for my children. I spent several evenings going through old writings of mine and letters and photographs, and put them into folders and scrapbooks. I arranged to have my bills paid electronically so that nothing would get disconnected or foreclosed. I phoned around to set up carpools to get my daughters to and from their schools. I wrote terrible letters to several friends who'd ignored me in the weeks since I got the first biopsy result, then decided not to send them. I dismissed these people from my mind. I told some other friends why I loved them, and told my ex-husband that I wasn't sorry I'd married him. I told my boyfriend I was going to be spending enough of my time with doctors and their ilk and didn't have any extra energy for the couples therapy we'd been having for several months; it wasn't doing any good anyway. Whatever happens, happens, I told him. I calculated when I would and wouldn't be prostrated from chemo, and started planning a party to celebrate my daughter's tenth birthday. The one thing I didn't know how to prepare for at all was saying goodbye to my daughters.

"Every so often during this period of filing, organizing, planning, and discarding I'd think: wait. Was this on the 'prepare for life' list, or the 'prepare for death' one? Sometimes I got very agitated because I couldn't remember, thus couldn't explain my compulsion to do these things. It was weeks or months before I realized the lists were the same."

Judy has just sent the second of her daughters off to college, is in good health overall, and is working full-time for a non-profit practice. Her memoir was written in 2002, nine years ago.

The third patient is me. Typical: I go to the doctor, he says "Oh, the prostate doesn't feel right. Go to the urologist, we ought to have a biopsy." A diagnosis, and I come home. I already know I have to do things a certain way or I start to feel "psychiatric," as I like to say. In other words, if I don't feel like myself I start to feel depressed, dissociated, anxious, etc. I have a maxim, "The more person, the fewer symptoms."

The first thing I did was to start studying. I looked on the Internet and started to learn about how people talk about prostate cancer. I don't have time to learn the science, but I know how to read and what people mean by what they say real well. I started to listen by reading and then listened to only a few people that I spoke to. I spoke with two friends who understand medical science. I spoke to a couple of people I know who had prostate surgery. I spoke to a couple of physicians who are friends of ours.

Then, I set a deadline, sometime in February or the beginning of March I would have a decision: surgery (several types) or radiation (several types). No physician can definitively recommend which type of which to do and no one else can either. After reading all of this for a couple of weeks, I started to have a fever of emotion, a whole range of feelings—anger, regret, sorrow, fear, love— the whole range in one pop. I understand that as the preparation to go through some treatment. When I work with people who are going through surgery, I almost always recommend that they will go through some storm of feeling at some point. And when it happens they know they'll be ready for the surgery or the trial or whatever. The night before my femoral artery surgery, I found myself up all night, crying, talking aloud to each person I loved, awash with emotion. About 2 a.m. I realized that this storm of feeling was the preparation for surgery. It washed through me and cleaned me out as surely as an antiseptic wash cleaned the skin at the incision.

I do not process my feelings or thoughts inside myself, I want them in inter-action. One of the things that is true about me is that I am interpersonal and not very intrapsychic. I'm extroverted. I plumb the thoughts of others' feelings, and it works better for me. I get to know a lot and I get to feel grounded with other people. I operate from the old *shtetl* principle that "life is with people."

I spoke with a radiation oncologist. I liked her as she volunteered about herself that she is very meticulous. She devised a computer program that will aim radiation beams, which are very narrow, into the body, avoiding damage to important parts of it to meet at certain points within the prostate.

I knew from the beginning I would take radiation and I knew that surgery would be more dangerous for me because I had had endocarditis. But I couldn't decide. And I was, for a day or two, woeful and unkempt. My wife, Lori, intervened. After a day or so she just said, "Decide. I have had enough of this." I decided what I had known I would do all along.

Throughout the course of the treatment I worked full-time, I went to the gym every other day, I drove 100 miles roundtrip to the radiation treatment, had a very good time. Really good delicatessen in the industrial park there. I liked driving the roads, challenging, narrow roads. I liked the radiation techs, had fun with them, talking cars.

Another thing: I don't like alternative medicines, foods as medicine; I have a lot of prejudices of thought. Only prejudices of thought, though, not against people. But there are certain thoughts and language I do not like. I like experi-ences but I don't like most explanations of experience.

I found something perfect because I knew Lori and a lot of friends and col-leagues would be recommending alternative treatments to me. I found someone I know, a woman from Brooklyn, nearly 80. She was a Sloan-Kettering oncolo-gist during her working life. Her partner is a homeopath. She had a recurrence of breast cancer in her later life and decided to use only homeopathic treatment, and flourished. So I signed up for the homeopathy. This pleased many of my friends, and I was pleased because side effects were less. The homeopath will think that is what worked, the radiologists will think that is what worked, Lori thinks vegetables worked, vitamins and supplements. I am convinced, and both my work and Erickson's demonstrate this, that change in emotion, thought and action can arise in interaction with others as easily as it can in introspection within oneself.

Also during this time, I noticed I lost my superstitions. If I missed a dose of medicine, I didn't think anything was going to happen, etc. I'm just not superstitious anymore. I think that's a consequence of how I am happy as a person. Except for a few days throughout this I have been happy this whole time. I think that has been pretty much it. When given a procedure, I like to follow it. I won't know for 10 years whether this all worked. It was caught early.

I thought, too, about doing some kind of something hypnotic. I realized, looking back on cases, I just did not know then that the life and death talk I had with Judy applied to me. I couldn't prepare any better than that for myself. The talk seemed to cover living normally until you die and those you love are cared for. It also implies that you don't back away from those you love because you're sick or scared, and that seemed to me most important. There was also working with Karen over those many years and learning to rely on your body to do what's required. She was a great example. In the middle of her cancer she went back to working with a personal trainer and was outdoing her age group on half a lung.

So, knowing what you can call on in yourself, whether it is intellect or physical strength or, in my case, connecting with people, is what you stand on when things are tough. (I am pretty sure that when I listened to doctors, techs, etc. I listened in a very narrow focus. If they said something I didn't want, I would knock it away—and sometimes forcefully.) That kind of hypnotic attentiveness on the main goal yet not knowing how to get there, is a scheme for hypnotherapy. I'm pretty sure I practiced that. I listened very very tightly to the people and read very tightly. Once I figured out what a mess the situation was, I was free from a lot of encouragement and sympathy because nobody really knows what to do and the outcomes of any treatment look good for five to ten years after.

Let's look at things the way I looked at things with Judy: she had reason to be very pessimistic, but she has just sent her younger daughter off to college—something she was terrified she would not live long enough to do. She says she'll sew her wedding dress, not believing it. At some point one starts looking ahead, and that's built into the Erickson approach. Even at the end of his life, Dr. Erickson looked at things with great courage and with hopeful curiosity about what is next. As he says at the end of the documentary videotape, *Milton H. Erickson, M.D.: Explorer in Hypnosis and Therapy* (Haley & Richeport-Haley, 1993), "I will be eternally grateful to my grandparents: they taught me that of course they had grand old times in the past, but the really good times are yet ahead of them." I find that very congenial emotionally. I like to see what's going to happen.

In approaching the fearful and uncertain landscape of cancer with my patients, I utilized their unself-conscious resources to interact with them hypnotically. Karen's automatic athletic strength and grace and her self-definition were keys to her struggle with disease. Her love for others and generosity with them situated her individuality in a warm, caring community. I utilized Judy's legal realism and craft to allow her to consider fully both aspects of the case—life and death—and to fully support her client, the mother of her two young children. And, in thinking like a hypnotist, with myself as the patient, I utilized Eric's ability to read, listen, and communicate and his extraverted interest in people to help him go through all those procedures, treatments and discomforts with strength, and without fear, and to enjoy life as he did so.

To realize oneself *with* others, rather than inside one's own consciousness, seems obvious to me, but would strike many introverted therapists as shallow, unconscious, or lacking insight. Yet, in hospitals and doctors' offices and at labs *I found myself* while interacting fully with each person I met. I must have seemed like Lucy from the Charlie Brown comics, wheeling my 5-cent consultation booth through the wards. But it worked for me to be like me: I recovered quickly and well from each medical problem in turn. Here's what I wrote after one hospitalization:

> My enterprise while a patient turned out to be an extended version of my spontaneous response to previous trauma. I became very engaged with the doctors, nurses, and housekeeping staff who visited me day and night and all around the clock to stick me, take temperatures and EKGs, listen to my chest, introduce the new shift, bring meals, change the bedding. This meant I got to know a lot of people. Since I felt good and was ambulatory, I managed to gather supplies I needed and contact people I needed, too.
>
> From the start, I decided I would need a pair of scrubs [the pants] to go with the awful hospital gown we [patients] were all given. Everyone [docs, nurses, staff] said that there were no pants to be had for patients. So, each conversation I had with anyone who came by my room, I ended by saying, "I'd like to have a pair of pants." I inquired of the night house-keeper, and was told, "There are no pants. They send maybe three with each ten tops. The day staff keeps them locked up. I don't have the key." A day later, the head nurse came by with a pair of pants.
>
> Next day, one of my doctors held out a pair to me. Two days later, another nurse brought a pair. I also read the book, *Endurance* (Lansing, 1999) about Shackleton's Antarctic trials, and a Dick Francis mystery, and the *Wall Street Journal*. Slept when I could, visited with Lori and other guests, ate hospital food with real appetite.

The notion of self, hence of self-knowledge, implicit in these stories rests within a network of concepts like styles, approaches, tastes, interactions, doings, procedures, and such. This family of loosely related ideas refers to ways of pro-ceeding more than to characteristics attributed to a static personality. It may remind one of Wittgenstein's (1958) notion that the meaning of a word relates to the entire environment of the saying of it. Persons may be similarly derived from the whole environment of their interactions. Finding ourselves in novel environments and interactions with others obliges us to select those constructs, as George Kelly (1955) called them, which help us navigate novelty and threat with a compass of the self.

In Erickson's terms, we think of using our unconscious resources to approach these challenges. What are these resources? I'd nominate three human processes as unconscious: ways of learning, neurophysiology of the mind-body, and interpersonal relations of more than two people. The first two are obvious. We learn much of great importance—breathing, smiling, language—without the ability or need to be conscious about them. Our bodies operate skillfully with enormous complexity, without the necessity or possibility of precise conscious control, even when we sleep.

The third candidate is non-obvious. Think of this: language is readily available for relations of two people, such as father and son, husband and wife, friends. With language, possible consciousness. Relations of three or more, like that of my grandmother with my father's brother's children, and their interrelations, are hard to speak of. So, novels are written, or we resort to collective nouns, like family, or class. The cloud of emotion which influences all children can be formed over generations, and is largely unconscious. Erickson's work shows what a great resource these extensive relational clouds provide for change in lives and persons. Erickson's life was situated in a large family of origin and a large extended family of his own. And he seems to have known almost everyone of interest in his time, from Mead and Bateson, to Huxley and Feldenkrais.

When a fellow graduate student first gave me an article by Erickson, I read it and said out loud, "Oh, *that's* how you do therapy!" *Utilization* is the awkward term for his graceful and powerful approach to persons, using the ways they do things to promote healing within them. After decades of practice I found myself utilizing my unselfconscious resources—ways of learning, the processes of the body, and complex interpersonal emotions—to guide my own healing and that of my patients. As another old saying (from Rabbi Hillel) has it: "If I am not for myself, who will be for me? If I am for myself only, what am I? If not now, when?"

References

Greenleaf, E. (1994). On the social nature of the unconscious mind: Pearson's brick, Wood's Break, and Greenleaf's Blow. In S.R. Lankton & J.K. Zeig (Eds.), *Ericksonian Monographs*, No. 10 (pp. 16–24). Reprinted in E. Greenleaf (2000), *The Problem of Evil* (pp. 45–51). Phoenix, AZ: Zeig, Tucker & Theisen.

Haley, J., & Richeport-Haley, M. (1993). *Milton H. Erickson, M.D.: Explorer in Hypnosis and Therapy.* [Videotape.] New York: Brunner/Mazel.

Hirshberg, C., & Barasch, M.I. (1999). *Remarkable Recovery: What Extraordinary Healings Tell Us about Getting Well and Staying Well.* Collingsdale, PA: Diane Publishing.

Kelly, G.A. (1955). *The Psychology of Personal Constructs.* New York: Norton.

Lansing, A. (1999). *Endurance: Shackleton's Incredible Voyage.* New York: Carroll & Graf.

Wittgenstein, L. (1958). *Philosophical Investigations* (3rd ed.) New York: MacMillan.

12

ON BEING BLACK IN WHITE PLACES

A Therapist's Journey from Margin to Center

Kenneth V. Hardy

Long before I knew exactly what a therapist was, I knew I wanted to be one. From the time I was in elementary school I was intrigued by the complexity of the human condition. I was perpetually curious about why certain things were the way they were. My parents and grandparents often attempted to provide me with satisfying answers but seldom did they, or did the insights they offered, succeed in soothing the soul of my incessant sense of curiosity. I always seemed to have had an endless stream of "why" questions that ranged from the absurd to the profound, from micro- to macro-related issues; from questions about the here-and-now to those about the afterlife ... assuming that such a phenomenon even existed. Beneath all of the questions was a blaze of curiosity, intrigue, and dogged determinism to gain a firmer grasp of the nuances that help to elucidate what made us tick as human beings. I wondered how twin brothers, David and Donald Watkins, family friends, could share the same parents, grow up in the same family, and yet be so fundamentally different. I had the same query about my family: how did my brother and I grow up to be so different, although we shared the same parents, were just two years apart in age, and did virtually everything together as children? I also wondered why my first cousin Johnny had no siblings and why his father was alive but not present in his life. Although these curiosities were persistent, they were fairly benign compared to the ones that constituted the major "haunt" in my life.

The haunting curiosities were almost always reserved for and related to the phenomenon of race. My questions about race and race relationships were recurring, disturbing, and emotionally disruptive. They felt very personal. Through the eyes of a young child it was always difficult to understand the many *whys* associated with the phenomenon of race. For instance, why did White men who were often 10-15 years my father's junior insist that he address them by using the term "Mister" while they routinely and consistently addressed him by his first name? Why? Why did they insist? And why did my Dad so willingly acquiesce? I wondered why my father, who often seemed so omnipotent and sturdy under some circumstances, especially within our family, seemed so small, fragile, and frazzled outside of the family, especially when in the presence of Whites? Why? Why were my mother, and other Black women like her, constantly treated as if they were servants? Why was she and other Black women like her never afforded the respect, deference, or regal treatment that was commonplace for their White female counterparts? Why did she often behave as if it were her duty to care for the very Whites who seemed to care little about her? The rules of race relationships in the world in which I was socialized supplied me with a multitude of phenomenological/existential questions—among those were questions about the meaning of Blackness in general and what did it mean for me specifically.

My great grandmother, Anna, the granddaughter of a slave, lived with my family until I was a junior in college and tried feverishly to help me answer all of my emerging questions regarding what it meant to be Black. She was one of the first and few people in my earlier life to talk to me so openly and candidly about race with the uncensored rawness befitting the topic. She recalled countless stories, devoid of any detectable emotion, of women she knew who had been raped at the hands of White men. Stories of young innocent Black men who were hanged, castrated, and terrorized for merely looking at a White female. She witnessed firsthand the brutality and inhumanity of the segregated South in this country; yet she neither harbored nor displayed any discernible expressions of hostility, rage, or hatred. Her sense of humanity and undying faith in God would not allow her to harbor ill feelings, she often noted. She was a deeply religiously devout person who believed in God and His capacity to rid the world of evil and sin. As her first-born great grandson, she made two requests of me: (1) "Make sure you get an education!"—an experience she had been denied by law—and (2) "Put your faith in the Lord." Because education, both in my biological and ancestral family, was considered the key to liberation, honoring this dimension of my grandmother's request was simple. The second request was far more challenging.

At that point in my life, I had already developed an ambivalent relationship with religion. In fact, I couldn't understand why the White, blond-hair portrait of Jesus Christ that was so prominently displayed in our home and the homes of virtually every Black person I knew were so revered. It was painfully difficult for me to differentiate between "the image" in the portrait and the picture etched in my young psyche of those who routinely belittled, humiliated, and disrespected my parents. My introduction and exposure to church, God, and religion only intensified my sense of curiosity. The more I learned of God and His holiness, the more I began to question life as I knew it and the harsh cold world of mean-spiritedness that I got a glimpse of on a daily basis. The set of questions and curiosities that I was left with were complex and even more difficult to discuss without high affect. Why, I wondered and asked on numerous occasions, was there so much hatred in the world if God was so good? Why so much suffering? What did it mean that Blacks were slaves and Whites their "masters"? Why did God allow slavery to last for nearly 300 years without intervening? Were I and other Blacks like me cursed, as some religious doctrines would assert? My incessant questions often left my parents, grandmother, and even some teachers and clergy worried and frustrated. Admittedly, I had a very difficult time reconciling the matter of race and all of its intricacies and complexities. At a very early and impressionable age, the plight of Black people had tremendous resonance for me. It was personal and quite intimately interwoven in my life. It lived robustly in the house I grew up in. It loomed large over the street where I resided. It permeated not just the school I attended, the church where families like mine congregated, but also every corner of the world in which I inhabited. My walks to school and church were rude reminders of a world divided, the impenetrable chasm that existed between the *haves* and the *have-nots*, those who were valued and devalued, and those who were spiritually alive as well as those whom had been cast aside to die a slow and irreversible spiritual death. Put my faith in the Lord? How did Great Grandmother Anna? How could I do so without feeling betrayed? Why didn't she feel betrayed? After being harshly reprimanded by several powerful and influential adults in my life for expressing such disrespectful and sacrilegious sentiments, I learned to conceal my thoughts and feelings about race and religion. In spite of it all, the questions remained.

The Pre-College Years

By the time I reached high school, I was certain of what I wanted to do in life, although I still didn't have a name for it. Full of adolescent naïveté, blind ambition, and race-related rage, I wanted to change the world! I was sickened by the absurdity and hypocrisy of the world in which I lived. My daily walk to high school was "inconvenienced" by the omnipresence of homelessness and people sleeping on the streets because they had nowhere else to go; yet houses seemed in abundance. Arriving at high school where most of the students were Black and most of the teachers and virtually all of the administrators were White was fraught with racially based complications. My school, like so many others, was one where well-intentioned teachers attempted to educate students without understanding or being educated about the complexities of their conditions. It was the place where the students saw race with impeccable clarity and felt the pangs of it with an undeniable sting, while the teachers denied seeing it at all. There was no space for common ground or any plausible possibilities for traversing the divide. The teachers were often considered right in their self-righteous and self-declared view that they were colorblind. They promulgated the notion in every possible way that race didn't matter, while the students were accused of using it as a crutch or excuse for their academic ineptitude, lack of interest, drive, and ambition. My high school then, like many urban schools now, was a type of slaughterhouse. It was a place where the hopes, dreams, and spirits of young children of color were routinely and systematically destroyed. There were two dominant educational tracks: one that prepared the precious few for future careers at prestigious colleges and universities like Harvard, University of Pennsylvania, and Yale; the other that prepared the critical masses for a future inextricably tied to the juvenile justice system, detention facilities, and ultimately jail. One of the most egregious offenses that could ever be exacted against young curious minds took place as a matter of routine at my school: well-meaning school personnel routinely placed expiration dates on the dreams and ambitions of young curious minds. Children's dreams, in my view, no matter how far-fetched, preposterous, or seemingly unattainable should never be discouraged or taken away.

Unfortunately, African Americans, and other students of color, were routinely discouraged from pursuing college by academic advisors and guidance counselors. The common and general belief was that "we were not college material." Several decades later I still have vivid memories of conversations that I had with my guidance counselor about going to college and my desire to pursue a psychology degree. The advice and "guidance" I received was to pursue trade school so that I would be equipped to pursue a career where I could use my hands. I received this "encouragement" on more than one occasion, which was extremely odd given that I was enrolled in a college preparatory curriculum and had no demonstrated skills "in using my hands." This is what it looks like to have your dreams, hopes, and ambitions eclipsed by the subtleties of race. It is a process that is akin to what educator and activist Jonathan Kozel (1967) referred to decades ago as a type of "death at an early age." Having dreams decimated, destroyed, and/or deferred has been a common experience for many African Americans both individually and collectively. It is in part, I believe, what inspired the poet Langston Hughes (1958/1994, p.268, emphasis in original) to pen his inspirational poem, "Harlem (2)."[1] Hughes asks:

> What happens to a dream deferred?
>   Does it dry up
> like a raisin in the sun?
>   Or fester like a sore—
>   And then run?

---

1   "Harlem (2)" from THE COLLECTED POEMS OF LANGSTON HUGHES by Langston Hughes, edited by Arnold Rampersad with David Roessel, Associate Editor, copyright © 1994 by the Estate of Langston Hughes. Used by permission of Alfred A. Knopf, a division of Random House, Inc.

> Does it stink like rotten meat?
> Or crust and sugar over—
> like a syrupy sweet?
>
> Maybe it just sags
> like a heavy load.
>
> *Or does it explode?*

The College Years

My life in college greatly enhanced my understanding, awareness, and sensitivity to what it meant to be Black and especially, to be Black in White places. No longer embedded within the familiar surroundings and security of Blackness that my family and community had afforded me in the mostly racially segregated margins of society I called home, college represented a new and sometimes harsh cold world. My life in college not only provided a jaundiced view of Blackness but of Whiteness, as well. I learned very quickly that virtually everything associated with being Black was framed as bad, pathological, demonic, and even dirty in some instances while "pure, wholesome, normal, and superior" often characterized Whiteness. These pro-racist notions about *Blackness* and *Whiteness* were present virtually everywhere from private peer interactions to the classroom and lecture halls. Even the living quarters on campus perpetuated the broader cultural narrative that Black was inferior and White was superior. The dormitories that "coincidentally" housed students of color were without fail less aesthetically attractive, poorly maintained with tiles missing from the floor, cracked windows, water-stained walls, a scarcity of toilet paper, and washers and dryers that were frequently inoperable. On the other hand, the dormitories that were inhabited by White students were very well maintained and adequately furnished with all necessary paper products and supplies. The floors were spotless and cleaned routinely, and not just during parents' week. The appliances were state of the art, and the ambience that permeated all of these dorms was one that invited, perhaps even demanded, honor, dignity, and respect. This is what it means to be Black in White places. According to Hardy and Laszloffy (2005, p. 149), "devaluation refers to a process by which an individual or group is stripped of the essentials of their humanity." At its core, devaluation assaults one's sense of dignity, while heightening sensitivity to disrespect, and elevating the demand (need) for respect. Devaluation is a driving and central force in the experience of Blackness. It is virtually impossible to feel respected in a context of devaluation.

Any effort to bring attention to the obvious inequities that existed based on race was pointless and perilous. The push-back by the White establishment—administrators, faculty, and students—expressed a familiar sentiment. Thus any claims of racial bias were considered unfair and unfounded allegations advanced by those who were "hypersensitive" about race and merely trying to "play the race card."

My journey to becoming a therapist involved attending three different large state universities, and completing two post-doctoral training programs in five different regions of the country. My professional journey mirrored that of many African Americans and other people of color of my generation and beyond: I never had a single classmate, professor, or mentor of color. While I had the pleasure of working with several supportive White mentors, and had some White classmates who became lifelong acquaintances, race was always the unspoken and unacknowledged dimension of these relationships. It was rarely, if ever, discussed. In our relationships, we understood intuitively that open discussions about race were off limits. We colluded in pretending, acting "as if" it didn't matter or that we had transcended it. Yet it mattered so much that we could never discuss it. In the rare instances when race was acknowledged, it was usually introduced by a White professor or student assuring me that they did not think of me, nor see me, as Black.

I have vivid memories of sitting in classes and wondering how many of my self-assured, confident, brilliant, eloquent and articulate White classmates could do what I was doing? How many of them, I wondered, would be willing to submerge themselves into a context where they would automatically be relegated to a non-negotiable, irrevocable *world of otherness*? How many of them would be willing to leave their *sanctuaries of sameness* to explore and experience the world of otherness … where the rules of engagement were not their rules, where their core values and values of the system were replete with tension and incongruity, where a sense of safety was not ensured by the familiarity of the surroundings? I wondered how many of them would be able to show up every day as *the only one*, and tolerate being the someone who was obviously noticed but never acknowledged? Would they be able and willing to endure the many microaggressive racial slights that occur almost daily (see Sue et al., 2007) or to bear the innocent acts of ignorance that were *never intended* to do harm but somehow always managed to do so? These were often the thoughts, self-reflections, and feelings of resentment that invaded and interrupted my thinking while sitting in class very visible but unseen.

On Becoming a Therapist (Who Happens to Be Black)

For many Blacks, and other people of color, on the path to becoming therapists, the journey is a rather emotionally tumultuous one that requires a constant sorting through the intricate entanglements of race and racial oppression. The process and experience demand so much more than mastery of an academic curriculum, successful completion of an internship, scholarly work and licensure. It also involves managing the emotional burdens of being Black in

White places … having to cope on a daily basis with the often painful and emotionally-laden experience of managing the dilemmas of race. Black and other people of color understand that the process of becoming a therapist, unlike with their White counterparts, requires mastery of two curricula—one explicit, one implicit; one for all trainees, and one for "minorities only."

The Dilemmas of Race

The *implicit, for minorities' only* curriculum, requires Blacks and other people of color to effectively deal with a myriad of racially charged issues and dilemmas that occur on a regular basis. Unfortunately, many of us are often confined to dealing with these matters in private, alone, and devoid of support. It is often this dimension of the process of becoming a therapist that leaves many therapists of color questioning their sanity, mental stability, and appropriateness for the field. After all, there is something potentially "crazy-making" about seeing and feeling racial slights, whether intentional or not, so potently while they are simultaneously denied and remain invisible by everyone around you. The *implicit, for minorities' only* curriculum requires that Blacks and other people of color continue to remain sane even while operating in the midst of (seemingly) insane places. We must always demonstrate the proper decorum, stay polite, remain a team player, and take the "high road" in response to racial slights and abuses regardless of how much pain we have to endure. The following vignette provides a brief example of the type of restraint, stamina, and internal fortitude that being Black in White places often requires.

Case of "The Ultimate Pathology"

In a doctoral seminar entitled "Dynamics of Family Processes," one of my White class-mates asked the professor: "Does illegitimacy or female-headed households constitute the ultimate pathology in Black families?" The professor received the question and after a few pensive moments said, "Well, I am not sure what you mean by ultimate pathology … pathology is pathology." The ensuing class discussion was devoted to how one measures degrees of pathology and the topic of race was never mentioned.

Unfortunately, neither the professor nor the students advanced a single comment devoted to the incendiary racial premise of the question. Several class members did glance at me as if anticipating a reaction, but experience had taught me to remain still and silent, no matter the emotional cost. The dilemmas of race are such that African Americans, as well as other people of color, are often expected to be the resident experts on a host of race-related issues (see Kirkland, 2011). The positions they posit, however, must be self-deprecating, affirm the views of the dominant racial discourse, and never implicate Whites. Any deviation from the aforementioned prescription for executing one's race-related expertise deems the African American an angry, polarizing, hypersensitive, self-proclaimed victim. Although I was overcome with emotions during the remainder of the class, for these reasons, I "chose" to remain silent.

As I recall the details of the class, I am still not sure, even as I commit these words to writing, what was more personally painful and disappointing: (a) the premise of the question; (b) the absence of any racial critique by a professor I admired and respected professionally; or (c) the utter silence of all my classmates. More importantly, the collective silence of the class made it clear that it was incumbent upon me to understand that the pain, agony, disappointment, and furor that the experience generated, belonged to me. There was no processing it in class, there was no discussion to be had regarding the inherent racism threaded in the question, or consideration of what the experience was like for me as the only one in the class who had grown up in a Black family. As is often the case, I, like many other people of color in similar situations, had to stay centered, not take it personally, don't play the race card, and "choose" whether I should speak up and be punished publicly—but allow my soul to thrive—or whether I should remain silent, thus allowing my physical self to be embraced and have my soul assaulted. Every conceivable effort you expend to extricate yourself from the cycle of "being defined" only serves to intensify and reinforce the dynamic. Blackness as an experience means standing in the midst of a double bind, where both one's passivity and assertion in response to being defined, for example, often renders the same outcome. Essentially, you are double-bound, "damned if you do, and damned if you don't." Demonstrating the ability to effectively confront and manage dilemmas of race, even when it is virtually impossible to do so, is a salient feature of the *implicit, for minorities' only* curriculum.

Early in my clinical career, during a family therapy session (reported in Kottler & Carlson, 2005, pp. 123–128) in which I was confronted with the overt racism ("I ain't goin' to see no nigger doctor") of a 9-year-old White boy and his parents, I was distressed by the intransigence of the patients, of course, but was even more angered by the response of my White colleagues who were observing through a one-way mirror when they advised, during a consultation break, "You can't allow this racialized interaction to distract you from the real issues operating here" and "You just gotta hang in there."

Ironically, I was recently contacted by a large university located on the West Coast to assist with a racial issue that was quite similar to the ones described above. According to the dean of the college, "The situation started out as a benign misunderstanding that has since become racialized by a few. Now it simply won't go away as it continues to spread like an untreated cancer." Consider the following summary of the major events.

Case of "The Facts"

The program in question is a doctoral clinical training program that prides itself on its commitment to diversity and social justice. Several African American students were outraged regarding a dynamic that occurred in one of their classes. During a class lecture devoted to HIV and AIDS, the professor noted, according to one of the students, that one out of every five Black women suffers with AIDS. Ironically, there were five Black females in the class who immediately drew scrutiny in the form of stares from the class as well as some scattered and intermittent laughter. Feeling over-exposed, embarrassed, and humiliated, one of the students immediately left the classroom in tears, while the others stared at the professor with disbelief. The professor responded by stating: "What do you all want me to do ... these are the facts, I'm giving you the facts here. I can't change the facts in deference to political correctness. In all due respect, this is the type of hypersensitivity to race that makes it impossible for all of us to move forward. I'm counting on all of you here to make a difference in the world out there and you can't do that if you overreact every time someone makes a statement about race that you disagree with or think shouldn't be stated."

The professor, a licensed therapist, seemed oblivious to the process of the class dynamics and how it was profoundly shaped by the nuances of race.

In these vignettes and countless others that have been omitted but could have been included, the African American students were left to deal with the racially charged, emotionally-laden burden of being Black in White places. It was their task, burden, and responsibility to stay present, not over-react, or personalize the issue at hand, regardless of how personal it was or felt. They must accomplish this feat while simultaneously managing deeply-seated feelings of hurt and shame for which there were no invitations or avenues to open and honest discussion. Regardless of the depths of the emotions experienced, the rules of race and racial oppression dictated that it was imperative that silence be the expression of choice.

The World of Work and "Coming Home"

In many ways my graduate and post-doctoral training prepared me well for my work as a clinician in the "real world." My first full-time permanent position as a clinician was in an outpatient Mental Health facility in Brooklyn, New York, where I also served as Director of Group and Family Treatment. My clients were largely lower-income and poor African Americans and Latinos whose mental health difficulties were compounded by the intersections of race, class, and the everyday social, psychological, and emotional hardships of life in the inner city. From a distance, and based on what was typically documented on referral sheets, my clients' presenting problems were similar to those one would expect to find in any behavioral health treatment center: anxiety and other affective disorders; psychoses; and a myriad of child-centered family dysfunctions, all compounded by trauma. However, in treatment, clients routinely discussed problems that were never taught throughout my graduate school training or treated in the many university-based clinics where I had worked. Their "problems" had no *DSM* diagnostic categories and often centered on a recurring list of social problems that seemed beyond the reach of the *psychological solutions* that constituted our preferred treatment protocol. So much of their reported suffering was rooted in what they reported as maltreatment by the police, teachers who preferred to punish and discipline their children rather than educate them, landlords who refused to repair the dilapidated, often rodent-infested buildings where many lived, and politicians who only saw them when it was in the politicians' best interest to do so. I heard the painful human cry of those who wondered why dialing 911, for example, was of no consequence while the blood of their children and other loved ones saturated the streets of East New York. Many of the clients, who frequented the Center were obviously depressed, both those who expressed a frightening sense of unbridled rage, as well as those who appeared sunken in a sea of sullenness. It was a detail that was too stark and keenly obvious to overlook. Yet, the clients' incessant experiences with oppression and the ways it was so intricately intertwined into every fiber of their daily existence was much harder for many clinicians to see. Efforts to uncover the roots of depression, rage, or other serious mental-health issues repeatedly focused on the clients' biology, psychology, and family-of-origin experiences, but almost never their *ecology*, that is, the impact of their environment and the sociological-cultural context in which they and their behaviors were deeply embedded.

Although I had never treated clients of color prior to accepting this position, there was something familiar about their experiences that extended beyond words or conscious recognition. For the first time as a practicing clinician, I was able to breathe a little more freely. There was suddenly no more anxiety about greeting a client in the waiting room and watching the shock on their faces and the temporary paralysis-like state they exhibited when discovering that "their doctor" was not White. Gone were the anxieties and awkwardness about having to hear denigrating references to Blacks and/or other minorities in sessions that subsequently exempted me because I "was different." I relished the idea of finally being able to practice in a context, as I assumed was commonplace for my White counterparts, where race didn't matter; where my anxieties and insecurities could be considered relative to my clinical competencies and not the color of my skin. In many respects, this job was a godsend. It was a kind of homecoming. It was what I believed I was called to do. It was exactly what, I believe, my great grandmother had in mind when she demanded that I "make something of my life." No, she wasn't referring to objects, things, or material wealth, she was speaking of giving back to the dispirited, the silenced, and the disenfranchised while never forgetting upon whose shoulders I climbed and stood to elevate and escape the walls of oppression. Furthermore, this job was exactly what I believed I needed to help repair the many wounds to my soul that were sustained from many years of training as a Black person in predominantly White settings.

The treatment population served, the essence of the work at the Center, and the neighborhood in which it was embedded was central to the early life curiosities that initially sparked my interest in the profession without a name. My life had come full circle. The questions, curiosities, and musings that I had about the world, particularly in regards to race, that had been such a catalyst for my chosen profession was now the centerpiece of my work as a therapist. I could not imagine another job for which I was more aptly suited.

Unfortunately, the seemingly intuitive understanding that I believed I had of my clients and their experiences did not easily translate into them understanding me or feeling understood by me. In a relatively short period of time several of my clients expressed apprehension, skepticism, and even suspicion about me. Both privately and publicly they wondered if I were "Black enough." After over 10 years of being "educated" in White places, this was a question I had privately asked of myself on numerous occasions, breathlessly fearing the answer. One Latino client eventually confirmed one of my greatest fears as he stated wryly: "Hey Doc, I don't really get you, man. You look Black but everything else about you tells me you're White … I really can't trust someone like you who has the complexion but not the connection … I feel I'm Blacker than you and technically I'm not Black!" A day earlier, my secretary, Janie, who was African American and a single parent, also confronted me regarding what she perceived as my lack of racial connection. Her words were carefully chosen, expressed with the utmost respect and sensitivity but cut liked a knife nonetheless. She noted that she was offended by the language and descriptions that I had used in a Psychosocial Assessment that I had written. She stated that she felt that I had equated single parenthood with "being dysfunctional" and that everything I had written about the family in question was what she thought White people thought, wanted to believe, and would delighted that "I" had written it. "Somehow I, as well as the others, here expected something different from you," she stated disappointedly. Both my eyes and my heart began to weep. She went on to say: "We were so proud of you and thought you would be different but you seem lost … you seem like all that book knowledge has ruined you." In many ways Janie reminded me of my great grandmother, Anna, not in terms of physical appearance or age but with regard to her centeredness, wisdom, and seemingly unflappable demeanor. She had a hearty wisdom and unshakeable clarity that all of my "book knowledge" had not equipped me with during my process of miseducation. Her words resonated with me intellectually and jarred me emotionally. Janie, as well as other clients and colleagues, were voicing externally what I already knew internally but found too painful to fully embrace. They were absolutely correct: I had been trained to be a good White therapist!

A Well-Trained White Therapist

I was once again reminded of the inescapability of race. In the world of work I was much too White to earn the trust of many people of color, and among Whites, I was always too Black to be taken too seriously. Janie was absolutely right, I had lost my *self*. After all, this was a precondition for successfully navigating and completing graduate school. How could someone like me, who was completely educated and trained by Whites, who was fully indoctrinated in Eurocentric ideology, whose clinical exposure was primarily to White clients, and who was consistently and systematically discouraged from paying too much attention to race throughout his training, be anything but a good White therapist? I was tremendously skilled at writing "great" case notes exactly the way I was trained to do. Unfortunately, so much of what I looked for, what I wrote, and what I was unable to see because of what I had been trained to look for, unwittingly maligned many of the clients of color that I endeavored to help. To my White colleagues, my notes were excellent, "professional," and "objective." To my clients of color, my notes, case summaries, and assessments were essays of betrayal, written by a good White therapist.

As a good White therapist, I had become what I now refer to as a GEMM (Hardy, 2010), a Good Effective Mainstream Minority therapist. To accomplish this feat, therapists of color, like me, must commit to never discussing or acknowledging race. We must understand that "being professional" and "being objective" are sacred virtues that should never be violated or compromised even when our souls are being murdered. Being "professional" means never discussing or reacting to personal issues like race. It means always having the unshakable ability to stay calm, composed, and centered especially in the face of egregious racial slights, microaggressions, and insults. "Being objective" often means not seeing what I believe I see but rather seeing what Whites believe I should see. Along the way, I have had numerous opportunities to demonstrate my sense of professionalism and objectivity, such as in the following scenario.

> *While employed as a senior level executive for a professional association representing therapists, it was an integral part of my responsibility to attend the Board of Directors meetings. The association president, serving as Chairman of the Board, became visibly irate during a rather spirited discussion at a Board of Directors' meeting regarding whether rehabilitated ex-felons should be allowed to join the association. The President made it unambiguously clear to the board that he was a strong advocate for the proposal in question.*
>
> *When the motion to adopt a policy to grant ex-felons admittance to the organization received little support, the President assertively pursued his argument with the Board even further. When the Board appeared unimpressed and unfazed by his impassioned plea, the President stated to the Board in a frustrated and terse manner: "Damn it, I feel like the nigger in this group." After a brief and silent pause, he turned to me and said: "Oh, excuse me, Ken! I guess I'm frustrated because all*

of you have stated that you want to increase our minority membership base and how in the world are we ever going to do that if we make it mpossible for (rehabilitated) ex-felons to join our organization."

Not surprisingly, not one of the 11 remaining Board members or any of the three staff in attendance said a word or even acknowledged the inherent racism contained in the President's heartfelt plea. After all, he was using "nigger" as a metaphor not a vitriolic racial slur. "His intention," I was later encouraged to consider, "was not to insult or malign Blacks ... he is just a passionate guy." I was once again told what I have often been told in situations such as this one: "Ken, you are too emotional—you can't afford to personalize these issues, they are not personal. You have to look at the big picture, stay professional, and be objective." While the commitment of the President—who was a well-educated, powerful, White, heterosexual male—to increase the "African American membership" was laudable, it was never questioned why his proposed strategy was relegated to admitting ex-felons and not targeting for recruitment the wealth of Historically Black Colleges and Universities located throughout the country, at least five of which were located within driving distance of the national headquarters of the Association. This interaction and all of its intricacies was a potent example of what it means to be Black, feel Black, and be in a "White place."

"White places" are those "places" where "normal, healthy, the standard" are code words and synonyms for Whiteness. In White places "White" and "right" are interchangeable. It is where it is commonplace and acceptable practice to negatively define the experience of others, deny their realities, and impose meaning on the lives of others regardless of how little is actually known about them. Both privilege and the privileges of privilege are strongly sanctioned in White places, including the privilege to: speak or not speak; to be seen or not seen; to define others' in accordance with one's image; to deny and/ or dictate the length of others' suffering; to ignore history; to obfuscate the critical distinctions that exist between excuses and reasons, explanations, and justifications; and to remain righteous about the rightness of one's position. Finally, "White places" negatively affect the lives of White people who are poor, gay/lesbian/transgendered, women, as well as countless others who are marginalized due to social location, stigma, or experience with trauma.

Over the years many of these experiences have become increasingly less toxic and painful. In a perverse way, I am grateful to have had all of these experiences. While being Black in White places has certainly been the epicenter of considerable pain, disappointment, hopelessness, and despair in my life, it has also contributed to my growth and development as a therapist and as a human being. It has provided me with a perspective that enables me to be in the world as it is and simultaneously aspire to help mold it into what it quite possibly could become. Perhaps this is why I see my role as a therapist in broad terms. It is not just a process that can or should be limited to the small, intimate, sanctuary known as the consulting room. There is a global imperative as well contained in this work, and that is for those of us aspiring to be healers to be wherever human suffering is and to recognize that healing the world is and has to be a fundamental aspect of the work that we do.

Lessons Learned

My great grandmother often encouraged me, sometimes while on the brink of tears, to "Do something with your life … make a difference in the world, even if it's a small one. Too many people along the way died for us for you or any of us to squander a precious life away." My great grandmother's words and the complex experiences of being Black in White places have profoundly shaped my worldview and how I practice as a therapist. The lessons I have learned along the way have been many and the contributions they have made to my evolution as a therapist have been extraordinary. The salient lessons I have learned have been: (a) the meaning of what it means to be Black; (b) the meaning of White places; (c) the meaning of what it means to be Black in White places; and (d) the meaning of what it means to be a therapist as healer.

Implications for Therapy and Beyond

Being Black in White places has had a profound impact on my life and how I view the human spirit and the process of therapy. It has underscored the importance of embracing positions of both/and in and outside of therapy. This perspective was a welcome relief from the segregated thinking that often left me, and especially those who had been entrusted to train me, feeling bleak about my future. It was the segregated thinking that made it difficult for many Whites in my life to see me as Black and a good student, friend, or colleague. Too often the visibility and recognition of my Black being was denied to create space for some other role, e.g., "Ken, I don't see you as Black, I see you as just another student!" It seemed near impossible to have both positions simultaneously honored.

Embracing *both/and* enabled me to continue to respect many of my professors for their wisdom and faith in me as a developing therapist, while having virtually no faith in their abilities to see the inherent struggles underpinning being Black in White places. It was essential that I had the ability to see them more complexly than they were able to see me. They were professors and White, and in this regard they were simultaneously trustworthy and untrustworthy. The most powerful lesson I learned was from interactions with the relatively small, albeit significant, number of Whites with whom I interacted over the years who did make a concerted effort to understand race and themselves as White people. These were the Whites who stood up, spoke up, and stretched themselves to reach beyond racial stereotypes to be allies to people of color while their White colleagues remained paralyzed by racial polarization and holding onto claims of colorblindness. As Whites, they listened and refrained from labeling; and they worked earnestly and assiduously to show respect while acknowledging their emotional reactivity. These Whites and my experiences with them taught me an invaluable lesson about the relevancy of embracing both/and and appreciating that there are always exceptions to dominant stories. The life lesson is that there is good contained in bad and bad embedded in good.

Therapist as Healer. Being Black in White places has also aided me in developing a rather sophisticated understanding of the human condition and how to work with it in therapy, and why it is imperative to work beyond the four walls of the therapy office. It has taught me in the most raw and brutal ways what it feels like to be locked out, stepped over, and at times stepped on. *In the spirit of my great grandmother Anna, I now understand how she could endure so much injustice and harbor so little anger or hatred. Perhaps like my great grandmother, I see absolutely no value in engaging in ways of being that relegate others to the margins of society, especially knowing what I know about life along the margins.* It is a place that can crush the spirit, puncture hope, and destroy dreams if those who are entrapped are ignored, deemed invisible, or stripped of inspiration. Hope and inspiration are essential keys to transforming and transcending life along the margins. Inspiration and hope can be derived from multiple sources and forces, but it has to be harnessed. My parents, grandparents, the teachers who believed in me as well as those who didn't, the professors, guidance counselors, and others who suggested implicitly and/or explicitly that I wasn't smart enough, good enough, White enough or even Black enough provided me an unwavering inspiration that became a life force unto itself. There is something uniquely transformative and transcendent in instilling a sense of inspiration and hope in someone for whom it has been denied and/or destroyed. It has a way of lighting the internal fire of our souls in a way that suddenly makes the impossible possible and the unimaginable, imaginable.

Consequently, I have learned the healing and transformative potential of inspiration, hope, and the restoration of dignity. I regard the resurrection of hope a major task of the therapeutic process and it has become a focal point of my work as a therapist regardless of the presenting problem. I believe as therapists we are actually stockholders in the *hope manufacturing business.* Our job as therapists is to help create a sense of hopefulness for those who are in places where inspiration has been placed among the deceased and hope has long since ceased to exist. The igniting of inspiration and restoration of hope cannot be achieved through acts of placation or the extension of platitudinous remarks and gestures but instead by looking for, and hence having the ability to see, the redeemable parts of all human beings no matter how egregious their transgressions or inferior we consider them to be. It is the insatiable hunger I believe each of us has to be validated and deemed worthy that unites all of us in our humanity, regardless of race, class, gender, or sexual orientation. It is through the recognition of one's inherent worth that we as therapists get to the deeply protected places where hope and inspiration reside within those we serve. For this reason, I believe therapy must essentially involve processes of healing and transformation. Healing is what we must do to bring comfort; to soothe; and to repair that which has been disrupted, fractured, and even broken. Transformation is what we do to help forge a new way and to alter the sociocultural conditions that nurture the lethal forces of racism, sexism, homophobia, elitism and all other conditions that devalue. It is my view that when therapy fails to address systems of domination and the multitudinous ways in which people's lives are significantly hindered and devalued by them, the process falls short of one of its greatest potentials—to uplift the human spirit and transform the human condition.

Therapy as I conceptualize it is not limited to a focus on emotions, cognition, and one's psychology, but on political and the contextual variables as well. Thus, attending to issues of social justice is integral to my view of therapy. I can no longer sit with women, gay/lesbians/transgendered, or poor clients without thinking critically about sexism, heteronormativity, and classism. I look earnestly for the possible linkages between the manifestation of individual suffering and the sociocultural circumstances in which the individual (and their problems) are embedded. I am now able to better understand that these clients, even when they are White or hold privilege in other ways, exist in "White places" and suffer the symptoms of "Blackness," although they are not Black. While I think it is crucial to create space for both the naming and honoring of these untold stories, talking is simply not enough. I believe it is crucial for us to take socially just positions in and outside of therapy that help to give voice to the voiceless and uplift those who have fallen or been pushed from society's grace because of the color of their skin, shape of their eyes, or whom they happen to love. The tensions between the ideals of my professional training and the practical realities of everyday life where I practice have invited me to reconsider some sacred truths of therapy.

I have spent years in recovery from many of the ways I was trained to do therapy. As a result, I no longer strive to achieve objectivity. I recognize that I am hopelessly biased. In fact, I am as biased as those who taught and trained me how to be objective. I am not a *tabula rasa*. I wear the human stain. The prism through which I see the world, both mine and the client's, is heavily jaded by who I am: African American, male, middle class, heterosexual, and so forth. Being Black in White places has taught me all too well about the perils of unacknowledged subjectivity disguised as objectivity. It is a misguided truth that often leads us down a path to prejudgment, righteousness, and a foreclosure of possibilities. My experiences along the way have taught me the importance of locating myself in all human interactions, because it is my location that dictates my perceptions. What I look for invariably dictates what I see. *Self-location* also enables each of us to engage in a process of self-interrogation and ultimately helps to deconstruct *the manufacturing of other.* This important concept has been crystallized and reinforced for me repeatedly over the years. Every time I have been asked incredulously and disdainfully by a White colleague, professor, student, etc., "Ken, why do you always have to bring up race?" I am reminded why it is important to locate ourselves. If the questioner were to engage in such a process, the answer would be profoundly simple: "Oh, maybe he always brings up race because I as a White person never do!" Unfortunately, it appears more expedient and righteous to ignore the influences and dislocation of the self while demanding accountability from the so-called Other.

Coming Full Circle

My journey as therapist and civilian has provided a sense of purpose to my life, work, and my life's work. It also has imbued me with an acute clarity regarding where I fit into the process. I, like many therapists, have had to make a critical choice regarding *who it is* and *how it is* I want to be not only in my role as therapist but as a citizen in the world as well. The choices are somewhat finite in scope: Helper, Jailer, and/or Healer. The role of the *Helper* is to meet those who suffer where they are and to provide comfort and a context for healing and recovery. It is usually outside of the self-proclaimed scope of practice of a Helper to get involved in applying one's work to the larger social order. The main role of the Helper is to be present and provide assistance to those in need. The principle role of the *Jailer,* by contrast, is to establish and maintain order; to promote personal responsibility and accountability, often using punishment, the establishment of firm boundaries, and control as the primary tools. The world of the Jailer is comprised of *Us* versus *Them.* There is a clear line of demarcation between those who are "good" and "right" and those who are "bad" and "wrong." Those who are wrong or bad, according to the ideology of the Jailer, should be punished. Those who are good can do no wrong. The *Healer,* on the other hand, like the Helper, provides comfort and the essence of one's being to those who are served, but is also vigilant in addressing the larger sociocultural forces that are interwoven into the everyday pain and suffering of those who are trapped in White places. The Healer recognizes that both the focus and force of our work must be directed towards both the micro- and macro-systems. The Healer recognizes the inherent challenges involved in continuously attempting to treat social problems with psychological solutions. The Healer never assumes that the way things are is the way that things have to be. The Healer recognizes and operates from the premise, as Martin Luther King, Jr. said in his 1963 "Letter from Birmingham Jail," that we are all "entangled in a web of mutuality" in which none of us can truly be what we wish or ought to be until each of us is. Thus if we have compassion for the poor, although we ourselves may not be poor, we must also have an undying resolve to address poverty and greed. It must become a part of our *work* even when it is not within the scope of our *job*. As a therapist I believe it is incumbent upon me to overtly give voice to these issues and not retreat behind the masks of neutrality, and objectivity. I owe it to myself, my ancestors, and especially to my great grandmother.

Catch the Fire[2]
by Sonia Sanchez (1995)

(Sometimes I wonder:
What to say to you now
in the soft afternoon air as you
hold us all in a single death?)
I say—
Where is your fire?
I say—
Where is your fire?

You got to find it and pass it on.
You got to find it and pass it on
from you to me from me to her from her
to him from the son to the father from the
brother to the sister from the daughter to
the mother from the mother to the child.

Where is your fire? I say where is your fire?
Can't you smell it coming out of our past?
The fire of living ... not dying
The fire of loving ... not killing
The fire of Blackness...not gangster shadows.
Where is our beautiful fire that gave light
to the world?
The fire of pyramids;
The fire that burned through the holes of
slaveships and made us breathe;

The fire that made guts into chitterlings;
The fire that took rhythms and made jazz;

The fire of sit-ins and marches that made
us jump boundaries and barriers;
The fire that took street talk sounds

---

2 From *Wounded in the House of a Friend* by Sonia Sanchez. Copyright © 1995 by Sonia Sanchez. Reprinted by permission of Beacon Press, Boston.

and made righteous imhotep raps.
Where is your fire, the torch of life
full of Nzingha and Nat Turner and Garvey
and DuBois and Fannie Lou Hamer and Martin
and Malcolm and Mandela.
Sister/Sistah Brother/Brotha Come/Come

CATCH YOUR FIRE … DON'T KILL
HOLD YOUR FIRE … DON'T KILL
LEARN YOUR FIRE … DON'T KILL
BE THE FIRE … DON'T KILL
Catch the fire and burn with eyes
that see our souls:
WALKING.
SINGING.
BUILDING.
LAUGHING.
LEARNING.
LOVING.
TEACHING.
BEING.
Hey. Brother/Brotha. Sister/Sista.
Here is my hand.
Catch the fire … and live.
live.
livelivelive.
livelivelive.
live.
live.

References

Hardy, K. V., & Laszloffy, T. A., (2005). *Teens Who Hurt: Clinical Interventions for Breaking the Cycle of Adolescent Violence*. New York: Guilford Press.

Hughes, L. (1994). "Harlem 2." In *The Collected Poems of Langston Hughes* (p. 268). New York: Knopf/Random House. (work originally published 1958)

Kirkland, S.L. (2011, September/October). The new face of racism. *Psychotherapy Networker, 35*(5), 17–18.

Kottler, J., & Carlson, J. (2005). Ken Hardy: Mister Black Doctor. In *The Client Who Changed Me: Stories of Therapist Personal Transformation* (pp. 123–128). New York: Routledge.

Kozel, J. (1967). *Death at an Early Age*. Boston: Houghton Mifflin.

Sanchez, S. (1995). "Catch the Fire." In *Wounded in the House of a Friend* (pp. 15–17). Boston: Beacon Press.

Sue, D.W., Capodilupo, C.M., Torino, G.C., Bucceri, J.M., Holder, A.M.B., Nadal, K.L., & Esquilin, M. (2007). Racial microaggressions in everyday life: Implications for clinical practice. *American Psychologist, 62*(4), 271–286.

13

UP THE HURRY STAIRS

Tobey Hiller

Chloe helter-skelters up the stairs. She drops her lunchbox on the lowest stair, her reading folder on the next, flings her sweater over the banister; behind her upward rush, it slides down the slick wood and drops to the living room floor. At last the school part of the day is done. She's almost frantic to get to her room, where everything, including time, will be soft and furry and belong to her. She feels it in her feet, in her belly, as physical and imperative as needing lunch or having to go to the bathroom. At the top of the stairs, two pink glops from the raspberry popsicle she grabbed from the kitchen drop on to the polished hardwood floor, and then a blob drops on to the Persian rug in the hall. Chloe is going too fast to notice. As she touches the handle on the door to her room, she hears the front door click, and knows her mother has just walked in.

Chloe's mother sits on the couch in my office. She's thin as a whippet, her hair a bonnet of bees. She is talking very fast, about Chloe. Her words have a staccato and rushed rhythm, with emphatic veers of pitch and twists of tone. "Every day, and I mean *every day*—not just some days or every third day or once in a while—every day she just strews all her stuff all over the stairs when she comes in. I really can't fathom it! I don't know *how* many times I've told her to put her lunchbox in the kitchen and take her homework upstairs, hang up her jacket ... but it's just useless, *use*less: she never listens. She WON'T listen. The days I pick her up, all the way home, it's 'I want this, I want that, I didn't like my lunch, I was wearing the wrong shoes' (I was wearing the wrong SHOES?! doesn't she know how lucky she is?) whining and whining, and by the time we get home we've already had three fights, and then once yet again, she REFUSES to remember to do what I've asked ..."

"Chloe! Get down here right away! You've left all your stuff on the stairs again!" Chloe hears quick feet on the stairs. "And dammit dammit godDAMMit Chloe look at this— there's pink glop on the floor. AND on the hall carpet! Can't you remember what I said about snacking in your room? You're the one who wanted a white carpet in your bedroom, and now I ... are you eating stuff on your bed again?" The door bursts open, and there she is, her mother, gripping the door handle hard, her face pinched into that snagged, tangled look Chloe thinks of as a knot she must somehow untie—by yelling. Or arguing. Or, sometimes, pleading.

Chloe's mother squinches up her face, leans forward intensely. She is dressed with flair and can give an impression of considerable vigor and acuity, both physical and intellectual, but around her there is often a zone of disturbed air, a climate of electrical storm, as though the tension she feels emanates palpably outward in energetic waves. She is very well educated and well-read and often enough speaks with considerable insight and scope of knowledge about her own life, the people in it, and her job—she holds an administrative post at a non-profit which provides tutoring and educational consultation to low-income families—as well as the world at large. When she is not spooked into her highest velocity by an anxiety about all the things she can't control (including herself), her native intelligence and resourcefulness make her both interesting and competent. She is a fighter for social justice, and she is good at what she does. If people need her help, she is reliable, hard-working and compassionate. But she is always in the trenches. She always knows best. There is a great deal wrong with everyone, and this annoys her incessantly.

When Chloe's mother is manic, she stays up all night planning campaigns in which a rival agency or an earlier romantic rival are brought down, or she gives away a great deal of money to good causes and buys some nice jewelry, with perhaps a car thrown in, or she goes to Hawaii to berate her relatives and argue about the will. Her husband has learned to recognize the signs of gathering storm and he does what he can—often with skill and compassion and a custom-made balance of comfort and direction born of experience—to stem the tide. And fortunately these extremities don't happen so much anymore. Chloe's mother has informed herself thoroughly about her bi-polar condition and taken steps, including using medication, to keep herself in better balance and avoid full-blown episodes. She's learned, over the years, to recognize the signs of approaching storm herself and collaborate with those who want to help keep her out of the pressure cooker. Now she wants to learn how to live more equably in the middle zone, and she wants a better handle, she says, on what drives her up the scale toward conflagration.

So Chloe's mother isn't manic at this point. What we are encountering here is her steady-state set of problems, the way she sees it: Chloe's constant recalcitrance, her husband's lack of sensitivity, the stupidity of people at work, not to mention the faults, legion and ever-present, of her various family members—and she has come to me to help her handle these difficulties better. Which at many points seems to mean to get them all—those idiots, shirkers and traitors—to straighten up and fly right. (An impossible task from where I sit, my own godlike abilities regarding the shortcomings of others—or even my own—having already been tested, many times, and found wanting.)

Though Chloe's mother's strengths and assets, as well as her good intentions, are evident, and sessions with her are always interesting, and I admire the bravery, even fortitude, with which she has dealt with her biomedical and temperamental condition, I sometimes find it difficult to connect with her. I am, more often than I would like to be, put off by what seems to be her hardness, the chitinous wall she puts up between herself and other people. The absolute wrongs and rights of things. The way she judges and condemns and controls. Not to say I haven't encountered these tendencies in myself; though traitors don't figure much in my inner psychic landscape, I have certainly been known to use the word "idiot" or felt that the right answer resides with, well, guess who? And all of us know how to convert hurt into anger. Nonetheless, Chloe's mother is clearly a person for whom an empathic extension into the worlds and feelings of other people is a far leap, and often beyond her psychic muscular power.

The trouble lies mostly in her intimate and collegial relations. As long as she's directing people, she knows where right and wrong stand, and her sense of compassion for the challenges people face is aroused. She is alert to all levels of unfairness and touched by—indeed, often infuriated by—social injustice and feels a strong interest in helping people less fortunate than herself, so that she's able to be skillful and persistent in her job, setting up good systems to help the clients her non-profit serves. But when it comes to family life, and to the inner lives of others whose needs and feelings might be in opposition to her own—or simply different—she's puzzled and hurt by the disappointing way people won't go along with her superior way of designing things. Then the sharp and often stabbing arrow of her assessment of others' shortcomings, arcing well over some reservoir of hurt, comes into play. Listening, ramping down, imagining someone else's meaning, letting it go, or taking it easy—these go out the window.

Though my orientation in therapy is collaborative, and I eschew, when I can, the life-expert's idea that I have an answer the client lacks, I have certainly done what I could to steer Chloe's mother toward a more empathic and sensitive view of others and a more nuanced spectrum with regard to motive and meaning in her intimate relations. We have worked together on finding ways for her to slow down in anxiety-provoking and conflictual situations—she has identified a feeling of tension in her head and neck that she's learning to use as a trigger for an inner voice saying something like "easy, easy there"—so that she can listen to the other person's conflicting ideas and ask questions to make sure she fully understands this foreign point of view and where it comes from.

I have also set up a number of role-playing situations for her, particularly with Chloe, where she explores what standing in her daughter's shoes is like, and she's expanded her understanding of Chloe's feelings and needs, though coming up against Chloe's disappointments or fears is hard for her. Luckily, she likes me, and we seem to have a good rapport, so she's willing to venture into areas she finds quite challenging. That does not mean, however, that the issues that bedevil her—the vagaries and debilities of other people and the prickling sense of the helplessness one has faced with the suffering and injustices of the world—have let up much since we've been working together. I've been trying hard to teach her to take it a little easier, but the pathway to easy still seems pretty overgrown. Or she tries—she has a very evident "good girl" side—and then it all goes—*whoosh*—back to steady state and the familiar inner mutter that keeps her lying awake at night counting the ways her husband has disappointed her and, the next day, screaming at her recalcitrant 7-year-old daughter on the hurry-up stairs.

"Oh oh," thinks Chloe. "I think Mom's home already." She hears commotion in the kitchen. Carefully, she hangs her coat up on the hat rack next to the door. She puts her reading folder on the hall table, where it's supposed to go. Feeling a longing now for the hurry up, for the warm spot on her bed where Ogilvie the Rabbit lives, she briefly contemplates going into the kitchen to deliver her lunchbox. But really, it's the stairs she wants. She doesn't want to talk, or tell about the day and what she liked or didn't like. She doesn't have to think, "I love my Mom" to make it okay—she does love her mom: she just doesn't want to talk. Or argue. Or help her clean up the kitchen. Quickly, she lays the lunchbox on the table in the hall alongside her notebook—maybe that will be good enough—and then she puts her shoes under the table for good measure. That will show how careful she is. She runs up the stairs.

"Chloe!" Just as she shuts the door. "What is your lunchbox doing here? Haven't I told you, again and again and yet once again, to bring it into the goddamn kitchen? Are you deaf? What's your problem, Chloe? Are you really deaf, dumb, and blind?"

Chloe's mother sits on the couch. She's leaning forward, her two hands placed on either side of her knees. I am always astounded by her hair, which leaps out of her skull in gold loops and tangles as though trying to explain what her thoughts do on the inside of her skull. I wonder if her daughter has hair like that, too. She's certainly a fighter, by all accounts.

"I thought to myself, *I don't want to do this*. Even while I was screaming at her—and I know I was screaming at her—I was thinking, *look at this, look at this, look at the jacket hung up, the notebook*. She was doing her best. So when I calmed down I told her I was sorry. And I think she was glad."

"But I do that too much." She looked up. "I always tell her I'm sorry, and I know it doesn't make up for it. So I've been thinking about what to do."

She looks at me, a blue gaze quite frank and deep; a silence ensues. This kind of quiet is quite rare in our sessions. Silence is not particularly welcome to her, and she pours words into it—buzzing, or brilliant, or hurried. Again, they make me think of bees. But now, I think of honey.

The silence lengthens. She looks away and shakes her head.

"Actually, I don't know exactly what I want to do. I'm afraid I can't get anywhere on this stuff. It's so … it feels like having a door slammed in my face when she does this stuff. Like she just won't do this one thing … So I can never seem to … But anyway I do have an idea. On this one thing, at least. And I want your help figuring it out."

"Sure. What's your idea?"

"My idea is that we should go up the stairs together, holding hands. Maybe we could talk about it in the car. Then she'd have to slow down."

"And you'd be slowing down, too, sounds like."

"Yeah, that's true. And I could help her put things away …"

"Help as in do it for her or something? Would she like—"

"No, no. Just be with her. She knows how to do it. I could just, you know, say, 'that's good' … or … Oh, I don't know—maybe it's a stupid idea."

"No, no, I think it sounds like a good idea. You being with her. Maybe not giving the stairway-after-school lecture or anything, but sort of making a game of it, the two of you going at the same pace. What do you think would help you to go slow, or have patience, just in case she doesn't do it right?"

"I don't know, just going at her speed, I guess, letting her lead."

"Holding her hand, like you said."

"Yeah."

We discuss what she might say in the car about trying this. We imagine, together, how Chloe might take to this idea and agree she'll have to see if Chloe's interested in trying it.

The door opens. Already they're holding hands. Chloe has her backpack and sweater in one hand. She steps to the hall table and glances up, bright-eyed, at her mother. "I have to let go of your hand for a second." Her mother smiles down from the aureole of her hair. Chloe unzips her backpack, takes out her lunchbox, grabs her mother's hand, and leads her into the kitchen, where she deposits the lunchbox on the counter. "C'mon!" She marches out of the kitchen, back to the hall, still holding her mother's hand, and takes out her homework folder, which she puts on the table. She hangs her sweater on the coat-tree. "See," she says, "this is how you should do it." She is grinning, and so is her mother. Chloe turns toward the stairs, then "Ooops! 'Scuse me for a sec," she says, and giggles. She zips up her backpack, one-handed, and pulling on her mother a bit, places it underneath her sweater very carefully. Then she tugs hard: "Let's go!" and starts up the stairs, fast. Her mother stays right next to her, clattering up the wooden stairs at a matched pace, and now they're both laughing. They burst into Chloe's room and dive, together, for the bed. "Boy, what a speedo!" says Chloe's mom. "Those stairs are hurry hurry," says her daughter, her face shining, "so I always run fast as I can."

"And then," says Chloe's mother, "we had this long talk, lying on her bed, about why she likes to run up the stairs, and why she likes to get to her room fast after school. I listened, she talked. It was great—she told me a lot of stuff about school I couldn't get her to talk about before. And the next day, she put everything away, on her own." She smiled. "I don't know if she'll keep on with it, but doing that, going up with her, taught me so much about her. And about how to get her to do things, in a different way." She looked at me, her face full of the pleasure of that moment with her daughter, which, no matter how many times other kinds of moments would still erupt—as we both knew they would—was the kind of moment she could have again, because she was the one who made it happen. The one who had imagined it, the one who had listened with her body to her daughter's pathway up the hurry stairs.

And I was filled with gratitude. To her, to the luck of my job, to the moment. To be in the presence of that deepest of change-makers in human beings: the expanding human heart. *Who's the helper here?* I thought. Because she was helping me to encounter again the best reasons for pleasure in being human: the unexpected, indeed almost miraculous, capacity for change, for tectonic movement, where none has been expected. In a spot where, if asked, the observer might even say: that door is unlikely to open, no light will enter there.

Nothing better than to be proved wrong about that.

And I felt how totally beyond what I did or didn't do—so long as I provided a welcome environment—the rise toward generosity, the reach toward another, the plan based on love a client made—really was. And how lucky I was to be party to this capacity and impulse in human beings, to facilitate it where I could, to be surprised and delighted by it when it arrived, to be comforted by its growth. Even on what seemed arid ground: the oasis, and not a mirage.

Chloe runs up the stairs, behind her on the steps a mess of lunchbox, coat and shoes. Her head down, Ogilvie in it. She hears the kitchen door swing, and a sort of stuffed silence below her. She stops. She turns. Her mother is standing down there, arms crossed tight across her chest, and Chloe can feel the frown, though it's silent. "Hold on, Mom," she yells. "Hold on! Hold on! I forgot." She clatters down the stairs. "Go in the kitchen!" yells Chloe, louder than she meant to, and for a second she sees her mother's face fill up with words, but then she turns and goes into the kitchen, though her back has that stiff-as-a-board look. Chloe runs down and puts her stuff away where it's supposed to go. Then, though it's hard and it feels like one thing too many, she takes her lunchbox into the kitchen. Her mother smiles and frowns at the same time, teetering on the edge of words. "Come upstairs and say hi to Ogilvie, Mom," says Chloe, depending on the smile part, and the smile grows wider and Chloe runs out of the kitchen and up the hurry stairs, thinking something that resembles, but is not exactly the same as, honey or butterscotch pudding or something like that.

Reflections

I could have written here about many things that have made the practice of therapy rewarding and worthwhile for me and stacked up solid against the grind or pain of it: the use of my capacities to connect to and help others, a boon; the miracle of being in the presence of someone who is undergoing a deep grief or transformation and witnessing and sharing that journey; the love-liness of being party to so many creative and interesting inner lives; the honor of being trusted. But in the end what I wanted to talk about is the way, time and again, the practice of therapy has broken me open, shattered my assumptions or plunked down hope where little or none had existed. In a way, this is what brought me into the field.

Thirty-five years ago, when I was studying Psychodrama, I watched a woman I had already decided, just from looking at her and without even naming it to myself, was a person whose inner life could never resemble my own, respond to a warm-up and begin to work with the student director. She was wearing a knit pant suit and a beehive-ish hairdo, and she'd said hardly anything in our classes so far, and what little she had said seemed critical and nitpicky to me. Not very far into the work, she broke down, and a torrent of feeling poured out. Well, you know the story, no doubt. In fact, her inner life—complex, delicate, full of terror and delight and unresolved pain, was fully as interesting as my own, and despite her beehive hairdo and my long, freestyle hair we were cousins not more than once removed.

Ever since then, I've been on the alert for my assessments of others—which, I admit, I still think of often as astute—to be broken open, and for the little laughing god of the unexpected and miraculous to leap out and run, faster than I can follow, up my hurry stairs.

14

ROAD TRIP[1]

Michael F. Hoyt

When I finished graduate school in 1976, my father flew East so that we could meet and drive back to California together. We planned to hook-up in Chicago and head West, taking our time, a father-and-son road trip. I filled my little Japanese-import station wagon with my few belongings—a Persian rug, a bent-wood rocker, a couple of boxes of books, and a certificate declaring me a newly minted Ph.D., said goodbye to New Haven, Connecticut (where I had gone to school), and drove to the Windy City, where my father was spending a few days visiting old friends and family. After a night at my aunt and uncle's, Dad and I headed out for our big adventure.

Route 80 took us across Iowa and Nebraska, then south to Denver. A long conversation ensued as we motored along a concrete and asphalt ribbon of changing landscape, roadside motels, steak houses and truckers' breakfast spots. Small talk, jokes, family histories and mysteries, silences, discussions about school and my future, updates on family news, some sightseeing. Passing the Rockies, we entered Utah and decided to press on to Las Vegas.

Somewhere in southern Utah, somewhere along the way, somewhere in the night, a sign said "Construction Ahead" and the road diverted. We turned off and took the side road, and then another. It was late and dark, and a sign directed us toward another detour. We were moving slowly on a dry scrabble dirt road. We passed fires in open oil drums and abandoned heavy equipment that looked like eerie dinosaurs in the shadows cast by our headlights. We

1 A version appeared, with changes, in J.H. Frykman and T.S. Nelson (Eds.), 2003, *Making the Impossible Difficult: Tools for Getting Unstuck* (pp. 62-65). New York: iUniverse. ©Michael F. Hoyt. 2003. Used with permission.

slowly drove on for what seemed a long time, maybe another 45 minutes or an hour, following the road farther into the dark. It grew increasingly desolate and forboding. We went further. There were no other cars, no more construction equipment. There had been no other signs, but we wondered if we had missed a turn. Just as we were discussing whether to turn around, it happened: The engine suddenly died!

"Oh shit!"

"Why'd you stop?" Dad asked.

"I didn't—the motor just stopped."

There was gas on the gauge. Turning the key did nothing. We tried, over and over. *"Don't flood it."* We sat, then tried again. Nothing. We got out and opened the hood. Nothing. We wiggled a few wires. Nothing.

"We're fucked!" I muttered.

"No. We're stuck."

"What do we do?"

"We wait" said Dad.

"For what?"

"Help."

"From who?"

"We'll have to see."

"What if no one comes?"

"We'll see."

A long time passed. Suddenly, a large truck, an 18-wheeler, came around the curve. We stood by our car, in his headlights waving as he approached … the truck slowed but just kept going.

"Shit!" I cursed. Dad shook his head, saying nothing.

More time went by, maybe another hour. I turned the key again—still nothing. It was very dark and getting colder. Suddenly, another set of headlights! This time a car. We waved, but it barreled by, going too fast, not even slowing. The driver honked his horn as he disappeared into the night.

Eleven o'clock came and went. We sat in the car, hood up. Not talking much.

Maybe an hour passed. Then another. It got even colder.

Then, headlights coming up the road toward us! We got out and waved. The pick-up truck slowed, then stopped. The driver rolled his window down.

"What's wrong?"

Dad spoke: "We're stuck. The engine stopped and won't start. We've got plenty of gas."

"Want me to take a look?"

"We'd sure appreciate it."

The man was wearing a jacket and a John Deere cap, looked to be in his mid or late 30s. His wife, bundled up, was sitting next to him. She was holding an infant or small child. Sleeping bundled up between them was a little girl, maybe 4 or 5, maybe a bit older.

He backed up his truck, faced his headlights under our hood, then got out and closed the cab door behind him. He leaned over the car and poked around, asking questions, wiggling this, checking that.

"*What do you think?*" Dad asked.

"*I don't know—all your connections look OK.*"

"*What do we do now?*" I asked impatiently. Dad slipped me a look.

"*It could be your gas line, but it sounds more electrical. Mind if I check a little more?*"

The man went back to his pickup, behind the cab, and returned with a flashlight and a toolbox.

"*Are you a mechanic?*"

"*Not really, but I like to fool around a little.*"

"*Let me hold your light for you,*" said Dad.

Spark plugs were unscrewed and reversed. Nothing. Connections were loosened and retightened. Nothing. Hypotheses were formulated and tested. Nothing. Finally, he announced:

"*Here it is! It's your rotator. It broke off. Too bad—I was hoping it was something we could rig up, at least to get you to town. There's nothing we can do—you'll need a new one. They should have one, but if not, they'll have to order it. You're going to need a tow into town.*"

"*How far is it?*" I asked.

"*Not too bad—maybe an hour, little more.*"

I knew to be quiet. I let Dad speak.

"*What should we do?*"

"*Well, your vehicle can't move, so I'll have to drive back and let them know you need help. It'll be better if I have them follow me to show them where you are.*"

"*That's taking you way out of your way—I really appreciate all of your help.*"

"*No problem.*"

The man went back to his truck, got in and talked with his wife for a few minutes. She listened, then nodded. He pulled up next to us.

"*It'll take us maybe an hour to get there. There's an all-night service station. At this hour we should be able to get someone to come right away, so unless there's some problem, we'll be back in a couple of hours.*" He turned around and drove off.

A couple of hours later, two sets of headlights appeared. The pickup pulled up next to us, followed by the tow truck. The driver got out.

"*That wasn't too bad. I've told Joe what the problem is, and he'll tow you right to the gas station. The parts store is right next to it, and it opens up at 8 a.m. They should be able to get you back on the road. There's an all-night coffee shop you can wait in until it opens at 8.*"

"*Thank you.*"

"*There's nothing more I can do. Like I said, you need a new rotor. You'll be OK with Joe. I think we're going to take off. We've got a way to go until we get home to Sacramento. But first, my wife's got some family in Los Angeles we're heading to see.*"

"*You've really helped us out.*" Dad reached into his pocket. "*I'd like to pay you for all of your time.*"

"Don't worry about it."

"That's very kind. But you really saved us, and it took you a long way out of your way in the middle of the night."

"I was glad to be able to help."

"I'd feel better if I could pay you—at least for your gas."

"Nahh."

"Well, then would you at least let me buy a little present for your girls?" Dad had a couple of $20s in his hand.

"It's not necessary."

"No, but you've really been great."

The man paused. "I don't want any money, but I'll tell you what you can do." We listened intently. *"Sometime, if you ever see someone who's stuck or needs a hand, help them out, OK?"*

Dad nodded. "I understand. You're a good man." I listened.

He shook our hands, wished us well, and drove off as we called out "Thanks, again!"

The tow driver hitched us up for the long ride into town.

"Wow! What luck! He wouldn't even take any money. That was far out!" I exclaimed.

"Nice guy, huh?" replied Dad.

"You know, we never even found out his name."

"Let's call him Sam, for short. Know what I mean?"

I did. I bought some battery cables. Paid for them myself. You never know when someone might need a jump.

15

BLUE ON BLUE

A Love Story

Chris Iveson

"And I thought you were dead!" I knew that it was the wrong thing to say but by then the words had left my brain and were on their way to my vocal chords. It was too late to call them back and in the slowly passing micro-seconds before they turned to sound I rewound the steps to this moment.

Six months earlier I had been asked to accompany a colleague on a home visit following a request for an emergency admission to residential care of an elderly woman suffering from Alzheimer's Disease (see Iveson, 1990). Martha had been cared for by her husband, Ralph, who a few days prior to the call had suffered a massive stroke and was now in a coma from which he was not expected to recover. Martha's daughter, Rosa, was caring for her mother temporarily but lived many miles away and was not in a position to carry on in this way. It was Rosa who had asked her mother's doctor to make the referral for residential care.

Surprisingly, Martha had been expecting us even though Rosa had not yet arrived. She was an elegantly dressed, well-groomed woman in her late 70s and had a tea tray already laid out. We were seated in comfortable chairs in a large, airy and well-furnished St. John's Wood mansion flat with china cups and saucers in hand. For half an hour we talked about the paintings on Martha's walls and the books that lined her copious shelves. We had much in common with both: books we loved and art that remained a mystery. Ralph was himself an accomplished artist though the paintings were not his but gifts from his friends.

Martha spoke knowledgeably about literature and publishing which had been her field, while we waited for Rosa, held up in London traffic. She eventually arrived flustered and concerned that her mother would be upset by our visit, as indeed she became as soon as Rosa joined us. "Who are these people? Who are these people?" Martha began to ask. "You're not going to let them take me away! Who are they?" These were distressing cries and did much to explain Rosa's worries. Nonetheless, Martha had clearly displayed an ability to care for herself sufficiently well to rule out compulsory admission to residential care. Rosa then became very distraught and angry that she was being left unsupported. My offer of counselling for her mother was spurned despite my belief that it was likely to help her cope. So we left behind an angry daughter and a confused mother and took with us a definite feeling of inadequacy.

The Story Continues ...

Six months later I received a call from a very friendly sounding Rosa saying her mother had finally agreed to come for counselling. I am constantly surprised at my failure to read my client accurately. I could have sworn that Rosa had totally dismissed the very idea of counselling yet here she was, eager for it to happen. "Will you be coming, too?" I asked. "No, my father will come with her," she surprisingly replied. His recovery had been a minor medical miracle.

Two weeks later, as arranged, I walked into the clinic waiting room where Ralph and Martha were seated. Maybe it was something about Ralph, dressed in a large grey herringbone overcoat, brilliant white trainers and a white peaked hat, that hinted at mischief and as my greeting formed I hoped I had read him correctly, otherwise it was definitely going to be the wrong thing to say: "You must be Ralph" I said, holding out my hand, "and I thought you were dead!" Ralph gave a large laugh, jumped to his feet and performed a little jig saying, "But as you see I'm very much alive!" Martha looked on with resigned amusement.

It was the beginning of a short and influential relationship.

"I hear you are an artist?" I asked Ralph as we settled into our seats. "What kind of artist?"

"I'm what we call a minimalist, but it's a bit of a dirty word these days," he replied.

"Me, too" I responded. "And it's a bit of a dirty word in therapy as well!"

This was a genuine question. Despite many concerted efforts, reading books and going to galleries, I had never found a way to look at abstract art with anything other than incurious bewilderment. I was a Philistine and this was too good a chance to pass up. Here was a horse's mouth from which I might learn:

"So what does minimalism mean in art?" I asked.

"We were all trying to get behind and beneath, get to the true essence of colour and form, reducing things to their bare essentials," began Ralph. "Then in the late 60s, early 70s we all, one by one, painted ourselves off the canvas with our whites on white and blacks on black. After that there was nowhere to go so many of us stopped painting. I didn't paint for 16 years."

"But you're painting again now?"

"Yes, for a couple of years. In fact I was working on a canvas when the stroke hit me, so I'm back to that now." Ralph went on to describe how he had painted a blue wash on a large canvas, then applied "layer upon layer upon layer of glaze," added a square of blue, more layers of glaze eventually leaving a number of squares set in a deep glaze, "So when it's finished you should be able to take a walk inside." Having concluded, Ralph waving his hand in an elegant spiral. It was a mesmerising description.

As was Martha's. Asked to imagine a "tomorrow" in which she had all the memory physically available to her, Martha began: "Well, the first thing will be that I remember Rosa is coming to take me Christmas shopping." Ralph's jaw dropped as he whispered, "She is, too!" Martha went on to describe the shock, relief and pleasure that she would see on her daughter's face when she arrived to find her mother ready and waiting. The description continued. They were going to take the bus into town because parking would be a problem and their first stop would be Liberty's where they would take morning coffee. Martha hoped her daughter would not dawdle too long after that because she was keen to get to Selfridges by lunchtime ("The Selfridge Hotel does such a good lunch!"). They planned to end the day in Harrods where Rosa was going to order her Christmas turkey. Ralph looked on in sheer amazement at his wife's lucid and totally accurate description of tomorrow's plan.

I then asked Ralph to describe what he would see different on Martha's return if her memory was still with her. She would remember where she had been, she would know what she had bought and for whom and he would feel that he had his wife back. Almost as an afterthought he went on to say, "But the thing that would really clinch it for me would be if she knew what was in the freezer without having to look!" It is not part of my usual practice to give advice or claim superior knowledge to my clients but before I could stop myself I cried, "Ralph! Nobody knows what's in the freezer without having to look!" Ralph was intrigued by this statement but accepting my expertise, waved his hand at the camera recording this meeting and called out, "Please strike my last statement from the record!"

Two weeks later Ralph and Martha came for their second appointment. Ralph jumped to attention as I came into the waiting room and declared himself to be still alive. He went on to say that they had not come for more therapy but just to thank me which they wanted to do in person. I was touched and asked what were they thanking me for.

"We don't know" said Ralph. "We can't tell if she's regained her memory or if we've just stopped worrying about her losing it! Either way it's no longer a bother, so thank you!"

It was the last I saw of Ralph.

A few weeks later I was teaching in Newcastle where the Laing Gallery had an exhibition of abstract art. For the first time in my life I went alone to an exhibition and for the first time enjoyed myself. Somehow I had found a way, not to understand but to look. There was a postcard of one of the paintings, a yellow on yellow and I sent it to Ralph with my thanks for his tuition and a joke I had been told about the minimalist musician, Philip Glass:

> Knock, knock.
> Who's there?
> Knock, knock.
> Who's there?
> Knock, knock.
> Who's there?

A few weeks later I received a card from Ralph with an equally obscure joke.

A year went by and I was reminded once again of Ralph while reading a very moving and minimalist account by Bruce Chatwin (1989) of his meeting with Nadezhda Mandelstam, an impoverished, bed-ridden Russian, who he also described as "one of the most powerful women in the world." In two pages (pp. 83-85) he brought his whole afternoon in her cramped, stale-smelling room alive as she talked of literature and art. As he left she asked Chatwin to straighten the painting on the wall by her bed. "The painting was all white, white on white … 'Weisberg,' she said. 'He is our best painter. Perhaps that's all we can do today in Russia? Paint whiteness!'" I sent the story to Ralph and he sent me a quote from the French minimalist philosopher, Derrida.

Another year or so and I was thinking of Ralph again. I had just opened with Evan George and Harvey Ratner our first clinic—the Brief Therapy Practice, which later became 'BRIEF'—with its unadorned white walls, and was thinking about contacting Ralph with a view to buying a painting from him. A few days later I had a call from Rosa. She had tracked me down to let me know Ralph had died. Apparently, according to his papers, our meeting and correspondence had been as important to Ralph as it was to me and she wanted me to know how her parents had enjoyed an Indian Summer in their last few years together. When I told Rosa of my hope to hang one of Ralph's paintings in the clinic, she said I was very welcome to choose one. In return, she asked for a copy of the videotape I had made of our meeting. This raised a confidentiality issue as Martha would need to give permission. Though she could not remember our meetings, we decided that if she watched the tape she could then give her consent, or not. She agreed to a joint viewing, and a few weeks later we all three met and watched the tape together. Whatever Martha and Ralph had been through together, and there were sufficient hints that their relationship had not been a bed of roses, in this video they were as close to the perfect couple as could be on this earth. All three of us wept throughout the whole hour. Promising to make a copy of the tape, I arranged to visit Rosa to choose a painting. When the time came, I could not bring myself to copy the tape; it seemed an original was the only fair exchange. And I knew which original I wanted. Visitors to BRIEF will see on the wall of our training room one of Ralph's last minimalist paintings: a blue on blue.

Two years later I was invited to a retrospective of Ralph's work, hosted brilliantly by Martha. Rosa laughed, saying what a pleasure it was to see her mother happy and though she would not remember the event the next day she was living and enjoying her life to the full.

Evolving Minimalism

Ralph continues to influence my work and my life. Perhaps his most precious gift was to help me find a way to share my wife's enjoyment of art. London's Tate Modern is no longer a place of anxious boredom, though it remained so for my greatest mentor, Steve de Shazer. We ate at the seventh floor restaurant, overlooking the River Thames and St. Paul's Cathedral, on one of Steve's visits. Leaving late, the galleries were empty, but still open. Steve marched through room after room of the world's best known modern art, eyes straight ahead. When challenged about his own minimalism, he said, "It's not the same!" And it isn't.

Harvey Ratner, Evan George, my partners at BRIEF, and I, are not alone in owing a great debt to Steve de Shazer. Though we were able in later years to joke with him that if he did our Diploma course, he would fail because we had messed so much with his original ideas, we have stayed true to his version of minimalism: the application of Ockham's Razor to everything we do. de Shazer's (1982, 1985, 1988) early writing and that of the team at the Brief Family Therapy Center in Milwaukee is particularly 'research' oriented. Almost every move was tested for its necessity: if not essential it was dropped. BRIEF has continued this tradition of experimenting and over the years have 'dropped' many of solution-focused brief therapy's traditional components (see George, Iveson, & Ratner, 1999, 2006; Iveson, George, & Ratner, 2012; Ratner, George, & Iveson, 2012; Shennan & Iveson, 2011). However, like Steve before us, we are not attempting Ralph's form of minimalism, we are not attempting to get to any underlying meaning or essential reality. Instead, we discover that each time we successfully remove what turned out to be an unnecessary component of our work a new realization and new practice emerges. It is an evolving minimalism in which every removal brings into focus something hitherto hidden. And it means that after 25 years of working together Evan, Harvey and I can still argue about where on earth we are!

And Back to the Story

Ralph and Martha were leaving the clinic after their first visit. Standing with them by the door I was whipped by an icy wind as Ralph turned with a protective arm around Martha and, pointing at her head with his other hand, asked

"Have you noticed anything odd about her?" I was not sure where Ralph was going with this and, as solution-focused brief therapists tend not to focus on oddness, I gave a non-committal shrug.

"She shakes her head all the time!" he cried, "can you do anything about that?"

It had been difficult not to notice Martha's violent head-shakes every two or three minutes. I once imitated her and gave myself a headache I shall not forget.

Martha demurred, "Oh Darling, don't be silly, I've done this all my life!"

"Can you?" insisted Ralph.

By now I was beginning to shiver so I suggested to Ralph that we talk about it next time. A look of such disappointment crossed his eyes that I relented and asked Martha how she controlled her head-shaking. She said she couldn't, she never had been able to.

"What about when you'd look a complete fool or end up bidding a million pounds for a picture?"

"Oh well" she laughed, "I know exactly what you mean."

"So what do you do then?" I persisted.

"Sometimes deep breathing helps. Not all the time though!"

"Okay, deep breathing can help—what else helps, even sometimes?"

"Counting to ten is another one, but that doesn't always work either."

By now I was close to hypothermic so I quickly asked them both to look out for all the other ways Martha had been controlling her head-shakes possibly without even realizing it.

As Ralph and Martha stepped out of the clinic for the last time two weeks later, Ralph put a protective arm around Martha and, pointing at her head with his other hand, asked "Have you noticed anything different about her?"

Not being skilled at noticing oddness, I wasn't quite sure and gave Ralph a non-committal shrug.

"She hasn't shaken it since we saw you last, so thank you for that, too!"

"Yes, thank you," said Martha. "It's such a relief!"

And as far as I can remember noticing, Martha was still not shaking her head five years later.

Discovering What You Already Know

As for Ralph's seminar on art appreciation, it turned out I already knew what to do but just hadn't realized it. It was a replica of solution-focused brief therapy. Don't go with a "diagnostic" framework in which you try to understand and explain what is going on; instead go with a sense of curiosity and the belief that if you are prepared to look, if you are prepared to ask questions of yourself and prepared to wonder, you will have an experience: that is the enjoyment, the appreciation of art. And therapy.

References

Chatwin, B. (1989). *What Am I Doing Here?* London: Jonathan Cape

de Shazer, S. (1982). *Patterns of Brief Family Therapy.* New York: Guilford Press.

de Shazer, S. (1985). *Keys to Solution in Brief Therapy.* New York: Norton.

de Shazer, S. (1988). *Clues: Investigating Solutions in Brief Therapy.* New York: Norton.

George, E., Iveson, C., & Ratner, H. (1999). *Problem to Solution: Brief Therapy with Individuals and Families* (rev. ed.). London: Brief Therapy Press.

George, E., Iveson, C., & Ratner, H. (2006). *BRIEFER: A Solution-Focused Manual.* London: Brief Therapy Press.

Iveson, C. (1990). *Whose Life? Community Care of Older People and Their Families.* London: Brief Therapy Press.

Iveson, C., George, E., & Ratner, H. (2012). *Brief Coaching: A Solution-Focused Approach.* London: Routledge.

Ratner, H., George, E., & Iveson, C. (2012). *Solution-Focused Brief Therapy: 100 Key Points and Techniques.* London: Routledge.

Shennan, G., & Iveson, C. (2011). From solution to description: Practice and research in tandem. In Franklin, C., Trepper, T.T., Gingerich, W.J., & McCollum, E. E. (Eds.), *Solution-Focused Brief Therapy: A Handbook of Evidence-Based Practice* (pp. 281-298). New York: Oxford University Press.

16

EXHILARATING COUPLE THERAPY

Singing to My Soul—Holding Steady to My Science—Filling Up My Heart

Susan M. Johnson

I practice Emotionally Focused Therapy (EFT) with couples, families, and individuals because it's the most fascinating and deeply moving activity I have ever discovered. Maybe that word, *discover*, is the key. In particular, working with couples from an attachment perspective is a constant voyage of discovery for me into what it means to be a human being. I watch and learn and often ache for my clients as they play out the drama of our deepest human emotions and needs. I watch them as they attempt to keep their balance and dance in tune with the most important people in their lives, and so often end up missing each other and falling into soul destroying isolation. In a therapy like EFT, focused on connection, the enterprise of therapy touches the therapist as well as the client. Some of my colleagues have just conducted research into the impact of EFT training on clinicians learning this model. They found that learning this model contributed significantly to personal growth, to healing and improved relationships for the trainees (Sandburg & Knestel, 2011). Trainees spoke of how meaningful the attachment framework was for understanding relationships, how amazing it was to be able to use emotion to transform relationships, and the sense of empowerment that comes from having a clear map to guide therapy. They also reported being more open and compassionate to their own feelings and with others (Montagno, Svatovic, & Levenson, 2011). This mirrors my own experience over the last 25 years as we have developed and tested EFT. As I and my colleagues, with the help of our clients, craft EFT, the practice of EFT shapes us.

An EFT session is nothing if not rich and integrative, as the therapist tracks how interpersonal dance and inner emotional experience come together to create a relationship. Sometimes in my couple sessions it seems like I am listening to a rich Bach quartet. I hear the steady repetitive beat of the recurring feedback loops of a couple's dance; other times, I hear the violins—the very personal ways of sensing, regulating, and expressing attachment fears and longings that guide each person's moves. An experiential therapist is nothing if not curious, and even though we have a clear map for the territory of love and loving, it is always a unique and satisfying experience to grasp how particular partners shape emotions and pull each other into distress or moments of connection. Finding the inherent logic and order in apparently bizarre moves or emotional responses still intrigues me, as we piece together a coherent image of their attachment story and how they recreate it every day. Creating a new story by helping partners risk and reach for each other moves me every time I do it. In the *strum und drang* of research studies, client sessions, meetings and teaching, just being able to be with two human beings as they find a way to truly connect takes me back to my center as a human being. And it allows me to be both scientist and, on my good days anyway, artist and poet.

It seems to me that the challenge of psychotherapy, which I see as a "growth for people" endeavor rather than a "fix that symptom' issue, is exactly this. Therapy is a conversation, pure and simple. The quality of connection in this conversation is the platform for any intervention, any way of guiding a client forward. I am not talking about therapeutic alliance as the general factor that defines therapy per se. The trouble with general factors is just that: they are general. In EFT we find that the quality of the alliance accounts for about 20% of the variance in outcome (Johnson & Talitman, 1996). This implies that a positive alliance is necessary but also that it is not sufficient for good outcomes. A good alliance that allows for a conversation that helps a client explore their world and their pain, in EFT terms, is an alliance wherein a therapist is emotionally present, accessible and responsive, much like a good attachment figure. The therapist's presence creates safety, allowing clients to touch distress and so reshape it, but not be overwhelmed by it. *Presence* implies authenticity and real connection. As one client put it, "Why am I still here letting you break the rules and chip away at my walls? I have wondered. It must be because you let me see you, too. I think I impact you a little." Clever lady. I believe that to be a good therapist, in whatever model you use, means to be present as a person, and, also to be a scientist. Science is the disciplined observation of pattern and the formulation of the structure implicit in pattern. Without presence, therapy can easily become empty advice giving or the teaching of coping techniques that clients do not own or integrate. Without data and discipline we can all persuade ourselves that we create miracles in our offices and lose our way in the superficial clichés of a culture drowning in quick fixes and self-help mania. My sense is that most therapists are drawn to this field because they want to grow as people and connect with others. This chapter is about how I learn as a human being, as a person and a scientist, as I take a couple through EFT, an approach that has tested its outcomes and theories of change extensively and is grounded in the only systematic scientific model of human connection we have yet formulated—attachment theory.

EFT—A Bonding Approach

Emotionally focused couple therapy (Johnson, 2004, 2008) does not directly teach coping or problem-solving or sketch out family histories or focus primarily on the creation of insight. It does not coach a set of "skilled" interactions to improve communication and reduce conflict. *The ultimate goal of the EFT therapist is to help partners reach for each other and create the attuned synchrony of emotional responsiveness that builds and maintains secure emotional bonds* (Bowlby 1988). The image of the tango might be useful here. There is evidence that empathy starts with body synchronization and that movement coordination both reflects and creates bonds (de Waal, 2009). Tango, like a love relationship, is a complex, close improvised dance, where each partner is able to intuit intentions, coordinate moves and together create what physicists call "resonance." Body language and emotional cues such as facial expression are the basic music of this dance. *Resonance* is defined as a sympathetic vibration between two elements that allows two elements to tune into each other and act in harmony. The neural duet (Goleman, 2006) of matched rhythms, pacing, intuited intentions and coordinated attuned responsiveness is what you see in positive infant-mother play and in positive interactions between adult lovers where it predicts future relationship satisfaction (Milkulincer & Shaver, 2007; Huston, Caughlin, Houts, Smith, & George, 2001). To continue the metaphor, dancers can only move together in harmony when they have a felt sense of secure connection, that is, when they can order and shape and attune to the emotional signals that are the music of this dance of love and bonding.

The creation of such an emotional bond has most often been an implicit goal or a hoped for by-product of couple interventions. Mackay (1996) makes the point that couple and family therapists have done everything except focus on how to create nurturance and love. This is reasonable given that when the founding fathers of couple and family therapy shaped this modality they had no systematic idea of what love was! Even now many sophisticated academics are still telling us that love is an intoxicating mixture of sex and sentiment that no one can understand or stating that love is essentially just frustrated sexual desire. At best, love was seen as a transitory and nebulous emotion! This has changed in the last decade. Old clichés about love are being challenged, and thus challenging our set ways of working with couples. Researchers are now suggesting that, apart from the element of obsession, romantic love is more robust and lasting than previously imagined (Avecedo & Arons, 2009) and that the therapy field needs to set "higher expectations" for itself than simply lessening conflict. Emotion itself is also more delineated and respected as a powerful survival information processing system rather than being seen as what happens when reflective cognition fails. More than this, over the last two decades the development of adult attachment theory and the neuroscience revolution have created a robust, tested theory of adult love that elucidates the nature of bonding (Johnson, 2009). It also, as required by Ludwig von Bertalanffy, the father of systems theory (1968), identifies the "leading" or organizing elements in a love relationship so that a therapist can focus laser-like on these transforming elements. This new science of love and bonding integrates a focus on self and system, that is, on the inner "ring" of individual experience, especially emotion, and on the outer ring of circular interactional patterns (Bowlby, 1973).

EFT is the first approach to couple and family therapy that is based on a broad well-researched theory and science of human love, that has proved its effectiveness across time and with many different kinds of couples (see www.iceeft.com for a comprehensive list of research studies on EFT). The new science of attachment gives us: (1) A new view of human nature where connection and the regulation of emotion with others is central; (2) A new sense of how humans grow, develop and change; (3) A clear model for what a healthy human being and a good relationship looks like; and (4) A pathway as to how relationships become derailed and the toxic damage this causes. As relationship therapists, it gives us a map to the dance of love and the inner emotional music that defines that dance. This map gives us a focus and a direction in the many-leveled drama of a distressed relationship and turns couple sessions into a fascinating mosaic of potential change moments rather than a struggle with chaos and the couple's recurring cycles of blame and withdrawal.

The core of the EFT understanding of love relationships rests on two principles: First, that adult romantic love is best understood as an attachment bond where emotional contact and proximity are crucial and dependency a given; and second, that significant change in therapy is about a corrective emotional experience that is integrated into new relationship responses and a new sense of self.

The principles of attachment, only applied to adult relationships since the 1990s, lay out the logic of love relationships. They turn couple therapy into a safe adventure, for the couple *and* for the therapist! Attachment theory tells us that the most primary need we have is for connection with a close and trusted other. Isolation is here the ultimate enemy of man and woman and our mammalian brain cries out in protest against it. In adulthood this isolation may not be an outer literal reality. It is often emotional isolation, an emotional starvation. A monk who lives alone on a deserted island who feels close to his God can flourish. A person who lives with many others and feels unimportant to and emotionally disconnected from others is at risk—mentally, emotionally, and physically (Johnson, 2008). For example, such a person is more likely to become clinically depressed or to suffer from heart attack and stroke. We are strongest, demonstrating a more positive and coherent sense of self (Mikulincer, 1995), when we have at least one safe haven and secure base relationship. Effective dependency is strength—emotional disconnection is a danger cue for our mammalian brain and elicits attachment panic and protest at separation. This panic and attempts to regulate it underlies most blaming, coercive responses in distressed couples. The withdrawal so often seen in distressed partners is a flee-and-freeze response fueled by the same panic about loss and helplessness and an attempt to contain conflict and hold onto a loved one. The anguish we feel at abandonment or rejection is encoded in the same part of the brain as physical pain (Eisenberger & Lieberman, 2004). Securely attached partners can regulate their emotion, recognize their needs, and use the primary attachment strategy—that of reaching for another. However, chronically anxious (sensitive to abandonment) or chronically avoidant (untrusting and sensitive to rejection), partners use the secondary strategies of demanding responsiveness or numbing, moving away and denying attachment needs. These secondary strategies end up perpetuating cycles like demand-withdraw that shape recurring disconnection and aloneness. Partners who habitually use these strategies cannot help each other move into a sense of safety and the physiological balance that is part of secure connection: The quality of an attachment relationship is based on emotional accessibility and responsiveness. Once this is in place, then models of self and other become more positive, moments of disconnection are manageable (for example, protests can be heard and dealt with positively), and problems can be faced together. Positive models or inner representations of loving attachment figures foster positive expectations of others and resilience in the face of stress and trauma (Mikulincer & Shaver, 2007). The other key elements of a love relationship, such as caregiving and adult sexuality, can then flourish (Johnson, 2003).

The goal of an attachment couple therapy such as EFT is then, in Stage 1 of therapy, to reduce the negative responses that constantly shape disconnection and anguish; and, in Stage 2, to choreograph positive patterns of emotional accessibility and responsiveness that create secure attachment. As each person has a felt sense of a secure base with another and a helpful partner in the regulation of emotion, each partner grows as an individual and in empathic responsiveness to the other. With the lens of attachment theory, suddenly I can make order of the drama in my therapy room. I see the impact that partners have on each other. I can tell Tim, a withdrawer, "Yes, I see that for you turning away when she is angry seems like the only way to survive. But when you shut down your emotions and there are no more signals from you, she feels shut out and panics. She begins to bang on your door harder, Yes? You turn from her anger and your dance goes on." I also have a clear goal—a clear way forward. My goal is to help people understand the dance of attachment and to create new awareness of the primary emotions that underlie this dance. This awareness translates into the formulation of attachment needs and fears, the key elements of new signals to the partner that foster a cascade of felt safety and connection. In this cascade, the answer to THE primary questions in love, *"Are you there for me? If I call will you come? Do I matter to you?"* is a resounding "Yes!"

EFT in Action

I often talk about relationships as a dance. If we extend the metaphor and think of therapy as a dance, the basic steps in EFT that recur again and again in every session are the therapist reflecting the process of interaction that is happening in the room, keeping the focus on the present moment and finding the pattern that impacts the quality of the couple's emotional connection. The point is *how they engage*, and how they misattune and miss each other on an attachment level. The therapist frames both partners as victims of the dance of disconnection. The therapist focuses on inner process, the emotions, and works to access and deepen emotion with one partner, using reflection, relentless empathy, simple process questions and small specific interpretations.

Once a new emotional sense emerges, the therapist distills this and turns it into a new signal to the other partner, setting up a simple specific enactment. (For example, "So, can you tell her, 'I am so afraid of hearing that I am disappointing you, of losing you, that I freeze and shut out the message. I don't know what to do.'") This new message and the resulting interaction are then processed with each partner and the whole sequence begins again. (An example of clarifying and deeping emotion to set up such an enactment is given below.)

If the therapist loses his or her way in a couple's fights or content issues, he or she simply returns to the basic steps and begin again. I find that this gives me a touchstone and allows me to find my way in even the most difficult session.

Working with Emotion

To be empowered and effective couple therapists we not only need to know how to understand love relationships—a task that philosophers and poets have struggled with for years—we need to know how to change these relationships. The model of EFT intervention focuses the therapist on the six primary emotions (Ekman, 2003): joy and surprise, anger (we mostly see reactive anger that pushes others away in couple sessions), sadness, shame, and fear of abandonment and rejection. Working with emotion to help partners into their deeper, more primary emotions and creating more and more contactful and positive interactions that build secure bonds are the two main tasks of EFT. When I work with a very distressed reactive couple, perhaps one where partners also struggle with post-traumatic stress disorder or depression or who have never experienced secure attachment or had a "Hold Me Tight" conversation (Johnson, 2008) in their 30 years of marriage, I can stand on the platform offered by the model. It offers me a secure base as a clinician so that I can confidently order what I see and move into the dance with my clients. I particularly need this secure base when working with the most powerful force in the room, strong attachment emotions.

As a society, we tend to distrust emotions. After all, Decartes saw them as part of our animal nature, and in a couple session they can indeed seem primitive and overwhelming. Many approaches to couple therapy have attempted to go around emotions or leave them out all together and focus on teaching skills and problem solving. But that is like leaving the chicken out of chicken soup! In the last few years, psychology has moved from an obsession with behavior and cognition to recognizing *emotion* as an adaptive and sophisticated information processing system that is essential for our survival and, because there is an action tendency in all emotion, a key part of motivation and cognitive decision-making. In EFT, emotion is a power to be recognized and shaped and the process of intervention is clear and systematic. Above all, emotion is to be used to literally "move" partners into new steps in their dance. Emotion puts us in touch with our needs, and vulnerability clearly expressed has a unique power to evoke compassion and caring. Positive psychology suggests that positive emotion has a "broadening and building" effect on experience and personal resources (Frederickson & Losada, 2005), and there is nothing that fills us with joy and contentment more than requited love. When the therapist provides safety and structure, powerful emotional longings move partners to reach for their partner and the joy and comfort of connection marks these "softening" or "hold me tight" change events as transformative. Such change events are predictive of freedom from distress at the end of EFT. As a researcher, my sense is that these positive change events and the joy and felt security they bring are the main reason why we find little evidence of relapse in EFT research and also find that couples continue to improve once EFT sessions end. Once partners find a way to create the joy of secure connection, they are home free. It is rewarding for therapist and clients when such transformation happens. Perhaps this is why, after so many years, I still love to work with couples. As Bruce Springsteen says, he cannot imagine ever retiring: "When I play—men weep and women dance. Why would I ever stop?"

Secure attachment interactions not only turn on cuddle hormones like oxytocin that shut down fear, ramp up our reward system, and tune us into others, they simply amplify positive emotion, as in play. Dan Stern (2004) reminds us that the evocation of the "vitality affects," pleasure and playfulness, heighten our engagement with and in the world. To feel more ALIVE is one of the great highs of love and this high is contagious for the therapist. We have made a difference! When Sam is able, rather than numbing out his anxiety, to turn to his wife and tell her of his fears and ask her for reassurance in a way that evokes loving-kindness in her, this is a high for everyone in the room!

However, if emotion has primacy in love relationships (if you do not believe this, try telling your partner you love him or her with a still flat face and see what happens!), and attachment is all about affect regulation, the therapists has to know how to work with the elements of emotion and not become flooded in order to stay focused and effective. It helps me always to look past the surface emotion—maybe critical anger or flat detachment, both of which are frustrating for the therapist let alone the other partner—and grasp the fear and profound aloneness that fuels and forms the deep structure of a demand-withdraw relationship. When Liza, who "wants closeness" with John but slams him with angry criticism as he risks and reaches for her instead of moving away, I am frustrated. After all, I have worked long and hard to help him emerge from his intellectual withdrawal. I know that for Liza closeness has been violating and she is never sure if loved ones are a source of fear or a solution to that fear. It also helps in our work that I grasp, from the research on emotion and on adult attachment that Liza is dealing with panic and emotional starvation and her guardedness with her potentially loving husband is a result of a history of violation at the hands of attachment figures. When I can tune into her ambivalence and recognize her terror of beginning to believe and need John, then I can stay responsive and help her face her fear. It is important to recognize that in EFT, I am also a process consultant leading people into more secure interactions. I don't have to be the all-knowing expert burdened by the weight of solving all Liza and John's problems with magical interventions; I just have to stay with them and help them take small risks on the journey of reconnection. When I train therapists, many find working with intense emotion or the lack of it, daunting. Working with emotion is like everything else. It is not hard when you see how it works and how to do it. We create a safe, non-pathologizing haven in each session and gently help emotionally reactive or numb clients focus on their deeper feelings by touching on the cues, the bodily sense, the attachment meanings and the action tendency in the emotion. As we access and order this experience with the client it is satisfying and an act of discovery for client and for therapist. Both can tolerate and explore what they can make concrete and specific, order and shape. So a moment of unfolding emotion in an "unemotional" man might look as follows (this example is used in the *EFT Externship Training Manual*, 2010)

Wife (to husband): You are so difficult—I can't tolerate your attitude.

Husband: *(Throws up his hands and turns to look out the window).*

Therapist: *(Softly and slowly.)* What happens to you as your wife says "........"?

Husband: *(He smiles.)* Nothing—I am used to this. She says this stuff all the time.

Therapist: You feel nothing as she says "..........."? *(Repeating the cue)*

Husband: This happens lots—I just try to roll with it—forget it. *(He describes his coping style.)*

Therapist: You try to forget these times when she tells you that you are too difficult for her to tolerate? *(He nods.)* But in that split second before you try to push it aside and "forget" her words, what happens to you? When she tells you, you are too difficult?
(Keeping focus, asking evocative questions.)

Husband: *(In a quiet voice.)* Don't know. I just move away.

Therapist: There is something here that is hard? Upsetting? You can't take it in; that is too hard? *(He nods.)* What do you hear her say? *(A small interpretation is made.)*

Husband: She's saying that I'm hopeless—this relationship is doomed—down the tubes. *(He goes into the attachment meaning he shapes from her comments—his sense of threat).*

Therapist: You threw up your hands—like this *(demonstrates)*; that is the hopelessness—the defeat? *(Follows his non-verbal body gestures and adds
meaning.)* *(He nods agreement.)*
It's like you throw up your hands and you give up. It's hopeless?

Husband: Yeah ... *(He looks down at his shoes. Quiet voice.)* There is nothing I
can do.

Therapist: You hear her say that you are too difficult. You feel hopeless. You try
to push it aside. But your body expresses the hopelessness and you
say to yourself, what? 'I have blown it, already lost her'? *(Therapist
summarizes the experience, heightening and clarifying the threat.)*

Husband: Yep. I have totally blown it. I'll never make it with her. She has her
standards and I can't ... I'll never ... *(He tears up).*

Therapist: So you withdraw to protect yourself. And then you *(to the wife)* get
even angrier *(she nods)* and that is the cycle that has taken over the
relationship and leaves you both very alone. And that brings tears for
you? *(Focusing on the action tendency in the emotion and how it helps create
the cycle of disconnection includes the partner here.)*

Husband: No—my eyes are just watering. *(He withdraws.)* *(The therapist stays
focused, empathic.)*

Therapist: You say to yourself, "I have blown it, lost her, I'll never make it with
her"? Some part of you wants to throw up your hands, like "I will
never please her—never have her love" —Is that it?

Husband: Right. My brother said, "There is a time to get married" and he told
me I was too young. But you do what you do. All my family got
married young. *(He emotionally exits.)*

Therapist: I'd like to go back. So when you hear your wife's anger you move
away. You try to forget it, and she sees "coldness" and "indifference." *(She nods.)* But, in fact, you are really trying to deal with a
huge sense of defeat and hopelessness; a sense of failure and a fear
that you can never please her.

Husband: Yes—that's it—I think that's it. I run. That is so hard.

Therapist: *(Shaping an Enactment.)* Can you tell her that, please. I will help you
if you need me to.

As a therapist, when delving into emotion in a session seems risky, it helps to
remember that the suppression of emotion, even in a good cause like learning
communication skills, is a very fragile strategy in love relationships. Suppression is physiologically HARD WORK. You tend to become more physiologically aroused in the process and so does anyone who is interacting with you
(Gross, 2001). The goal in EFT is to create a vibrant safe relationship where,
as my colleague, Jack Kornfield notes (2009, p. 131): "We can let ourselves be
carried by the river of feeling—because we know how to swim." We can then
engage trustingly with our own emotional experience and with our loved ones.

Apart from working with emotions, the second task of EFT is to create emotionally vibrant enactments that move partners towards closeness and responsiveness. Therapists can find this daunting. However, once you learn that you can indeed "catch bullets" when enactments go wrong (Johnson, 2004), turning to the unresponsive partner and exploring their inability to respond, and you see how they powerfully shift how partners dance together, then creating them becomes exciting. This task is dealt with in more detail in the EFT training literature (Johnson et al., 2005). These enactments are often very moving for everyone in the room. As Liza turns to John and tells him, "I hear you. I am trying to trust and risk but I am so scared. Part of me just wants to get into my tank and stay fierce. To never be hurt again. I am afraid to ask—to let myself long for connection again," he reaches out his arms to her and she folds into him. My mammalian brain and heart sing and I replay this moment as I drive home. It makes me softer when my husband comes to greet me at the door.

The Soul in Couple Therapy

What does EFT couple therapy have to do with the soul, for the therapist or for clients? The science and theory of attachment has huge implications for how we see human nature in general. The key issues EFT address have obvious existential implications, especially if we consider that connection to another is perhaps the main way we can effectively deal with existential anxiety and our need to find meaning in our lives. More secure bonds grow more healthy adaptive human beings who can deal effectively with the trials and terrors of life. Securely attached individuals are more emotionally balanced and able to flexibly regulate their emotions, more able to be curious and tolerate uncertainty, more able to trust their experience and integrate experience into a coherent whole, more positive in their sense of self and able to be open, responsive and collaborative with others. They are also more compassionate. Frans de Waal (2009) in his book, *The Age of Empathy: Nature's Lessons for a Kinder Society*, notes that the essence of morality is feeling with and for others.

To use a popular framework, couple therapy is now at the point where it can foster more "mindful" individuals who are better partners and parents. Mindfulness comes from the Pali word *sati*, implying open awareness, focused attention and acceptance that translates into an ability to be present in the moment with self and others in a flexible, responsive way. Theorists have pointed out that experiential therapies like EFT are strikingly similar to mindfulness in their focus (Germer, 2005; Bradley, Furrow, Johnson, & Amadeo, 2011). Germer notes, for example, that mindfulness is not detached witnessing; rather it is experiencing the mind and body more intimately. Both mindfulness and experiential therapies are growth oriented, focused on awakening or increased awareness of the present moment and how we all create our own experience. The self is viewed as a process and many coping strategies are seen as creating or perpetuating suffering. In many ways experiential interventions reflect the statement of the poet Rumi: "The cure for the pain is the pain." In EFT terms the cure is to reprocess the "pain" within and between people in a way that creates new realities and new response options. EFT allows people to regulate their emotions and reflect, seeing the meta-perspective, cultivates compassion for self and other and acknowledges our interdependence.

The Greek word for soul (*psyche*) translates as "vital breath," essence and aliveness. Attachment and experiential therapy perspectives tell us that the essence of humanity is our need to connect with others and this emotional connection renders us vital and alive. In this sense, for me, a therapy such as EFT can be thought of as soul-searching. To move through EFT is to move deeper into your experience and, finding your balance, to make it whole (the words *holy* and *health* have roots in this concept of wholeness) or integrated, so that you can be more intensely authentic and alive. EFT is a collaborative therapy, so this process also impacts the therapist. As we help others grow, we grow. de Waal notes (2009, p. 68), "The evolution of attachment came with something the planet had never seen before—a feeling brain. The limbic system was added to the brain allowing emotions such as affection and pleasure." Thus he concludes, "We are pre-programmed to reach out." From this perspective doing EFT—as client or therapist—is a lesson in accepting human vulnerability and the need to reach and to know that another will answer. It is a lesson in how to be human.

References

Avecedo, B., & Arons, A. (2009). Does a long term relationship kill romantic love? *Review of General Psychology, 13*, 59–65.

Bowlby, J. (1973). *Attachment and Loss: Vol 2. Separation*. New York: Basic Books.

Bowlby, J. (1988). *A Secure Base*. New York: Basic Books.

Bradley, B., Furrow, J., Johnson, S., & Amadeo (2011). Spirituality and emotionally focused couple therapy: Exploring common ground. In J. Furrow, S. Johnson, & B. Bradley (Eds.), *The Emotionally Focused Casebook: New Directions in Treating Couples* (pp. 343–372). New York: Routledge.

de Waal, F. (2009). *The Age of Empathy: Nature's Lessons for a Kinder Society*. New York: Random House.

EFT Externship Training Manual. (2010). Ottawa, Canada: International Center for Excellence in Emotionally Focused Therapy (ICEEFT).

Eisenberger, N.I., & Lieberman, M.D. (2004). Why rejection hurts: A common neural alarm system for physical and social pain. *Trends in Cognitive Science, 8*, 294–300.

Ekman, P. (2003). *Emotions Revealed*. New York: Henry Holt.

Frederickson, B.L., & Losada, M. F. (2005). Positive affect and the complex dynamics of human flourishing. *American Psychologist, 60*, 678–686.

Germer, C. (2005). Mindfulness. What is it? Why does it matter? In C. Germer, R. Siegel, & P. Fulton (Eds.), *Mindfulness and Psychotherapy* (pp. 3–27). New York: Guilford Press.

Goleman, D. (2006). *Social Intelligence*. New York: Bantam.

Gross, J. (2001). Emotion regulation in adulthood: Timing is everything. *Current Directions in Psychological Science, 10*, 214–219.

Huston, T.L., Caughlin, J.P., Houts, R.M., Smith, S.E., & George, L.J. (2001). The connubial crucible: Newlywed years as predictors of marital delight, distress and divorce. *Journal of Personality and Social Psychology, 80,* 237–252.

Johnson, S.M. (2003). An introduction to attachment: A therapist's guide to primary relationships and their renewal. In S.M. Johnson & V. Whiffen (Eds.), *Attachment Processes in Couple and Family Therapy* (pp. 3–17). New York. Guilford Press.

Johnson, S.M. (2004). *The Practice of Emotionally Focused Couple Therapy* (2nd ed.). New York: Brunner-Routledge.

Johnson, S.M. (2008). *Hold Me Tight: Seven Conversations for a Lifetime of Love.* New York: Little Brown.

Johnson, S.M. (2009). Attachment theory and Emotionally Focused Therapy for individuals and couples: Perfect partners. In J.H. Obegi & E. Berant (Eds.), *Attachment Theory and Research in Clinical Work with Adults* (pp. 410–433). New York: Guilford Press.

Johnson, S.M., Bradley, B., Furrow, J., Lee, A., Palmer, G., & Tilley, D. (2005). *Becoming an Emotionally Focused Couple Therapist: The Workbook.* New York: Brunner-Routledge.

Johnson, S.M., & Talitman, E. (1996). Predictors of success in emotionally focused marital therapy. *Journal of Marital and Family Therapy, 23,* 135–152.

Kornfield, J. (2009). *The Wise Heart: A Guide to the Universal Teachings of Buddhist Psychology.* Bantam/Random House.

Mackay, S. K. (1996). Nurturance: A neglected dimension in family therapy with adolescents. *Journal of Marital and Family Therapy, 22,* 489–508.

Mikulincer, M. (1995). Attachment style and the mental representation of self. *Journal of Personality and Social Psychology, 69,* 1203–1215.

Mikulincer, M., & Shaver, P. (2007). *Attachment in Adulthood: Structure, Dynamics and Change.* New York: Guilford Press.

Montagno, M., Svatovic, M., & Levenson, H. (2011). Short-term and long-term effects of training in EFT: Professional and personal aspects. *Journal of Marital and Family Therapy, 37,* 380–392.

Sandburg, J. G., & Knestel, A. (2011). The experience of learning emotionally focused couples therapy. *Journal of Marital and Family Therapy, 37,* 393–410.

Stern, D. (2004). *The Present Moment: In Psychotherapy and Everyday Life.* New York: Norton.

von Bertalanffy, L. (1968). *General System Theory.* New York: George Braziller.

17

THE BODHISATTVA

Tending the World[1]

Jack Kornfield

Forty years ago, I arrived at a forest monastery in Thailand in search of my own happiness. A confused, lonely young man with a painful family history, I had graduated from Dartmouth College in Asian studies and asked the Peace Corps to send me to a Buddhist country. Looking back, I can see that I was trying to escape not only my family pain but also the materialism and suffering—so evident in the Vietnam War—of our culture at large. Working on rural health and medical teams in the provinces along the Mekong River, I heard about a meditation master, Ajahn Chah, who welcomed Western students. I was full of ideas and hopes that Buddhist teaching would help me, maybe even lead me to become enlightened. After months of visits to Ajahn Chah's monastery, I took monk's vows. Over the next three years I was introduced to the practices of mindfulness, generosity, loving-kindness, and integrity, which are at the heart of Buddhist training. That was the beginning of a lifetime journey with Buddhist teachings [....]

In the traditional training at Ajahn Chah's forest monastery, we were sent to sit alone in the forest at night practicing the meditations on death. Stories of monks who had encountered tigers and other wild animals helped keep us alert. There were many snakes, including cobras. At Ajahn Buddhadasa's forest monastery we were taught to tap our walking sticks on the paths at night so the snakes would "hear" us and move out of the way. At another monastery, I periodically sat all night at the charnel grounds. Every few weeks a body was

---

1   Excerpted from *The Wise Heart: A Guide To The Universal Teachings of Buddhist Psychology* by Jack Kornfield, copyright © 2008 by Jack Kornfield. Used by permission of Bantam Books, a division of Random House, Inc.

brought for cremation. After the lighting of the funeral pyre and the chanting, most people would leave, with only monks remaining to tend the fire in the dark forest. Finally, one monk would be left alone to sit there until dawn, contemplating death. Not everyone did these practices. But I was a young man, looking for initiation, eager to prove myself, so I gravitated toward these difficulties.

As it turned out, sitting in the dark forest with its tigers and snakes was easier than sitting with my inner demons. My insecurity, loneliness, shame, and boredom came up, along with all my frustrations and hurts. Sitting with these took more courage than sitting at the charnel grounds. Little by little I learned to face them with mindfulness, to make a clearing within the dark woods of my own heart.

Mindfulness does not reject experience. It lets experience be the teacher. One Buddhist practitioner with severe asthma learned to bring a mindful attention to his breath. By becoming aware of the stress in his body and being patient as the muscles in his throat and chest relaxed, he was able to limit his attacks. Another man undergoing a cancer treatment used mindfulness to quell his fear of pain and added loving-kindness for his body as a complement to his chemotherapy. Through mindfulness a local politician learned not to be discouraged by his attackers. A frazzled single mother of preschoolers used mindfulness to acknowledge her own tension and feeling of being overwhelmed, opening the space to become more respectful of herself and her boys. Each of these practitioners learned to trust mindfulness as they entered the difficulties in their lives. Like the Buddha in the thick of the forest, they found healing and freedom [....]

The Bodhisattva

> The problem with the world is that we draw our family circle too small.
>
> —Mother Teresa

Bodhisattva is the Sanskrit word for a being who is devoted to awakening and to acting for the benefit of all that lives. The way of the bodhisattva is one of the most radical and powerful of all Buddhist forms of practice. It is radical because it states that the fulfillment of our happiness comes only from serving the welfare of others as well as ourself. Our highest happiness is connected with the well-being of others.

The bodhisattva's path is a striking contrast with the common Western modes of therapy that so often reflect the excessive individualism of our culture. Everything can get focused around me: my fears, my neurosis, my happiness, my needs, my boundaries. We can get so caught up in our own drama that we stop our own growth. Reflective self-absorption can be valuable for a time, but we don't want to stop there. Therapists talk about how clients eventually become sick of listening to themselves, which is actually a good sign. It means we are moving beyond the identification with our personal suffering. We are ready to care for a world larger than our own.

Every wisdom tradition tells us that human meaning and happiness cannot be found in isolation but comes about through generosity, love, and understanding. The bodhisattva, knowing this, appears in a thousand forms, from a caring grandmother to the global citizen. Meditators often recite the bodhisattva vows when they sit, offering any benefit of their practice for the sake of others: "Sentient beings are numberless; I vow to bring liberation to us all." Like the ancient Hippocratic oath, the vow to serve the sick taken by every physician, the bodhisattva vows to serve the welfare of all. In a more poetic fashion, the Dalai Lama takes bodhisattva vows based on the words of the beloved sixth-century sage Shanideva:

> *May I be a guard for those who need protection*
> *A guide for those on the path*
> *A boat, a raft, a bridge for those who wish to cross the flood*
> *May I be a lamp in the darkness*
> *A resting place for the weary*
> *A healing medicine for all who are sick*
> *A vase of plenty, a tree of miracles*
> *And for the boundless multitudes of living being*
> *May I bring sustenance and awakening*
> *Enduring like the earth and sky*
> *Until all beings are freed from sorrow*
> *And all are awakened.*

Psychologically this is an astonishing thing to say. Does this mean that I am going to run around and save six billion humans and trillions of other beings? How can I do so? When we think about it from our limited sense of self, it is impossible. But when we make it an intention of the heart, we understand. To take such a vow is a direction, a sacred purpose, a statement of wisdom, an offering, a blessing. When the world is seen with the eyes of a bodhisattva, there is no I and other, there is just us [....]

"We are not separate, we are interdependent," declares the Buddha. Even the most independent human being was once a helpless infant cared for by others. Ajahn Buddhadasa instructed all those in his forest temple to do a daily contemplation of interdependence. With each breath we interbreathe carbon dioxide and oxygen with the maple and the oak, the dogwood and redwood trees of our biosphere. Our daily nourishment joins us with the rhythms of bees, caterpillars, and rhizomes; it connects our body with the collaborative dance of myriad species of plants and animals. Nothing is separate. Biologist Lewis Thomas explains, "The driving force in nature is cooperation....The most inventive and novel of all schemes in nature, and perhaps the most significant in determining the great landmark events in evolution, is symbiosis, which is simply cooperative behavior carried to its extreme" [....]

This is a principle of Buddhist psychology:

There is no separation between inner and outer,
self and other. Tending ourselves, we tend the
world. Tending the world, we tend ourselves.

Envision Liberation and Justice

[....] Do not confuse Buddhism with withdrawal from the world. The Buddhist teachings about wise society and wise leadership are taught from childhood onward throughout the Buddhist world. In hundreds of popular tales, the Buddha-to-be often appears as a prince or an animal. In one story, the Buddha-to-be is born as a Banyan deer king who nobly offers his life to a human king in place of a pregnant doe that has been caught. His gesture so inspires the human king that the hunting of deer and other forest animals is forbidden throughout the kingdom. In another story, the Buddha-to-be is born as a small parrot, who tries to save the animals around him from a forest fire. Repeatedly dousing his wings with river water, he flies into the great flames to find and wet his frightened friends. His bravery touches the heart of the rain god, whose tears fall, quenching the flames and rescuing all the creatures from a fiery death. For those who grow up in a Buddhist culture, these beloved tales of wise leadership are recounted a thousand times.

At a more sophisticated level, Buddhist psychology shows how training in mindfulness, integrity, generosity, and respect can create a healthy society. From village schools to community meetings, Buddhist practices of right speech, right action, and right livelihood foster moral character and the creation of harmony.

Buddhist temples model this psychology. They are among the oldest living social institutions in the world. For over two thousand years, temples have served as seats of education and service, offering help with community government, community projects, social organization, and the mediation of disputes. Villagers go to the monasteries to be reminded of this healthy way to live, and the whole society is nurtured and benefited by the example of the monks and nuns. Today the Southeast Asian environmental crisis has led Burmese and Thai monks to turn their forest monasteries into wild animal sanctuaries to help preserve the remaining tigers. In Cambodia monks and nuns run addiction treatment centers and AIDS hospitals. In Thailand monks wrap their robes around the most ancient trees to "ordain them" and save thousands of acres of disappearing forest.

Even when there is conflict in the monastery, it is dealt with as a practice. There are councils of reconciliation, vows of non-harming, trainings in mindful listening, and formal methods of confession, repentance, and release. The work of both Gandhi and Martin Luther King Jr. was founded on these principles, on *ahimsa*—or non-harming—as a path to happiness [....]

Tending the World

[....] When Zen master Thich Nhat Hanh took a stand for peace in the 1960s in Vietnam, he understood that true peace would grow only from building schools and hospitals, not from taking sides. His book *Lotus in a Sea of Fire* described how the Young Buddhist Service Movement, which he helped to found, chose to support everyone, regardless of their politics. Martin Luther King Jr. was so inspired by this work he nominated Thich Nhat Hanh for the Nobel Peace Prize. But back in Vietnam because the Young Buddhists refused to swear allegiance to either the Northern or Southern faction, they were considered an enemy by each faction. "If you're not with us, you must be with the enemy." Many of the Young Buddhists were killed by both sides. In spite of these deaths, Thich Nhat Hanh and his colleagues continued their work. A bodhisattva commits to heal suffering undaunted by outward periods of failure and success [....]

We are limited only by our imagination. Yes, there will always be a shadow. Yes, greed and fear and ignorance will be part of our psychology. But there are ways we can live wisely. For the bodhisattva, raising a family, running a conscious business, and righting an injustice all can contribute to the fabric of the whole. Every one of us can sense this potential. Human beings can live with more compassion, with more care for one another, with less prejudice and racism and fear. There are wise ways of solving conflict that await our hands and hearts.

Practice: Bodhisattva Vows

Consider undertaking the vows and practice of a bodhisattva. In taking these vows you will join with the millions of Buddhists who have done so. As is traditional, you might seek out a Buddhist center or temple and take the bodhisattva vows in the presence of a teacher. Or, if you cannot do so, you can take them at home. Create a sacred space and place there the images of bodhisattvas or Buddhas who have gone before you. If you wish, invite a friend or friends to be your witness. Sit quietly for a time and reflect on the beauty and value of a life dedicated to the benefit of all. When you are ready, add any meaningful ritual, such as the lighting of candles or the taking of refuge. Then recite your vows. Here is one traditional version, but there are many others:

> *Suffering beings are numberless, I vow to liberate them all.*
> *Attachment is inexhaustible, I vow to release it all.*
> *The gates to truth are numberless, I vow to master them all.*
> *The ways of awakening are supreme, I vow to realize them all.*

You can change the wording of these vows so that they speak your deepest dedication. Then you can repeat them every time you sit in meditation, to direct and dedicate your practice.

18

HERMAN'S WAGER[1]

Murray Korngold

According to George Bernard Shaw, there are only three subjects intelligent people talk about: sex, politics, and religion. So let us embark on a conversation about religion. In polite society these subjects are taboo, of course, since they lead, when discussed intelligently, to passionate controversy and occasionally bitter disagreement. It's my hope that you and I constitute a humane community but not a polite one. It has been my experience that a truly intelligent mind can hold two or more conflicting ideas at the same time without losing consciousness or succumbing to shock. Actually, when I speak of religious thought I don't refer only to theology, or for that matter the question of the existence or non-existence of a deity. I refer to the general philosophical notion of the largest, most inclusive possible context; a context that includes all possible contexts. From that standpoint Einstein's relativity theory in transcending Newton's mechanistic theory was a more religious approach because it is clearly more inclusive. When Wittgenstein, who was no slouch as a logician, declared that it was a wondrous miracle that anything existed at all he was making a religious statement. When Chesterton insisted that there was no lack of wonders in the universe, but only a lack of wonder he was making a religious statement. Schrodinger, a founder of quantum physics, said, "Consciousness is a singular of which the plural is unknown. There is only one thing, and that which seems to be a plurality is merely a series of different aspects of this one thing, produced by a deception ... as in a gallery of mirrors." To my mind, this is a profoundly religious statement.

1 Excerpted from Murray Korngold (2005), *First Draft: A Life to Talk About* (Chs. 9 & 10). Paris: Valmy Press. © 2004 by Murray Korngold. Used with permission.

How I came to my present outlook is a rather embarrassing saga. From my adolescence until well into my middle age, I was more of a mechanic than I was a gardener. Like the geometers on the Isle of Lilliput in *Gulliver's Travels*, I distrusted anything which didn't fit between my vernier calipers. I am still a skeptic in the sense that I truly believe only on the basis of evidence, but also a mystic in that I know with absolute conviction that, to paraphrase Hamlet, there is more between heaven and earth than can be dreamed of in any philosophy. In fact my personal definition of mysticism is the total acceptance of reality, without any reservations, whether we know how it works or not.

There is an old joke about the hick who went to a zoo for the first time and when he saw a giraffe said, very simply, "there ain't no such animal." I was that kind of a hick who denied the evidence of my senses for the first six years that I was experimenting with psychedelics. During the trip itself, I knew with conviction that there was a giraffe, namely, that I was a part of a single consciousness of which existence in all of its glory was a manifestation. However, when I came down off the trip I regarded those realizations as an exotic drug experience. I was of two minds. I felt happier and more whole when I was tripping but I couldn't take care of business very appropriately in that state. If I had been completely honest with myself, I would have seen everything in a different light. Between 1963 and 1969 I moved more firmly into the one-mind reality as a result of experiences that I could not ignore or rationalize away in the service of a world outlook that saw everything as separate from everything else.

Let me set the stage for what led to abandoning my previous dogmatism in the service of what I have come to see as the wildest and most joyous adventure of my life for the last 48 years. It was the spring of '63. I was 43, a university professor of psychology, a teacher and practitioner of individual and group psychotherapy. I had a substantial private practice and was conducting seminars for my colleagues in existential psychotherapy. Whenever the subject came up anecdotally of prophetic dreams, clairvoyance, miraculous healing at a distance—what are still referred to as "anomalous events"—I would be impatient. Anyone who put any stock in the validity of such accounts, in my view, was a fool, an eccentric skirting the thin edge of madness.

This is a brief snapshot of the man that the director of the UCLA Extension Division, Ed Monsson, telephoned one April morning. "How would you like to co-present a five-day workshop at our Lake Arrowhead campus?" He mentioned a handsome honorarium and access to vacation facilities. As it was scheduled for July it sounded very attractive, but before agreeing I asked what the subject was. He said, "Frontiers of the Mind." I asked, "What is Frontiers of the Mind?" and Ed said, "Oh, it's the psi phenomenon, parapsychology, that sort of thing. By the way, you don't have any bias about this field do you?" "Certainly not," I said, lying like hell, "but I really don't know anything about it." Ed said, "So much the better. Read up on it. It's good that you have no bias because the other guy, a philosophy professor from Stanford, is rabidly pro." I thought about those words, "rabidly pro." It seems that I had my work cut out for me; defending the cause of rational thought, of the scientific method against all this medieval obscurantism and superstition.

It turned out to be a pleasant experience. About a hundred people showed up—a mixed bag of professionals, mostly artists, teachers, physicians, and housewives, all apparently quite sane. For the most part the reason they had enrolled was that they had had personal experiences that were startling and incomprehensible and were looking for help. They had paid a large fee for this help. In most respects they knew more than I did. I felt embarrassed and a little guilty. I kept telling myself that at least they were getting a nice alpine holiday with good food, mountain hiking trails, boating and campfires. Despite my library research I still didn't really know a great deal about this subject, so I opted to act as a facilitator and moderator of discussion. I couldn't actually bring myself to suspend my disbelief, but I did pretend to suspend my disbelief out of simple courtesy and professional obligation. At the end of the five days I returned home Sunday night as convinced as I had been before that there was really no ESP. In the morning just before awakening I dreamed that a patient of mine was standing in my kitchen and after apologizing in advance for her presumption in making a request of me, asked me for a character reference that she planned to take to Europe. In the dream I expressed surprise that she was leaving the country. She explained that she hoped to be working for a Dutch psychologist who was expanding into media in Holland and Britain. When I awoke I related the dream, which was a rather inconsequential one, to my wife. At that point the phone rang, and I listened in some shock as this same patient played out the same dialogue on the phone, precisely as she had done in the dream. That morning my first appointment was a young psychotherapist who was just starting his own private practice. As a rule he began by relating his dreams. He was a colorful dreamer. But this time, he said that the previous weekend he had gone to a party at a young woman's apartment, a person I had never heard of. With some excitement he said, "You have no idea what a weird pet she had." "I know," I said, "it's a baby boa constrictor." I blushed with embarrassment. I had no idea why I had said such an absurd thing and his jaw dropped. "How did you know?" he said. Of course I had no idea. That's exactly how it all began.

Opening to Experience

Since that time, there have always been events of this sort in my everyday life. Often I hear myself saying something that I didn't know I knew until I heard myself saying it. When the impulse to say it is strong I know that the information will be correct. I also have dreams that frequently correspond to events in the lives of people with whom I'm involved, such as relatives, friends, colleagues, and clients. At other times the converse is the case. For example, one

Sunday in the late sixties two young woman, one Black and the other Asian, were having lunch with me in my house during a record-breaking heat wave. We were considering whether to go swimming in a public pool or perhaps go to an air-conditioned movie. In the end we decided to go to a movie. I remember the movie was quite boring, *The Blue Max*, with George Peppard. At any rate, we spent a couple of hours at the height of the heat in a cool environment. The following morning a psychotherapy patient who was a graduate student at UCLA related the following dream: "I had three small children, two daughters and a son. He was the son and the two girls were Black and Asian. He wanted to go swimming. They wanted to go to the movies, so he was left behind while the rest of us went to the movies." At that time I was still having difficulty believing this was happening to me, and I interrogated him at some length, asking him what he had done the previous day and if anyone had talked with him about me. He was baffled and irritated by this unusual line of questioning and I subsequently apologized, realizing that his dream was incorporating information from my life into his particular pattern of wishes and fears. It was as if reality had simply gotten its foot in the door of my attention. Once the genie was out of the bottle there was no stuffing it back in. Somewhere along the line I realized that this was real and I wanted to have some kind of disciplined mastery over this power.

For the next eight years I looked for a mentor, a teacher who could help me understand how this worked. There were plenty of volunteers for this role but every one of them insisted on teaching some dogma or doctrine or theology of which these phenomena were a part. By this time I was approaching my fiftieth birthday and no longer had any tolerance for dogma of any sort. In retrospect it's clear that I was reacting to these events in a peculiarly American way. Whether in medicine, philosophy, science or technology, the American way is extremely mechanistic. The first question I had to ask is how does this work? Naturally, if you're dealing with lathes or carburetors or electronic software to know how something works is a *sine qua non*. But too often, as was true of me, the demand for a mechanical explanation is simply a self-mystifying form of resistance to the new. As a working acupuncturist I still encounter this form of resistance on the part of many physicians who first ask, how does this stuff work? Not DOES it work, but HOW does it work? Michele de Montaigne once, when asked why he had loved a dear friend who had recently died replied, "If you ask why I loved him, it was because he was he and I was I." Smart fellow, that Montaigne. I remember once about 25 years ago needling the hand of a clinical neurologist in order to relieve a shoulder pain and he exclaimed that he had felt a jolt of something like electricity run up his arm. When I asked him to trace the pathway of this sensation he traced the exact pathway of the Large Intestine meridian (see Beinfield & Korngold, 1991). When I pointed this out he denied the possibility of such a pathway because, in his experience of dissection, he had never seen it. Therefore it did not exist. *Q.E.D.*

I remember an event in the summer of 1969 in London when I saw clearly the uselessness and utter futility of demanding an explanation as a way of defending against something mysterious. For a couple of months in Belsize Park Gardens I had been house-sitting R.D. Laing's house, and was also seeing some of his patients while he was away. Francis Huxley, a friend of mine, lived nearby, and we had numerous conversations. He was an anthropologist whose particular interest was shamanism. I was fascinated by some of his first-hand observations but I was in the position of Nicodemus in the New Testament (John 3: 1-21) who in essence said, "Lord, I believe. Help thou my unbelief." One day he invited me to a soiree at his home. The visiting dignitary was a Brazilian shaman, Loreval de Freitas, a 38-year-old Indian taxi driver from Rio. He was ordinarily a somewhat melancholic chap who now and then appeared to be possessed by the spirit of Nero Caesar or at other times by Nero's sister, Messalina. On those occasions he was said to have miraculous healing powers. Also at those times he would undergo a radical personality change. Usually he was a non-smoking and modest teetotaler. When he was possessed he would chain-smoke cigars and would guzzle whisky and brandy from the bottle. He would generally have a boisterous rip-roaring time dancing and flirting with all the young women. When I heard this description it seemed to be a classic dissociative pattern typical of multiple personality disorder. Francis' reply to this view was, "I don't know what he is, but I have seen what he does."

At the appointed time, Loreval de Freitas arrived with an entourage from the Brazilian Embassy. There were about thirty people present, including a number of physicians and psychiatrists and a number of people in the arts, sciences and professions in Northwest London. One woman who was there that evening, Anne Dooley (1974), describes the evening in one of the chapters of her book, *Every Wall a Door*. I was not indulging in alcohol or cannabis nor was I under the influence of any medication because I very much wanted to be a fair witness. About an hour after his arrival Loreval did undergo a dramatic personality change and got quite drunk and boisterous. As he spoke only Portuguese one or another of the bilingual attendees would translate into English. What he said was not particularly noteworthy. What he did, however, can only be described as mysterious, miraculous and utterly incomprehensible. Let me describe, briefly now, one of the events that positively stunned us.

Try to imagine the *mise-en-scene*. There was a very large L-shaped space with tables laden with drink and refreshments at one end. Along the walls were couches and chairs, and at the other end a record player playing Bossa Nova. We all stood around watching Loreval dance with one woman after another. There was a sweet and attractive young woman, Mona Lisa Boysen, wearing a chic backless blue dress sitting on the couch. Her mother, Gerda Boysen, a well-known Reichian therapist in London, was also present. We were aware that Mona Lisa had been suffering intermittently from agonizing back pain for which she had visited a number of specialists without relief and without a diagnosis.

She seemed on this occasion to be in remission. Loreval asked her to dance and after a couple of minutes he commented that there was something wrong with her back and that he would like to fix it. He had her kneel down on the floor with her elbows on the couch supporting herself. He began cupping areas of her back with an empty inverted glass and found a spot to the right of her thoracic spine, in the middle of her back. He left the glass on her back and called for a razor blade. There was a bit of a to-do, after which someone unearthed a used single-edged razor blade from the medicine chest. He removed the glass and squirted some whisky from his mouth onto her mid-back and began to hack away, attempting to make a vertical incision. I can only speak for myself when I say that this was extremely alarming and my first impulse was to interfere in order to make him stop. But I figured that there were physicians present and that it wasn't my place to interfere. I wandered over, put my hand on her shoulder, and asked if she was all right. She murmured calmly and cheerfully that she was fine. When he laid open the top layers of skin there was a surge of pinkish body fluids to the surface of her back, but there wasn't any bleeding, then or later. He couldn't make as much headway as he would have liked with the blade as it was too dull, so he called for a pair of scissors. Someone brought him what appeared to be fingernail scissors with which he finished the job. Throughout this procedure Mona Lisa appeared to be in a trance. She was completely relaxed and didn't appear to be experiencing any pain or distress. In the end there was a ragged incision that was about four inches long and about an inch deep. He then put his mouth to the incision and sucked vigorously for a while and then spit out a lump of tissue into the glass. It was a grayish pinkish tapioca-like lump about the size of the tip of my thumb. He wiped her back with his hand and called for a needle and thread. Someone brought him a sewing needle and a spool of black thread. He was apparently too drunk to thread the needle so someone did it for him. Loreval took a few stitches that held the lips of the incision together. He then pulled her to her feet and they resumed dancing with the needle and thread swinging freely behind her. After a minute or two he pulled the stitches out and tossed them aside. After about five minutes by my watch the incision was solidly closed. There was no sign of swelling or discoloration. What it looked like was a fingernail scratch along her back. In a half hour there was no evidence at all of the procedure. I took the liberty of putting my hand on her back and palpating the area. She claimed that she felt nothing amiss, that it was indistinguishable from the rest of her back.

I couldn't deny the evidence of my senses but I still wanted and needed to find some way to explain it. I remember on that occasion talking with Ted Allan, a Canadian author and playwright. "What does all this mean?" we kept asking each other. "How did he do it? How can we understand all this?" It was sometime during the course of that evening that I realized that my view of reality and my life would never be the same. A doorway opened for me that night into a limitless space containing more wonders than I could ever imagine.

I realize now how hard it was to finally, finally get my attention! I really am too stubborn for my own good. How I resisted realizing the power and scope of Mind with a capital <u>M</u>! It is obvious now how extremely distasteful it was for me to change my mind. Given my stubbornness and deeply ingrained egotism, I'm very lucky to have lived long enough to learn what many young people already know and intuit about the nature of reality. Since then my experience of the sacred is more incandescently real than my experience of the profane, and the undermining of the feeling of being in a separated state has relieved me of a heavy burden.

In those days I hadn't yet learned to get comfortable in this new godless, self-created, incredibly friendly universe. I was still groping. I remember in 1970 having been invited to spend a month in India. I had been invited to speak at the First (and as it turns out, the last) World Congress of Scientific Yoga in New Delhi. In the course of that visit I was invited to stay with friends in the Himalayas near a mountain village called Almora. I used to hike into the village and hang out on Bindhu Joshi's veranda. He was an interesting man, an alchemist, an herbalist, and also a man of affairs.

While chatting with Bindhu, what was I really thinking? I was thinking, "Maybe I don't belong in San Francisco. Maybe I don't belong in this marriage. Should I leave San Francisco and go back to London or maybe resume my practice in Los Angeles? Santa Barbara might be nice—I was a real hit there." Then I thought, "What a schmuck I am. I've come halfway around the world seeking enlightenment and here I am thinking about leaving San Francisco." And then Bindhu, who by the way knew of me only that I was American and a psychologist, said, "Hmm, San Francisco. If you don't mind my saying so, just so long as San Francisco needs and wants you, you should stay there and when it no longer needs you or wants you, you should leave." Then he called to one of the boys and sent him off to fetch a tray of tea and sweets. Jesus! I was speechless. It only takes one swing of the bat to knock the ball out of the park and so far as really getting my attention goes, Bindhu had just hit a home run. I had occasionally found myself doing exactly what Bindhu had just done, but somehow it had not felt real. Because of my constant wish to be extraordinary it felt more like a party trick. But at this moment I felt the reality of unmistakable sharing of mind. I knew then that what I needed was a little less theory and a little more practice. There were other "anomalous" experiences to come (see Korngold, 2005), but it was then that I knew not how, but where I was headed.

Spirit

By this time you must be aware that my truest religious striving is synonymous with what many people call the spiritual path, whether Western or Eastern. But increasingly in recent decades I have felt an instinctive kinship not with the lifestyles of the East but certainly with their world outlooks. Whether it is the nature spirit called *prakriti* which manifests in existence, or the all-inclusive *Tao* which gives rise to "the ten thousand things," or the Buddha-nature pervading all mind, there is in these outlooks something in common that drew me away from the alienation of the three Western monotheisms. I realized that in the West grace or *baraka* descends from above like a Christmas basket for the poor. It is philanthropic and corporate and hierarchical and lends itself to oligarchy, whereas in the Eastern modes grace or salvation or enlightenment come from within. The Eastern view is that we are all fed from a single common root system of awareness. It is this awareness that gives rise to individual awareness and it is the transaction between the single drop and the sea of which it is a part from which we all emerge individually. I understood at last what the cabalists implied when they argued that if there were one drop of water less in the sea that the whole ocean would thirst. My direct and undeniable experience is of the sacrament, which is the common reality.

The concept of God as a person who is separate from his creation was and is repugnant to me. It rings hollowly with nightmares of separated states. The earliest Vedas, despite their use of metaphor to point to different aspects of consciousness, were clearly according to Mircea Eliade (1961) non-theistic at their core. This direct experience is sacred not only because it is steeped in what Aldous Huxley (1954) called "suchness" but also because it is ineffable. It transcends the limits of the profane or what could be called the mundane because it is unlimitedly magical and endlessly creative. At such moments the "I" that is personal is a faceted reflection of the supreme "I." This supreme "I," by whatever name it is called, is the grandmother of us all and as the primary singularity ceaselessly creates what John Wheeler (Misner, Thorne, & Wheeler, 1973) calls "super space" that contains innumerable universes, which effect and leak into each other and for all we know may have different laws or habits. Jorge Luis Borges (1964, p. 28) in "The Garden of Forking Paths" describes this reality as "an infinite series of times, in a growing, dizzying net of divergent, convergent and parallel times. This network of times which approached one another, forked, broke off, or were unaware of one another for centuries, embraces *all* possibilities of time. We do not exist in the majority of these times; in some you exist, and not I; in others I, and not you; in others, both of us. In the present one, which a favorable fate has granted me, you have arrived at my house; in another, while crossing the garden, you found me dead; in still another, I utter these same words, but I am a mistake, a ghost."

Every instant of time is a miraculous event. It you had electron microscopes for eyes you could then see physical reality as either discontinuous or continuous, either particle-like or wave-like, but not both. Nils Bohr overcame Einstein's classicism. Einstein insisted that there really was an "out there" out there which had its own unalterable laws. But the Copenhagen interpretation which is now the dominant view of physicists says that it is not only true of subatomic reality but also true of macrocosmic reality, that we participate in creating the reality we are observing. However, there are many, myself included, who feel that we not only create reality by the way in which we observe it and how we affect it in the act of observing it, but also that we create reality by what we think, feel, fear, wish, expect, and pay attention to. In a word, our individual and collective consciousness participates in creating new realities.

One thing is clear to me and has been for the past several decades, and that is that consciousness, states of mind, moods, intuitions, are the connective tissue binding us all together. I think that we, all humanity, are influencing each other all the time on many levels in our waking states and in our dreams. We are creating personifications that act with us, for us, and against us. Indeed, not simply humanity but all life is a single dance and that consequently we, as thinking beings, are not only responsible for our actions but also for our thoughts.

There are moments when a place, an event, an object becomes sacred—an unmistakable sacrament takes place. One becomes aware of the sacred because it shows itself. It strongly reveals itself. It gets right in your face. It is wholly other. Nor does it even have to be as spooky a movie as the events that I have described. Mircea Eliade (1961) makes the same point. He says, "The sacred tree, the sacred stone are not adored as stone or tree; they are worshipped precisely because they show something that is no longer stone or tree, but the sacred, the *ganz andere* (i.e., the wholly other)." So, who created this hierophany, this self-revealing sacredness? The answer is, you did. I did. What do we feel inside an old Renaissance cathedral? We feel a living prayerful presence, a presence that resounds through our very beings. To put it plainly and outrageously, I know it may sound insane to the untutored ear, but it's my truth. Take it or leave it. But first try it on for size before you chuck it out. If there were 20 million people who believed in a God named Vladimir and endowed him with particular powers and attributes and envisioned him, communicated often with him, after some period of time, be it a month, a decade, or a century, there will be a functionally autonomous God with these virtues and shortcomings who thinks of himself as Vladimir and who plays an active part in human affairs.

Place Your Bets

I have a personification who is my guardian angel. His name is Herman. He helps me find parking spaces. He assures me when I run out of money that money will appear, either from new patients or some other source. Thus far it has always happened that way.

I have conversations with Herman, who is also quite witty in the bargain. He is my link with the divine. I'm too limited in my scope to get any idea of the whole picture, so Herman explains it to me, always in a way that my little brain can grasp. He is unfailingly kind but never lets me get too big for my britches. One time I told him what a great idea it was for me to invent him and Herman replied, "What makes you think it was your idea?" In the sense that I've just described, God and Gods do exist exactly in the form that we create them. My tribal desert chieftain ancestors created Jahveh. According to Moses, Abraham, and the author of the *Book of Job*, Jahveh is a jealous and vindictive god. Simply to show off he made a bet with Lucifer in the course of which he killed Job's family, bankrupted him, made him intolerably sick, and tormented him. When Job had the audacity to ask what he had done to deserve this, Jahveh proceeded to "bully him into submission." Now, from where we sit, that's not a very nice god. Moreover, Jahveh is still around, alive and kicking. He's still raising hell and sometimes speaking through the mouths of Islamic mullahs, Christian ministers, and Jewish rabbis.

Jung (1970), in his celebrated *Answer to Job*, in 150 eloquent pages reminds us that it is our human responsibility to help God to evolve, to mature out of his childlike narcissism, jealousy, and vicious tantrums. It is our job to civilize him, to tame him, to teach him morality. Who else would have this job, if not us? What I get from Herman isn't simply what he tells or shows, but also the choices he creates, from which I get to pick. It's quite elegant. As you can imagine, I play an important part in this relationship. Herman is not exactly my mentor. You can have your angel be your mentor, if you wish. There are certain things I would rather do for myself. Herman doesn't seem to have an agenda. He is my genius helper. If I decide, perversely, to go to hell in a hand basket, Herman will be glad to pack me a lunch, so to speak. Herman is always gentle, not pushy, intrusive, or judgmental. He is not given to moralizing. He won't allow himself to get dragged into hurting anyone. He simply wants to help me achieve my desire. Though he has no theology he has a much broader perception of possibilities than I do. I'd much rather look through his kindly lens which is non-dogmatic and tailored to my comprehension than through the eyes of any pope or rabbi or imam. For the first half of my life I was singularly lacking in curiosity about what happens after death. But now what I would truly like to know is what sorts of things do happen. Herman seems to feel confident that something does continue after death, not only in humans but also in other sensate creatures.

Naturally, at my age—92 on New Year's Day 2012—I'm deeply interested in such matters. Although logically death is possible at any moment starting from the day of one's birth, in old age death is crowding one a bit. There is a Yiddish saying that "A young one may, but an old one must." So, if you start from the assumption of some continuation beyond biological death then it may be advisable, I reason, to prepare for it. The most developed psychotechnology for negotiating this stygian passage appears to be the Tibetan Buddhist approach to the *bardo*, which is the interval between biological death and one's next assignment, so to speak. I have to confess that I have a few doubts about the technology, but I don't know of a more appropriate method. I distrust all dogmas, even the ones that work for me. Once burned twice shy, as the saying goes. But still, the Mahayana rationale is plausible. The *bardo*, which means "between the two," between death and rebirth in some human or non-human form, is a dreamlike process that has no grounding in any soma. Like a vivid dream, it feels like a substantial reality. But like a dream, it is a contrivance of the mind. You're not actually being eaten alive by a shark or being seduced by a movie star or being trapped in an avalanche. You're dreaming. But waking up out of the *bardo* is very different from waking up in an embodied state. The traditional custom is to have someone who is communicating with the dreamer guide him through it and remind him of what is really happening. The practice of lucid dreaming while one is still alive might be useful. I work at that, but I'm not very good at it. The ideal scenario is, according to the *Bardo Thodol* (also known as *The Tibetan Book of the Dead*—see Evans-Wentz, 1960; Leary, Metzner, & Alpert, 1964), to awaken and discover immediately that you are simply Mind. At that point you may elect to be reborn in the form of your choosing or at the very least to be reborn in a more auspicious situation in which you might have, say, a whole lifetime to prepare for the *bardo*.

Naturally, I can't help doubting this particular metaphysic. It feels plausible, but how do I know for sure that I'm not heading toward simple extinction? Under similar circumstances a few centuries ago, Blaise Pascal (1623–1662), the great mathematician who invented probability theory, in his *Pensees* made a wager with himself that ever since is known as Pascal's Wager. He argued with himself as follows: If it is the case that accepting Jesus as my savior will be my salvation and will lead to eternal life, then even if it's a long shot, perhaps a hundred to one against it, since I have everything to gain by backing this long shot and nothing to lose by backing it, it would be foolish, even insane, not to bet my life on this wager.

So, even though my situation is quite different and the terms of my bet are quite different, I think that it is well worth my while to make a kind of Pascal's Wager. Because if my consciousness can continue to create reality after death just as it does after breakfast, even though I don't know for certain that that's the case, it certainly feels like that's the case. So I would be taking a proactive part in my life after death and have nothing to lose by taking this course. If it isn't the case then I'll simply be extinct and there wouldn't be any me around to be a problem. In that case, my having elected to bet my life would have cost me nothing. On the other hand, if because of my doubt I bet on extinction then I may unnecessarily be consigning myself to extinction. I'd be foolish, therefore, not to bet my life since I have absolutely nothing to lose if I'm going to be extinct anyway. I suppose you could call this Herman's Wager.

References

Beinfield, H., & Korngold, E. (1991). *Between Heaven and Earth: A Guide to Chinese Medicine*. New York: Ballantine/Random House.

Borges, J.L. (1964). The garden of forking paths. In *Labyrinths: Selected Stories and Other Writings* (pp. 19–29). New York: New Directions.

Dooley, A. (1974). *Every Wall a Door: Exploring Psychic Surgery and Healing.* New York: Dutton.

Eliade, M. (1961). *The Sacred and the Profane: The Nature of Religion.* New York: Harper & Row.

Evans-Wentz, W.Y. (Ed.). (1960). Tibetan Book of the Dead: or, The After-Death Experience on the Bardo Plane. Oxford: Claredon Press.

Huxley, A. (1954). *The Doors of Perception and Heaven and Hell.* New York: Harper & Row.

Jung, C. (1970). Answer to Job. In *Collected Works of C.G. Jung (Vol. 11 – Psychology and Religion: West and East).* Princeton, NJ: Bollingen/Princeton University Press.

Korngold, M. (2005). *First Draft: A Life to Talk About.* Paris: Valmy Press.

Leary, T., Metzner, R., & Alpert, R. (1964). *The Psychedelic Experience: A Manual Based on the Tibetan Book of the Dead.* New York: Citadel Press.

Misner, C.W., Thorne, K.S., & Wheeler, J.A. (1973). *Gravitation.* New York: Freeman.

19

LOVE IS A FOUR-LETTER WORD IN THERAPY

Jeffrey A. Kottler

For decades I have been struggling with, and writing about, the inner journey of what it means to be a therapist, not only in terms of professional development but also the personal changes that we experience as a consequence of our work. I have been a big fan of the ways that clients become our teachers in a multitude of ways. Of course, they provide valuable feedback on what we do that is most and least helpful; it is just as significant that they influence and affect us on a deep personal level. Our clients remind us about issues we have yet to resolve. They help us to explore some of the most mysterious and confusing life conflicts. They push us to look at aspects of ourselves that are less than pleasing. They teach us about resilience and courage, but also test us with regard to setting limits. Most of all, they help us access greater compassion, caring, and yes, love.

"Love" has been the forbidden word in our profession, largely because of its associations with exploitation, sexual improprieties, countertransference, codependence, and personal indulgence on the part of the therapist. Instead we use terms like "alliance," "unconditional positive regard," and "empathy" to describe the relational connections that develop with our clients. And certainly there are some people we see who we don't much like at all; in fact, they work pretty diligently at making themselves as unlikeable as possible. Nevertheless, I have long believed—and kept this pretty much to myself—that it is love that drives a lot of our therapeutic work.

I know there is a preoccupation with techniques and interventions in our field. There is a search for variables that produce positive outcomes, especially those that can be standardized and manualized and broken down into their component parts. I like concrete strategies and reasonably foolproof techniques as much as the next person. And yet what has kept me most energized, excited, creative, enthusiastic, and wildly passionate about the work that I do as a thera-pist and teacher is love. I am talking about the kind of love that has been described as non-demanding, non-exploitive, non-romantic, but more than what it is not, it is love that represents genuine, authentic, and deep caring for those we help. For me, that is the origin of my commitment to helping others, and it is what sustains me. I'd like to think that beyond anything I offer to my clients, students, and supervisees in the way of constructive advice, input, feed-back, insights, and content, that many of them also felt loved by me.

Multiple Dimensions of Caring

Some of the most kind, caring, and loving people I know are therapists. On the other hand, there are other practitioners, remarkably effective in their own right, who appear downright withholding, if not mean. They appear to have the interpersonal skills of a toad, croaking in an annoying tone, demanding, self-justifying, and sometimes rude. Yet I'd like to think that in their own way these professionals just have a rather unique way of expressing their caring for their clients, one that is no less powerful. Even among those who don't explic-itly acknowledge that caring is an integral part of their work, and that it may even lead to nonproductive pity, they still leak their compassion and love in other ways that their clients would describe.

When I was a graduate student eons ago, one of my heroes was Albert Ellis who had just reached the status of superstar on the workshop circuit. I showed up at one of his "performances" and found a room filled with over 300 partici-pants; the only seats left were in the front row so I was delighted to have the best view. I had been learning and practicing Rational Emotive Therapy (as it was then called) so I was eager to see the master demonstrate these techniques that already had been so useful to me.

Boy, was I surprised to learn that the front row seats were reserved for vol-unteers who were going to come on stage as clients! I watched in awe as Ellis plowed through the sessions, one after another, "fixing" each client with a wave of his magic disputing of irrational beliefs. The thing that surprised me, though, is that he looked mostly bored with the routine, as if he had been through this procedure thousands of times (and he had!) and it was just a mat-ter of reciting the script. It seemed to work well enough but it seemed like something else was going on which I tried to figure out as I waited nervously for my turn on stage.

Ellis talked about his theory, his assumptions, his technique, the research that supported this approach, and it was really all about following the regi-mented steps—describe the activating event, list the emotional consequences, identify the irrational beliefs, and so on. It seemed like a recipe that was fairly easy to memorize and not that difficult to put into practice. Perfect for a begin-ner like me.

Finally, it was my turn and I bounded up on stage absolutely terrified. Here I was a lowly student, in my second semester of training, and here I was in the presence of the great master, surrounded by all these hundreds of professionals. But I tried to block out all those distracting thoughts, using what I already understood about RET, and it wasn't that difficult to do. As it turned out, I was smack in the middle of a major crisis: my mother was dying. But here's the thing: rather than feeling terrible anticipatory grief and loss, I was actually relieved that she would be gone soon. My mother had always been a burden in my life, a depressed alcoholic who was often suicidal. She was dying of cancer and I was secretly relieved. But my major problem is that I felt terribly guilty that I was such a terrible son. I assumed there was something wrong with me, that I was a bad person because my responsibility for taking care of her would finally end.

I'm sure you can guess the kind of thing that Ellis would have used with me—challenging my beliefs about what constitutes a "good" son, disputing my irrational thoughts regarding "appropriate" behavior, and so on. I went along with the program—after all, we were on stage in front of all these people. Ellis was talking to me in that screechy, annoying voice. I was more than a little intimidated by him, especially considering that he began the day by addressing a group of nuns sitting in the back of the room, scolding them that if they were going to be offended by his "fucking" language, they might as well leave now. They did.

There is nobody else in the audience who could really see or feel what was happening during my session on stage. When audience members were asked to comment afterwards they identified all kinds of different techniques and interventions that Ellis used with me—and it really was a pretty stunning conversation that forever changed the way I thought and felt about my mother's death and my relationship with her. But when I was asked then, and afterwards, what it was that Ellis did that was most helpful, my response was simple and straightforward: "Nothing." It really wasn't about what he did that seemed to have the most impact; it was the way we felt connected and the way I felt understood during that interaction.

When I later reviewed the tape that was made of our session, I became more convinced than ever that it really wasn't the RET that helped me: it was Ellis—as a person. I don't think there was anyone else present that day who could sense and feel how much it seemed he cared about me during the brief time we were together. We were sitting close together, our knees almost touching, and I felt truly heard by him. I felt his compassion for me. I felt that he *knew* me in those moments.

This was an absolute breakthrough for me, not only as someone who was suffering from the impending death of a parent, but as a student who was learning to be a therapist. I realized after that experience that as important as I imagine technique might be, it was really this feeling of caring, of compassion, dare I say *love*, that was so incredibly powerful.

Owning Personal Motives

It is now more than three decades of practice, and dozens of authored books later, that I still struggle to make sense of what happens in that mysterious, complex, multidimensional world of psychotherapy. I have since left the confines of my office and now spend much of my professional life working in the field, conducting service visits with students and colleagues in remote regions of the world. We have begun to specialize in rescuing and supporting lower caste girls who are at greatest risk to be sold into slavery (www.empowernepaligirls.org), as well as visit orphanages, schools, and community agencies in parts of South Asia and Africa. Yet in spite of the money we raise to support our efforts, the scholarships we award, the resources that we bring, the teaching, consultation, mentoring and interventions we initiate, I remain convinced that it is the love and caring that we offer that helps our clients feel valued and supported. The love is hardly enough—but it sure helps to intensify the other work that we do.

During the ensuing years, I have since completely reconceptualized my work. Whether I am doing a home visit in a remote village, volunteering in a school or orphanage, leading a service trip to a disadvantaged community, teaching, coaching, supervising, or conducting a therapy session, much of what I'm trying to do is communicate my caring and compassion to those I am assisting. This is love without pity, without reciprocal demands, without (mostly) meeting my own needs. I inserted "mostly" because I reluctantly acknowledge that what I do isn't just about helping others, but also fortifying myself. I *need* to feel wanted, so to speak. Although I prefer to have my efforts appreciated and explicitly expressed, sometimes that feels like a need as well: I'm frustrated a lot of the time because I can't really tell whether my work is doing what it was intended to do.

I would also be less than honest if I didn't acknowledge that my interest and passion in the work I do, as well as my focus on love, is to fill a vacuum of intimacy that I have longed for in relationships outside of my family and friendships. I became a therapist in the first place, at least in part, because I so enjoy the close connections developed with clients, especially in a context in which I get to be in charge and I'm not the one who is vulnerable. Having felt pretty worthless and inept as a child—a marginal student, a poor athlete, socially awkward and insecure—being a therapist provided just the opportunity for me to feel loved and appreciated in such a way that my own life would feel redeemed. The therapy experiences I've most enjoyed, and felt most satisfied, have been those in which not only that the clients were helped significantly (and expressed gratitude for the help), but also that there was mutual affection and respect and caring in the relationship.

When We Lose Our Compassion

Looking back, most of my own teachers, supervisors, therapists, and influential mentors, taught me "stuff," meaning that I learned certain skills, knowledge, content, and wisdom from them, but I also felt loved—or at least respected—by them. This wasn't always the case, of course. I can think of a few who not only didn't much love or respect me but they didn't even seem to like me. But that taught me some important lessons as well, painful ones that also shaped what I've become.

I would be remiss if I didn't mention that there are exceptions to almost everything, including the rather obvious supposition that compassion is a significant part of therapeutic work. We have all encountered clients who could care less if we care about them or even *like* them. This is business for them and they just want some answers—or action. Some are completely oblivious to relational issues, either because they were born that way or trained from childhood. When we might try to demonstrate some modicum of empathy for their predicament, they just shrug as if to ask, "That's great you feel that way, but how is that relevant to what we're doing right now?" And they genuinely believe that.

There was a time when I was in private practice full time and was feeling frustrated, maybe even burned out, by the futility of my work. I was questioning whether what I was doing made any kind of important difference in the world, given that most of my clients at the time were among the "worried well," relatively middle-class working professionals struggling with adjustments to all the stresses in their lives. I felt replaceable, that so many others could do what I was doing. I also had some serious doubts about whether my work even had much lasting value. How did I know my clients were really changing? Among those who were truly suffering, what could I possibly do for them for 50 minutes each week? I had lost my therapeutic "faith." I had also somehow misplaced my compassion, more often seeing my clients as noncompliant and resistant. It was during this time that I had this great idea for a new book that would be called, "Clients from Hell," in which each chapter would be about a different kind of client who tortures us with their manipulative games, noncompliance, or stubborn instructiveness. Admit it: wouldn't this be a fun, validating book to read? Anyway, upon completion the book was sent out for review and one reviewer hit me pretty hard with the observation that it seemed like I had lost my compassion, feeling like clients were being sent from hell to make my life miserable (I swear—they were!). That single comment helped me to change my perspective, and the title of the book, to ... "*Compassionate Therapy: Working with Difficult Clients.*"

By the way, you'd never guess who the reviewer was who made that comment that I'd lost my compassion and love for my clients: Albert Ellis.

Rekindling Passion and Commitment

One of my friends who worked in community mental health somehow found the means to remain inspired and energized by his work. This was particularly interesting because he worked with the most difficult population imaginable: dual-diagnosed, homeless patients who presented symptoms of schizophrenia, addictions, mental retardation, or all of the above.

"How do you manage to keep working with these people?" I asked him one day. "I mean, what can you possibly do for them?"

"What do you mean?" he said, genuine puzzled by my question.

"Well, these people live on the streets. They are actively hallucinating. They have borderline intelligence. Most of the time they're high, either on streets drugs or Haldol they get from the clinic. They can barely focus on a conversation, much less participate actively in a meaningful therapy session. What the hell can you do for them?"

My friend looked thoughtful for a moment. He nodded his head and at first I thought he was agreeing with me. But then he said something to me that I will never forget and hold dear to my heart to this day: "My hope is that for at least one hour each week they feel like someone really cares about them."

I am haunted by these words, just as I am by the previous observation that I became most dispirited and disinterested in my work when I had lost (or misplaced) my compassion. Anyone who has been in this field for awhile knows well the challenges of keeping ourselves fresh, energized, and passionate about what we do. It is so easy to function on autopilot, to listen to our clients with partial attention, repeat the same well-worn stories and anecdotes, use the same time-tested techniques that have worked previously. It takes considerable commitment and energy to truly remain engaged in sessions, to co-create individually designed, unique therapeutic masterpieces that not only promote lasting changes, but inspire clients to maintain the momentum long after the work ends. We all have to find our own path to doing so, one that helps us keep things fresh. For me, that has been about accessing and expressing love in what I do, love for the people I help, love for the work that I do, and love for the gratitude I feel in what I've been privileged to learn from my clients and students over the years.

20

THE JOURNEY OF A LIFETIME

Or, the Adventures of Being a Therapist

Judith Mazza

It is hard to know when the idea of becoming a therapist first began. It seemed as if I always had an interest in learning about people. I recall that one of my first experiences in trying to systematically understand the people around me took place when I was in fifth grade. I had purchased a paperback book on handwriting analysis at the local library's used book sale; it probably cost 5 or 10 cents. Fifth grade was the point when we were expected to write in cursive, and I was fascinated seeing the different handwriting styles of my friends. I wondered if these different styles represented something about their personalities. I brought a handful of blank paper to my all-girls physical education class and asked each person to write a sentence. I collected the papers and then used my newly purchased book on handwriting analysis to try to understand more about each of them. At the end of the school year, I asked them to write another sentence and was able to compare it to the first. I was astounded to see how much some of them had changed! Of course, I didn't take into account that my friends in the physical education class were experimenting with their handwriting at the time. They would first slant one way and then the next. Sometimes the "dot" over an "i" would become a bubble or a heart. Sometimes, they would write in black pen, sometimes in peacock blue pen, and other times in pencil. I would ask myself, "What did it all mean?" I would once again consult my little paperback book on handwriting analysis, but did not find that it gave me the definitive answers I sought.

The library in the Village of Croton-on-Hudson, New York, where I grew up in the 1950s and 1960s, was in the municipal building. For much of that time, it was just one large room. Since I was not drawn to sports, reading became one of my most treasured activities. I was a very fast reader, often reading an entire book a day. I decided that it was realistic to try to work my way through the entire one-room-library! I would just pick a shelf and read every book on it. In the course of attempting to read the entire library, I stumbled upon Freud's *The Interpretation of Dreams*. I was fascinated at the meanings attributed to dreams as I began reading. Of course, I only understood what I read in the most superficial way (I was probably around 13 years old), but as I read this book, I hoped I would gain an increased understanding of myself and others. It didn't really turn out that way since I was just too young, but I gave it a try.

I created my first behavioral intervention when I was asked to help tutor a boy for his Bar Mitzvah. I was 16 years old with limited time due to the pressures of school. My student had little interest in studying Hebrew. When he heard we had to work one hour a day, he thought we could just use the time in a playful way and not really study. I didn't want to waste our time and felt responsible for his success. I took my uncle's darkroom clock which started and stopped like a chess clock. I set it for 60 minutes and put a sign on it which said, "No work! No tick!" The moment the young man would get off-task, I would stop the clock. When he was ready to work, I'd start it again. It soon became obvious to him that that one hour of actual work could end up taking all evening! He soon buckled down, our time was used efficiently, and he ended up doing a great job at his Bar Mitzvah. I felt an immediate sense of satisfaction in finding a creative behavioral solution to the problem that resulted in change in the young man's approach to his Bar Mitzvah studies. This was a moment of inspiration for me and made me more curious about "what made people tick." When I was completing a college application two years later, and was asked on the application what department interested me, the Department of Psychology seemed like a natural choice.

I was the first in my family to go to college, and although I was very excited about being on a college campus, our family didn't have much in the way of financial resources. It was 1965, and information about where to apply and how to pay for it was not organized in the way it is now. I had decided I would only apply to schools in New York State, since I had been awarded a Regents' scholarship for four years of college. I stumbled upon *Lovejoy's Scholarship Guide*, a compendium of scholarships and grants available to college students. I went through it with a fine-toothed comb, and applied to EVERY scholarship I could possibly qualify for! I wrote essays on any topic presented to me. As a result, I was awarded many scholarships, such that at my high-school graduation, I was being called to the podium far more often than any other student. I was a moment of personal triumph. When deciding how to deal with the scholarships, my parents and I decided to deduct the scholarship credits from the fees due to the University of Rochester, and split the balance, so that I paid half and my parents paid the other half. I always felt proud that I had been able to contribute as much as I did to financing my college education.

The Mentors and Being Part of a Community of Therapists

I believe that having a relationship with a mentor and becoming part of a community of like-minded therapists creates excitement that persists long after a course of study is completed. I was fortunate that at several junctures in my career I formed such relationships. Each relationship changed my point of view and gave me additional skills as well as lasting friendships. These mentoring relationships also led to my becoming part of a network of therapists who were interested in the same approach to creating change that I was.

It wasn't until my sophomore year at the University of Rochester, when I took my first class in Applied Behavior Analysis (a new and very exciting area at the time), that I felt that I had found my intellectual home. It seemed as if a light bulb went on and suddenly I had a paradigm to help me make sense of the world and the people in it. I was greatly influenced by two professors at the time, Drs. Stanley Sapon and Ralph Barocas. Their enthusiasm for the application of behavioral principles to people was infectious. I was fortunate to know both faculty members in and outside of the classroom.

When it was time to apply to graduate school in psychology, I didn't know where to begin. I started applying to a variety of doctoral programs in the northeastern part of the United States. By the first of the year, I had submitted applications to several different programs. It was a lot of work, especially since there were no word processors and each had to be typed individually. I eagerly awaited the results. I had a strong grade point average even though I was working about 30 hours a week as a cashier in the Strong Memorial Hospital gift shop. I was heartbroken when I received rejections from all programs! I couldn't understand what had gone wrong. Men who had lesser credentials than I did were being admitted to similar programs while my application was being rejected. I consulted with Dr. Emory Cowen, a senior member of the faculty who had written letters of recommendation for me. I will never forget the conversation we had as we walked down the hall. He put his arm on my shoulder and said, "Well, dear. You must understand. We need those places for the men." I frankly did *not* understand. The year was 1970, and the Vietnam War was at its height. The Women's Movement had not yet erupted. Men were still able to get graduate school deferments from the draft, so admissions committees, I was told, were reserving as many places as they could for male graduate students in order to keep them out of the war. I wasn't sure where to turn, so I turned to the graduate students who assisted in the applied behavior analysis courses I was taking. They (Walter Rucker and Ronald Wolf) suggested that I apply to a terminal Master's program and subsequently, as soon as I arrived at the Master's program school, I should apply as a Master's-level student to doctoral programs. They had some specific suggestions for me, as they had a good grasp as to where exciting behavioral work was being done at the time. As a result, I applied for a Master's degree in Experimental Psychology at

Western Michigan University, then known as a "hotbed" of radical behavioral psychology. I was delighted to be accepted with financial support. I knew that it meant I would need to re-take the GRE's and apply for doctoral programs as soon as I arrived, because Western Michigan University did not offer a doctoral program in psychology.

Through networking with my fellow graduate students at Western Michigan University during the first semester, I learned about a new doctoral program with a behavioral orientation that had been created at the University of Maryland. So I applied and was subsequently admitted to that program. Meanwhile, I expected to complete my Master's degree in one calendar year. It would be quite an endeavor to complete 30 hours of coursework in addition to an experimental Master's thesis, but I was resolute and determined to complete the program in the time frame I had set, so that I could enter the University of Maryland doctoral program the following September.

The program at Western Michigan University was quite unusual in that one theoretical orientation dominated the entire program. The faculty, through example and a shared vision, encouraged everyone to speak a type of "behavioral operant language" in normal social interactions. It was like being in a total Berlitz immersion program in applied behavior analysis. Some faculty members wore devices on their wrists to count behaviors. You never knew when speaking to them whether they were counting the behaviors of a person they were speaking with or counting some personal behavior that only they were privy to. The whole gestalt created a micro-culture where the students and faculty felt that we were in on the ground floor of something quite interesting and exciting. Dr. Frederick P. Gault, who was in charge of the physiological psychology laboratory at Western Michigan University, had taken me under his wing and became a mentor to me. Under his guidance, I made the transition from being just a college student to thinking of myself as a professional psychologist. As my friendships with the other graduate students in his lab deepened, we would have very intense discussions about behavioral theories which lasted for many hours.

My excitement was compounded when, during that year, I had the opportunity to meet B.F. Skinner, the much acclaimed father of behaviorism. Dr. Skinner attended a dinner reception which was intended for graduate students only. However, at that reception, my fellow students were shy about approaching him. I remember thinking that I would not lose this opportunity, and spoke with him about his hobbies, and things he was reading and thinking about, rather than his latest scholarly articles. I was delighted that he was interested in speaking with me. As I got to know him, his friendship contributed to my feeling that I was on the right track with my career. We became friends and corresponded and met regularly until his death. In fact, Dr. Skinner was kind enough to allow me to do a videotaped interview with him in 1975, entitled "Personal Reminiscences" (Mazza, 1976).

It was during some late night conversations with my fellow students in experimental psychology at Western Michigan University, that we discussed our favorite schedules of reinforcement, as only earnest graduate students might. I decided that my favorite was the variable interval schedule of reinforcement since it maintained behavior for long periods of time. I created a behavioral bumper sticker fashioned somewhat to mimic the spine of the Appleton Century Croft psychology series of books. The bumper sticker said, "God is a VI" (meaning variable interval schedule of reinforcement). We all found it quite amusing. When I got to know B.F. Skinner, I sent him one as a present. A year or so later, I was surprised to find that the phrase, "God is a VI" was the title of an interview of Dr. Skinner in *Playboy Magazine* (August 1972). I contacted the author and found that he took the title of the article from my bumper sticker which was on Dr. Skinner's bulletin board. I then sent the author his very own copy of the bumper sticker, which he was quite pleased to receive. It seemed funny and ironic to me that even though I was a mere graduate student, at that time just a neophyte in the field of behavioral psychology, nonetheless the whimsical bumper sticker that I created had become the title of a national magazine's interview with the renowned behaviorist B.F. Skinner.

The doctoral program at the University of Maryland was headed by a very wise and humorous mentor, Dr. Donald K. Pumroy. He was looking for students with a behavioral background, and my Master's degree from Western Michigan University was just what he wanted. I was able to bring ideas I had learned at Western Michigan University to the University of Maryland, and became his research assistant. Dr. Pumroy was behaviorally oriented, but his stance was softened by his clinical experience. He allowed me to shadow him in his private practice, and was a model of creating change without rigidity. He introduced humor into our work, and was adept at creating a sense of camaraderie among the graduate students in his program, which has lasted to this day.

I had a background in theater and theater costuming and used those skills to "invent" a character known as "Behavior Queen." She dressed somewhat like Wonder Woman, with a cape and tights. The cape was fastened with a chain which joined the symbols for positive reinforcement and punishment. The name "Behavior Queen" was appliqued on the back of the cape in sequins like a prize fighter. Inside the cape were behavioral bumper stickers, which were in fashion at the time. "Behavior Queen" would give M&M chocolate candies as reinforcement whenever she observed someone doing something nice. Dr. Pumroy asked me to appear at various ceremonies in my "Behavior Queen" costume to present awards to deserving graduate students.

Who says therapy can't be fun? There was a sense of joy and the realization that we could be playful while learning and helping others.

After I finished my doctoral coursework, I began working in various staff positions at a State of Maryland residential treatment center for children 12 and under in Baltimore. I was fortunate to have another wonderful mentor during this stage of my career, Dr. Norma Hauserman. She was superintendent at the Regional Institute for Children and Adolescents (RICA) where I worked, and appointed me as Clinical Director of the facility. She supervised my clinical and administrative work, and together we created a new vision for the facility. We had the hope that we could create a therapeutic environment that would be a place of healing for children. Despite our best efforts, after a few years, we found ourselves amidst state budget cuts which limited the resources RICA could provide. Furthermore, despite the good support and supervision I had, I was worried that I did not have enough training and experience to expertly guide the children and staff. At the time, I was only 28 years old, and began to look for a post-doctoral program.

Once again, serendipity led me to a wonderful opportunity, a two-year post-doctoral program under the supervision of Jay Haley and Cloe Madanes at the Family Therapy Institute of Washington. I found that Haley's strategic therapy and the behavioral orientation I already had were quite compatible (Mazza, 2000). While in this training program, I noticed that some distinctions which I had previously paid attention to no longer seemed important. It was less important whether someone was a psychologist, a psychiatrist, or a social worker. The most important thing was that we were all *therapists* and that any of us were in a position to create interesting interventions. I found that my inspiration during those years not only came from Jay Haley and Cloe Madanes, but also from my colleagues, my fellow trainees. Once again, I realized I had the good fortune to become part of a community of therapists who were excited about the work that was being done. Although Jay Haley's approach to creating change was different from the approach used in my graduate programs and in my job at RICA, I was fascinated with his interventions and theoretical orientation. I subsequently became a supervisor at the Institute, and ultimately became the Institute's Clinical Director, a position I held for several years.

Early in my training, I recall a moment behind the one-way mirror with Jay when my theoretical orientation shifted. We were observing a case of a young man who had dropped out of school, was living at home, and couldn't quite manage to get to his one academic class. In my behavioral frame of reference, I said to Jay, "He needs a self-management program." I thought that perhaps we could arrange for some rewards to be given to the young man when he met his goals of keeping to his schedule. "No," Jay said. "He needs a job." "A job?" I asked. "If he can't get to his one class, how in the world will he also manage a job?" Jay Haley looked at me and said, "Do you know how hard it is when you're on vacation at the beach and you have one postcard to write and to mail? You need to find the postcard, you need to find the stamp, you need to decide what you're going to say, and then you need to take it to the Post Office." Jay went on to say, "And do you know how easy that is to do in your everyday working life when you have many other things to do as well? If I want something done, I'll give it to one of the busiest people I know. I know they'll do it quickly." I thought about what Jay said and I realized he was right. This young man was seemingly on a metaphoric "beach vacation" with little to do and a lot of time in which to get it done. It all conspired to make each goal difficult to accomplish. Jay instructed the therapist to have the young man get a job and sign up for some additional classes. Sure enough, once the young man had a job, he was more energized and attended all his academic classes regularly. It was a moment of inspiration for me, and one which I will never forget. I wanted to learn how to think of interventions like that. It didn't exactly fit into the model I had been using when working with my clients. I was intrigued.

Another moment which shifted how I approached my clients was when Jay Haley said that it was the therapist's job to learn the client's language, and not the client's job to learn the therapist's language. It seems so obvious when I say it now, but at the time, it was monumental. I had spent a considerable amount of time trying to teach parents whose children were in residential treatment how to speak my technical behavioral language. It seemed somehow important that they be able to define the difference between negative reinforcement and punishment. The thinking of the time (in the late 1970s) in behavioral circles was that if only parents thoroughly understood behavioral principles, that would enable them to understand what they were doing and raise their children with more positive reinforcement. My clients humored me by trying to use my jargon. However, I always felt like I was swimming upstream. Once I realized that I had it backwards--that as the therapist, it was my job to speak the *client's* language and to customize my interventions to fit the *client's* frame of reference—the creativity in my work began to soar, and the outcomes improved.

Creating Interventions

While involved with Jay Haley at the Family Therapy Institute, I became fascinated with the notion of symptom utilization (Mazza, 1984). I realized that when I am able to use a symptom in a new way to create flexibility in someone's life, not only was the result effective, but also the process of developing the strategy was immensely satisfying. It was the same sense of satisfaction one has when figuring out the answer to a complicated puzzle. Mihaly Csikszentmihalyi (1998) describes this feeling as "flow." It's when you are "in the zone" and so focused on something that you might lose track of time. When creating an intervention in session, it can be easy to lose track of time. I feel very much "at one" with my clients. I've sometimes described it as feeling as though the tumblers in a lock have just clicked into place and the door now swings open.

Let me give you a few examples. A family came to see me because their youngest child, now a young man of 18, had just returned from his first time living away from home. Apparently, when he got to college he basically did nothing. He didn't go to many classes and he didn't even socialize with others. When he returned home at for the holidays, his parents decided not to send him back. They explained that he has a diagnosis of Asperger's Syndrome, and despite his obvious intelligence, they were at a loss as to what he might be able to do with his life. He was working at a menial job in his father's business, a job which he performed well but was uninterested in. In fact, the entire family seemed somewhat depressed because the parents had looked forward to enjoying being "empty nesters," and now were once again becoming hands-on parents. They feared they would turn into "helicopter parents," who hover closely over their children and are intensely involved in the minutia of the children's lives (which they had been during his high school years). I asked what the young man liked to do. After some prodding, they admitted that he enjoyed all things digital, but that his parents had restricted him from the Internet and using devices with screens because they thought it was a waste of his time. When involved with these activities, he showed enormous concentration and attention span, but with other activities that didn't interest him, he was easily distracted. The parents told me that he had previously been diagnosed as having attention deficit hyperactivity disorder. I asked if they had ever considered that he might use his interest in things digital as a career path. I began to reframe his Asperger's as a potential asset in this career path since he had a type of laser sharp concentration and focus when working with computers. I suggested that they might seek out people who are currently developing video games and other software programs, to learn what skills and education are needed to pursue that type of job. They all brightened. I suggested that although social interactions might be somewhat more difficult for him, the facility and fluency he had in the digital world was, in part, due to his Asperger's, and therefore a potential asset. In fact, the Mom said that this exploration of possibilities in a digital career sounded like fun. They left the session with a renewed sense of purpose, and I, as a therapist, felt invigorated. His neurological condition had been reframed as an asset.

After they left, I reflected on why that interaction was stimulating for me as a therapist. I certainly enjoyed the change of mood in the room as the young man's deficit morphed into an asset. The parents had arrived to the session expecting to be blamed for the young man's problems. They had read quite a bit of family/systems literature and wanted to know if there was a problem in their family system that resulted in this young man's "collapse" back to his parents' home. When the parents found that his "condition" was given a positive connotation, and that they were not blamed for his problems, they were relieved and empowered. My interaction with them while engaging in this very practical creative problem solving was immensely satisfying. For me there were two aspects that I found reinforcing: there was the creative process for me personally, and the knowledge that through this intervention I contributed to new successful possibilities for my clients.

In another case, I received a call from a concerned mother. It was September in Washington, D.C., which can be a time of turbulent weather. Her eight-year-old daughter had become obsessed with weather forecasts. If there was rain or a thunderstorm in the forecast, she became extremely anxious, crying and upset, and refused to leave the house. This was a huge departure from how she once was. I asked both parents to come to a session with their daughter. They explained that this problem had started a few months before. There had been two very strong storms a few weeks apart. Each storm had resulted in the loss of power for several days and some property destruction in the neighborhood. When school resumed after these storms, there were school-wide safety drills held. In the event of a severe storm warning, the children had to leave their classrooms, line up in the hallways, sit on the floor, and cradle their heads. (This reminded me of the air raid drills my generation had experienced in grade school in the 1950s.) They were to stay away from windows. It appeared that these safety drills had a big and rather unsettling effect on this little girl. She became preoccupied with the weather. When she arrived home, she began to check the weather on the computer and did this with great frequency, to the point that it became an obsession. It interfered with her going to sleep, it interfered with her playing with friends, and it interfered with her getting her homework done. The parents had tried to talk "sense" into her (she was quite bright), but had run out of ideas. I discussed this with the girl in front of her parents. I said that she had taken on a very important job, trying to protect her family. She agreed. She said that she wanted to make sure that no one in her family would be hurt by a big storm. I said to her that even people with the most important jobs take vacations from time to time. She nodded. I asked her if she would be willing to take a short vacation from her responsibility of checking on the weather. Was she willing to trust her father and then her mother to do this job for her? She said that she trusted them and that she would be willing to take a vacation from her job. We discussed at what times it was most important to check the weather and that her parents would let her know what they learned. She gave them a schedule to follow, which we carefully wrote down. I asked each parent to take one week to be the family weather-checker and scheduled our next appointment two weeks later. At the next appointment, I asked the girl if she thought her parents had done a good job. She nodded and said they had. I said to her that we had agreed that she would be on vacation for two weeks and that now the two weeks were up: I wondered if she would like to have her job back as family weather-checker, or did she want her parents to continue with this important responsibility. She said that she didn't want the job back anymore. She thought they had done a good job. During the two weeks, she had not experienced any incidents of crying or being upset about the weather. We had experienced two weather events during that time, but neither seemed to occupy her in the same way as they had previously. She had gone back to being her cheerful pre-weather-checker self. I made one more follow-up appointment with the family six weeks later and found that the parents had continued to do their jobs, albeit not as diligently, and that their daughter no longer was preoccupied with the weather forecast.

I reflected on my own reaction to this intervention. The non-linear change was enormously satisfying to me as a therapist. The parents were amused to some extent with the intervention, and realized that once their daughter returned to her age-appropriate eight-year-old interests, she was unlikely to give those up for the sake of again becoming the family weather-checker. The girl's actions were not diagnosed or pathologized; her motives were given a positive connotation and framed as "protecting her family." Her "work" as a weather-checker was taken seriously and then she agreed to go on "vacation." I had enjoyed my interaction with the family, and the parents were relieved not to be blamed for the girl's difficulties. I was energized by the success of all and pleased that the problem was solved in such a brief manner.

Some years ago, I was consulted by a married couple who said that the husband had gotten the flu and was very ill several months before. However, after his flu symptoms abated, he continued to vomit, and didn't seem to have control over this. It turned out he had vomited in all of their favorite restaurants. The involuntary vomiting had become so severe that he had been hospitalized and had lost more than 80 pounds. As he had once been quite obese, he did not appear to be too thin; however, his electrolytes were out of balance and his physicians were worried about him. No medical interventions had worked, so he and his wife sought therapy. When I asked about their families of origin, it appeared that he came from a family which was quite chaotic and dysfunctional. He had a handicapped sister in her 20s who had never been to school and had never been toilet trained. His parents were supportive of him and his marriage, so I asked if they would invite his parents to attend the next session. I had asked him and his wife to keep data on the vomiting pattern, which they did, and in the second session, I used that data to set up times when he was supposed to vomit—scheduling the symptom as a paradoxical intervention. I further said that if he vomited at a time other than a scheduled time, it was an indication that he needed more support from his parents, and that he would need to spend 24 hours in his parents' home. His parents, who had attended the second session with his handicapped sister in tow, were only too happy to oblige. When they returned the following week, not only was he unable to vomit on the established schedule, but he never had to stay at his parents' home. The vomiting problem was solved, but more difficult marital issues soon emerged. I have always wondered whether the vomiting was a metaphoric comment on his marriage or something else. He and his wife never referred to the vomiting after we started to work on other issues. I never knew for sure why the vomiting had persisted in the way it had. In fact, I don't believe that it is necessary to know precisely why a problem emerges to create change and solve it. Sometimes, after a problem is solved, the clients develop theories about the problem.

I believe that whatever insight they have is theirs to keep, and as long as the problem does not reoccur, I do not need to add my thoughts to theirs.

I often tell therapists I am training, that one of my goals is to empower them to become more creative in their work. If they are going to remain as therapists in this field for a number of years to come, they should be free to continue to customize their interventions and approaches to the client and the situation. It would not be optimal if five or ten years from now, they were intervening in precisely the same way as they are intervening today. Being creative is fun and energizing. If they were to spend decades implementing the identical interventions over and over again, they will invite burn-out (see Mazza, 1995).

Teaching and Becoming a Mentor

I have always found it quite satisfying to teach others and to share whatever knowledge I have. The mentors I was fortunate to have taught me much about therapy and how to think about creating change. In virtually every setting I worked in I eventually became a supervisor of others and a mentor to some, which has been a very satisfying part of my career. For the supervisor or mentor, training a therapist can be much like doing therapy. The interventions given have to fit not only the client but the supervisee or mentee as well (Mazza, 1988). It is an opportunity for a supervisor or mentor to share information (and hopefully some wisdom) acquired over years of practice.

For me, *mentoring* is a voluntary relationship which both parties enter into with the express purpose of honing the skills of the mentee. A *supervisory* relationship has the objective of improving the work of the supervisee, but the relationship may in fact not be voluntary, in the same way that a mentoring relationship is. A trainee-supervisee may be a participant in a program where he or she is assigned a supervisor; neither trainee nor supervisor usually makes the choice, inasmuch as they are typically assigned to one another.

I believe that to be a good mentor or supervisor, one should not judge the trainee or mentee. Jay Haley was a master at conveying new ways to approach cases without making the trainee-mentee feel inadequate or stupid. Haley used to say that his therapy was a "therapy of courtesy," and that it is rude to tell people things they already know, and that a supervisor or mentor should be courteous in the same way. I believe that being a good mentor or supervisor is similar to being a good therapist. It is as important that the trainee-mentee feel as comfortable sharing their moments of indecision, despair and triumph with their mentor or supervisor as it is for a client to share the same with their therapist. Watching therapists I have trained expand their skills, and analyze and approach cases in new ways, has been highly satisfying to me. It has motivated me to continue to teach and give workshops even when I might experience greater financial rewards by instead using that time in my private practice.

For example, therapists who had completed the training program at the Family Therapy Institute approached me around 1981, and asked if I would continue to help them with their cases via a case consultation model, inasmuch as the Institute's live supervision was no longer available to them. I said I would, and at one point ran four different consultative supervision groups, each consisting of several therapists. Each group met once a month for two hours, and cost each therapist a nominal amount. I never charged these therapists for my travel time to the seminar site, as I thought it was important to assist them in their work. My goal was not primarily financial—I felt I had a higher purpose. I was interested in teaching a particular model of brief therapy. One of those groups continues to this day. We now meet in my office, but the nominal fee charged has not been raised since 1981. The therapists who were once trainees are now dear friends and colleagues. We meet monthly to discuss cases and other matters of importance to our work. It is deeply satisfying and stimulating.

Since 1984, I have been on the faculty of the National Naval Medical Center or Walter Reed Army Medical Center (and, for several years, both) where I have been training psychologists, psychiatrists, and social workers in strategic therapy. These military training programs presently are among the few places where therapists can still receive live supervision. I first consulted at Walter Reed for about four years beginning in 1984, giving seminars and doing live supervision through a one-way mirror. As a result of my work, I was invited to teach at a multidisciplinary conference run by the U.S. Army in Heidelberg, Germany, in 1987. I also began training psychologists at the National Naval Medical Center in 1987, and I continued consulting to the psychology department there for twenty years, until 2007. At that time, the mission of the Psychology Department changed, and psychologists began spending more and more time doing neuropsychological evaluations due to the injuries incurred by active duty service members in Iraq and Afghanistan, rather than providing family and marital therapy services to military families.

In 2003, I was contacted by the Social Work Fellowship program at Walter Reed and began training social workers and the occasional psychiatrist in marital therapy. This program was unique in that the first semester was didactic and the second semester consisted of live supervision through a one-way mirror. During the live supervision semester, the therapist used a wireless "bug in the ear" earphone to receive instructions from me while seeing their clients. There were other trainees behind the mirror with me, discussing and strategizing about the case. It was very satisfying to me to have some of my former trainees continue in their military career to positions of authority where they were able to invite me to teach at the multidisciplinary European Regional Medical Conferences in 2005 and 2009. It is one thing to know that your teaching is influencing trainees in the moment, but there is yet a higher level of satisfaction when a former trainee you haven't seen recently invites you to give a series of lectures in Europe! Thankfully, my husband has been very supportive and we enjoy exploring new countries and cultures in conjunction with my and his international business travel.

I remember thinking (earlier in my career) that being a therapist is one of those professions where one is assumed to have greater wisdom the longer one is in practice. It is unlike being in some fields where it is assumed that recent graduates have the most relevant knowledge. It is a field where maturity and life experience can be an asset as long as you continue to be open to learning new techniques and ideas.

I believe that it is important for any professional to engage in a variety of activities as a way to reduce stress. I have thought for some time that staying current by learning new technologies keeps one open to new possibilities. Furthermore, digital technology today provides an interesting contrast to the analogic world of therapy. As we age, it is critical that we challenge ourselves to continue to learn something new. This process keeps our brains active and stimulated. If what you are learning has a practical application, it is all the better, because then you will use what you have learned. From the time that I used my uncle's darkroom clock at the age of 16 to motivate a young man to study efficiently, to the present, I have incorporated the technologies available to me to support my work.

My first job after I finished my doctoral courses was Director of Staff Development at RICA. The then-superintendent, Dr. Roger Olsen, had secured a grant to purchase state of the art reel-to-reel video recording equipment. When I was hired, he took me to a room which was piled floor to ceiling with unopened equipment boxes and said, "Make it work." I jumped in and did just that. Two years later, I was given permission to borrow this video equipment to tape the interview I did with B. F. Skinner in 1975 in Boston. I was also able to borrow it to videotape the teaching seminar I attended with my fellow trainees at the Family Therapy Institute in 1979 when we visited Dr. Milton Erickson in Phoenix shortly before his death. Today, I continue to educate myself to make sure that I feel comfortable with evolving digital technologies. I currently use a tablet PC to take handwritten notes when I see my clients, have a website (www.familytherapy.com) where clients can download and complete necessary forms prior to the first appointment, and I aspire to develop a paperless private practice. To this day, I use computers in all aspects of my practice, including creating presentations, editing videos and still photographs, and helping colleagues who are less fluent in this area to do the same.

Coming Full Circle

My journey of being a therapist has extended over several decades. Some ask if I am ready to retire, and this question has caused me to reflect on what gives meaning to my life. To help answer the question of what contributes to giving meaning in one's life, I recently read a book by Susan Wolf (2010), a philosophy professor at Princeton University, entitled *Meaning in Life and Why it Matters.* Her conclusion was that "meaning arises from loving objects worthy of love and engaging with them in a positive way" (p. 75). Thus, to have meaning in life, it is not enough to be personally fulfilled. What you engage passionately with must have worth outside of oneself, that is, it should have objective worth, and serve a higher purpose. As a therapist, creating change in clients' lives so that they find increased satisfaction, are no longer encumbered by symptoms, and report increased happiness is, in my view, an endeavor of great objective worth. I have found that the passion I have for this work has been maintained not just by the success experienced when working with clients, but has also come from interactions with generous mentors willing to share their knowledge, and from grateful mentees and trainees, as well as staying in close contact with a network of like-minded professionals.

Furthermore, I believe it is also important to have interests and activities that contrast with that of being a therapist. Obviously, these interests and activities will vary from person to person, but they should be stimulating and also good for your health. One might travel and learn about other cultures, or develop hobbies that have nothing to do with therapy. I believe it is important to continue to be open to learning new skills, in addition to physically moving and staying active; to continue to make new friends while at the same time nurturing life-long relationships. Needless to say, I take my own advice. I make a point of seeing clients, teaching, staying active with colleagues, maintaining relationships with both my mentors and mentees, using new technologies, and developing hobbies and interests apart from being a therapist.

I continue to find the work of a therapist to be endlessly interesting. No two clients are exactly alike and their dilemmas and problems continue to fascinate me. When that is no longer the case, I know it will be time to retire.

References

Csikszentmihalyi, M. (1998). *Finding Flow: The Psychology of Engagement with Everyday Life.* New York: Basic Books.

Mazza, J. (1976, May). *B.F. Skinner...Personal Reminiscences.* Presented at convention of Midwest Association of Behavior Analysis, Chicago, Illinois.

Mazza, J. (1984). Symptom utilization in strategic therapy. *Family Process, 23*(4), 487–500.

Mazza, J. (1988). Training strategic therapists: The use of indirect techniques. In H. Liddle & D. Bruenlin (Eds.), *Training in Family Therapy* (pp. 93–109). New York: Guilford Press.

Mazza, J. (1995). The top ten ways to burn out as a bureaucrat. *The Public Manager, 24*(1), 46–48.

Mazza, J. (2000). The making of a strategic therapist. In J.K. Zeig (Ed.), *Changing Directives: The Strategic Therapy of Jay Haley* (pp. 139–153). Phoenix, AZ: The Milton H. Erickson Foundation Press.

Wolf, S. (2010). *Meaning in Life and Why It Matters.* Princeton, NJ: Princeton University Press.

21

AT MY MOTHER'S KITCHEN TABLE

Who Are We, But the Stories We Tell?

Donald Meichenbaum

Interviewer (Int): Dr. Hoyt has asked me to interview you for this volume in search of any words of inspiration, passion, and renewal that can be conveyed to psychotherapists. I have been working as a psychotherapist for 25 years. I also teach and train new psychotherapists. I have been asked by these neophytes to submit questions that they would like you to address. Is that okay with you?

Dr. Meichenbaum: I am honored to be included in the present list of distinguished therapists. Your timing is quite good since I am about to celebrate my 72nd birthday and I had some occasion to reflect on my personal journey as a psychotherapist and researcher.

Int: Let's begin with your personal journey. My students want to know how did you go from undergraduate training at City College in New York to being rated as "one of the ten most influential psychotherapists of the 20th century"?

Dr. M: You are referring to the survey of clinicians that was reported in the *American Psychologist* (Smith, 1982). Well, I entered City College in the hopes of becoming an engineer. I remember that all entering freshman had to attend a session with the Dean of Engineering, who told us to look around the room, because in four years only one in four of us would graduate the engineering program. My reaction was to immediately begin to console my three friends about how to cope with failure and disappointment. I soon learned that I was better at offering support and advice than I was at engineering.

Int: So you graduated City College as a psychology major instead of as an engineer. What was the next step on your journey?

Dr. M: Your students may be interested in what happened next. Well, I took the Graduate Record Examinations (GRE's) and did <u>not</u> do well and I began to receive rejection letters from graduate schools. So I decided to write a letter to all of the remaining grad schools that I had not heard from questioning the validity of the GRE's in predicting future professional success in psychology. I did a literature search and quoted Lee Cronbach (1960) who had written the textbook *Essentials of Psychological Testing* that there is always an "outlier" who scores poorly on tests, but who succeeds. I signed my letter: "The Outlier"!

Int: What *chutzpah*!

Dr. M: Actually, the saga continues. I was accepted at the University of Illinois in Champaign in the psychology program where Cronbach had taught. Upon my arrival I was ushered into the office of the Chairman of the Psychology Department, Lloyd Humphries, who greeted individually all incoming grad students. He was a psychometrician and when he opened my application folder, he said, "There must be some mistake, we do not accept students with GRE scores like that. You have to take the GRE's again."

Int: Did you take them again?

Dr. M: Yes, and my scores did not improve that much. The GRE's are reliable, but I do not think they have much predictive validity. Four years later, I graduated with honors and with a Ph.D. in clinical psychology. Once again, I found myself in Lloyd Humphrey's office, now doing an "exit" interview. I had waited four years for this moment to ask him to reopen my application folder, and now I said goodbye as the "Outlier."

Int: My students will get a kick out of your story of grit. But that seems to be the story of your professional career. I recall the flack you encountered, breaking the mold in the area of psychotherapy in the form of Cognitive Behavior Therapy.

Dr. M: Well, when I left Illinois clutching my diploma, I was very fortunate to take a teaching position at the University of Waterloo in Ontario, Canada, where I taught and did research for 35 years. It was a new and vibrant university and had great young, bright faculty and graduate students. I thrived and began a research program to explore the role of cognitive and emotional factors in the behavior change process.

Int: Before we discuss the "flack" you encountered, can we take a moment to discuss the factors and influences that led to your developing a cognitive-behavioral approach to psychotherapy?

Dr. M: In retrospect, it is difficult to determine how all of these influences played out. I can recall that as an undergraduate at City College, which was a hotbed of psychoanalytic thinking, they had a visiting professor give a lecture and I sat enamored of his account of people's functioning. His name was George Kelly (1955) of Personal Construct Theory fame. At the University of Illinois, I had a chance to listen to and meet Victor Frankl, the author of *Man's Search for Meaning* (1963) and the developer of logotherapy. In fact, over the years, as a presenter at the Evolution of Psychotherapy conferences, I had several further opportunities to meet with Frankl. I arrived on the scene when the *zeitgeist* was filled with folks like Albert Ellis, Aaron Beck, Arnold Lazarus, Michael Mahoney, and others. I was also influenced greatly by the work of Richard Lazarus and his colleagues on the role of appraisal processes in coping, Irving Janis on decision making, and Norman Garmezy on resilience. This is quite a "Who's Who" list, all of whom inspired and influenced me. But, when it comes down to *the* most substantial influence … it would be my mother.

Int: So, *nu*? Doesn't it all go back to one's mother? How did she impact your career path?

Dr. M.: When she visited me before she died, I noticed something very interesting. I would ask her, how things were going in her life? She was a very good storyteller, but she had an interesting way of telling her stories. Not only would she describe the events in her life, but she would tell you what thoughts and feelings she had in the situation, and moreover, she would incorporate in her accounts an evaluation of what were good or productive thoughts versus those that were maladaptive and stress-engendering. Moreover, she would include what different thoughts, feelings and behaviors she could have engaged in to achieve a better outcome:

> So I did X and felt Y and I thought it is bad enough what happened and then I told myself, "Why make the situation worse?" so I changed what I said to myself—Florence Meichenbaum

It dawned on me that I ate dinner with Flo my entire childhood, through college and that this style of thinking became part of my fiber.

Int: Are you suggesting that Flo was one of the founders of Cognitive Behavior Therapy?

Dr. M.: I think she would be willing to share credit with others. Also, keep in mind that I grew up in New York City and everyone there talks to themselves, everyone has a story to tell. As the adage goes, it is a city of 10 million stories. In fact, when I went to the University of Illinois, I did my doctoral dissertation on "How to Train Schizophrenics to Talk to Themselves." I figured that they were doing this anyway, so perhaps I could influence what and how they talked to themselves.

Int: So this developmental experience was the beginning of your self-talk or cognitive-behavioral therapy approach.

Dr. M.:   As I reflect back on my 35 years of research at the University of Waterloo, I essentially was teaching people in Ontario to do what New Yorkers do, and what my mother was doing all the time. I called it Cognitive Behavior Therapy and became "one of the 10 most influential psychotherapists of the 20th century." I do not understand what is the big deal. In fact, I have come to view my entire professional research career as a way of validating my socialization process.

Int.:   Actually, you are making light of the distinguished research program that you conducted. Your work on self-instructional training with a variety of child and adult clients with impulse control disorders, your work on stress-inoculation training, your work on cognitive narrative perspective of psychotherapy with traumatized clients, your current work with returning service members and their families on ways to bolster resilience, go well beyond your mother's storytelling style.

Dr. M.:   That is a very gracious comment. As you know, I took early retirement some 15 years ago from the University of Waterloo and I am now a Distinguished Visiting Professor at the University of Miami in the School of Education and Research Director of the Melissa Institute for Violence Prevention and Treatment of Victims of Violence which is located in Miami. Please visit our websites www.melissainstitute.org and one for educators www.teachsafeschools.org. I am very proud to report that these two Melissa Institute websites have had over two *million* hits worldwide. I am into what Erik Erikson called the "generativity phase" of life where one tries to "give science away" and leave a legacy. In fact, you can visit the Melissa Institute website and click on the Author Index on the left side and scroll down to my name and read book chapters and conference Handouts that provide a description of my recent work. I welcome your feedback on these papers. You can e-mail me at dhmeich@aol.com.

Int.:   I thought you said you were "retired."

Dr. M.:   You are starting to sound like my wife.

Int.:   I do couple's therapy, but we do not have time to go there. Let's pick up on the flack you received as you and others began to introduce and advocate for a cognitive-behavioral approach to psychotherapy.

Dr. M.:   It may be difficult to envision what the field of psychotherapy was like back in the 1960s and 1970s, where a strict behavioral approach was dominating the field. Eysenck, Skinner, Wolpe, and many leaders of AABT (American Association of Behavior Therapy) had eschewed the notion of thoughts and feelings, or at least conceptualized them as operants and conditioned responses, subject to so-called "laws of learning," like other behaviors. Into this mix, I arrived employing a different set of metaphors that moved the field from conditioning to information processing to a constructive narrative approach. This new stance was not welcomed. In print, I was called an "oxymoron" for trying to bridge the gap between cognition and behavior. I recall attending a Behavior Therapy conference and being told I had made "the list." My immediate reaction was that somehow I had made President Nixon's list of who should not be invited to the White House, with Eartha Kitt and others. "No, no, you made Joseph Wolfe's list of 'malcontents' in behavior therapy." I had surely arrived! Today, Cognitive Behavior Therapy has emerged as the most evidence-based approach to psychotherapy and the organization has added a C, for Cognitive. They are now called the Association for Behavioral and Cognitive Therapies (ABCT).

Int.:   Your mother would be proud of you.

Dr. M.:   But, here is the rub. While cognitive-behavioral approaches have emerged as an important source of psychotherapeutic interventions, the more recent meta-analyses of cognitive-behavioral therapies versus bona fide comparison groups have questioned the relative efficacy of CBT approaches. (See the recent papers by Wampold et al., 1997; Wampold, Imel, Laska, & Benish, 2010, listed in the Reference section.) These authors seriously challenge the mechanisms of change proposed by myself and others. Moreover, the excellent work by Michael Lambert (2010) and his colleagues highlight the critical role of the therapeutic alliance and ongoing feedback mechanisms as key to psychotherapeutic behavior change. Thus, we have come full circle in the field.

Should your students learn and master therapeutic manuals designed to treat patients with specific psychiatric disorders as advocated by some, or should they focus on the transdiagnostic commonalities across patients with varied psychiatric disorders and the common mechanisms of change? You know, there are no winners in the so-called race of which treatment procedures work best (Luborsky, Singer, & Luborsky, 1975). After being a psychotherapist for 40 years, and a consultant/trainer giving innumerable workshops in all 50 U.S. states and around the world, and as a researcher for a similar period of time, I am still challenged by the question of "What makes psychotherapy work?"

Int.:   Where does your passion for research come from?

DR. M.:   Although it is not very fashionable at the present time, when I was in graduate school at the University of Illinois (1962-1966), the clinical training program embraced the Boulder Model. We were trained to wear two professional hats—first being a contributor and critical consumer of research and the second to be a culturally sensitive practicing clinician. Each arena should inform the other. My research derived from my strong desire to test out my hypotheses

	and to play "detective" and to be an "honest broker" when training clinicians.
Int.:	I am also reminded that Michael Lambert (2010) observed that in about 10% of cases patients get worse as a result of participating in psychotherapy.
Dr. M.:	Yes, that concerns me greatly, since I continue to train psychotherapists. My solution to this dilemma of negotiating between those who advocate for "evidence-based interventions" and those who highlight the role of non-specific factors (the so-called "dodo bird effect") is to highlight the role of expertise. Some therapists are "experts" in getting positive results, more so than others (interested readers may want to listen to the dialogue between myself and Scott Miller that took place at the 2009 Evolution of Psychotherapy, available at www.miltonhericksonfoundation.org).

When I present workshops on "expertise" in psychotherapy, I usually begin by asking the question:

> What is the most important skill that psychotherapists need in order to achieve positive results, to have a rewarding practice and to maintain a good reputation?

Int.:	What is that skill?
Dr. M.:	An analysis of the research literature clearly indicates that the most important skill a psychotherapist needs in order to have good treatment outcomes is—get ready for this—the ability to choose one's patients carefully. Patient characteristics account for the largest portion of the variance in treatment outcome. If you could delimit your practice to what are called YAVIS—Young, Attractive, Verbal, Intelligent, and Successful—folks like yourself, then you will have positive treatment outcomes. YAVIS folks will get better with, or without, your help—so you might as well take credit for the change.
Int.:	But most of us do <u>not</u> treat patients who are YAVIS. My practice is filled with folks who have a history of victimization, present multiple comorbid problems often involving substance abuse and have high-risk unsupportive environments.
Dr. M.:	That is my clientele as well. In fact, you can view various training films that I have made with such challenging clients (e.g., see my film on Cognitive Behavior Therapy available from www.apa.org). So then, what are the various core tasks of psychotherapy that "expert" therapists engage in?
Int.:	That is *the* key question my students want an answer to.
Dr. M.:	In formulating my answer, you need to know that I love doing psychotherapy or counselling. I just love it and the reason I love it so much is that I love the way I think about cases. I am totally enamored with my head. I love the "detective work," the "art of

Socratic questioning," the ability to help patients "restory" their lives and develop intra- and interpersonal coping skills and bolster their resilience and build upon their strengths.

Int.: It sounds like your inspiration, passion, and renewal come from your clients.

Dr. M.: Definitely! Most recently, working with returning service members and their family members is inspiring. Seventy percent of those who have been through horrific combat experiences, often with injuries, will evidence resilience and, in some cases, posttraumatic *growth*. They have so much to teach us. I am their student.

Int: But how do you help the 30% who evidence chronic disabilities, both psychological and physical?

Dr. M.: This is where the Core Skills of being an "expert" psychotherapist comes into play. These Core Psychotherapeutic Skills include:

1. The ability to establish, maintain and monitor a trusting, supportive, nonjudgmental *therapeutic alliance*, in a culturally and gender-sensitive manner. In addition, there is a need to address any "ruptures" in the therapeutic alliance. The quality of the therapeutic alliance is the "glue" that makes everything else work. But, from my perspective, the quality of the therapeutic alliance is a necessary, but not sufficient, condition in order to achieve psychotherapeutic success.

2. There is also a need to provide ongoing psychoeducation. I do <u>not</u> mean using a didactic lecture, but rather the art of questioning, which is your most valuable tool. It involves collaborative formulation of a Case Conceptualization Model, the dispelling of myths, and the need to assess and provide ongoing feedback. There is a need to probe for the clients "implicit theory" about his/her presenting problems and notions of what is needed to change. The "fit" between the patient's and therapist's models is critical to foster the patient's therapeutic engagement and participation. Note that ongoing assessment and session-by-session feedback is critical to outcome. Assessment and treatment are critically interlinked throughout.

3. The "expert" psychotherapist is effective in nurturing the key ingredient of *HOPE*. There are a number of ways to do this, but one of the best ways is to engage clients into collaborative goal-setting that provides "SMART" goals: Specific, Measurable, Achievable, Realistic and Time-limited goals.

   There is also the need to use the "Art of Questioning" in order to solicit the "rest of the story" of what clients have been able to achieve, to survive, *in spite of* their stressors and life experiences. There is a need to obtain multiple timelines of what they have been through, but also a timeline of what they were able to accomplish *in spite of*—namely, the signs of strengths and evidence of individual, familial, and community-cultural resilience that they possess and can call upon.

I encourage the clinicians I train to emulate that fine inquisitor, Peter Falk playing the character, Detective Columbo. I encourage clinicians to "play dumb," using their befuddlement, confusion, and Socratic questioning style. For some clinicians, of course, "playing dumb" comes naturally. The trick is how to be inquisitive, without giving up your "placebo value."

4. Cognitive-behavioral techniques can be called upon to address the next psychotherapeutic goal of nurturing and teaching direct action and emotionally palliative coping skills. The expert psychotherapist does <u>not</u> merely "train and hope," but builds into treatment the technology and guidelines designed to increase the likelihood of generalization and maintenance of treatment and training effects such as relapse prevention, self-attribution training (client taking credit for change), and putting the client into a consultative mode of teaching others, demonstrating his or her coping skills and soliciting the reasons why engaging in such behavioral acts will help them achieve their treatment goals.

In addition, for those clients with a history of victimization or current risk of revictimization, there is a need for the expert psychotherapist to ensure safety, to help clients avoid revictimization, to allow them to disclose their "story" at their own pace, and assist them to (re)consider the conclusions they draw about themselves, others and the future as a result of such life experiences. It is not that "bad" things have happened, but *what is the story that clients fashion and construct about such events that is critical.* There is a need for individuals to engage in a meaning-making mission. For some clients this may entail some form of spirituality or religious healing activities.

In short, what I am proposing is a Constructive Narrative Perspective (CNP) of psychotherapy that helps clients restory and integrate their traumatic victimization experiences into their autobiographical memories and personal accounts. Recent research highlights the value of such a CNP approach to psychotherapy that can be integrated and blended with the skills training components of cognitive-behavioral interventions. [See the Reference list for some descriptions of this research.]

Int.:   You are suggesting that we are all storytellers and that we can live by the stories we tell.

Dr. M.:   Exactly. This book is filled with psychotherapists sharing their stories. This is exactly what our clients do. My job is to listen attentively, nonjudgmentally, and compassionately to the stories my clients have to tell and collaboratively help them develop more adaptive stories and the accompanying skills to achieve and live their more functional accounts.

Int.:   So, renewal, inspiration, and passion are not only for the readers of this book, but for your clients, as well.

Dr. M.:   I have often asked myself, what contributed to my effectiveness as a psychotherapist? One of the answers I have come up with is that no matter how bad off are my client's presenting problems, psychiatric conditions, or life situation, I refuse, as a psychotherapist, to get depressed. No client leaves my office without my helping him or her to find some "nuggets," or signs of strength and resilience. No matter what the client does, or does not do in psychotherapy, I can help him or her view it as "buying into treatment." I can capitalize on the fact that the client's behavior can be reframed. I believe that my collaborative realistic planfulness, my efforts at joint goal-setting, my meta-communication of hopefulness are some of the key ingredients to successful treatment outcomes. As I say to my clients:

> Let me explain what I do for a living. I work with folks like yourself and try to find out how things are right now in your life and how you would like them to be. How can <u>we</u> work together to help you achieve your goals?
>
> Moreover, I would like us to be informed by what you have tried in the past. What have you tried? What worked as evident by? What difficulties did you have and how did you anticipate and handle these challenges? What were you most satisfied with that we can build upon?
>
> Moreover, if we work together, and I hope we can, how would we know if you were making progress? What would we see changed? What, if anything, would other people notice?
>
> May I ask one last question, if I might? Can you foresee, can you envision, anything that might get in the way of your achieving your treatment goals? How can you learn to anticipate and handle those barriers should they arise?

Int.:   Whenever I have watched you work with a client (on videotapes at conferences) I have always been struck by how present you are and how much you *care* about the person—as well as how thoughtful and constructive the questions are that you ask.

Dr. M.:   Thank you. That's the "glue" I was referring to. The therapeutic alliance is built on a foundation of caring and respect—it's not enough to just go through the motions of asking good questions.

Int.: I also noticed a couple of things about your client message. First, all your questions are "What" and "How" questions and you do not use "Why" questions. Second, I see you bathe your social discourse with a number of "we" statements.

Dr. M.: Yes, both of these strategies are intentional on my part. I do not find "why" questions very productive, while "what" and "how" questions pull for the process of thinking and behavior and accompanying feelings that can be addressed in treatment. The heavy emphasis on "we" statements reinforces the notion of collaboration and strengthens the therapeutic alliance. I am at my psychotherapeutic best when the clients I see are one step ahead of me offering the advice or suggestions I would otherwise offer. Clients are more likely to implement strategies they came up with, and as a result they feel more empowered and more self-efficacious. I guard against becoming a "surrogate frontal lobe" for my clients. "Expert" psychotherapists do not see themselves as infallible experts, but continually ask their clients for feedback and for ways to improve the working psychotherapeutic journey.

Int.: There is one last question that my colleagues and students have. What do you see as the future of psychotherapy in addressing the extensive mental health needs of the general population?

Dr. M.: As Research Director of an institute, this is something to which I have given a lot of consideration. Recently, this issue was also addressed in a thoughtful article by Al Kazdin and Stacey Blasé (2011). They asked how can psychotherapy be rebooted, using computer technology? As I mentioned, I have been consulting for the National Guard and I have recently completed a book entitled *Roadmap to Resilience* (Meichenbaum, 2012), enumerating various ways to bolster resilience in six domains (physical, interpersonal, emotional, cognitive, behavioral, and spiritual). We have been working on ways to put this information online (see www.warfighterdiaries.com), where you can download coping stories by returning service members onto your iPod, iPad, cell phone, and the like. This is a way to take "teaching stories" and turn them into modeling films.

Int: Could you give an example or two of the kinds of stories soldiers (and/or clinicians) might see?

Dr. M.: There are now a number of resources (websites and videos) that use storytelling as a means of helping service members listen to healing accounts of other veterans who have returned from deployment. In each of these narratives, the returning service member describes some "traumatizing" event such as being injured due to an improvised explosive device, descriptions of their accompanying injuries, both physical and psychological. Most importantly, they also continue to relate the "rest of the story," of resilience and personal growth with the help of others. They relate how such events contributed to stronger interpersonal relationships, increased personal strengths, a greater appreciation of life and spiritual renewal. The interested reader can visit the following websites to listen to stories of resilience: www.warfighterdiaries.com,www.MakeTheConnection.net/stories-of-connection, and www.realwarriors.com. They should also view the HBO video *Alive Day Memories*. These are each effective demonstrations of the power of a Constructive Narrative Perspective as a psychotherapeutic tool.

INT: Wow! I can imagine how having these easily available to download on your phone or computer could help someone who was discouraged or despairing.

Dr. M.:   Yes. I am also involved in a number of other computer-based training programs for clients, their family members, and for psychotherapists. Imagine that as a psychotherapist you would be able to access demonstrations of "expert" psychotherapists implementing each of the Core Skills of treatment—short vignettes illustrating ways to build and repair a therapeutic alliance, how to collaboratively establish therapy goals, how to ask useful questions, how to nurture hope, and so on. Moreover, you would be able to submit to the website your ways of implementing that psychotherapeutic skill to be shared with others, as the website goes viral.

Int.:   Are you suggesting that what you learned at your mother's kitchen table could be given away worldwide?

Dr. M.:   I have often wondered what psychotherapy would be like if, instead of B.F. Skinner (1948), my mother had written *Walden 2*.

References

Cronbach, L.J. (1960). *Essentials of Psychological Testing* (2nd ed.) New York: Harper & Row.

Frankl, V. E. (1963). *Man's Search for Meaning: An Introduction to Logotherapy*. New York: Washington Square Press.

Kelly, G.A. (1955). *The Psychology of Personal Constructs*. New York: Norton.

Lambert, M.J. (2010). *Prevention of Treatment Failure: The Use of Measuring, Monitoring, and Feedback in Clinical Practice*. Washington, D.C.: American Psychological Association.

Luborsky, L., Singer, B., & Luborsky, L. (1975). Comparative studies of psychotherapies: Is it true that 'Everyone has won and all must have prizes'? *Archives of General Psychiatry, 32*, 995-1008.

Kazdin, A.E., & Blasé, S.L. (2011). Rebooting psychotherapy research and practice to reduce the burden of mental illness. *Perspectives in Psychological Science, 6*, 21-37.

Meichenbaum, D. (2012). *Roadmap to Resilience*. Clearwater, FL: Institute Press.

Skinner, B.F. (1948). *Walden 2*. Indianapolis, IN: Hackett Publishing Company.

Smith, D. (1982). Trends in counselling and psychotherapy. *American Psychologist, 37*(7), 802- 809.

Wampold, B.F., Modin, G.W., Moody, M., Stah, F., Benson, K., & Ahn, H. (1997). A meta-analysis of outcome studies comparing bona fide psychotherapies: Empirically, "all must have prizes." *Psychological Bulletin, 122*, 203-215.

Wampold, B.E., Imel, Z.E., Laska, K.M., & Benish, S. (2010). Determining what works in the treatment of PTSD. *Clinical Psychology Review, 30*, 923-933.

22

THE POETICS OF PRACTICE

Becoming "Well Versed" in Loss and Grief

Robert A. Neimeyer

Few psychotherapists choose to devote a career to working with loss and grief simply out of curiosity. Typically, the wellsprings of engagement with such existential issues as death, impermanence and the quest for meaning in their wake run deep, usually deeper than our conscious narratives. Such was the case, at least, for me. When my father opted to end the growing darkness occasioned by his encroaching blindness and financial ruin 10 days before my 12th birthday, the life he ended ushered my mother, brother, sister, and me into another life entirely, one characterized by little of the innocence, predictability, and security that we had long taken for granted (Neimeyer, 2011). Ironically, it also launched me into an experience that made more intelligible the tragedy and transcendence of those people who would later become my clients, whose worlds were often shattered by similar loss. Though I scarcely recognized it at the time, my pursuit of a career in psychotherapy in general and grief therapy in particular represented my intuitive effort to step into the alien terrain into which I was introduced by loss, to map its contours, and if I could, to help survivors—myself included—stretch the boundaries of lives that seemed foreclosed in a single fateful moment by the traumatic loss of another (Neimeyer, 2009).

This chapter offers two snapshots of the resulting journey, conveyed conventionally in brief clinical vignettes, and unconventionally in my poetic response to them. In each instance I will try to sketch some of the terrain my client and I negotiated together, and then share a poem that arose for me in the midst of the work that attempts to give voice and verse to a poignant moment of meeting. Of course, I recognize that poetry, perhaps as much as any literary or artistic medium, speaks uncertainly across the divide of different aesthetic preferences, and that figurative depiction of our clients' realities is uncommon in clinical discourse. But this is an uncommon book, and in inviting soundings from the hearts of therapists who love their practice, editor Michael Hoyt challenged each of us to go beyond convention to conviction and candor about how we are moved by the work we do. The poems and meditations that follow are my response to this invitation.

Case 1: The Presence of Absence

When Cara lost the infant daughter she had carried inside her for seven hopeful months, she was disconsolate. A loving mother of three other children, she had prepared them for the baby's arrival, and her youngest daughters, Alexis and Alia, in particular, looked forward to becoming "big sisters," just as her husband Alfonso eagerly anticipated an expanded fatherhood. When Cara awakened in panic one morning to the concerning quiescence of the previously active baby in her womb, and when the child's death was confirmed in medical examination, she was catapulted into her worst nightmare, just as her family began to deal with the apparent double loss of the child to death and her mother to an isolating grief in its aftermath. Together, Cara and Alfonso decided to name their stillborn daughter Spirit, because, as he said, that was how she came to them, as a spiritual being, rather than a physically living child. Ironically, Cara returned from the memorial service to a house filled not only with funeral bouquets but also to wilting Mother's Day flowers, given to her the day before she had entered the hospital. Broken but proud, Cara hid her tears behind the closed door of her bedroom, the first day of an apparently endless series of days that she would spend there to buffer her contact with a world that had wounded her deeply.

At the point she came to see me some months later, Cara had quit her work, discontinued her schooling, and beyond mandatory functioning in the home, cut off substantially from both friends and family. Seemingly every restaurant was filled with thriving babies, and even the eyes of the babies she saw in framed photographs on visits to her ob/gyn for post-partum care seemed to accuse her of having done something wrong to lead to the death, prompting her to discontinue even this follow-up care. Greatly compounding her suffering were the pregnancy of her best friend, due to deliver within a few weeks of our initial visit, and much more problematically, the parallel pregnancy of Cara's oldest daughter, Jasmine, just 16, unmarried, and wholly unready for motherhood. Being unaware that her daughter was even sexually active, it was literally at Spirit's funeral that Cara observed that Jasmine was beginning to "show," and soon experienced a grief alloyed with anger, guilt and envy, all of which prompted her to keep contact with the girl to a bare minimum, despite Jasmine's clear need for a mother at an anxious and life-changing time. It was in the crucible of this complicated grief that Cara was referred to me for a planned six-session therapy across a two-month period, every session of which was captured on video, with accompanying commentary (Neimeyer, 2008).

Returning from my first session with Cara, which was held in a distant city, I found myself stirred by her suffering, and in need of time to process the anguishing story she had shared, with all its hurtful reminders of her bereavement during her waking hours, and the symbolic reenactment of the loss in her dreams as she slept. Most of all I was struck by her need to make sense of the seemingly senseless death of her daughter and to form a continuing bond with her, the twin quest for meaning and attachment at the heart of grief (Neimeyer, Baldwin, & Gillies, 2006; Neimeyer & Sands, 2011). I therefore sat in my hotel room, conjured a state of mindfulness in which the words could come, and penned the following poem, titled in honor of Cara's child (Neimeyer, 2009b):

Spirit[1]
She was seven months in you
wrapped snug in your house of flesh
when she came to rest,
turned her face to the dark wall.
Beyond your high hard hope
you knew in your heart that she was gone,
this sliding shift of gravity
in your belly, in your bed.

You named her Spirit
because this is how she came to you—
there and not there,
a doll baby with eyes
painted shut. Instinctively,
your hands reach out,
grasp at air,
try to pull the light toward you,
into you, disperse the darkness.
A silent cipher, no one
can know what you have lost.

Now she stares at you
with the indifference of the angels
through the paper eyes, smiles
of baby pictures in your obstetrician's office,
the glazed gaze of newborns nursing
in restaurants at their mothers' breasts.
One after another, she tries on lives,
in the frames, in the arms of strangers.

---

1   From R.A. Neimeyer (2009), *The Art of Longing.* Charleston, SC: BookSurge, pages 24–25.
    © R.A. Neimeyer, 2009. Used with permission.

She leaves each like a pair
of discarded shoes.

And so you seek her
in the misty maze to which she has retreated,
the shadow flash of dreams,
the sudden sightings of a body,
small and dark as a polished stone,
and as cold.
Left still on the couch,
found wrapped in a box,
she practices dying until it is perfected,
until you find a new way

of holding on.

In the remaining five sessions of therapy, in the second month of which Jasmine gave birth to Cara's granddaughter, we stood close to the very present absence or void Cara felt within her and around her, seeking practical and spiritual reorientation in a life transformed by loss. In one particularly moving session we reviewed the photographs taken of the birth and funeral by Cara's sister—the first time that she had done so—trusting me to examine and describe each to prepare her for the image that was to follow. Layer after layer, we drew closer to the core of the painful question of why her child was "taken," an urgent issue brought into sharp focus by the mysterious image of a "woman" in her four-month ultrasound of her living baby, the apparent harbinger of her daughter's looming death. Grappling with the disturbing spiritual implications of this "thing," we sharpened the questions in a narrative assignment without offering saccharine answers. What emerged from our work and the family conversations it sparked was ultimately a more expansive, less "Cara-centric" view of the universe, in which she was able to recover trust in a beneficent cosmos, even as she also came to more intimately know the suffering of other bereaved women who shared an analogous loss. As therapy concluded, Cara had reentered school, begun once more to mother Jasmine and hold her grandchild in loving arms, and experience a return of occasional joy, hope and appreciation for the life she had and again began to value. A qualitative research study of the "innovative moments" of reflection, action and reconceptualization that made this possible can be found elsewhere (Alves, Mendes, Gonçalves, & Neimeyer, 2011).

What did my encounter with Cara across our six sessions of work teach me? In a phrase, a great deal. At one level it reminded me of the core lessons of loss: life is ephemeral, anticipation is uncertain, and grief may come calling at any point. But it also affirmed the reality of resistance, the durability of love beyond death, and the power of compassionate companionship as we traverse a dark terrain. As we completed our work, I was left in awe of this brave woman who somehow trusted me, across the divides of race and gender, to accompany her in one of the most intimate passages of her life. And with a sense of shared sacred space constructed in our secular encounter, I felt once again the grace, the gift, of being a therapist.

Case 2: Dialogue with a Dead Daughter

The cold March morning brought chilling news from a distant state: Tricia and Scott's 19-year-old daughter, Christine, was found dead by overdose after a turbulent few years marked by treatment-unresponsive depression and previous attempts to end her life. Yet even with this dark drum roll, the announcement of her death was shattering, leaving the couple blindsided by its seeming impossibility. Always before, they would somehow coach her through the crisis; always before, things would improve, if only for a time. Now there would be no more opportunities and no hope: only burning questions about why she didn't call, and the indelible guilt left behind.

By the time they consulted me some months later, Tricia was drowning in despair, and Scott felt helpless to reach her. As religious people, both struggled to understand the will of a God who could create a child who once seemed so perfect that she was the envy of her teachers, who somehow went "so wrong" during adolescence. Nearly as unsettling as the crisis of faith engendered by Christine's death was the way the world moved blindly forward: the birds would keep singing, people would get in their cars and go to work, all oblivious to the hole in the universe left by their daughter's departure. As Scott worked to reestablish some sense of order and control in a life turned upside down, Tricia retreated into a world of private pain and self-soothing, leaving both partners wondering whether their marriage would survive. It was at this point of painful standoff that I penned the poem *Survivors* to capture their emotional position as we began our work together (Neimeyer, 2009b).

> **Survivors**[2]
> He has stopped trying
> to grasp her remoteness
> that he mistakes for calm,
> this cooling that accompanies
> the wintering of her grief.
>
> Since their daughter's explosive
> departure, its echo
> like a slammed door,
> she has pulled in, and in,
> away from the pain,

---

2 From R.A. Neimeyer (2009), *The Art of Longing*. Charleston, SC: BookSurge, pages 22–23. © R.A. Neimeyer, 2009. Used with permission.

away from him.
What he cannot know is how
she slips inside the sleeve
of her music, the lyrics
of angels
              touch
                     return,
draws down into the bubble
of her hope.

Alone in her car,
the music builds a room
around her, around the room
a house through which
she strolls.
It is in the nursery
that she feels the peace,
rocks her child, rocks herself,
restores the bond.

Too soon, the car turns itself
into her drive, slides
into the vault of garage.
Her hand finds the latch,
pulls her out. She takes the steps
like a condemned man.

The forced hello fades,
yields to the distance.
She glances up at him,
sees the eyes,
the terrible mirrors,

and turns again to stone.

As we sought ways together to clarify and address their grief as well as miti-
gate it, we approached the burning question mark at the heart of most suicides,
the mystery of why a loved one chooses to die rather than live, which was
experienced especially acutely by Tricia, for whom it echoed in the hollow of
her life on a "24/7" basis. When paired with the seemingly impossible goal of
restoring an attachment bond with their dead daughter, this struggle for meaning at spiritual, psychological and relational levels was so preoccupying that it
eclipsed even memories of Christine's life. As Tricia tellingly noted in an early
session, "All I can remember is the bookends of her life. I remember her birth
and her death, but I can't recall a single image of her as a little girl or a growing

teenager." The heavy shadow of her Christine's suicide seemed to threaten all that remained of her daughter's existence, effacing even her memory.

A turning point in our work came when we stood at the intersection of the quest for meaning and a restored bond with Christine, and invited Tricia, in Scott's silent and supportive presence, to address the questions burning in her heart directly to her daughter, projected imaginally into an empty chair placed before her. As I coached her toward honest and immediate dialogue, Tricia sobbed out the questions proliferating in her heart: *"Why did you do this? Why didn't you call me? Why didn't you reach out? Why, why, why?"* Accepting my suggestion to lend her daughter her own voice in the facing seat, Tricia quickly assumed a younger tone of voice and expression, and replied, *"Mom, this is so not about you."* She went on to invoke a stunning metaphor: when she was a child, Tricia had been her sun, and Christine revolved around her. But as she grew toward adulthood, Tricia was no longer her sun, but rather her moon, orbiting around her. Completing the interaction in a few conversational turns, Tricia spontaneously processed its implications, including the possibility that her daughter had fallen into the thrall of a darker star, and that she was not as a mother directly responsible for her death. In the weeks that followed, Tricia's conversations with Christine continued in her head in the kitchen, the shower, when walking, when doing housework. And in each case, she sensed she could hear and see Christine's loving and reassuring response to the repeated or residual questions, until the unburdening answers were consolidated at a level that gave her peace. Scott soon reported that it was as if he got his wife back, and along with that shift an opportunity to walk together a difficult road that each previously had been walking alone. A fuller telling of this clinical vignette can be found elsewhere, along with a usefully integrative Tripartite Model of Suicide Bereavement that can organize psychotherapeutic work with survivors (Sands, Jordan, & Neimeyer, 2010).

What was the "take-home message" of my six-month therapy with Tricia and Scott? Again, as with Cara, the learning was multifaceted: I was brought into vivid awareness of the intricate inter-braiding of our lives with those we love, and particularly with those to whom we owe a duty of care; the power of experiential work in session to foster changes that could then be harvested and integrated in subsequent processing (Neimeyer, 2009a); and the significance of symptoms, like grief, to achieve essential, if initially unconscious ends, such as maintaining loyalty to the deceased as the only perceived alternative to forgetting. I was also impressed once again with the human capacity to construct in imagination what no therapist can provide, but only guide—in this case a healing dialogue with a daughter made more urgent, but apparently impossible, by the intervention of her death. In the end I was reminded of the tragedy that is human life, but also of the transcendence of which people are capable.

Coda

In 35 years of practicing the art form that is psychotherapy, inspired but never directed by the evolving scientific literature (Neimeyer, Harris, Winokuer, & Thornton, 2011), I am regularly struck by the capacity of my clients to confront the abyss that opens in the wake of losses of many kinds, and to find a way to bridge the chasm between what was and what will be in ways that cannot be specified in any psychotherapy manual. In this, I view myself as leading from one step behind, following closely the subtle clues in the therapy process—verbal, co-verbal, non-verbal—that inform us precisely about what a given client needs and is capable of in any given moment. My goal, when I am centered and receptive, is to discern the place where pain meets readiness, that spacious moment where a next step can be discovered and taken in the safe container of our relationship. Like free verse poets improvising jointly on a theme, we find a way forward, often with astonishing efficiency, from a reading that feels defeated, discordant or deafening to one that is clear, coherent and creative. To be a frequent, if not inevitable, party to such progress continues to astound me, and validates weekly my once naïve but hopeful anticipation that I would find meaning in this astonishing career of psychotherapy.

References

Alves, D., Mendes, I., Gonçalves, M., & Neimeyer, R. A. (2011). Innovative moments in grief therapy: Reconstructing meaning following perinatal death. *Death Studies, in press.*

Neimeyer, R.A. (2008). *Constructivist Psychotherapy Over Time* [DVD]. Washington, D.C.: American Psychological Association.

Neimeyer, R.A. (2009). Constructions of death and loss: A personal and professional evolution. In R. J. Butler (Ed.), *On Reflection: Emphasizing the Personal in Personal Construct Psychology* (pp. 291–317). London: Wiley.

Neimeyer, R.A. (2009a). *Constructivist Psychotherapy.* London: Routledge.

Neimeyer, R.A. (2009b). *The Art of Longing.* Charleston, SC: BookSurge.

Neimeyer, R. A. (2011). Suicide: A personal construction. In M. Pompili (Ed.), *Suicide in the Words of Suicidologists.* Hauppage, NY: Nova Science Publishers.

Neimeyer, R.A., Baldwin, S.A., & Gillies, J. (2006). Continuing bonds and reconstructing meaning: Mitigating complications in bereavement. *Death Studies, 30,* 715–738.

Neimeyer, R.A., Harris, D., Winokuer, H., & Thornton, G. (Eds.). (2011). *Grief and Bereavement in Contemporary Society: Bridging Research and Practice.* New York: Routledge.

Neimeyer, R.A., & Sands, D.C. (2011). Meaning reconstruction in bereavement: From principles to practice. In R.A. Neimeyer, H. Winokuer, D. Harris, & G. Thornton (Eds.), *Grief and Bereavement in Contemporary Society: Bridging Research and Practice* (pp. 9–22). New York: Routledge.

Sands, D.C., Jordan, J.R., & Neimeyer, R.A. (2010). The meanings of suicide: A narrative approach to healing. In J. R. Jordan & J. L. McIntosh (Eds.), *Grief After Suicide* (pp. 249–282). New York: Routledge.

23

NATURAL COMPASSION[1]

Ram Dass and Elizabeth "Shakti" Gawain

I was in about forty feet of water, alone. I knew I should not have gone alone, but I was very competent and just took a chance. There was not much current, and the water was so warm and clear and enticing. But when I got a cramp, I realized at once how foolish I was. I was not very alarmed, but I was completely doubled up with stomach cramp. I tried to remove my weight belt, but I was so doubled up I could not get to the catch. I was sinking and began to feel more frightened, unable to move. I could see my watch and knew that there was only a little more time on the tank before I would be finished with breathing! I tried to massage my abdomen. I wasn't wearing a wet suit, but couldn't straighten out and couldn't get to the cramped muscles with my hands.

I thought, "I can't go like this! I have things to do!" I just couldn't die anonymously this way, with no one to even know what happened to me. I called out in my mind, "Somebody, something, help me!"

I was not prepared for what happened. Suddenly I felt a prodding from behind me under the armpit. I thought, "Oh no, sharks!" I felt real terror and despair. But my arm was being lifted forcibly. Around into my field of vision came an eye—the most marvelous eye I could ever imagine. I swear it was smiling. It was the eye of a big dolphin. Looking into that eye, I knew I was safe.

It moved farther forward, nudging under, and hooked its dorsal fin under my armpit with my arm over its back. I relaxed, hugged it, flooded with relief. I felt that the animal

1   Excerpted from *How Can I Help?* By Ram Dass and Paul Gorman, copyright © 1985 by Ram Dass and Paul Gorman. Used by permission of Alfred A. Knopf, a division of Random House, Inc. Dolphin story from Elizabeth Gawain (1981), *The Dolphin's Gift* (pp. 233-234). Mill Valley, CA: Whatever Publishing. © 1981 Elizabeth Gawain. Used with permission.

was conveying security to me, that it was healing me as well as lifting me toward the surface. My stomach cramp went away as we ascended, and I relaxed with security, but I felt very strongly that it healed me too.

At the surface, it drew me all the way in to shore. It took me into water so shallow I had began to be concerned for it, that it would be beached, and I pushed it back a little deeper, where it waited, watching me, I guess to see if I was all right.

It felt like another lifetime. When I took off the weight belt and oxygen, I just took everything off and went naked back into the ocean to the dolphin. I felt so light and free and alive, and just wanted to play in the sun and the water, in all that freedom. The dolphin took me back out and played around in the water with me. I noticed that there were a lot of dolphins there, farther out.

After a while it brought me back to shore. I was very tired then, almost collapsing, and he made sure I was safe in the shallowest water. Then he turned sideways with one eye looking into mine. We stayed that way for what seemed like a very long time, timeless I guess, in a trance almost, with personal thoughts of the past going through my mind. Then he made just one sound and went out to join the others, and all of them left.

At times, helping happens simply in the way of things. It's not something we really think about, merely the instinctive response of an open heart. Caring is a reflex. Someone slips, your arm goes out. A car is in a ditch, you join the others and push. A colleague at work has the blues, you let her know you care. It all seems natural and appropriate. You live, you help.

When we join together in this spirit, action comes more effortlessly, and everybody ends up nourished. Girding against the flood … setting up a community meeting … preparing a funeral...people seem to know their part. We sense what's called for, or if we don't, and feel momentarily awkward, someone comes quickly with an idea, and it's just right, and we're grateful. We babysit the kids while the parents move possessions to homes farther from the rising river … we bring a comfortable chair for an older person who might attend the meeting … we call the rabbi with a favorite psalm of the one who just died. Needs are anticipated, and glances of appreciation among us are enough to confirm that it's all going well.

We take pleasure not only in what we did but in the way we did it. On the one hand, the effort was so natural it might seem pointless or self-conscious to make something of it. It was what it was. Yet if we stop to consider why it all felt so good, we sense that some deeper process was at work. Expressing our innate generosity, we experience our "kin"-ship, our "kind"-ness. It was "Us." In service, we taste unity [...]

Caring for one another, we sometimes glimpse an essential quality of our being. We may be sitting alone, lost in self-doubt or self-pity, when the phone rings with a call from a friend who's *really* depressed. Instinctively, we come out of ourselves, just to be there with her and say a few reassuring words. When we're done, and a little comfort's been shared, we put down the phone and feel a little more at home with ourselves. We're reminded of who we really are and what we have to offer one another.

When the experience of helping seems so natural, it's not surprising we find ourselves wishing or wondering if things could be like that more or even most of the time.

24

THE TAO OF A WOMAN

Michele Ritterman

I was a psychology Ph.D. intern at the Philadelphia Child Guidance Clinic in the early 1970s, studying with Salvador Minuchin, Jay Haley, and Braulio Montalvo. I was trained in structural family therapy (Minuchin, 1974; Minuchin, Roseman & Baker, 1978), intervening from the "outside," and because of Jay Haley, I was introduced to the broad concepts of the "ecology of mind" (Bateson, 1972), both models that acknowledged that the family gets under the skin of the patient. I had been sneaking in trance inductions in my structural and strategic family therapy sessions, drawing upon case studies from Haley's (1967) collection of Erickson's papers, *Advanced Techniques of Hypnosis and Therapy*, like the sorcerer's apprentice, but without any map to integrate the unconscious and the systemic. Then one day—which changed my life—my mentor Sal called me in to a private showing of a videotape a colleague and friend of mine, Herb Lustig, M.D., had just produced, one of the first available studio produced demonstrations of Milton Erickson's current work (Erickson & Lustig, 1975/2000).

It was a tape of Erickson working with Monde, a young woman who suffered anxiety when she walked into a room filled with people. Today, in a 10-minute appointment with a psychiatrist, Monde would be diagnosed with Social Anxiety Disorder and prescribed Paxil. What I saw then on that tape was *how* Erickson actually got permission to enter into Monde's mind. Once there, he did what I would eventually call "Stopping the Clock" and "Taking the Vertical Plunge" (Ritterman, 1995). He entered specifically into *the moment before* Monde would enter a group. Inside the treasure trove of her mind, he found a vivid recollection of a beating with a hair brush by her mother when she was a little girl. So he was now privy to the specific memories and emotions that Monde brought to her pre-group-entry sense of self, the terrible feelings of humiliation and shame that she was projecting on to the group she had not yet encountered.

In the video Erickson methodically and respectfully tracked her observable physiological responses—including changes in rate of respiration, tension in the face and body, changes in body temperature as Monde visibly re-experienced her spanking again and again. Each time, the spanking actually hurt—she winced and gasped and even got angry with Erickson for letting her go there. Then he taught Monde to work her own mind—to use her very own trove of experiences again, but now to locate a memory in which she felt powerful. She recalled playing with abandon, chasing ducks. He trained her to switch from the humiliated child to the carefree child inside of her mind, *within the pre-group-entry moment*, using subjective time to do so, and to do all this within the clock time that it took her to blink. She was trained to use her own eye-blink to automatically shift to the right mental state.

It was then and is now the best piece of clinical work I've ever seen. Many years later it is a centerpiece in my development: use the therapeutic relationship purposefully to help a person enter into a state of subjective time and add on another piece of track of natural experience that is helpful to them in changing their existing sequence of experiences that lead them off track. This use of trance to shift the inner conditions for a person to attain a proper stance has become almost four decades later for me, in this nanosecond era in which we live, a cardinal facet of psychotherapy.

After Sal and I finished watching Herb Lustig's video of Monde, I vividly recall Sal saying in his Argentinian-Yiddish accent to Herb: "She was *heepnotized* by the video!" It was true. I needed to learn more! How did what I had just seen fit with all the family systems learnings I had? My two publications in the field prior to and during internship very much addressed the idea of synthesizing psychological models. I needed to integrate all that I had learned from systems thinking and from hypnosis into a unitary theory of consciousness and human connection … but how?

My other mentor, Jay, suggested I go visit Erickson, "bringing hugs and kisses from Jay." I approached Harry Aponte, the Director of the Clinic, and asked if I could use my educational travel stipend to visit Erickson in Arizona, rather than spending the money to attend the annual convention of the American Psychological Association. Bless him forever, he said: "Yes."

After my first visit, Milton asked for his gift from Jay. I had no idea what he meant. But then, I laughed and gave him a hug and a kiss on the cheek and that began a warm student-mentor relationship that lasted until his death six years later. After I finished in Philadelphia and moved to Seattle (and then on to Oakland and Berkeley, California), I continued to go to Phoenix a couple of times a year, until Erickson passed away in 1980. Sometimes I stayed at his office cottage. He and his wife, Betty, became godparents to my two children, Miranda and Judah. They never missed a birthday, and we had a strong correspondence between visits. When Miranda was born, I had a C-section. Milton wrote: "Not from under the Verandah came Miranda, but from the Belly of

Shellie." A gift I'd made for him showing a favorite puzzle of his hung in his bedroom beside a copy of Miranda's birth certificate even many years after he'd died. (I'll have more to say on that later in this chapter.)

During one visit I told Erickson about my revelation that *the individual's symptom was a trance state* produced by the multi-voiced and multi-layered hypnosis of context. I had been watching a family therapy videotape of my work as an intern so that I could use it to teach in Seattle. At first, I was upset to see that in the session the young man who was the identified patient came in symptom-free and within 10 minutes manifested all his symptoms. I was in trouble. Things got worse with me sitting there! I'd taken too long to intervene … But then I realized: "That's it! That's what happens!" I watched to study how this family had specifically suggested his symptoms of chest pain and difficulty thinking from one thought to the next. And before it was even published, this family had naturally employed the Erickson and Rossi (1976, 1979) induction paradigm, but instead of there being one hypnotist, all the family members induced the symptom trance through sequence and through structural messaging. I realized that there was something much, much more important than my ego going on here, and anyway, I did eventually wake up from the family trance and help the young man and his family—so I did have my teaching tape after all. When I woke up, I intervened into the sequence of family hypnotic steps in such a way that synchronously, each member shifted to a slightly new piece of mental track and a new liberating pattern was available to them that did not trigger the young man's vulnerabilities. (See Ritterman, 2005a, pp. 117–142 for the transcript of this family induction.)

It was then that I went to Milton as soon as possible with my revelation: "Milton, family and society are the 24/7 ongoing daily life hypnotists and symptoms are just suggested trance states. We need to track the inductions for the symptoms trance and counter them with our systemic hypnosis." He gazed at me and said: *"If I were you, I'd develop that idea."*

So I've spent the rest of my life doing just that.

I began this understanding in the late 1970s, when I was about 27 years old, and developed it into hypnotic family therapy and an in-depth analysis of many forms of collective reverie. I pioneered the concept of group inductions, and performed three of them to large audiences at Erickson Congresses: to counter the hate movements, to breathe in what is useful to you in the world and let the rest go, and to deal with the problem of evil without becoming tainted. I also created the notion of *Shared Couples Trances* and *Couples Separate Track Trances* (Ritterman, 2005b). All of these developments are rooted in my evolving grasp of the spells we cast upon one another through the structures and systems we are part of—the voodoo of daily life (see Cannon, 1957).

After writing *Using Hypnosis in Family Therapy*, the first systematic integration of hypnosis and family therapy (Ritterman, 1983/2005a, 1985), I also came to recognize that governments can use collective (social/cultural) trances to subjugate their population. I decided to research how the state suggests health or illness for its citizens. Like Franz Fanon (1961) before me, I studied the role of torture in the *willful social induction* of mental derangement (Ritterman, 1987). My political commitments led me to Chile, where I worked with victims of torture and with those who sought to help heal them, experiences I describe in my book *Hope Under Siege: Terror and Family Support in Chile* (Ritterman, 1991). I was honored that Isabel Allende provided the Foreword to the book. The book ends with this conclusion (p. 237): *"Who loves and is loved deeply is hard to be robbed of dignity."*

Talk about inspiration: Jose Quiroga, M.D., had been the cardiologist of the democratically elected president, Salvador Allende, and had been with Allende in the palace in Chile as the planes of Pinochet took over and his friend, colleague, and mentor ended his own life rather than be taken prisoner. Dr. Quiroga was an exiled cardiologist-researcher in Los Angeles when I met him. Simply because *no one else* was doing it, he treated torture survivors at night every week-night for free in a clinic he created that exists to this day 40 years later. I said to him, "These clients must adore you." He said that in all the years, not one of them had ever thanked him ... except one: "But that one thanked me for all the rest." *That* is inspiring to me!

To tell you about how I came up with the idea of group inductions, mass collective meditations for the good of humanity, I remember wondering what my style of hypnosis would be. My teacher, Erickson, was a storyteller, but I am a poet. Back in the United States, at the Erickson Congress on Hypnosis and Psychotherapy, held in Phoenix in 1992, instead of telling metaphorical stories, I presented "A Five-Part Poetic Induction in Favor of Human Decency (Countering the Hate Movements)." This was the first large group induction done at an Ericksonian Congress. Because I am a human-rights activist, Erickson had spoken with me in my language, if you will, but about his views of political rights and responsibilities. So I was aware of some of his values and I began my group induction, by quoting from an article that Erickson had written:

> Throughout the ages people have tried to believe that normal psychological behavior includes only that which is good at the social level.... At times, man's inhumanity to man is given some euphemistic label, but no effort is made to investigate scientifically the extremes to which the normal, the good, the average, or the intellectual person or group will go if given the opportunity: consider the Spanish Inquisition, the Salem witch trials, or the introduction of slavery into a country dedicated to the right of everyone to equality and freedom.... How did it happen that noble purposes of the Pilgrims led to the position that "The only good Indian is a dead Indian"? (1968, pp. 277–278)

I went on, blending prose and poetry (mine and others'), to discuss hate movements, the collective mind and synchronous musings, social suggestions, the need for the witness to look away for the abuser and hatemonger to do their dirty work, the need for promoting human decency, and ways we can celebrate our senses and our constructive strengths. I finished my talk saying (Ritterman, 1994, pp. 480–481, emphases in original):

I ask the most important thing of you
you there listening to my voice today
enjoying as much as I hope
and more than I can know
all your faculties and senses,
that you REMEMBER *me when you are packing your suitcase*
as you put the clothes you brought back into the suitcase,
that you put your own ideas of beauty
into the folds,
that you fill the sensuous corners with humor,
and your shoes
with an expanding compassion
to lengthened your gait.
When you return home and are unpacking,
won't you remember me,
my message to you?
And when you wake up
the next morning,
will you not allow your eyes and ears
to fill with beauty
so that you will have,
let's say in five years, little room for hate,
in a decade, no time or space to waste on hate.
When we talk about the heart of Erickson,
is not the bottom line
that we *have the courage*
to stand up
for the best that human nature is capable of,
whether or not we see that best around us.
[…]
For those of you
who like to travel light,
five words: (I hold up my hand)
Hate harms.
Caring can repair.[1]

---

1   Excerpted from M. Ritterman (1994). A five-part poetic induction in favor of human decency (countering the hate movements). In J.K. Zeig (Ed.), *Ericksonian Methods: The Essence of the Story* (pp. 465–481). New York: Brunner/Mazel. Copyright © Brunner/Mazel Publishrs, 1994. Used with permission.

More Learnings from Erickson and My Idea of the "Slo-Mo" Effect in Therapy

Erickson taught me that in therapy we create the circumstances under which a client can respond spontaneously and make the smallest possible change, positive or negative, and that heartened by the possibility of change he or she will go on to make other changes. When therapists think of change, we may think of actions that are too big, like changing a personality or life philosophy or style of interaction. I once asked Erickson: "Why do you get people to levitate a finger?" (He would sometimes make suggestions for automatic responses to communicate with the hypnotist without speaking, saying for example, "You have expressive hands and your right index finger is your 'Yes' finger and your left is your 'No' Finger.") He answered my question: "If someone doesn't receive a suggestion to lift a finger, do you really think you can effectively make a suggestion that will enable him to make change in his life?"

Years later, in my book *The Tao of a Woman* (Ritterman, 2009, pp. 130–131), I wrote:

A Daily Practice[2]
When I was a girl, while I waited for
a train, my gaze fixed upon the place
where a set of railroad ties diverged
from the other tracks. A kindly
coachman, observing me, approached
where I stood to tell me that if you
followed the old track, it went on into
our town. But if the train turned off
from the roadbed onto this new track,
it led to another town, and eventually
another country, far away.
How marvelous that such a tiny change
in angle, added right on to the old
track, could carry us to a brand new
place! How I longed to go there!
Sometimes we think that a musician or
a yogini "practice". But isn't the point
of any practice to help us live better?
Why not create your own emotional
way, tailor a routine to suit your own
particular needs? As the pianist plays

---

2   From M. Ritterman (2009). *The Tao of a Woman*. Berkeley, CA: Skipping Stones, pp. 130–131.
    © Michele Ritterman, 2009. Used with permission.

scales and the yogini greets the day
with a sun salutation, you can develop
a sequence that strengthens you, day
by day.
Thanks to your simple personal practice,
little by little, you will add on new pieces
of mental track that will help you to
move from the small town of your big
dreams to their realization in the world.

Erickson co-wrote a book, *Time Distortion in Hypnosis: An Experimental and Clinical Investigation* (Cooper & Erickson, 1959) on clock versus subjective time. He really understood the microcosms of the mind. He had his finger on the pulse of how people have control over themselves and how they lose control over themselves. It happens in a heartbeat. It happens in the blink of an eye. In this sense, his appreciation for the role time would ultimately play in our lives—now critical to good therapeutic intervention, which needs to help people make quick and profound emotional and behavioral shifts while the force of time speeds on around them—was ahead of his time.

In Puebla, Mexico, I recently (November, 2011) worked therapeutically, speaking in Spanish, with a woman who had only a week before experienced a bus hijacking. My years of experience working with torture and trauma before the diagnosis of PTSD had been created taught me that the closer in time the treatment to the traumatic assault, usually the more effective. She had already talked to many friends about it, but no one had stopped the clock, helped her enter into what I now call "*Slo-Mo*," and found out *what bothered her?* What bothered her was not that the driver could have been in on it, not that a gun was held to her neck, not that they stole her cell phone. She had digested and eliminated those poisons. What bothered *her* was that she heard an older woman behind her on the bus cry and she couldn't help her because she had to sit statue-still with her head down. She knew that there were two children up front and she feared that they would cry out and get killed. As soon as the hijackers left the bus with the passengers' money and cell phones, she was the person who took charge of the situation and got everyone calmed down. The undigested part of the trauma, obtained only *by my withholding the idea* that I understood or could guess what bothered *her,* and by *stopping the clock to enter into her meticulous recounting* of the micro-moments of the event, revealed that this woman felt bad that she couldn't be who she is, during the assault. In half an hour of talking with me, she was a bit improved and less depersonalized. As she finally cried with release, she told me, "You came inside. You got it. You helped me get to the real injury underneath the obvious." I also read her a poem from *The Tao of a Woman* (2009, p. 157; translated beautifully into Spanish by Leandro Wolfson in *El Tao de Una Mujer*):

My Teacher's Last Gift[3]

My teacher received a visit
from a very old Japanese man.

The visitor told my teacher that he saw his life
as he stood on the top of a mountain
looking down over the climb that he had taken.

The jagged rocks and sharp weeds
that cut him along the ascent
had become overgrown with moss
and wildflowers.

Therapy is like time-lapse photography—it can be like watching a flower open. There is beauty unfolding every day in your office. I urge therapists to slow down their observations enough to see these magnificent openings and unfoldings. It is a great inspiration to behold!

Another piece of my inspiration comes from helping therapists see alternatives to psychopharmacology that prevent people from entering into those desperate moments in which they reach for the quick fix instead of developing a new skill. Again, as an intern at Philadelphia Child Guidance clinic, I was also permitted to carry out my doctoral dissertation research with the clinical population there (Ritterman, 1978). There was a new medication out called Ritalin, and I was doing a huge four-year NIMH-funded study comparing the use of Ritalin versus family therapy and placebo with a newly created diagnostic category: hyperactive boys. What I learned from my study was that (a) families needed to put their child in a different trance if they were jumpy, and (b) the jumpy boys needed to learn to concentrate. There was no substitute for that. Many of the boys in other studies who were drugged ("pills, not skills") became delinquents. There may be a neurological substrate for some, but a lot of what was then called "Minimal Brain Damage" (MBD) and is now called "ADHD" is really the failure to engage the attention of children.

As I described earlier, I put together the family work Haley and Minuchin had taught me about how to carefully track and observe sequences and patterns of interaction with Erickson's demonstrations of subjective time, and I realized that as people interact with each other they go in and out of subjective time. And that in a state of subjective time, or slow-mo, people are more open-minded about new ideas. So I developed a model of therapeutic observation and intervention that I feel offers some antidote to the notion that the causes of human suffering are underlying biochemical imperfections that need a pill to fix them. Medicate the greedy, the violent, the sadistic … maybe … but not those who

---

3   From M. Ritterman (2009, p. 157). © Michele Ritterman, 2009. Used with permission.

suffer powerlessness and loss of self-control because they are oppressed and marginalized and driven to such desperation that only a pill seems the answer. First and foremost, help people get unstuck from the contexts that demean them, steal their jobs, take their houses, shut down their schools. Diagnoses in so many cases end up becoming a means to objectify and distance ourselves from the underlying social unfairness that suggests the derangement of its victims.

My life work is about how to help people wake up from these bad trances, and enter into alternative states of consciousness. Be it a person from New Orleans after Katrina, a couple dealing with infidelity, a woman whose husband turns her off, or a man who panics when he dances—the underlying approach can be the same. This realization, *the need to be here now*, led me to write a book of poetic meditations, *The Tao of a Woman: 100 Ways to Turn* (Ritterman, 2009).

Virginia Satir (1983, 1988), the mother of family therapy, used to say: "What's the problem with the problem?" Hypnotic phenomena can utilize the keeping of different information in different channels of the mind. For example, an amnesia—a forgetting—really entails one part of the mind keeping something from the other. So it appears that one has forgotten, but rather, the memory is placed somewhere else, out of the interfering reach of the analytic brain. (As you get older, the brain loves to play with this skill of hiding things, like people's names!)

What I am proposing is that we help our clients learn where their *inner* channel changer is, and learn what other channels are already available to them. They can learn to search, and learn to go from the automatic channel that may not be showing them the right programming for the situation at hand, automatically to another, more benign channel. Don't stop at the channel that shows humiliation or loss or violence and bloodshed, but when you arrive there, shift to the channel about survival, about how a seed takes root in darkness, and about courageous citizens. Our work is to help clients to fill a channel with all their useful programs they already have that may be dispersed across many different channels; and to stay longer in that newly created helpful channel and to let the feelings and ideas of that channel trigger in them a different state of mind or trance, and thus produce automatically a different stance: the stance of the urban warrior, not the stance of the defeated weary. Add on to the good old track a new piece that can take them all the way to their dreams.

I have a cell phone and a computer. The new technologies are helping us become a global culture. But there is a gigantic price we pay. When faxes and emails began streaming into my house during what was still called "The Dinner Hour," we bought our first microwave oven. My then eight-year-old son was playing Nintendo in the living room and asked when dinner would be ready. I looked at this new dial and instead of saying " 'Half an hour," as I always had, I said "35 seconds"—and Judah said, "That's too long!" And I understood, even as I threw out the microwave in protest, that my son was already living in a dimension of time that was different from what I had known (Ritterman, 1995). But this is the way of the world, so we need to learn to help clients shift *quickly.* The paradox is, as I've said before, that we need to do that quick shift using subjective time or what I call "Slo-Mo." Get your slo-mo working! I give out egg-timers at my classes to show how quickly we can shift mental states and adopt a new stance for action to counter the inductions destructive to us in our contexts, *by using Slow-Mo.* In just three minutes of clock time, if we use for the good the same mind we get into when shocked … the slow-mo mind, we can shift from a state of mind that leads to sorrow, to a state of mind that leads where we need to go.

Once human beings lived by the rising of the sun and the rising of the moon, and went out or stayed inside, ate specific foods because of the seasons of the year. The natural rhythms of the environment in which we lived synchronized the bio- and body rhythms of the creatures, including us humans. We were daytime animals, unlike the owl, who is nocturnal, and so we slept when it was dark and woke like the rooster with the light. There was synchronicity to our relationship with nature and also with each other. Humanity has a Nature Deficit Disorder! Add that to the tome of the *DSM.*

In musical notation there is a symbol called a *rest.* No matter how fast the piece, the rest takes the place of a note that is played and heard in the rhythm of the music, but the rest is not played or heard. It is a silence that is essential to good music.

The Joy of the Future[4]
The only road to bring you
from yesterday to tomorrow
is the one that passes through today.
Live in the present
for the joy of the future.
(Ritterman, 200, p. 154)

We need to help clients learn to bring their trance states and their *rest* notes right into the ongoing interactions in their lives, right into the environments that trigger them unconsciously and automatically to get stressed and overwhelmed. I call this *being in your mind* instead of letting others who are behaving in an unfair, greedy or nonreciprocal manner take over and drive you out of your own mind.

Occupy Your Mind

This brings me to the 99% and the movement I hoped to have catalyzed this year (2011) in October, the "Occupy Your Mind" movement. I live near Oakland,

---

4   From M. Ritterman (2009, p. 154). © Michele Ritterman, 2009. Used with permission.

California, one of the homes of the OCCUPY Movement. So I say: OCCUPY YOUR MIND. IT IS YOUR FINAL AND OWN TERRITORY. Don't let anyone conquer your mind or hypnotize you into something you don't want. Don't let any THEM define YOU, that's your job here on planet earth, to be yourself. Since Thomas Szasz (1961) wrote *The Myth of Mental Illness*, various authors have sounded the alarm. Psychiatrist William Glasser (2003) aptly titled his book *Warning: Psychiatry Can Be Dangerous to Your Mental Health*. There may be a (limited) role and time for medication, but "The medicating of Americans for mental illnesses continued to grow over the past decade, with one in five adults now taking at least one psychiatric drug such as antidepressants, anti-psychotics and anti-anxiety medications" (Wang, 2011, p. A3). And one out of four children medicated! Too often 10 minutes and a prescription refilled for life! It takes time to understand the context, the reasons, the alternatives—and to offer human help. There is growing evidence (see Whitaker, 2010) that the overuse of medications can launch someone on a lifelong career of psychiatric chronicity and more and more medication. There is a massive effort by the psychopharmaceutical-industrial complex to reduce or eliminate psychotherapy, both individual and couple/family (see Caccavale, 2011; Hoyt & Gurman, 2012), and replace it with more pills. Think for yourself! Hold your ground!

When I was in training, one of my supervisors told me that I was too personal, that I worked "too close." I told him that I needed to have a different supervisor. And so I got Jay and Sal and Braulio—and Milton.

Gifts To/From the Heart

Sometimes I do embroidery, stitching stories on to cloth. After Erickson conducted a sort of remarriage ceremony for me and my then-husband under some desert mistletoe hung on the *palo verde* tree out back of Erickson's house, I got pregnant on a camping trip with my first child, Miranda. During that fruitful river raft trip, I made a very special embroidery for Erickson, which he and his wife Betty said was one of the favorite gifts of their lives. Betty wrote that not a day went by when Erickson didn't show that embroidery and a copy of Miranda's birth certificate to visitors. The embroidery used 10 figures to depict some key moments in Erickson's life, with the word *Love* written beneath, and the design of it held the answer to a riddle he liked to ask highly intelligent people to demonstrate to them that they had a rigid mental set, that they were stuck with a perspective that didn't work, that they needed to change channels in their mind to find the useful programming: "What has 5 rows of 4 each, with 10 total? Now how is that possible?" He liked to say, "There is no trick in what I am saying. The challenge for you is created by your adding a word that is not there."

(Another teaching: You have to think outside the box—the rows form the shape of a star, not lined up in parallel lines.)

FIGURE 24.1 Love Star. Original 9½ diameter. ©Michele Ritterman, 2012. Used with permission.

I learned so much from Milton. When we were near the end of our time together, the second to last time I saw him, he surprised me by asking "How are you going to repay me?" I gulped. It was true that for six years I had studied with him, stayed at his house, received a steady correspondence from him and Betty ... and had never once paid a penny. He told me his story. He was a farm boy. A rich aunt offered to meet with him. He was such a hayseed that he had read when you visit rich people you wear gloves, so when he first met her he wore his farm gloves. Well, long story short, this aunt, at his request, put him through college. After he did so well there, she paid for him to attend medical school. After all that, she said to him, "So, Milton, how will you repay me? The cost in dollars would be such-and-so." And Milton said, "My reaction was a lot like yours today. And then my aunt said, 'Or you can repay me by becoming a great healer.' So I ask you today, *How will you repay me?*" Well, I knew I was broke. So, with tears in my eyes, my heart forever accepted the challenge

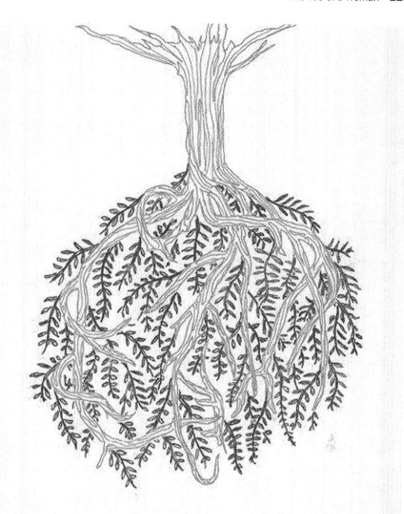

The Tao of a Woman

MICHELE RITTERMAN

FIGURE 24.2 Heart. ©Michele Ritterman, 2012. Used with permission.

of giving healing everything I've got. THAT was inspiration! To make sure I'd keep my promise he gave me an ironwood bird. I'd said to him, "What if I never see you again, how will I go on?" When he handed me the ironwood bird he said, "Indestructible."

I also made and mailed him another embroidery, of a special tree, just prior to the birth of my second child, Judah, and only months before Milton died. He enjoyed it. A variation of this tree is on the cover of my latest book and below.

To understand what this book cover is about, let me explain that I wrote the last verse in *The Tao of a Woman* (2009, p. 156) on trance and stance in the face of death and loss. Personally, it was about my carrying on after my great mentor died.

A Lesson from the Heart[5]

I embroidered for my Teacher
a gift that he received
weeks before he died.

It appears to be an ordinary apple tree,
like one he described from his childhood,
but it is a representation
of the coronary arteries.

Your heart is an upside down tree
giving nourishment to the earth
and rooted in the divine.

Even your broken heart
can be port of entry
for one who grieves.

If you turn the figure upside down, you can see that it is a representation of the coronary arteries. Your heart is an upside down tree that branches out to sustain the body and is rooted in the light.

References

Bateson, G. (1972). *Steps to an Ecology of Mind*. New York: Ballantine.

Caccavale, J.L. (2011). Failure to serve: The use of medications as a first-line treatment and misuse in behavioral interventions. In N.A. Cummings & W. O'Donohue (Eds.), *Understanding the Behavioral Healthcare Crisis: The Promise of Integrated Care and Diagnostic Reform* (pp. 327–341). New York: Routledge.

Cannon, W.B. (1957). Voodoo death. *Psychosomatic Medicine*, *19*(3), 182–190.

Cooper, L.F., & Erickson, M.H. (1959). *Time Distortion in Hypnosis: An Experimental and Clinical Investigation*. Baltimore, MD: Williams & Watkins. (Reissued 2002 by Crown House Publishing, Williston, VT.)

Erickson, M.H. (1968, October) The inhumanity of ordinary people. *International Journal of Psychiatry*, 277–279.

---

5   From M. Ritterman (2009, p. 156). © Michele Ritterman, 2009. Used with permission.

Erickson, M.H., & Lustig, H. (1975). *The Artistry of Milton H. Erickson, M.D.* Video/DVD. Bala Cynwyd, PA: Swan Multimedia, Inc. (reissued as Silver Jubilee edition 2005)

Erickson, M.H., & Rossi, E.L. (1976). Two-level communication and the microdynamics of trance. *American Journal of Clinical Hypnosis, 18*, 153–171.

Erickson, M.H., & Rossi, E.L. (1979). *Hypnotherapy: An Exploratory Casebook.* New York: Irvington.

Fanon, F. (1961). *The Wretched of the Earth.* New York: Grove Press.

Glasser, W. (2003). *Warning: Psychiatry Can Be Hazardous to Your Mental Health.* New York: HarperCollins.

Haley, J. (Ed.). (1967). *Advanced Techniques of Hypnosis and Therapy: Selected Papers of Milton H. Erickson, M.D.* Boston: Pearson, Allyn & Bacon.

Hoyt, M.F., & Gurman, A.S. (2012). Wither couple/family therapy? *The Family Journal:Counseling and Therapy for Couples and Families, 20*(1), 9–13.

Minuchin, S. (1974) *Families and Family Therapy.* Cambridge, MA: Harvard University Press.

Minuchin, S., Roseman, B., & Baker, L. (1978) *Psychosomatic Families.* Cambridge, MA: Harvard University Press.

Ritterman, M. (1978). *Family Therapy vs. Ritalin vs. Placebo Treatments of Hyperactivity: An Open Systems Approach.* Unpublished doctoral dissertation, Temple University, Philadelphia, PA.

Ritterman, M. (1985). Family context, symptom induction, and therapeutic counterinduction: Breaking the spell of a dysfunctional rapport. In J.K. Zeig (Ed.), *Ericksonian Psychotherapy: Clinical Applications* (Vol. 11, pp. 49–70). New York: Brunner/Mazel.

Ritterman, M. (1987, January-February). Torture: The counter-therapy by the state. *Family Therapy Networker, 11*(1), 43–47.

Ritterman, M. (1991). *Hope Under Siege: Terror and Family Support in Chile* (Foreword by Isabelle Allende). Norwood, NJ: Ablex.

Ritterman, M. (1994). A five-part poetic induction in favor of human decency (countering the hate movements). In J.K. Zeig (Ed.), *Ericksonian Methods: The Essence of the Story* (pp. 465–481). New York: Brunner/Mazel.

Ritterman, M. (1995, January/February). Stopping the clock. *The Family Therapy Networker, 19*(1), 44–51.

Ritterman, M. (2005a). *Using Hypnosis in Family Therapy* (2nd ed.) Phoenix, AZ: Zeig, Tucker & Theisen. (work originally published 1983)

Ritterman, M. (2005b). *Shared Couple's Trance* [CD]. Available at www.HypnosisNetwork.com.

Ritterman, M. (2009). *The Tao of a Woman: 100 Ways to Turn.* Berkeley, CA: Skipping Stones Editions. (Available in Spanish as *El Tao de La Mujer.*)

Satir, V. (1983). *Conjoint Family Therapy.* Palo Alto, CA: Science and Behavior Books.

Satir, V. (1988). *The New Peoplemaking.* Palo Alto, CA: Science and Behavior Books.

Szasz, T. (1961). *The Myth of Mental Illness.* New York: Harper & Row.

Wang, S.S. (2011, November 16). Psychiatric drug use spreads. *Wall Street Journal*, p. A3.

Whitaker, R. (2010). *Anatomy of an Epidemic: Magic Bullets, Psychiatric Drugs, and the Astonishing Rise of Mental Illness in America.* New York: Broadway/Random House.

25

CREATING PATHS WITH HEART

Teresa Robles

All paths in life are the same and they do not arrive at any place. This is one of the main teachings Carlos Castaneda (1968, 1971, 1972) received from his Master, Don Juan, the Yaqui *curandero* (indigenous healer). Don Juan said, however, that some paths make you curse life at each step. If so, you have all the right to abandon them no matter what anyone says. Other paths, when you walk them, fill you with joy, peace and a sense of well-being. You are one with the path ... they are paths with heart. Don Juan (Castaneda, 1968, pp. 105-106) advises his disciple: "Look at every path closely and deliberately. Try it as many times as you think necessary. Then ask yourself, and yourself alone, one question.... Does this path have a heart? If it does, the path is good; if it doesn't, it is of no use."

I really identify myself with these teachings (Robles, 1990). As an explorer and a dreamer, I always like to try new paths and invent others. I am a rebel and I only follow those paths which vibrate with my heart. I also enjoy being in contact with people. Looking for new paths and new forms of being and living, I came to Social Anthropology. There, I had the opportunity to know several indigenous groups in Mexico and Ecuador, and I lived with them, particularly with the Tarahumara and the Mazahua. The Tarahumara live in the State of Chihuahua, in Northern Mexico in a very mountainous region. The Copper Canyon is part of it. Their houses are so isolated that often you cannot see a house one from another. Towns in this region are *mestizo*. The Tarahumara are very special people: they have never been conquered. They feel proud of their traditions and believe that, by keeping them alive, they save the world from a collapse. They used to stand without moving for hours looking at the horizon... meditating? ... or feeling part of Nature?

During my first fieldwork, I had to explore their food habits. Early in the morning, I came into a small house, and invited a girl about my age (by that time 20 years old) to have a talk with me. We sat at the border of the cliff looking at the horizon, having a marvelous sight in front of us. Starting the evening that my workmates came to pick me up, they were worried because I had not arrived at the meeting place. I don't really know what happened. The Tarahumaran girl and I did not exchange a word with each other. By the time I realized where I was and what time it was, I felt we had had an intense communication and I felt we were indeed very similar inside and very different outside.

Because of different life situations, my family and I went to Mexico City to live. My anthropology became a "Book Anthropology" without any field research. I was unsatisfied very soon, so I tried new paths. I began to work in Psychoanalysis study groups. The theory was fascinating to me and I decided to include it as a theoretical framework for research I was about to begin on Mexican leaders.

I visited the Faculty of Psychology of the National Autonomous University of Mexico (UNAM) with the purpose of attending some listener courses. When I entered the office and looked at the posters announcing: Training in Group Psychotherapy, Child Psychotherapy, Psychoanalysis, etc., I spontaneously went into a trance and started to imagine myself as a therapist. Again in contact with people! I was there, when I heard a voice asking who was going to apply for the Doctoral Program in Clinical Psychology. I raised my hand and paid the exam fee, did it, and passed.

"I'll be a therapist," I said to Roberto, my husband, as soon as I got home. He immediately began to wonder where in the house we could build my office. At that moment, Pepe arrived, my brother-in-law, who is an architect and offered to build the office for me beside the entrance to the house.

To become a therapist was a long path, but with heart. I had to take many courses in Psychology before I could formally be part of the Doctoral Program, but I enjoyed all of them. I also worked in different study and supervision groups, because I wanted to be well prepared. Marie Langer, a psychoanalyst from Austria who had lived in different countries, used to coordinate one of these groups. She was an open-minded person and I loved and admired her very much. I wanted to become a psychoanalyst. In fact, psychoanalysis was the most prestigious approach in Clinical Psychology in Mexico at that time, and almost the only one. To reach this goal I had to go through an individual and group psychoanalytic process.

Neither I nor my psychoanalyst had a good time. Through the sessions, I learned that what I used to see as natural was considered pathological. I also learned that looking at the good side of things was called "Denial," and that if I did not recognize what the psychoanalyst interpreted, it was because "I was resistant and the content was repressed." As this path was making me curse life, I left it, and changed my training from psychoanalyst to psychotherapist.

Finally, the time to treat my first patient came. By the time my psychotherapy office was almost finished, Anita, the person who used to help me clean the house, had gone on holiday. She came back home with her sister, who had attempted suicide. She introduced her to me saying, "I told her you were going to cure her."

Anita and her sister, María Alejandra, are indigenous Mazahuas. They come from the region where I did my Master's thesis in Social Anthropology. I already knew most of their culture, traditions, and beliefs. Anita's sister came from a small village which is more than two hours away from Mexico City. She had no money to come back and forth. I called the supervisor that had been assigned for me, I continued attending Marie Langer's supervision group, and I began Maria's psychotherapy.

Working with María Alejandra, I broke all the rules that I had learned I was supposed to follow. María Alejandra stayed at my home because she did not have a place to spend the night. Of course, her sister had already told her all about my life. Sometimes, I didn't charge her and even gave her money so she could get back home again. She wanted to repay my work by cleaning a part of the house and occasionally she used to bring me some wild herbs named *corazones* ("hearts") that the Mazahuas used to eat with tortillas

During the first session, she told me: "I feel like a *cántaro* [a huge, round pottery jar used by indigenous women to carry water over their heads or shoulders] not sealed ... you can always fill it but sooner or later it remains empty." And we began to talk about *cántaros,* that we all have, and how we can fill them with water from different persons and activities; we argued we might also give a little of our water to fill *cántaros* from other persons, and concluded that it was better then to allow our *cántaro* going empty so that we could always fill it instead of having it full of stagnant water. This therapeutic process is described in my book, *Revisando El Pasado para Construir El Futuro* (*Revisiting the Past in Order to Construct the Future*; Robles, 2006).

At the supervision I commented what I had done with Maria Alejandra, and everybody jumped on me saying that I should have interpreted the *cántaro* as the maternal womb that rejected her without giving love to her. However, Marie Langer said, "She is a different client. Teresa did something different. Let's wait to see what happens." María Alejandra came back to my office in a much better mood. We continued working with metaphors, rites and ceremonies of her culture, and she continued improving to the surprise of my supervisor and colleagues.

I learned to work with metaphors, symbols, rites, and anecdotes with María Alejandra. I learned that all of us have different parts (a similar concept to "ego states") and that we can work at having each part communicate with the others in order to become a team looking for the welfare of the complete person. In this team, each part offers the best it has to the others. For her, "María" was her traditional part, and "Alejandra" the woman that desired to be integrated into the culture of the city.

My name is María Guadalupe Teresa. I have discovered that "Teresa" is the successful woman, "Guadalupe" is my traditional part, and "María" is my spiritual part.

The work done with María Alejandra was a wonderful path with heart, one that we both enjoyed step by step.

My work with other patients from the University with my personal supervisor was quite different. I had a lot of difficulties to repeat the interpretations that my supervisor had asked me to do. And when the patients left the therapy because "they were resistant," I used to think "I'm glad they left." Sometime after, I also left my psychoanalysis before I started cursing life.

Marie Langer suggested to me that I attend a training course in Systemic Family Therapy with a friend of hers, Ignacio Maldonado, who was just coming from Argentina. I did so and was part of the first group of the Instituto Latinoamericano de Estudios de la Familia (ILEF). There, I learned that noting the good side of life is called "positive connotation" and that doing this was indeed a useful tool in therapy. This approach was a better path for me. I learned many things and made a lot of friends there.

As soon as I finished, I associated with three colleagues to do research, create new techniques and adapt others to Mexican culture. One day, one of these friends, Rosemary Eustace, shared the book *Trance-Formations: Neuro-Linguistic Programming and the Structure of Hypnosis* (Grinder & Bandler, 1981). We read it with a strong interest, and started to practice those techniques. I also began to look for their origin.

My Path with Heart

By that time, I knew about a Congress that the Milton H. Erickson Foundation had organized in Phoenix, Arizona. I registered, went to Phoenix, and decided that this was my path with heart, a path that made me enjoy life and be one with it. Since then, I've been walking it, step by step, making the path as I walk. And this path has become richer and more pleasant as I join other Ericksonians' paths in different countries, which have enriched my own path. This path with heart has transcended into my personal life.

Those paths are too many to name each one of them. However, all these friends fill my *cántaro* and I share my waters with them.

I studied Dr. Erickson's life and work. I travelled to the Milton H. Erickson Foundation to look at his videos. I immediately identified myself with his work during his last years of life. At that time, he offered seminars on hypnosis. He demonstrated the hypnotic phenomena in a particular subject … but while observing, *all* participants entered in a hypnotic trance and changed. I have had the opportunity to know some persons who attended those seminars. All of them coincide in that their life radically changed after that experience. They changed without it being necessary for them to talk about their lives or their problems.

I believed that if you do not ask anything personal of clients, therapy becomes more respectful and comfortable. For Dr. Erickson it was not necessary to interpret anything, even less touching wounds. Week after week, Dr. Erickson repeated the same inductions to new groups: "To become a mind without a body....", "How we learned the alphabet....", "To stand up at the polar star...." among others. During the 1950's, Dr. Erickson remarked on the importance of tailoring therapy to each person, proposing that each human being is unique and unrepeatable. By the time he was in a wheelchair, he was asked why he used to repeat the same inductions if he affirmed that each person was unique and different. He answered: "I usually say the same, but I tailor it to each one."

Universal Themes

Dr. Erickson was indeed doing group therapy using *universal themes*. Universal themes touch every one of us only because we are all human beings sharing the same basic experiences. Observing his videos, I remembered that day when I was sitting at the border of a cliff with the Tarahumaran girl ... so different outside but so similar inside. As a tribute to Dr. Erickson, I began to work with universal themes and to apply this work to groups where nobody speaks out about their personal situation--instead, they share their desire to grow up and to be better in their lives, or, for example, to learn how to deal with stress and burn out. Universal themes, presented as metaphors are, for example, the wounds we always suffer along our life ... and all wounds heal if you let them heal. We can also say: in the same way we have a skin that distinguishes that from it to the inside is Me and from it to the outside is not Me, we always need something like a fence in order to distinguish that from it to the inside are my desires, my difficulties, my projects and from it to the outside are the desires, difficulties and projects of others. My fence, your fence, must also be a protection that keeps outside whatever is not me or can hurt me. But like my skin, it would have entrances for receiving what is good for me and exits to take away whatever could hurt me or is not a part of me.

Another universal theme is the disguises that our family put on us, for example: "The Smart One," "The Crazy One"; or those that society puts on us, "The Latinos," "The Grandmothers." And each disguise has a description of it and a script telling about how to act and what we can expect from it.

By the last years of Dr. Erickson's life, his sight and hearing were diminished, and it was hard for him to move. He was not able to distinguish the minimal cues to tailor his interventions as he was years before. Observing his later videos, I realized he could connect the inside of the persons and he could perceive them beyond his own senses, with an amplified perception.

Many years after, I listened to his daughter, Betty Alice, saying: "The Ericksonian therapist should accept himself as vulnerable, in order to open himself to the client and so, to invite him to open, too. Once they are open, Universal Love comes from the Universe and begins to flow through them." I believe that happened between the Tarahumaran girl and me.

I also heard Betty Alice saying: "My father used to say that life is hard, it is unfair, pain exists, but the way we live it depends only upon us." Although life can be hard, we can always build paths with heart and Dr. Erickson's life was an example of this.

I'm not certain if he used to do it, but I began to play with the proposal that life is unfair, but it is unfair in both ways, for the good and for the bad. I began to say to the clients, or to any person around complaining about their lives: "Yes, life is unfair, very unfair: How many years have you lived? And how many babies die each day? You are right, life is unfair: How many persons in Mexico City have a car like yours, or can travel to other countries? Life is very unfair."

When I was a girl, my family used to meet every Sunday for lunch at my grandparents' house. After lunch, the men used to play chess or cards while the women were talking and knitting. I was always curious to listen to their conversations. They continuously used to repeat stories about other members of the family or friends. They were usually stories with a tragic end. For example, the aunt that fell in love with someone, but he never dared to ask her hand in marriage because he had no money, and therefore, he could not give her the life she was used to living. And so both got old alone, believing their love was impossible. I used to listen to those stories and said to myself: "It would have been very easy if he had asked her if she accepted him without money or not," or maybe if she had told him, "I love you so and want to live with you."

I immediately identified myself with Dr. Erickson's thoughts that "Life is simple," "We learned to act in a wrong way but we can learn to act in a good way," and "Problems appear because of a lack of options"—as it was the case with the aunt.

Milton Erickson proposed that our Unconscious Mind is like a Wise Part because in it all our life experiences are registered. These experiences are learnings and resources that we can use to solve any difficulty that life presents to us. Life presents difficulties to us; if we are able to solve them, we grow, develop new abilities; if not, the difficulties become problems.

Universal Wisdom

Around the year 2000, I read a paper about Quantum Physics entitled "Universe as a Hologram" (see Talbot, 1991). The proposal was that if the Universe is like a hologram, the Universe will be a projection of us, as Conscious matter-energy. In addition, a characteristic of a hologram is that all the information of the hologram is in each one of its parts, like the DNA in each one of our cells that contains the information of the complete person.

All the information of the Universe is in each one of its parts. All the information of the Universe is inside me and inside you. It is the same information that is in each drop of water or in the whole sea. It is the same information that is in the sun, the moon, stars and in the whole Universe. I, myself, complete, I am my Wise Part. And this Wise Part is like a Universal Wisdom because it is the same everywhere. Universal Wisdom in each one of us is part of a Universal Absolute Wisdom, the whole Universe.

To me this Universal Wisdom is like the Creative Force that makes possible the fact that the union of two cells, an ovum and a sperm, triggers a process of differentiation and growth, ending into a complete individual, with all the complexities involved.

I use this explanation with my clients—going into details, through hypnotic conversation, and then, as a first exercise in a natural trance, I put the person in contact with Universal Wisdom inside him or her (Robles, 1998). From that moment on, we always put the work during the session in the hands of the Universal Wisdom, of the client and of mine. At the end of the session, we also leave the process in the hands of Universal Wisdom.

And, as Betty Alice Erickson proposes, I open myself to the Universe, inviting my client to do the same so that Universal Wisdom, which we can also name Universal Love, flows through us, healing, solving, transforming. Before I begin to work I ask Universal Wisdom to put the right ideas and images in my mind, to put the right words in my mouth, to fill my heart with Light, Love and Peace.

When we are stuck in a process, I propose to my client to leave the problems and the solutions in the hands of Universal Wisdom. Or, if I am working with a couple and we are stuck, I propose to them to leave their conflicts in the hands of Universal Wisdom … and extraordinary changes always occur through the most unexpected paths.

Years before, I used to propose that therapy was a relationship between two experts: the expert in techniques, and the expert in oneself, the client, working together for his or her welfare. Now I look at therapy as an encounter of two parts of the same Whole, for the growth of both. And each one changes according to his or her needs.

My relationship with Universal Wisdom is now part of my life and an invaluable tool to grow with. Ericksonian Psychotherapy is also part of my life—my way of speaking, inviting one to imagine, to remember, to change—when I am in the company of my children, my grandchildren, with friends, everywhere.

And my life has two strong axes. Both are part of my mission and great paths with heart. One axis is to spread Ericksonian psychotherapy, Dr. Erickson's teachings and the work with Universal Wisdom, for contributing to a better world. The other axis is growing together with my family, a gift of life, with whom I often escape to enjoy all the free moments I have. This is also a part of my mission, as it was when I raised my children and as it is now to give to my grandchildren all I can to help them to be better in life. And they actually teach a lot to me. Frequently, I use anecdotes about them in my therapies. I enjoy them very much.

Invitation

Before finishing, I would like to invite you, dear reader, to try all the paths that life presents to you and to ask yourself: *Is this a path with heart for me?* If so, the path is good; if not, the path will make you curse your life. *Follow only paths with heart, enjoying each step you make, and create the path as you walk.* I also invite you to make Universal Wisdom be part of your life. Put yourself in Its hands and work in a team with It to solve any difficulty that life might present to you, to make you grow.

References

Castaneda, C. (1968). *The Teachings of Don Juan: A Yaqui Way of Knowledge.* New York: Ballantine.

Castaneda, C. (1971). *A Separate Reality: Further Conversations with Don Juan.* New York: Simon & Schuster.

Castaneda, C. (1972). *Journey to Ixtlan: The Lessons of Don Juan.* New York: Simon & Schuster.

Grinder, J., & Bandler, R. (1981) *Trance-Formations: Neuro-Linguistic Programming and the Structure of Hypnosis.* Moab, UT: Real People Press.

Robles, T. (1990). *A Concert for Four Brain Hemispheres in Psychotherapy.* New York: Vantage Press.

Robles, T. (1998) Recovering Your Life Force [CD]. Mexico City: Alom Editores. Visit www.hipnosis.com.mx

Robles, T. (2006). *Revisando El Pasado para Construir El Futuro.* Mexico City: Alom Editores.

Talbot, M. (1991). *The Holographic Universe.* New York: HarperCollins.

26

GET OFF YOUR HIGH HORSE

Reflections of a Problem Solver in Palo Alto

Karin Schlanger

Caminante no hay camino. Se hace camino al andar.
(Wayfarer, there is no way. The way is made by walking.)

—Antonio Machado (1875–1939)

I arrived at Palo Alto and the Brief Therapy Center at MRI (Mental Research Institute) from Argentina in the early 1980s. I had survived two things: the *Guerra Sucia* (the Dirty War) led by the military junta during my teenage years; and then, my psychoanalytic schooling at the Universidad de Buenos Aires. The first had happened by not getting too involved in politics; and the second by reading *Pragmatics of Human Communication* (Watzlawick, Beavin, & Jackson, 1967). Both, in a way, taught me something about right and wrong, good and evil and, ultimately, what works.

Back home a military junta ruled the country, and young people my age, particularly psychology students, were being tortured and "disappearing." For safety, you would lay low, trying to attract as little attention as possible and plan to leave the country on your terms. The other option was to go in the middle of the night because you had gotten a warning from a friend saying you *had* to leave if you wanted to live. Human rights simply didn't exist, but nobody in the whole world seemed to notice. News trickled in from abroad through the grapevine—there was no Internet yet—that there were concentration camps three blocks away. Nah! *That* could not be true!

Pragmatics of Human Communication guided my departure plan because it gave me a professional North. I realize now, many years later, that my interest in *Pragmatics* helped me to put together a plan that quite literally saved my life, since I was closely associated with some friends who had disappeared. I simply *had* to go to Palo Alto to see what these people practicing problem-solving brief therapy were doing. This was aided by a random event: I was offered, towards the end of my university studies, to come to Stanford to live with a friend. I knew Palo Alto was in the vicinity so I would be able to go to the Mental Research Institute. Carlos Sluzki was the Director then and he, as it turns out, had gone to medical school with my father in the 1950s. He greeted me warmly on my unscheduled visit and almost immediately found something for me to do. He was the editor of the journal *Family Process* at the time, and incorporated me into that activity as well. I am still very thankful for his generosity.

In hindsight, meeting him meant that I would stay in this strange land where seasons are inverted, they speak English most of the time, and a close friendship doesn't give you license to just show up at someone's house uninvited and stay until the wee hours of the morning. One thing led to another: I met my husband, had two kids, and now only go to Buenos Aires occasionally to visit. I am a citizen of the world.

It is now almost 30 years later and things have changed: I am now the Director of the Brief Therapy Center at MRI. I have become much wiser after living in a country that is, and will forever be, foreign. However, an important piece has remained the same: I am still in love with the way of looking at reality that I learned from my respected teachers—alas, all now deceased—Paul Watzlawick, John Weakland, and Richard Fisch. These learnings are applicable both within the office and in the wider world because they are about interacting with others within certain contexts and especially about a different way of listening. This way of listening allows me to be positive, see possibilities, give hope and, above everything else, allows me to relate to people respectfully. It is all about solving problems, promoting change, and helping people live better lives within *their own* context. It almost seems like, through experience, I can sometimes "hear" what people are going to tell me before they say it. I feel like Cassandra in Greek mythology. It is said that Cassandra spent a night in Apollo's temple, where snakes cleaned her ears so she would be able to hear the future clearly. When she did not return Apollo's love the next morning, he cursed her with no one believing her predictions. Why Cassandra? Because after working in the field for a number of years and because our clients are always of the human species, stories begin to repeat themselves in theory and you can start to hear repetitions. Those repetitions allow older, experienced therapists to appear to "see" the future and, from there, to ask questions that can clarify situations for clients.

Just last week, a student with whom I had worked when she was in high school called me to say she needed to see me for a "delicate issue." With me imagining all sorts of scenarios from gang activity to unwanted pregnancy, we arranged to meet a couple of days later. She looked great and was continuing to struggle with full-time college, work, and a difficult home life. She wanted to see me because, in her new relationship, the boyfriend had told her that he had been raped when he was six. The perpetrator, I immediately inquired, had returned to Mexico and was now dead. I asked why she wanted to see me, since there were several possibilities in my mind: not knowing how to help and/or shock at being the first person in his life to be told as they were just a new couple. It turns out her reason was quite different: "If I help him, then he becomes indebted to me because I know and he then becomes the person I have to spend the rest of my life with. It is a very new relationship and I don't know that he is the one. After all, I am only 20 and want to do something with my life other than marry, have kids, and not be able to move away from this bad neighborhood" (Schlanger, 2011). As a therapist, I did not see that one coming but because I was willing to listen to where she was at and she felt secure in our relationship, I was able to help the process of her clarifying what *she* wanted to do.

Situations that are in the open can be seen more clearly and that, almost immediately, makes them less scary and uncontrollable. That sets a more positive tone for the client, almost magically. But I have digressed into matters of how I use my toolkit without having explained what it contains.

The Problem-Solving Origins

Allow me to describe what I do and what is in my toolkit: what is problem-solving brief therapy all about? It is a very simple model to explain and quite hard to implement well, due to its simplicity and all the doors it leaves unopened in the quest for a problem to solve. It is profoundly based in constructivism, cybernetics, communication theory, the language of hypnosis á la Milton Erickson, and systems thinking. The genius of the model developed in Palo Alto is that it seamlessly takes pieces of all this thinking and translates it into practice (see Fisch, Weakland, & Segal, 1982; Watzlawick, Weakland, & Fisch, 1974; Fisch & Schlanger, 1999; Fisch, Ray, & Schlanger, 2010). Systems theory was originally developed in the fields of biology and physiology. It starts with Berntalanffy's General System Theory and in practice is closely related to cybernetics. Through Gregory Bateson (1972, 1980) and his interpretations therapists took the concepts of *homeostasis, closed and open loops,* and *feedback*—to mention but a few—and started to see families as complex systems. With the development of second-order cybernetics, Bateson included the subjective nature of the observer in the system that is being studied: it is cybernetics examining cybernetics, systems looking at systems. Heinz von Foerster, an engineer by training, was also interested in systems thinking and, together with other theorists of his time—Ernst von Glassersfeld, for example—he put forth the theory of *radical constructivism* (see Watzlawick, 1984; Watzlawick & Hoyt, 1998). An example of this thinking, in von Glassersfeld's words, is that a good teacher can never assume he or she can transfer knowledge to a student in a linear way. Students have to build their own knowledge. It is a process rather than a simple transfer of something ready-made into someone else's head. This method is the one that teaches people to think for themselves. It gives them the "why" behind the way things are and therefore enables them to use the concepts in a practical way. Students actively build their knowledge—anomalies sometimes can be very refreshing and mistakes are always a part of the process. This point of view leads to reflection, which in turn is crucial in understanding a new concept and making it your own. Talking fosters reflection, reflection fosters understanding and understanding fosters reflection ... a circular process, which allows for systemic thinking because all these premises constitute a circle, a system that continues to feed itself. It is about learning to learn: reflecting on what you learn and applying it and using it in practice.

Cybernetics is the science that looks at the structure of regulatory systems and is therefore closely related to systems theory: an action by a part of the system causes some change in its environment and that change is fed to the system via information (feedback) which causes the system to adapt to the new conditions. The system's changes affect its behavior. In practice, this means that the main focus of therapy is to produce one small change in one member of a family or system so that the problem that was brought in as a complaint can no longer continue to operate in its usual fashion. Inertia will have set in and motion will have been redirected: it is up to the therapist, as the leader in promoting the desired change, to guide this new direction.

The influence of *hypnosis* alluded to here is what Watzlawick (1982; Erickson, 1974) used to refer to as "hypnosis without trance." It is a way of talking during sessions based on Milton Erickson's slow, deliberate way of interacting with his clients. It is based on carefully listening to clients: what words they use, what concepts keep coming back in the session, as a way of ascertaining what is important to *them* (Fisch, 1982, 1994; Weakland & Fisch, 1992). This *taking them seriously*, listening to what is important to the *client*, not what is or should be important according to the therapist, is the basis for the intense work the problem-solving therapist does (see Hoyt, 1994/2001). I will come back to this concept because it is important, not only in becoming a good therapist, but also for becoming a good supervisor and teacher. After all, if you are in tune with what the other person is saying, the other person will feel heard and understood and will be more willing to open up, work, and trust the relationship. It is *in the relationship* that change will occur. The young woman student mentioned above who called me after two years felt that she could do so based on my previous willingness to be there when she needed to tell her mother that she was starving herself and didn't quite know how to deal with it, as well as my willingness to go out for a walk around school when she and her previous boyfriend were having trouble. I could be relied upon to listen without judgment. From my point of view, this is also the basis for a solid friendship at a more personal level.

Communication theory is the base for all our work: (a) One cannot not communicate. Any perceivable behavior, including the absence of action, has the potential to be interpreted by other people as having some meaning; (b) Every communication has a content and relationship aspect such that the latter classifies the former and is therefore a meta communication: each person responds to the *content* of communication in the *context* of the relationship between the communicators. For example, I recently visited a self-sustaining agricultural high school in Paraguay where kids get dual diplomas for academics and working in agriculture. It's a boarding school during the week and kids can choose whether to go home for weekends. While there, I approached a senior girl and asked her if the school could benefit from having a counselor who students could talk to about their family problems. When I briefly explained what I meant by "counselor," she lowered her head and said: "Yes, I could definitely use that. There is a lot of violence between my parents at home. I know there is not much I can do about it but I stay at the school even on weekends so I don't have to see it." I was unable to *not* see the way she spoke: just by her lowering her head, looking down and defeated, before she opened her mouth I had an idea as to what the emotions were that went with the words. In fact she was unable not to communicate and was also metacommunicating, if I chose to "listen" to it; (c) The nature of the relationship is dependent on the punctuation of the partners' communication procedures; (d) Human communication is both digital and analogic; and (e) Inter-human communications are either symmetric or complementary, depending on whether the relationship of the partners is based on differences or parity.

All the tools mentioned above are just that: tools of my trade. I will use them as a starting point to explore a couple of thoughts I have been considering lately.

How to Get Off Your High Horse

An explanation for "getting off of one's high horse" is to *stop acting as if one is better or more intelligent than someone else*. Students are implicitly taught in psychology school that a degree on the wall gives them the knowledge to know better than the client what said client is coming in for. Later these students do practices under the careful eyes of supervisors and they, in turn, have to teach the "right" way of listening. What I have been thinking lately is that a lot of young therapists are tentative and do things because they have learned it is "right" and not because the *client feels* it. At some point a therapist learns to distinguish between what is technically "right" and what is going to work because it *feels* right. For example: a female client comes in complaining that she is unable to say "No" to people around her, at home, in relationships, even at work and therefore her life is miserable. We start by defining what "No" means to her. She is able to say "No" if she is offered more food, but she is unable to say "No" to going out with someone on a date, even if she thinks that it is not a good match for her. She is also unable to say "No" to her sister who asks her to babysit too often. Her "No" is in the context of relationships with other people. The reader may be already making all sorts of hypotheses as to *why* she is unable to say "No" and those may be perfectly valid. Exploring all those reasons will extend the length of therapy. There is nothing wrong with such an approach, except there is a high risk that the client might perceive the therapist as being on his or her high horse: they know better than she does why she is unable to say "No." What she is looking for from a therapist is something that will help her to say "No" when she needs to, in a given interactional situation. If a therapist were to ask directly, they would probably be repeating what other people have already asked her to do. Instead, after several sessions it might be more useful to ask her, as homework, to practice saying "No" to at least one person every day and take notes on what happens. The immediate response, in this case, was "No! I cannot do that!" The funniest part, however, was that, as she was telling the therapist this, a grin came over her face: "I just did, eh? It *felt* good!" Always within the limits of the law, allowing young therapists to explore styles that fit them is where a lot of learning actually happens. Along with gentle reminders that what was learned in school can only function as a guide: it can be the map but doesn't have to actually *be* the route to take.

Another useful tool can be "agreed upon" (particularly when working in other cultures than our own) humor. Speaking in a language that is understandable to the client is always crucial. This is more specific than the words used—it is about cultural mores. It is about using words that the clients themselves have used: it is a language they can understand, can relate to. This "being in tune" will make the client and the therapist feel comfortable in the session. Being comfortable is what is going to make us sound genuine and *that*, particularly if working with teenagers, will give us credibility: we sound "real" as opposed to "fake." Young therapists also need to find what *they* feel comfortable with. This might even take the form of the therapist asking the client often if they are making themselves clear and understandable.

As a rule, when working with people who are very different from ourselves we tend to feel more uncomfortable. For example, working with low-income families with low education levels and irregular immigration status in the United States where restrictions are becoming tougher and tougher is something very hard to relate to. These situations can be a big challenge to the work done by therapists, psychologists, social workers, teachers, or staff at inner-city schools (Schlanger & Baske, 2007). When family members are invited to come to school to talk about ways to better support their young person from dropping out of high school, stories emerge in these people's backgrounds that are truly hair-raising: extreme physical violence suffered as children, abuse, and even incest. Often, this is the first time these folks have talked about any of this. In these cases, it is crucial to refrain from using words that were learned in school: "I know what you mean," "I understand," or even, "I know how you feel." Even if the intention is positive or innocuous, these phrases will never ring true unless the therapist has suffered abuse to that extent. Instead, a respectful silence, followed by "I cannot even imagine" might be more appropriate. In the case of a young therapist talking to an older mother about her lack of discipline with her kids, "I am too young to know this, but you might want to give this a try to see how it works ..." might be a credible way to approach the mother. In my small, cozy office at the school I had been listening to a mom tell me about abuse, neglect, and running away from home at the age of 15 to escape the nightmare. A couple of sessions later she told me how it was strange that she was the only light-skinned person in her family, except for her much older brother, who used to beat up their mother when he came home drunk. She muttered under her breath how she looked a lot like him, and not as much like her own father. She raised her head, looked at me for a long while in silence and then said: "Now do you understand why I will take the side of my teenage son against the rest of the world? Nobody protected me so I have to protect him."

While graduate school provides the tools needed in the form of books, it is practice and real life experience that develops seasoned human beings and thus better therapists. As supervisors then, one of our missions has to be to teach young therapists how to keep their heads above water when their enthusiasm makes them want to solve all the problems that clients come in with. One way in which this can be achieved is by accepting that clients, no matter how different they are from the therapist, are resilient and *will* manage. Therapists are there to tweak things and listen, to help clients do it for themselves more successfully. This can only be done with a profound belief on the part of the therapist that respecting other people's beliefs, particularly when they are different from their own, is a more useful approach to helping promote change. It makes the therapist more humble in terms of what changes they can help promote: as callous as it sounds, "We win some and we lose some." Sometimes it is easier to work with these extreme situations if there is something about the therapist's own life, which is inherently different from the client's. For example, I was recently supervising a social worker who mainly works with cases of child abuse. He has no kids of his own and said that working with these kids and their families is a great job for him. I pondered aloud that after I had had kids of my own it had become difficult for me to work with child abuse. I asked him how much of a difference it would make in his working with this population if he had kids of his own. He was quite surprised to say he had never thought about it before and that it would make a big difference in his being able to work with this hard population effectively and be able to sleep at night. His not having kids of his own meant that he would never have to worry about them being abused. Moral of the story: if a therapist is able to, it is helpful to pick a population to work with that will maximally use the therapist's strengths so that he or she can be the best therapist he or she can be!

Henry Ford once said, "If I'd asked customers what they wanted, they would have told me, 'A faster horse!'" When people come to see a problem-solving therapist they usually want their own methods perfected: they want therapy to make them better at implementing their failed solutions. If a therapist does that, they will have a lot of unhappy customers because, by problem-solving therapy definition, what clients have been trying to do maintains the painful status quo: "The [attempted] 'solution' is the problem" (Weakland & Fisch, 1992, p. 308). Second-order change is what allows therapists to see the problem from "outside the client's perspective" and thus makes them able to suggest something, from this outside, that the clients could never have thought of by themselves. It is from this "outside perspective" that therapists will give directives, usually in the form of homework to be implemented after the session, which will produce the desired change in behavior. It is more often the case that people don't know what they want until the therapist is able to show this new point of view to them: it is not what they were looking for but an improved version, which allows them to live better. Therapists are in a better position to achieve this if they have their feet firmly planted on the ground, speak the clients' language, and understand their context rather than looking down at the clients with an air of superiority from a high horse.

A Few Final Thoughts to Do with Love

A therapist having to correct a course of action, even if it seems common sense to the client, is a difficult place to be in. It ties back into being Cassandra and being able to see a future that is hard for people to believe is possible. But boy! Does it feel good when it does work! A "Thank You" note from an intern who was rigid in her approach to clients when she started but who became more flexible exemplifies this success: "You taught me that it was OK for me to be myself with my clients. I now know that I can even use humor carefully and, rather than be offensive, make clients feel more comfortable with me so that they open up sooner." That can only be taught by supervisors who have experienced it themselves and are flexible and confident enough in their own abilities that they are able to guide the learning. That, in turn, means that supervisors need to care about what they are doing.

Which brings me to *"What's love got to do with it?"* Being a therapist is all about loving what you do. Not every case will be easy. There are pieces of the job that will be hard, but overall, you have to care and love the way of approaching people that you have chosen to work with. With the problem-solving approach that I learned from John (Weakland), Dick (Richard Fisch) and Paul (Watzlawick), I often see "miracles" unfold in front of me if I am curious and patient enough to watch. It is an example of how problem-solving therapy is more about seeing strengths in clients and focusing on them, so that the clients can see those strengths, too. One of the clients I am most proud of today, as I write this chapter, is a Latina woman in her 50s, who had been diagnosed many years ago as being "bipolar." Margarita had a history of being hospitalized and believed deeply that she was "mentally ill." She also felt stuck in a life she did not enjoy. Margarita's daughter, now in her 20s, was living alone, but there was also a younger son, and she was concerned about how he saw her. She was seeing a psychiatrist who monitored her medications and who kept encouraging her to become a different person. We all saw in her a different person from what she was able to see herself. She had suffered serious sexual abuse as a child; one of her three younger siblings had been diagnosed as schizophrenic. The deck was stacked against her and yet she kept going. Picking up her son at school was impossible because she was certain that other moms were talking about her behind her back. Similarly impossible was doing the shopping for groceries. In spite of all this, and because she did not want to set a bad example for her son, with whom she had a good relationship, she kept coming to therapy. She wept uncontrollably for many sessions, recounting her everyday life and how powerless she felt. She was also guided by an intense feeling that there had to be something better out there. Little by little she managed to make small changes that felt empowering. After a while, we did not see each other every week. She was able to drive herself to pick up her son. She no longer thought that people at the art supply store were talking about her when she went to buy supplies for her work, and the other students at her art class did, in fact, think she had talent. So did her teacher, who encouraged her to do more and maybe try to sell some of her work. She was very surprised. But art was not how she was going to make her first million! She had other talents: she is bilingual; maybe she could help other people by being an interpreter. And that, too, required going to classes. That was very hard at the beginning. Classes went on for a whole year, and there would be a hard oral exam at the end of the journey. Possible? Oh so hard! But, little by little, one class at a time, with frequent phone calls for reassurance to her mother on the other side of the country, the course was done … and she failed the exam! With encouragement, she went to talk to her professors and obtained a special dispensation that allowed a second chance at the exam: her nerves had played a bad trick. This time she passed the exam, went out job searching, and is finding out being in the world is proving to be much more enjoyable than she could have ever imagined. On a personal level, the journey has not been an easy one. Will she make it? I am sure! Will it continue to be an uphill battle? I am also sure. In fact, the whole struggle cost her a short self-hospitalization a few weeks ago because she realized that she was in a bad place: she needed a break for a weekend. Her medications were re-evaluated and reduced. She was back at work, albeit reluctantly, after 4 days.

This story is one of those "miracles" that I have seen by helping people with their strengths. I have seen Margarita now for several years, on and off. Sessions were weekly for a few months, then biweekly, then monthly. Sometimes she would go live life on her own and, when she required help with the next step, she would call. This has been the pattern. It has been brief problem-solving therapy because it has always looked at her in the context of her difficulty and listened to what *she* wanted changed in *her* life. Lately, with the availability of e-mail, she writes "updates" and requests sessions when she needs them. She often writes e-mails with "I am doing fine" in the subject line and tells of her latest accomplishments, or asks for advice or for a meeting. I smile.

Equal "miracles" are stories of my interns at the high school where we work, where 75% of the low-income families speak Spanish in their homes. We have worked for three and four years, encouraging them when they are faltering, helping with college essays, going to soccer games when no family member would or could and cheering the kids on to graduate from high school because that will give them a stab at a better life than that of their immigrant, "illegal" parents. In America, at least in theory, they CAN achieve the dream.

So, when I ponder on *"What's love got to do with it?"* and what makes my job the best in the world, the response that most often pops into my mind is that a lot of it has to do with "just being there" in an open, honest, non-judgmental way in the relationship. Being willing to answer difficult questions, sometimes being willing to go the extra mile in showing that we care, and admitting that we certainly do not have all the answers and it is fine to show ignorance and willingness to learn, even from our clients. That is certainly how I got off my high horse—and it was particularly high being from Argentina! I worked with many women whose values were to stay at home, cook for their husbands, and be model wives and mothers, in spite of being bright and sometimes more educated than the husbands. So I listened to recipes, tried some of them, and heard the stories of what little piece they wanted to change in their lives. I would never have chosen to live life the way they were living it, but, in listening, I learned a lot, too.

Problem-solving brief therapy is more than just a way to do therapy; it is a more positive way of looking at the world. As Dick Fisch wrote (1982, p. 157): "Therapy should be measured not by its brevity or length, but whether it is efficient and effective in aiding people with their complaints or whether it wastes time." Supporting people in their journey through life makes us human and, therefore, wise and worth listening to. Does our job sound grandiose? No. It is about being "real," knowing the limitations to what we can change and what we cannot accomplish—and listening to a lot of music to take care of ourselves so that we can take care of others.

References

Bateson, G. (1972). *Steps to an Ecology of Mind*. New York: Ballantine.

Bateson, G. (1980). *Mind and Nature: A Necessary Unity*. New York: Dutton.

Erickson, M.H. (1974). Foreword. In P. Watzlawick, J.H. Weakland, & R. Fisch, *Change: Principles of Problem Formation and Problem Resolution* (pp. ix–x). New York: Norton.

Fisch, R. (1982). Erickson's impact on brief psychotherapy. In J.K. Zeig (Ed.), *Ericksonian Approaches to Hypnosis and Psychotherapy* (pp. 155–162). Philadelphia: Brunner/Mazel.

Fisch, R. (1994). Basic elements in the brief therapies. In M.F. Hoyt (Ed.), *Constructive Therapies* (pp. 126–139). New York: Guilford Press.

Fisch, R., Weakland, J.H., & Segal, L. (1982). *The Tactics of Change: Doing Therapy Briefly*. San Francisco: Jossey-Bass.

Fisch, R., & Schlanger, K. (1999). *Brief Therapy with Intimidating Cases: Changing the Unchangeable*. San Francisco: Jossey-Bass.

Fisch, R., Ray, W. A., & Schlanger, K. (Eds.) (2010) *Focused Problem Resolution: Selected Papers of the MRI Brief Therapy Center*. Phoenix, AZ: Zeig, Tucker & Theisen.

Hoyt, M.F. (1994). On the importance of keeping it simple and taking the patient seriously: A conversation with Steve de Shazer and John Weakland. In M.F. Hoyt (Ed.), *Constructive Therapies* (pp. 11–40). New York: Guilford. Reprinted in M.F. Hoyt (2001), *Interviews with Brief Therapy Experts* (pp. 1–3). New York: Brunner/Routledge.

Schlanger, K. (2011) Problem-solving brief therapy: The Palo Alto approach to working with a Latino couple. In D. Carson & M. Casado-Kehoe (Eds.), *Case Studies in Couples Therapy* (p. 133–144). New York: Routledge.

Schlanger, K., & Baske, A. (2007) The fight club: Staying away from what does not work. *Journal of Brief Strategic and Systemic Therapies, 1*(2), 67–80.

Watzlawick, P. (1982). Erickson's contribution to the interactional view of psychotherapy. In J.K. Zeig (Ed.), *Ericksonian Approaches to Hypnosis and Psychotherapy* (pp. 147–154). New York: Brunner/Mazel.

Watzlawick, P. (Ed.). (1984). *The Invented Reality: How Do We Know What We Believe We Know? (Contributions to Constructivism)*. New York: Norton.

Watzlawick, P., Beavin, J.B., & Jackson, D.D. (1967). *Pragmatics of Human Communication: A Study of Interactional Patterns, Pathologies, and Paradoxes*. New York: Norton.

Watzlawick, P., & Hoyt, M.F. (1998). Constructing therapeutic realities: A conversation with Paul Watzlawick. In M.F. Hoyt (Ed.), *The Handbook of Constructive Therapies* (pp. 183–197). San Francisco: Jossey-Bass. Reprinted in M.F. Hoyt (2001), *Interviews with Brief Therapy Experts* (pp. 144-157). New York: Brunner/Routledge.

Watzlawick, P., Weakland, J.H., & Fisch, R. (1974). *Change: Principles of Problem Formation and Problem Resolution*. New York: Norton.

Weakland, J.H., & Fisch, R. (1992). Brief therapy—MRI style. In S.H. Budman, M.F. Hoyt, & S. Friedman (Eds.), *The First Session in Brief Therapy* (pp. 306–323). New York: Guilford Press.

27

FINDING HUMANITY IN DARKNESS

Dan Short

What is it like to be absolutely alone in your suffering? What is it like to be without strength or resource in an incredibly dark place where no one else cares to go?

This was exactly where Sergeant Joshua Brennan found himself on the night of October 25, 2007. While leading his troops through the Korengal Valley, Afghanistan, he walked into an ambush and was cut down in a storm of bullets. Having been hit by eight rounds, and separated from his fellow soldiers by a barrage of heavy fire, there seemed to be no hope for him. To make matters worse, two Taliban insurgents rushed in to drag him off, into the black of night. This was going to be the worst possible way to die. However, Specialist Salvatore Giunta, recognizing that his friend was missing, jumped up from his position of cover and ran into the crossfire. Cresting a hill, Giunta spotted Brennan and the two insurgents, whom he shot down as he sprinted through the heavy weapons fire. Dragging Brennan behind a rock, Giunta applied first aid and reassured his friend that he would hold off the insurgents until help arrived. Later the next day, Brennan died during surgery. His body was flown back to the States for a hero's burial, and Giunta became the first living person to receive the military's highest decoration for valor, the Medal of Honor.

As spectacular as Specialist Giunta's actions were, the person he risked his life to rescue still died. So, was it a meaningful endeavor? Given the fact that we are all eventually going to die, and that suffering is an unavoidable aspect of living, can any of us really be rescued?

Seeing Through Darkness

Knowing my role as a counseling psychologist, friends and acquaintances often applaud me for my work, saying things such as, "I do not know how you do it. I do not think I could listen to other people's problems day after day." It is true. I have listened to many horrible life events, some so disturbing that I will not repeat them in print. In some instances, I have witnessed terrible suffering for which there are few practical solutions. However, I do not view my work as a burden. My actions are not heroic, not in the same way that a soldier demonstrates courage, but to reach those who have fallen into psychological peril, it is necessary to leave a position of comfort and journey into some incredibly dark places.

While still a young graduate student, I fulfilled practicum requirements for my group counseling class by going to the county jail to meet with inmates. The meeting space for my group had a large concrete floor, cream-colored concrete walls, and an ominous two-way mirror behind which guards monitored all our interactions. My group members, 13 male inmates, were all dressed in misfit orange jump suits. I remember feeling threatened at this place, but it was not the incarcerated men who made me feel uncomfortable. Instead, it was the institution, the hopelessness that lingered in the corridors and the dehumanization that buzzed overhead in the artificial lighting. I also remember being surprised at how eager the men were to come in and talk about themselves. After listening for awhile to the group members describe the disempowering circumstances in which they lived, and the impoverished childhoods from which they had come, I decided it might be helpful to teach some self-hypnosis. I wanted to show the group how to locate a self-determined, internal reality, a powerful subjective experience that, to some extent, would supersede the immediate sensory world.

Having everyone stand in a circle, with their eyes closed, I began, "You are about to go on a journey ... to a very important place. You carry in your *right* hand a great deal of baggage, heavy baggage. *Unfortunately*, the train station you are standing in has a very long line, and there really is not a suitable place to set down your belongings ... I am so sorry that you have to carry this burden alone ... and even more sorry that time is moving *so* slowly... As your muscles tense up, you can notice the baggage becoming heavier. Right now, you want nothing more than to set it down." This type of suggestion, one that was likely to elicit a physical reaction, allowed me to scan the room and see who was listening. Almost all the men were leaning to the right and some had an uncomfortable look on their face. So I continued, "*Finally*, it is time, the time has come to set your baggage down. And it comes as such a relief! Now your body can relax. Now you can focus your emotional energy on other things." I then went on to describe a journey where new discoveries are made and important relationships are formed. This was the type of journey in which a person's sense of self is expanded and empowered. After ending the exercise, and returning to their chairs, most of the men expressed their enjoyment of the experience. As one man put it, "I was really glad when you told us we could set the bags down. My arm was starting to hurt!" However, off to my left, I noticed one man was sitting motionless. The expression on his dark face was difficult to interpret. This being my first practicum experience, I was concerned I might have made some type of mistake. So I carefully asked him what was happening.

Without lifting his head, he reached for his chest, and said, "It's gone. It's not there anymore." After a brief moment of staring into vacant space, as if in a state of absolute disbelief, he slowly turned my direction and explained, "After 30 days of horrible pain in my chest, while I slept, while I ate, this constant pain … now it is gone!" The look that swept over his face reflected such delight that, for a brief moment, I wondered if he was mocking the group activity. However, after hearing his story, his response made perfect sense. As the inmate recounted, "There was an intense *stabbing* pain … in my heart … the day the judge slammed down his gavel and sentenced me to 99 years in prison. This all started when my fiancée told me she was ending it. She was the first person I had ever allowed myself to love, to really fully need. Now she was leaving me and it was so she could be with another man. So, without thinking, I went to the hotel where he worked … I had a knife in my hand … I saw him … jumped over the counter … and stabbed him, again and again. It was when the judge slammed down his gavel that I realized there was no hope for me, no hope for my life."

The pain reflected in his face, as he told his story, was not the type that is easily simulated. Feeling confident in his sincerity, I sought to learn more about what he had experienced during the group exercise, "Do you feel comfortable telling the rest of us what happened, why your heart stopped hurting?" He continued, "You started talking … and your voice was just sort of annoying, so I went in my own direction … I wasn't listening to what you were saying anymore. I was absolutely alone … surrounded in complete blackness. I really did not want to be in this place. Then … really far in the distance, I saw a small glimmer of light. I walked in the direction of the light and when I got close enough, I could see that it was a tunnel. It was difficult to look in the tunnel, because it was so bright, but when I did, I saw an angel at the other end. Slowly, this angel came drifting toward me … and as she moved in, the darkness began to fade, it was replaced by light."

At this point, most of the men in the room were entering into their second trance. As he spoke, it was difficult not to follow the man's gaze up to the ceiling and look for the angel yourself. The expression on his eyes, forehead, and checks, was such that it seemed he must be looking at something divine. He then said, "The angel spoke to me. She told me that I am forgiven. She said, 'You can have a new life in Jesus Christ.'" Focusing his eyes on the rest of the group, he said, "That is exactly what I am going to do. The first thing, when I arrive at the state penitentiary, I am going to be baptized!" Though his physical history and sentence remained immutable, something significant had changed for this man during the course of this encounter. He was no longer surrounded by darkness. I had not rescued him. However, I did witness a self-transcendence that occurred not only for him, but for others in the room, including myself. This event confirmed for me that this type of work would be one of the most meaningful activities I could pursue.

Though not everyone is inclined to feel concern for a man who has committed a horrible crime, as citizens of humanity, we are inextricably bound through our common capacity to suffer and to need others. This is especially true during childhood, a time when a person's vulnerabilities are more numerous. Childhood is a time when we so desperately need help from a mother, father, and the many others who come into a new budding life. My experience is that there are few who would be content to witness the suffering of an innocent child and do nothing. But at what point do we decide a person no longer possesses innocence, and is therefore no longer worthy of concern?

How does a universal human attribute suddenly disappear? According to Joan Didion (1961/1968), innocence ends when one is stripped of the delusion that one likes oneself. This idea points toward the human need to form a positive relationship with one's self. How much of an impact can another person really have on the general knowledge of oneself and the experience of innocence and personal strength? And, assuming that outside relationships really do make a difference, how much exposure is needed to make a lasting difference? Is it a matter of days, weeks, months, or can something significant transpire during a brief moment of interaction?

One day a concerned father brought his 13-year-old son to me for help. Looking at the father, I was immediately aware of a remarkable contrast. This man had a strong bulky frame. His hands were large and his shoulders almost as broad as the doorway opening. Yet he sat in front of me with a look of helplessness and desperation.

He wanted to protect his son from a sinister force that was causing the child great distress. But there was nothing he could put his hands on. His child was living in fear of vicious attacks that occurred every single night, by a perpetrator who remained at large, and absolutely untouchable.

For the past two weeks, the boy had been experiencing a recurring nightmare during which he was being anally raped. According to the father, his son was now unable to sleep. He had become socially withdrawn, unable to enjoy time with friends or family. When asked, the boy gave me the following description of his dreams: "I am in what seems to be the back of a semi-truck. It is all metal and I am being raped, anally, by a guy (I only saw his face once). I am being raped and it just seems to go on and on." After saying this, the boy's face flushed with a look of pain and shame.

The father was at a complete loss. As he put it, "This came out of the blue.

We have not seen a movie with anything like that. We have not discussed anything like that." The father indicated that his first concern was that someone was touching his son. If so, he wanted to know who it was so he could eliminate the problem. Looking into his eyes, I had no doubt he would kill in order to protect his much-loved child.

With his father sitting next to him, I questioned the boy at length. Without any hesitation, he insisted that there was no recent trauma, no illness or accidents, and no other significant problems in his life. He only wanted the nightmares to end. When I asked for more details, the boy told me that every night he had the same dream. When I asked what happened on the day that the nightmares began, he could not recall anything of significance. However, the father suddenly made a connection: "He has a girlfriend. He found out that day [that the nightmares started] that she would be moving away." Hearing this, I suggested that the dreams might be a symbolic representation of a real-life experience, an emotional experience that was otherwise suppressed. The father was insightful, immediately catching my line of reasoning: "Such as helplessness from his girlfriend moving away?" At this point, the father confessed his own feelings of helplessness. I acknowledged his dilemma: "It is hard to protect someone while they are sleeping," to which the father responded, "Amen!"

As mentioned earlier, I feel that an important part of my work with clients is my willingness to meet them at their core of darkness or distress, so I offered to the boy: "I may try to go into your dreams and help you ... Have you seen the movie *Inception*? [He shook his head 'No'] ... Nonetheless, I will do it using hypnosis, if you are comfortable with this idea. If not, we will not do the hypnosis." This idea was followed with a few minutes of small talk and humor, so that my young client could get used to the idea of intentionally walking back into his nightmare. Then, I questioned the boy a little further so that I could carefully tailor my suggestions: "To use hypnosis to make the nightmare go away, it would be helpful if I knew more about you. I need to know what you really like or what you are really good at, such as a particular sport." Without any hesitation, he replied, "I like baseball. I like hitting the ball with the bat!" This was perfect.

Next, I had the boy speak aloud as he closed his eyes and relived the nightmare, "The man is behind me ... and I am just getting anally raped ... feeling fear and shame as it is happening ... I am screaming, sometimes for help, sometimes for him to stop." Then, the boy suddenly opened his eyes. Having acknowledged his efforts, I offered a solution, "Okay. Let's see if we can make it so you don't have that dream tonight."

After instructing him to again close his eyes, and listen to me, I began to narrate the nightmare, "There is a man at the other end of the trailer. You see, through a flash of light, the look on his face. You realize he does not have good intention. And there is just enough light in that trailer that you can look on the floor and see a baseball bat laying there. [pause] And, I would like you to see that you can get to that bat far quicker than he can get to you. [pause] And, you take that bat in your hands, and you hold it up above your shoulders, just like you are ready to hit a homerun. [pause] And, at that moment you feel the strength in your hands. [pause—switching to a deep serious tone] And, you know what damage that bat can do. [pause] And, you know what would happen if you landed it on his skull. [pause] And, you are a decent enough fellow that [long pause] you decide not to use it unless you have to. But you let him know that you are serious and that you are strong. So you say to him, 'Do not take one step closer to me. I am absolutely serious about this, not one step closer to me.' [pause] And you ready the bat, just to make certain he understands that you mean business. [pause] And, you see him backing away. So you take a few steps toward him, not to hurt him, just a few steady steps. And, he steps back, eventually falling off the back of the semi. And, then he picks himself up and you see him start to run away. Everything is now out in the daylight. Now he is not only scared of you but he is also scared of being caught, of being identified. Everything has gone wrong for him. He is confused. And, you watch him run away."

Seeing a look of ease come over his body, I shifted from crisis intervention work to a focus on the boy's future development. "And at that very moment, as your muscles calm down and go back into a relaxed state, you loosen up your grip on the bat, and right then you make a new decision about who you are, that you are a person of power, and what you can handle in life, and how cool you can be in a crisis. It is hard to explain, it is hard to describe, but there is some sort of good feeling that starts to build up inside of you. [pause] You are someone who has just won a really difficult game against an opponent that you shouldn't have been able to beat. And this feeling sticks with you. It sticks with you for the rest of your life! And, you can dream that dream, I just described to you, over and over again. That same dream can keep playing itself out. But your unconscious mind can elaborate on it. It can add new details about what happens, what you say. It can even change up the context, the location, and your unconscious mind can continue to develop the dream in a way that is pleasing, in a way that meets your needs. And, you can keep having that dream, again and again, as I continue to talk to you."

At that point, I began to tell the young boy several stories. I told him about a girl I knew in high school, who was nearly raped in her home. Fortunately, her mother was able to frighten-off the intruder, almost immediately after he forced his way into the home. I told other similar stories of dangerous individuals being stood-down by courage alone. With the boy still slumped over in a trance-like posture, I explained to him, "When you take these things head-on, an interesting thing happens, the threat itself tends to back down. Anxiety tends to run away when you face it head-on. And that is something you can do in real life, at school, on the baseball diamond, while you are with your friends, or later on when you get a job. And it is something you can do in your dreams, at night, this very night! You can be surprised by how much personal power and strength you find inside yourself."

After the boy awakened, I asked him how the experience was for him. His one-word reply was, "Interesting." The father gave a more enthusiastic response: "That is the weirdest damn thing I have ever seen! So how ... when ... when did he go under? That was tremendous! Does he need to come in and see you again?" I told the father that there was no need to bring his son back to my office, not unless he still had problems with nightmares.

It has been over a year since this meeting. I have not heard from the father or his son. Fortunately, the mother decided to send me an email and provide me with some follow-up. She wrote, "I wanted you to know [her son] has not had any more nightmares. He is back to his wonderful, funny self. He turned 14 yesterday and it was a great day!" This email was a delight for me. It allowed me to know that, in this instance, I had done something to help reduce human suffering. Because of his age and vulnerability (especially in regard to identity development) there is the possibility that my moment with him may have far-reaching consequences. He now has a set of protective ideas that may stay with him for the rest of his life.

A Gateway to Compassion

Though I mostly do clinical work, I have occasionally volunteered my services for foreign-born children seeking protection or asylum inside the United States. Once, while testifying as an expert witness in such a proceeding, I found myself listening to a convincing attorney argue all the reasons why a boy, who was seeking asylum in the United States, needed to be returned to his own country, Guatemala. She made a compelling argument for why more American tax dollars did not need to be spent on a child who had illegally slipped through the borders just so he could have a more comfortable life. Her main argument was that this person was already 16 years of age, and, not speaking a word of English, was probably better off growing up in a culture to which he was accustomed, surrounded by people whom he already knew.

I had been invited by the court to provide my testimony by speaker phone. This put me at a disadvantage. I could not see the faces of the people that I was wishing to engage. The boy had someone there as his advocate, but she was an inexperienced law student, volunteering her time. Her English was slightly broken and she spoke with a thick Asian accent.

When it was finally my turn to speak, the judge let me know he had read my affidavit and that he was curious about a statement I had made indicating that there were no indications of malingering. To clarify, I explained, "Of course it is impossible to know with absolute certainty if someone has given an accurate accounting of events. However, there are some types of responses, coming from the autonomic nervous system, that come from exposure to trauma.

Most of these are outside a person's conscious control and some can be easily observed." During the forensic interview I had done with the boy at the detention center, I had taken the approach of asking questions about symptoms unrelated to trauma, to see if the young boy was simply endorsing all the questions I asked about possible difficulties. On the contrary, he had insisted that many of the symptoms I described he had not experienced. He was an uneducated Guatemalan Indian, living up in the mountains, who had not even learned to speak Spanish, much less English. (We had a translator on a speaker phone at the detention center.) There was no way he could have trained himself in the nosology of the *DSM* in order to fake the symptoms associated with Post-Traumatic Stress Disorder (PTSD).

As I spoke to the court, I used a voice that was monotone and unemotional. I did not want to be dismissed as a "bleeding-heart." I did want everyone in the courtroom to hear the boy's story. So with the defendant listening to my testimony, as it was translated into his native tongue, I continued: "In order to make sense of the unusual behavior demonstrated by this child at the detention center, you have to know something about the precipitating events. For instance, during my interview with him, the boy begged me for permission to stay at the detention center. The boy told me that the staff treats him very well. In his words, 'I feel safe here. No one is beating me. I want to learn how to read and write.' Allegedly, his mother began beating him with heavy sticks and ropes when he reached 10 years of age. These beatings, that were reported to have occurred as many as two or three times a day, provide some explanation for the scars and rope-burn marks you see on his arms and face. If he was, in fact, only allowed to attend elementary school for three years, before being forced to go work in the fields, then it would help explain why the detention center is viewed by the boy as some sort of home. However, more interesting to me was his explanation for the vertical scar you see on his right elbow."

After waiting a brief moment for everyone to gaze over at the boy, I continued: "When I asked him if this was from the beatings, he corrected me explaining that it was from a bicycle accident at the detention center. When asked to provide more details, he recounted that he had been riding his bicycle feeling very happy but then he had thoughts of his uncle and was no longer able to stay balanced on his bike, thus sending him crashing to the ground. This type of sudden loss of muscular coordination is known as 'freezing.' It is an automatic response triggered during traumatic events or during the recollection of such experiences. Although the boy seemed to be blocking much of his traumatic memories during our interview, and therefore unable to explain many of the scars on his body, when I urged him to tell me more about his uncle, he recalled an episode during which the uncle came to his house with a machete. This uncle allegedly made the threat, 'I will cut your head from your body,' at which time the boy ran into the jungle to hide. According to the child, the uncle came to the house more than once seeking to kill him. Allegedly, because the boy's father is dead, there is some disputed property that the uncle does not want the child to inherit. But as I was saying, the boy would stay out in the jungle for as long as 12 hours, without food or water. On several occasions, he would begin to vomit. After one such episode of vomiting he felt tremendous pain in his body and nearly lost consciousness." At this point, my testimony was interrupted by the judge. "Doctor ... doctor, there is something happening here ... the child is shaking. He does not look well. What do you think is happening to him?" Maintaining my dispassionate tone, I replied, "For us, this is another day of doing business. At the end of the day, we will go home and everything will be fine. But for the boy, this is a discussion about whether he will live or die. I believe he is convinced that if the court decides to send him back, he will find no one in Guatemala to defend him. He fears that his uncle will eventually kill him. He also seems to be fearful of the people in the village, to whom he owes money."

Knowing the child's emotional triggers, I pushed on ahead. "If you look on his arms and neck, you will probably see evidence of muscle spasticity. This boy responds with unusual distress and hypersensitivity to touch, especially on his left leg." During my previous interview with the child, he had recoiled and suddenly started rubbing his leg at the first mention of his uncle. This suggested that this part of his body contained strong implicit memory associations. It was this type of obvious somatic reaction that I believed would be the court's most compelling evidence. So I continued: "This part of his body was probably..." but before I could finish my sentence, the judge again cut me off. He said, "Doctor, you cannot see this, but something is seriously wrong with this child. He is not well. I am stopping the proceedings."

This was a welcome outcome. I did not want the child to suffer any more than necessary. It had been difficult enough to watch him decompensate during the forensic interview.

That interview had taken place a few weeks before the court date. Having been allowed only 60 minutes to establish rapport and gather the necessary clinical data—information that would determine the course of this child's life—I worked relentlessly and without delay. These were the types of disturbing memories that I would normally allow a client months to piece together and slowly integrate into conscious awareness.

To make matters worse, as a forensic investigator, I was not to do therapy with the boy. After taking him to a point of absolute psychological vulnerability and distress, I was supposed to simply end the interview and leave. For me, this was unacceptable. So at the end of our encounter, I did my best to humanize the process. After the child became reoriented to his immediate surroundings, I asked the interpreter on the speaker phone to say to the boy, "I am very sorry these bad things happened to you. You are a good person. You did not deserve to be treated this way." As the interpreter spoke, I looked deep into the boy's eyes. I did not dare say much else. I was being monitored by the detention staff and did not want to say anything that could be misconstrued as creating false testimony.

Now the courtroom proceedings had not lasted even half as long as the forensic interview. After the judge spoke, the prosecuting attorney made a brief frustrated response. She had not been given the opportunity to cross-examine me and she had not been told on what date the court would reconvene.

Three days later, I received a call from the boy's pro-bono attorney. She was happy to report that the judge had determined that no further evidence was needed. He had decided to grant the boy asylum inside the United States. She told me that another nonprofit organization was stepping in to help his transition to foster care and to provide him therapy for trauma.

Looking back, the greatest reward I took away from this experience was the lesson this 16-year-old child taught me. During the interview, I was intrigued by the boy's gratitude and subsequent happiness. Though severely traumatized, he was not a depressed child. He had not lost his humanity. He was grateful for his new life in the Arizona detention center. He was grateful for the opportunity to attend educational classes. He was grateful for his haircut and the food he was given. He was grateful for my help. And I, in turn, was grateful that I had the opportunity to meet him.

Love: Shining Light into Darkness

As mentioned in the opening paragraphs, pain and death are relatively inescapable aspects of the human condition. The extension of life and the reduction of suffering are, of course, worthy objectives. In many instances, I have seen psychotherapy succeed to this end. However, unlike medicine, a poignant human encounter will not only bring reprieve, but will also address the human need to make sense of one's suffering.

It is true that to understand the client's subjective reality, it is necessary to feel some of what he or she feels. However, it is also necessary to remain partially dissociated from the client's reality so that one's own ability to create new perspectives is not curtailed. More simply put, I do not want the client's disturbing reality to become my own. Although I truly care, if I am fully empathetic while dealing with traumatized clients, I am less able to help. That is because my own perspective would be contained within their narrative of helplessness.

This is an important means of protecting oneself from secondary traumatization. While listening to a highly distressed client, I will allow myself to feel physically a small amount of what he or she is feeling, perhaps at 25% of the intensity they experience. Depending on how disturbing their experiences are, this may only last for brief moments, followed by full detachment. This way my problem solving is not inhibited by fear, anger, shame, or whatever it is that has been dominating the client's awareness. Rather than being overwhelmed by highly challenging situations, I find this allows me to then take delight in the opportunity to exercise my problem-solving abilities.

Since I have been writing about a willingness to journey into dark places, I should also make some mention of how to re-emerge, unharmed. As mentioned above, I intentionally maintain a partial dissociation from the client's realities so that my own psychological resources are protected. I also limit the number of hours I spend with clients during a given day. Six hours is my preference; however, I can handle seven without having my defenses start to weaken. Anything past seven hours will cause me to run the risk of emotional contamination. My resilience has limits and I have learned to recognize when I am reaching the edge.

Another important strategy for those who do this work is having someone else to talk to. Fortunately, there are several therapists in my office suite. On occasion, we will consult with one another or, if needed, we will debrief after hearing something difficult. For those who do not have this type of resource, I strongly recommend finding a therapists' consultation group. Just 90 minutes, once a month, can do a great deal to preserve one's health.

The third strategy that has been essential for my own peace-of-mind is the collection of outcome data. This way I have physical evidence of the good that is accomplished. By collecting and studying outcome data, I am able to continue my professional development in a way that cannot be achieved by reading books or attending lectures. In order to closely monitor the transformation process, I make an attempt to collect written feedback on a session-by-session basis. The forms I use have been designed to illuminate what is needed and most helpful for each individual client. (These assessment tools are available for free at my website: www.IamDrShort.com.) In this way, I learn more about doing therapy with each and every session I conduct. Any data collection device can be a useful tool, but more importantly my clients know that I really care how things turn out for them. It is this felt human connection that causes the individuals I see to send me cards or call me on the phone, sometimes years later, so that I continue to share in the good that has been accomplished.

While looking for a way to conclude this chapter, I asked my 9-year-old daughter, Elise, "What do you think a hero is?" After thinking a moment, she said, "A hero is someone who is so kind they can give up themselves to help someone else, even though they may get hurt. You don't have to have super powers or anything like that. You just have to be brave and really kind." I think this definition fits well for those who have dedicated their professional pursuits to the practice of therapy or counseling. The designation of hero is especially applicable for those who work in shelters, community mental health centers, refugee camps, or any other psychologically demanding setting in which financial gain is clearly not the individual's primary motivation. The fact that there are some people willing to voluntarily journey into dark places and potentially expose themselves to secondary traumatization does not fit with the ordinary logic of self-preservation. It might even seem crazy to some. However, we not only help others experience safety and love by meeting them in their dark places, but we as care providers discover strength within ourselves as we participate in our species' quest for humanity.

Reference

Didion, J. (1968). On self-respect. In *Slouching Towards Bethlehem* (pp. 142–148). New York: Farrar, Straus and Giroux. (work originally in *Vogue*, 1961)

28

IN SEARCH OF THE SPIRIT

A Therapist's Journey

Terry Soo-Hoo

I am standing at the podium at California State University East Bay preparing to speak to the Marriage and Family Therapy Program graduating class of 2011. There is excitement in the air. Family and friends of the graduates are all sitting attentively waiting to hear what I have to say. As I look out into the audience, I wonder how many people are here. There seems to be a lot of eager, happy faces. Graduation ceremonies are wonderful events. They celebrate hard–won achievements as well as important transitions, the closing of one chapter in life and the beginning of another. I ponder silently to myself: *How did I get here?* How did I become a professor of counseling after more than 20 years working as a psychologist in the field? This is my 11th year teaching at this university. But I started as a counselor, then became a psychologist. How did that happen? Thoughts flow through my mind like scenes of a movie in fast motion. Certain images stop and linger briefly, then move on.

Coming to California

I am six years old, feeling lost, confused, and so scared. Everything was strange coming to California from Hong Kong. Nothing made sense. Why did we leave our home? What happened to our friends and relatives? No one even explained where we were going and why? I feel so alone, so different. Nobody looks like me. What is it that everyone was speaking? English, what kind of language was that? Does anyone speak Chinese here? What are they saying to me? I am feeling scared. The teacher is talking. Sounds are coming from her mouth but I only make out she is saying my name. She gestures towards one of the seats. I need to sit down at that desk? Class is beginning? OK, I better sit down. It is going to be a long day.

Running Scared

I am running as fast as I can. Five older kids are chasing me. Who are they? They look big and mean, like "gang" kids. What do they want from me? Don't they know I have no money? They are yelling "Chink" and "Slant eyes!" I get that "scared" feeling again. I am alone and there is no one to help. Why do we have to live here where there are no other Asian kids to join up with? Why do I have to be the smallest kid in the neighborhood? Why do I feel so weak and helpless? I wish I was at least Six Feet Tall. Then, I would stand and fight. But I find the strength to run faster. I am really fast! I am too fast for them! I deliberately take the long and out-of-the-way route home to be sure they don't know where I live.

The Lean and Mean Years in China

When I arrived home my mother is upset. When she was younger, China was in the midst of internal turmoil and under external threat. There was great poverty spreading across the land. Her village had to send their men and older teenage children away to find work. My father came to California at age 17 to work and save enough money to return many years later to marry my mother. My mother survived the "lean and mean" years in China. She suffered poverty, famine, vicious bandits, the Japanese invasion and physical abuse by her mother-in-law, and much more. After the marriage, my father had to return to California to build his business, leaving her behind for many years. She tells horrendous stories of survival those years while alone. She had to escape from the invading Japanese army. This was a time of great cruelty and savagery. Whole towns were devastated, men, women, children massacred. She had to escape by running up into the mountains. My older brother was strapped to her back, while she dodged machine gun bullets from strafing Japanese fighter planes. An incredible survivor, she and many of her generation are examples of the power of the human spirit. She has seen the destructive power of prejudice and racism, one race claiming superiority over another. But the lean and mean years have taken their toll. She is worried and afraid. On the outside, she was a powerful woman who needed to be in charge. On the inside was a wounded spirit that longed to be healed. She is saying to me: *There is great danger out there. There is no one to turn to. You have to rely on yourself.* I feel more alone. *You can never let up. You must work hard and focus only on your studies. Do not be foolish and think of small pleasures and having fun. When you become successful and famous you will have all that you can hope for.* There is a heavy feeling that weighs me down. Life is serious and dangerous. But I am determined to succeed.

The Search for Physical Strength

I am in Kung Fu practice. At 19 years of age, I still feel smaller than those around me. I want to become stronger and learn to fight to defend myself. I want to stop feeling so scared. I am fast and learn the techniques quickly. But something is missing. I still cannot defeat those who are bigger and stronger than I am. Even with superior technique and speed I still feel vulnerable when encountering a much larger opponent. Size does matter in sheer physical strength. I try many different styles of martial arts over the years, still something is missing. I want to feel more *powerful!*

The Wrong Direction

I am in college, studying electrical engineering. I like electronics. There is something rewarding about building a radio and listening to music through something I built myself. But I do not like the calculations! Why am I calculating the speed of an electron flowing through a wire!? What does this have to do with my life? The counselor is saying you need to expand your experiences, take different classes to experience different fields of study.

Exploring Psychology

I am in a Group Process class. Someone is talking about his father never being there for him. This feels very familiar. I know this feeling. I say to him: *"It is like there is an emptiness inside."* Yes, he says that is exactly how it feels. I am good at this! As I listen to the others in the group I am struck with how many of the issues are similar to what I have gone through. I am able to get in touch with other peoples' feelings and experiences. There is a student saying that all through high school he felt invisible, that no one could see him. There is an Asian American that is saying he hates himself because he is so short. He wishes he was six feet tall and could play basketball and football like some of his White friends. *"I don't think I will ever find a girl who will like me because I am so short and ugly."* I think to myself, does that sound familiar? I think I have come a long ways!

I left the group feeling I have been there, in the *"darkness,"* filled with self doubt, confusion and fear. *Maybe I can help people navigate where I have been and find a path out of the darkness.*

The Mind Fist

I am practicing standing meditation, a Chi Kung practice. A friend told me about a Chi Kung master (Sifu), Chuek Fung, who specialized in chi energy martial arts practice. It is called *Yi Chaun* (The Mind Fist). He teaches Chi Energy not only for health and healing but also as self defense and martial arts. He is saying:

> You can activate your energy and it will expand within your body and become so full it swells and you feel like a "Giant." We call this the "giant body" experience. It is just one of many experiences that will lead to freeing your mind, body and spirit. With this new freedom you can give expression to many different parts of your spirit, one moment the "ferocious tiger" spirit, the next moment the "playful monkey" spirit, and yet another moment the "soaring eagle" spirit. You have an infinite number of spirits waiting to be expressed.

I feel light as air as if I am floating but at the same time I am solidly grounded to the earth. I have never felt so centered and solid, so strong and powerful, yet so at peace with myself. Suddenly, my body is shaking. My energy is being activated and I need to learn how to let it flow evenly and naturally through my body. Fung Sifu is saying:

> It is not enough just to be an intelligent person. You also need "eyes to see." Do you have eyes to see what is "real" versus "illusion"? While it is important to cultivate a strong and healthy body, in martial arts a person with a large body and big muscles does not always possess superior strength. That is why we practice Hunyuan strength, oneness, whole body strength or six surfaces strength. This method integrates the mind, body, energy as well as spirit. It is the highest level of strength. When done correctly there is no grunting, straining or excessive tensing of muscles. The exertion of strength feels effortless.

I am able to bounce people away with ease, even people much larger. At last I have the answer, what was missing. Yi Chaun and Chi Energy! Sufi Fung continues:

> Understand that in any encounter your greatest resource is the quality of your "character." Remember that "true power" comes from the strength of your "inner spirit." We develop and nurture our inner spirit by cultivating a "loving heart." That is the path towards freedom and liberation. That is where the "light" leads us!

Now my mind, body, and spirit are one. Gone is the heaviness that had been weighing me down since childhood. At last I am on the right path towards the "light."

Something Is Still Missing

I am now a graduate of the University of California, Berkeley, a new Ph.D. in Clinical Psychology. It is surprising how much more confident I feel transitioning from a Masters Degree in Counseling to a Ph.D. in Psychology. Somehow I feel more empowered to take on more challenging jobs. Some of the cases are really tough. But after a time in the new, more challenging job, that old feeling is back. There has to be something I am missing. I am good at my work but I feel I can be so much better. Clients are getting better, but progress in therapy is moving very slowly. So many people are suffering and in pain. I need to be able to help more people than I am doing now. There must be a better way, a better method, and a quicker, briefer way to help people change.

The Mental Research Institute and Enlightenment

I am at the Mental Research Institute (MRI), listening to John Weakland, one of the founders of MRI (Weakland, Fisch, Watzlawick, & Bodin, 1974) He is saying: *"Most people who come to therapy are not really sick or pathological. Rather they are stuck and do not know how to find effective solutions to their problems. So the goal of therapy is not to cure sickness or pathology, but to help people get unstuck and find solutions that work better for them."*

Such a simple idea yet it has such profound effect on my clinical work. This is what was missing! The key is not just a systemic view but a "relational" or "interactional" perspective to working with human problems. The goal is to disrupt the ineffective interactional cycle or pattern and find solutions that work better. New, more effective solutions usually take a significant turn (often 180 degrees) from the ineffective "attempted solutions." Culture is important because how people get stuck is very specific to their culture and therefore, the solutions must be consistent with their cultural context. Culture shapes people's frame of reference, or the meaning that is attributed to their problem situation. For people to change, we need to help them not only change their ineffective behaviors but also change this meaning that is keeping them stuck.

So the very first task of a therapist is to "enter the client's world" and to work within that unique world as opposed to forcing the client to work within the world of the therapist. In this way all therapy can be considered "multicultural therapy," since every client brings to therapy a unique world.

As I listened and watched John working with a client, I am struck with his uncanny ability to activate the clients' strengths. One day he said: *"In therapy it is important to understand the duality of life. On the one hand, we need to acknowledge the client's pain and suffering. Yet on the other hand, we can appreciate what clients do in their attempts to solve their problems can be absolutely ludicrous. So in therapy we can empathize with the client's pain at one moment and at another moment laugh with the client at how what has happened is so ridiculous. So humor should be a part of therapy as it is in life."*

Thank you, John: Because of you I am more alive, natural, and human when I am seeing clients.

Just as Yi Chuan has opened my internal energy and inner spirit, MRI has opened my eyes to see the world of psychology and psychotherapy in new and wonderful ways. I feel enlightened. I like "thinking outside of the box"! Certainly, it has helped me be a more effective therapist. Now it was time to integrate the "energy and spirit" concepts of Chi Energy practice with the ideas of strength-based relational/contextual psychotherapy.

The Meaning of Life

I am in a church and standing next to Natalia, my wife to be. As I look at her I am thinking how beautiful she is and how lucky I am to have such a wonderful woman to be my wife. Natalia has been my inspiration and support. Our love for each other has helped me understand what has true meaning in life. I am a better person because of her. The birth of our son and the years since has further opened my heart. Who was it that first stated, "The therapist is the therapy"? Who we are as a person plays a huge role in terms of how we are therapists, healers, helpers or facilitators of change. Beyond the theory and techniques, beyond the science and research, psychotherapy involves a person in a relationship with another person (or persons). What we say to psychotherapy clients makes sense only within the context of who we are and how the client experiences us. Thus, as I become a better person a better therapist emerges.

Commencement

I am now speaking to the Commencement audience. How am I doing this? How can I be speaking to the audience at the same time I am reviewing my journey to becoming the therapist and teacher that I am now? Milton Erickson (Rosen, 1982) would probably say that the mind has infinite capacity and I must be in some kind trance—or maybe multiple trances.

I hear myself saying:

> Welcome everyone. Let me begin with an old Chinese proverb: If you want to be happy for one day, buy an expensive toy. If you want to be happy for three months, get married. If you want to be happy for a lifetime: Serve others!
>
> We are here today because our graduates have chosen to serve others. They have chosen to become counselors and therapists to help those in need. This path has not been an easy one. There have been many challenges. It has been filled with hard work, hardship and sacrifice. We are all proud of their perseverance and commitment to becoming full-fledged counselors and therapists."

An Integrationist

What is my psychotherapy approach? What theory do I ascribe to? I am an *"integrationist."* I call what I do *"Strength-Based Multicultural Integrative Therapy."* What is that? I have written some articles that have focused on some of my ideas (Soo-Hoo, 1998, 1999, 2005a, 2005b). I integrate different theories and techniques to form a coherent therapy approach that activates people's inner strengths and works towards finding solutions to their problems within their cultural context. I also look for ways to activate people's sense of spirit and energy (Soo-Hoo, 2000, 2003). I still need to write the definitive book on my approach.

Milton Erickson was a legend in his own time for his powerful psychological cures, often in just one or two sessions. He was a remarkable innovator and pioneer in both brief therapy and hypnotherapy. As a teenager, he lay in his bed listening to the doctors tell his mother through the bedroom door that her son Milton was not going to survive the night (Rosen, 1982). That night he consciously determined that he was going to see the sun rise in the morning no matter what the doctors had said! Each day for many years he gave expression to this very powerful *will* or *spirit*. Even though he was in a wheelchair much of his life, he cultivated a very powerful spirit and lived life with great energy and vitality. Despite his own pain and hardship, he was able to help so many people to overcome their obstacles and hardships. He referred to this as activating the power of the *unconscious*. I refer to it as the power of the *inner spirit*. How do I use this in therapy? It is hard to explain. Perhaps a few examples would help.

Darkness Everywhere: How to Find the Light

I am talking to Gerald, an African American teenager. He just lost his brother to gang violence. He looks lost, defeated, sad and very angry.

Gerald: Why should I bother with school? It makes no difference. All those A's I got in all those classes don't mean a thing now. Gang violence got my uncle, my cousin and now my brother. It will eventually get me!

He looks so scared and lost. I know that feeling! At times I can still feel it inside me. But I have learned not to be afraid of the "fear" but to let it pass through me. I use it to connect with others. I sense the "force" is strong with him. But he does not know it yet. How can I reach him and activate that force, his inner spirit?

Soo-Hoo: Life is a series of battles; you have to be strong to survive!

He looks at me as if to say "This guy knows something. I am listening."

Soo-Hoo: Have you heard of the *"warrior spirit"*? It is not enough to be physically strong—you have to be strong mentally and spiritually.

There is curiosity in his eyes. He likes this idea.

Soo-Hoo: Each culture has its own tradition of the *warrior spirit*. You can discover your own cultural tradition or I can share with you my training in the *warrior spirit*.

He is curious.

Soo-Hoo: Darkness is everywhere. You can give in to the Darkness. Or you can fight it and follow the path towards the Light!
Gerald: My brother tried to fight it but couldn't do it! I am so tired, why should I keep fighting everything, it gets you nowhere?
Soo-Hoo: Yes, I can see you are tired and exhausted. But being tired is not the same as being weak! You have fought many battles with great strength and courage. You have endured more than many people can even imagine. However, even great warriors can be wounded in battle. We call this "trauma." Trauma is an injury to the mind, body and spirit. Feeling "tired" is your spirit saying it needs to be healed.

He looks at me as if to say at last someone understands.

Soo-Hoo: But to heal the spirit means to allow yourself to feel the pain. Because the pain represents the love you have for your brother, as well as the other family members you have lost to violence. You can speak openly about that love or you can acknowledge that love inside without words. You can cherish that love and be proud of it on a spiritual level.

There are tears in his eyes. But he does not want to stay with the pain too long, so we move on.

Soo-Hoo: You can be stronger still by activating your *warrior spirit*. This will make you mentally tougher and smarter. A strong *warrior spirit* can endure hardship and suffering, yet also guide us to honor and respect our family and be gentle, caring, and loving to those who love us.

His eyes begin to sparkle again. Gone are the dullness and haze around his face that reflect his feelings of defeat and hopelessness.

Soo-Hoo: You love your brother, so the *warrior spirit* guides us to honor him. How do we honor him? The *warrior spirit* would say we honor him by continuing the path he would have wanted you to pursue. Do you think he would want you to "give up" on school and to go the path of the "Gangs"? Or do you think he would want you to go to college and make the family proud and make him proud?

His aura is changing, becoming more radiant yet smoother and calmer. His face is softening, yet there is a new sense of determination there.

Soo-Hoo: "Your spirit is strong—do you feel it?"

Yes, he can feel it and he is pleased and proud. He wants to honor his brother. We continue with the practice.

The Scared Little Boy Inside

I am talking to Derrick, a 28-year-old Chinese American computer programmer complaining of feeling anxious and fearful around people.

Derrick: I get so anxious and nervous. I am so afraid to talk to people that I have trouble even looking at the person I am talking to. Just thinking about social situations triggers so much anxiety and fear that I feel overwhelmed. That is why I work at home on the computer, to avoid interacting with other people. Psychologists have told me I suffer from "anxiety disorder" and "social phobia." But these therapists have not been able to help me stop being so fearful. Medicine is also useless. Nothing seem to be working!

He looks so vulnerable and scared. How do I help him not be afraid of the fear?

Soo-Hoo: We all have many parts inside. There is a strong and confident part as well as a *scared little boy* part. However, we need to feel fear if we are to know courage. It is the *scared little boy* part that allows us to be vulnerable, sensitive and gentle. And it is sharing this vulnerability and insecurity that leads to intimacy and closeness.

Derrick: How can feeling scared and vulnerable be a good thing when it causes me so much trouble?

He is being smothered by fear and self doubt. How can I help him free his spirit?

Soo-Hoo: The goal is not to eliminate the scared little boy part, but instead to have greater control over when that part is activated versus when the strong and confident part is activated. Look into this mirror while we talk about your strengths. Focus on your eyes. What do you like about yourself? What are your areas of competence and what are some of your successes? What would your friends say about you?

As he spoke his eyes began to sparkle and shine brighter.

Soo-Hoo: Do you see the energy that is shining in your eyes? That is your spirit being activated.

He was surprised yet pleased that he could so easily see the sparkle in his eyes.

Soo-Hoo: Think of the times in your life in which you felt a great sense of joy and satisfaction, you felt "on top of the world," "in charge of your life," or you had just accomplished something you were proud of. See how your eyes are even more radiant and shining brightly now as you think of those moments. Your homework is to practice activating your inner spirit by thinking of your strengths and past moments of joy and accomplishments.

In session two he got in touch with deep feelings of pain from years of feeling rejected and oppressed by his parents in his childhood. Every time he tried to express himself he was crushed. So it was not safe to express himself or to show others his true self.

Soo-Hoo: As we proceed to the next step, the goal is not to totally eliminate your fears but to gain mastery over them. It sounds like you do not give yourself credit for having the courage and strength to survive a very harsh and difficult childhood.

Derrick: But how can I be courageous when I am afraid all the time?

Soo-Hoo: Courageous is the ability to do what you believe is right despite being afraid.

Derrick: But I am afraid all the time with people and just become frozen. I can't even talk!

Soo-Hoo: It is a wise person that recognizes danger. The negative experiences in your past have heightened your perceptions of danger. So you are very good at sensing danger. However, it is important to develop an effective method to cope with these dangerous situations. It is only when we feel safe and secure that we can express ourselves. So the challenge is to create a sense of safety and security when we are faced with these difficult situations. Are you open to exploring the idea that we possess an energy that can give us strength and protect us?

Derrick: I am willing to try anything that will help me feel safer and less afraid.

Soo-Hoo: The Chinese call this Chi Energy. It means "life force" or "life energy." This Chi Energy has been measured as an electromagnetic force. All living things possess this energy. We can mentally activate our energy field to create a protective barrier that can give us a sense of safety and security.

He is intrigued by this.

Soo-Hoo: We are going to practice activating an energy field about three feet out around you and completely surrounding you. You will feel completely safe and secure behind this energy field. No one can harm you behind the energy field. You can observe others and even reach out to touch others but they cannot touch you without your permission. Once you feel comfortable in activating your energy field, the next level of practice is to integrate the activation of your strengths and inner spirit with this sensation of your Chi Energy that surrounds you.

Derrick was surprised that he could feel his Chi Energy as a physical force, something he could touch and sense around him.

A few months have passed. Derrick's aura is glowing radiantly. His eyes sparkle with energy and vitality. There is a new found sense of confidence.

Derrick: I feel really different. When I feel safe and secure, I am able to be myself. And when I am myself I can be natural and my good parts come out. People seem to like me. At times I still feel some anxiety. But I just activate my energy field and I feel safe and secure again.

The Child Becomes the Parent

I am listening to Helen, a 42-year old divorced mother of two daughters. She emigrated from Germany as a teenager.

Helen: My 67-year-old mother treats me like an incompetent child. She is intrusive, controlling and demeans me all the time. She tells me I am a bad mother and I have messed up my life. I married a no-good alcoholic husband that abused me. She constantly beats me over the head with this. I am extremely frustrated, angry and depressed. I feel so beaten and defeated. Some nights I have to drink myself to sleep.

Soo-Hoo: Sounds like you feel helpless when you are with your mother. But are there times she relies on you?

Helen: She has arthritis and I try to help her at different times but no matter what I do I cannot satisfy my mother. I can't do anything right! I went to one therapist who told me I need to think of myself and not be so involved with my mother anymore. He told me to stop talking to her. But that feels like abandoning her!

There is so much "darkness" here, so much pain and suffering. How can I shine a light here and activate mother and daughter's healing energies?

Soo-Hoo: You are a very caring person. Despite the pain and suffering that comes from these encounters with your mother you still care and love her deeply and are still concerned about her.

Helen: Yes, despite everything I still worry about her. She is alone and has nobody to care for her.

Soo-Hoo: It sounds like in your mother's family harsh, abrasive, and critical messages were accepted ways to raise children. Is it possible that your mother actually loves you and cares about you but cannot say it in ways that are comforting and reassuring?

Helen: Yes, my mother has taken care of me when I have been sick and has always given me material things. But she has never given me emotional support or positive praise. I know she gets this from her own family. I heard that my grandmother was a cruel tyrant!

Soo-Hoo: Is it also possible that your mother is expressing deeply felt frustrations, disappoints, and great pain in her own life?

Helen: My mother was physically abused as a child. Also, my father was an alcoholic and was very abusive to my mother. He abandoned us when I was six.

Soo-Hoo: Do you think your mother is worried that you might suffer the same fate that she had experienced?

A light appears in her eyes and spreads across her face.

Helen: She does not want me to suffer like her! Yes, you are right—despite the negative criticism and venting of anger and frustration on me I still love her and care about her.

Soo-Hoo: Is it also possible that even though she puts you down, in her own way she needs your strength?

Helen: There are times when I really worry about her. Sometimes she just acts irrational.

Soo-Hoo: With great insight and understanding comes great responsibility. You have the power to decide how to relate to your mother. You can model for your mother the type of relationship you want. As a loving daughter, what would your mother need from you?

Helen: She needs my understanding and support.

Together we worked out some responses to her mother's abrasive, negative criticism of her. When her mother says negative things about her, Helen would say: "I know you care about me. I know you worry about me." *If her mother tried to tell her what to do with her life, she would say:* "I know you want the best for me. I know you want me to have a better life. I know you are there for me." *If her mother tried to lecture her about how she was not able to take care of herself, she was to say:* "I appreciate you sharing your wisdom with me."

Her energy was quickly changing. Gone were the defeated look, and the pained and helpless demeanor. In its place was a new found strength and determination that she could be the strong one in this family.

At first her mother was surprised by Helen's completely different and surprising responses to her criticism. Her mother tried to deflect her comments by asking: "Are you feeling right? You are acting strange." *Ordinarily Helen would feel wounded by these comments. However, something had shifted inside. She was able to see beyond the angry, critical women who was venting on her. Then one day when her mother was particularly angry and mean to her, Helen said to her mother:* "When you are like this I really worry about you. I can hear and see the pain that is coming out. I know I need to do a better job of taking care of you!"

Her mother became speechless and did not know what to say. Then she said: "It is about time you are sensitive to others." *Then, after a few weeks of Helen's continued positive responses, her mother said:* "It sounds like you are finally growing up."

Helen felt a heavy weight lifted from her. Gone was the feeling of the incompetent child. The transition has been achieved. The child has become the parent! Her aura was glowing brightly.

In Closing

I have been speaking to the Commencement audience for 25 minutes. I hear myself say:

> I will end with this story. A great religious leader lay gravely ill in his bed. His followers gathered around him. They said to him: How will we go on without you? You are our light! Who will guide us?
>
> Then he replied: It is time. YOU are the light!
>
> So I say to all of you who are graduating today: It is time. YOU are the LIGHT! Go out and guide others to find their way. Where there is darkness shine your light!
>
> It has been an honor and a privilege to be your teacher. Thank you.

There is great applause, and I am smiling and am grateful for where life has taken me. My passion for the work is still glowing brightly and hopefully will be a beacon to guide others to follow their path.

References

Rosen, S. (1982). *My Voice Will Go With You: The Teaching Tales of Milton H. Erickson.* New York: Norton.

Soo-Hoo, T. (1998). Applying frame of reference and reframing techniques to improve school consultation in multicultural settings. *Journal of Educational and Psychological Consultation, 9*(4), 325–345.

Soo-Hoo, T. (1999). Brief strategic family therapy with Chinese Americans. *Journal of Family Therapy, 27,*163–179.

Soo-Hoo, T. (2000, October). *Integrating Mind, Body and Spirit in Psychotherapy: The Use of Chi in the Treatment of Children Who Have Experienced Trauma.* Presented at Conference on Spirituality and Psychotherapy, San Francisco.

Soo-Hoo, T. (2003, September). *Integrating Eastern and Western Approaches to Treat Children with Trauma II.* Symposium presented at Eighth International Conference on Family Violence, Working Together to End Abuse: Advocacy, Assessment, Intervention, Research, Prevention and Policy, San Diego, CA.

Soo-Hoo, T. (2005a). Transforming power struggles through shifts in perception in marital therapy. *Journal of Family Psychotherapy, 16*(3), 19–38.

Soo-Hoo, T. (2005b). Working within the cultural context of Chinese American families. *Journal of Family Psychotherapy, 16*(4), 45–63.

Weakland, J. H., Fisch, R., Watzlawick, P., & Bodin, A. (1974). Brief therapy: Focused problem resolution. *Family Process, 13*(2), 41–68.

29

CONSCIOUS PURPOSE AND COMMITMENT EXERCISE[1]

Michael White

Hoyt: Why do you do therapy? Why do you do this work?

White: This is not a new question. Way back in my social work training, which I began in 1967, we were required to address this question.... At that time, in response to such questions, only certain accounts of motive were considered acceptable. These were psychological accounts of motive. Accounts of motive that featured notions of conscious purpose and commitment were not fashionable and were marginalized. Responses to this question that emphasized a wish to contribute to the lives of others in some way, or that were put in terms of a desire to play some part in addressing the injustices of the world, were considered expressions of naiveté. Attempts to stand by such expressions were read as examples of denial, lack of insight, bloody-mindedness, etc. On the other hand, to traffic in psychologized accounts of motive was to display insight, truth saying, a superior level of consciousness, of maturity, and so on. And invariably, the psychologizing of motive translated into the pathologizing of motive. "Which of all of one's neurotic needs was being met in stepping into this profession?" "How did this decision relate to unresolved issues in one's family of origin?" "Did this decision relate to one's attempts to work through an enmeshed relationship with one's mother?" "Or did this decision relate to one's attempt to work through a disengaged relationship with one's

1   Excerpted from M.F. Hoyt (1996), "On Ethics and the Spiritualities of the Surface: A Conversation with Michael White and Gene Combs." In M.F. Hoyt (Ed.), *Constructive Therapies* (Volume 2, pp. 33–59). New York: Guilford Press. Used with permission.

mother?" And so on. I'm sure that you are familiar with questions of this sort, and that we could easily put a list together.

I always believe that this privileging of psychological accounts of motive to be a profoundly conservative endeavor, one that is counter-inspiration, one that could only contribute significantly to therapist experiences of fatigue and burnout. For various reasons, I could never be persuaded to step into the pathologizing of my motives for my interest in joining this profession, and mostly managed to hold on to what were my favored notions of conscious purpose and commitment. I have no doubt that over the years that expressions of these notions have been a source of invigoration to me, and in recent years I have been encouraging therapists to join together in identifying, articulating, and elevating notions of conscious purpose and commitment. To this end I have developed an exercise.... Readers might be interested in meeting with their peers and working through this together.

Conscious Purpose and Commitment Exercise

Introduction. We have discussed the extent to which the privileging of psychological accounts of motive has marginalized statements of conscious purpose and commitment to this work. We have reviewed the extent to which such statements are pathologized in the culture of psychotherapy, as well as the implications of this in regard to the stories that we have about who we are as therapists. The following exercise will engage you in acts of resistance to this—acts that are associated with the elevation and reclamation of statements of conscious purpose and commitment. I suggest that you invite another person or two to join you in this exploration, for the purposes of sharing your responses to this exercise, or for the purposes of being interviewed about these responses.

1. Talk about any experiences that you have had that relate to the psychologizing and the pathologizing of your motives for choosing this work, or any reinterpretations of this choice that may have encouraged you to mistrust your statements of conscious purposes or your personal commitment to this work.
2. Review what you can assume to be some of the real effects or consequences, in your work and your life, of this psychologizing of your motives, and of this pathologizing of your accounts of your conscious purposes and commitments.
3. Identify and retrieve some of your very early statements of conscious purpose that relate to your chosen work, however unsophisticated these might have been, and reflect on what they suggest about what you are committed to in this work.

4. Share some information about the significant experiences of your life that have contributed to a further clarification of your conscious purposes and commitments in taking up this work—that have generated realizations about the particular contribution that you have a determination to make during the course of your life.
5. Discuss the experiences that you are having in the course of this exercise: those experiences that are associated with engaging in giving testimony and in bearing witness to expressions of conscious purpose; those experiences that are associated with the honoring of statements of commitment.
6. Talk about how the elevation of your notions of conscious purpose and the honoring of your statements of commitment could affect:
   a. Your experience of yourself in relation to your work.
   b. Your relationship to your own life.
   c. Your relationship to your colleagues and to the people who seek your help.
   d. The shape of your work and of your life more generally.

30

THEMES AND LESSONS

The Invitation Revisited

Michael F. Hoyt

The authors in this volume repeatedly tell stories and recount experiences that elicit interest, admiration, laughter, wonder, and understanding—and occasionally, sadness and grief. The contributors—who are of diverse races, nationalities, and ethnicities—hold different psychological theories, but all are united by their concern for love, service, and kindness. Each reader will have his or her favorites, ones that "speak" especially to them; although there are certain common themes and lessons to be derived. Let us consider a few.

Connection: The Importance of the Therapeutic Relationship

The authors repeatedly emphasize the significance of *caring* and *alliance*. As Sue Johnson writes, "My sense is that most therapists are drawn to the field because they want to grow as persons and connect with others." Psychotherapy is primarily a relationship between two (or more) people (Short, 2010; Szasz, 2005). Regardless of the author's particular theoretical orientation, relationships are personal—even if a psychiatric diagnosis is mentioned, *we hear about real people, not stereotyped "cases" or "symptoms." The therapist-authors are present as real people, too.* Long ago it was Carl Jung (1931/1966a, p. 72) who commented: "The doctor is as much 'in the analysis' as the patient. He *[sic]* is equally a part of the psychic process of treatment and therefore equally exposed to the transforming influences." The Australian poet Gwen Harwood (1975/2001, p. 110) quotes Ludwig Wittgenstein: "Thought is surrounded by a halo." Peter Lomas (1973) noted that personal contact made for the difference between *true and false experience*. Carl Whitaker (1989, pp. 164–165) referred to this process as *co-transference*. Elsewhere (Hoyt, 2001/2004, pp. 8–9, emphasis in original) I have suggested that "processes of responding to the client that sometimes are termed *countertransference* also inform the connections we call *presence, attunement, empathy, rapport, resonance, inspiration, caring, compassion,* and the like.… *Client-inspired therapist contributions* can be very useful, although there needs to be keen recognition of the power gradient and the importance of honoring clients' goals and not imposing our values while maintaining a collaborative client-therapist relationship." Numerous examples of how clients energize therapists appear in the preceding pages: Laura Brown and Eric Greenleaf describe ways their clients teach and inspire them, Joe Goldfield and Sue Johnson recount the joy and delight they experience connecting with clients, and Jeffrey Kottler (also see Kottler, 1993, 2000) and Ram Dass and Shakti Gawain highlight the deep satisfaction derived from caring and doing good service. All of the authors take genuine pleasure in helping others.

Stephen Gilligan (1997; Gilligan & Simon, 2004; also see his Foreword in this volume) describes the importance of *sponsorship* (from the Latin *spons* = "to pledge solemnly"), a vow to help the person (including one's self) to use each and every event and experience to awaken to the goodness and the gifts of the self, the world, and the connection between the two. Numerous authors in the volume in hand—including Art Bohart, Jon Carlson, John Frykman, Eric Greenleaf; as well as myself, and Ram Dass and Shakti Gawain—illustrate the vital impact of having at least one person who supports you on your journey.[1] Even if we don't go so far as to accept Jack Kornfield's invitation to take the official vows of a *bodhisattva*, are you really there for your clients?

Lesson: The therapeutic alliance is the soil in which various techniques may (or may not) take root. Prepare and tend it well.

Feeling and Passion

As Sue Johnson eloquently notes, it is emotion that connects us and makes us feel human.[2] Bob Neimeyer resonates as he works sensitively with the grief and sadness of his bereft clients. Judy Mazza, Laura Brown, and others find rejuvenation in the joy of seeing clients make healthy changes, as well as in mentoring and supervising students. Jon Carlson speaks his truth the night before

---

1   Long ago, the social psychologist Solomon Asch (1956) conducted classic studies in which a subject was asked which of two lines was longer, and then heard from a group of other people—who were, unbeknownst to the subject—all confederates of the experimenter. When the others all unanimously contradicted what the subject saw and said, the subject would often change; but if one person (or more) stood with the subject, the subject seldom wavered or changed what he or she knew to be true. The implications for the therapeutic alliance are myriad and profound.

2   Thus, the French poet Charles Baudelaire (1857/1998) described emotionally disconnected inner boredom ("*ennui*") as "the worst crime." Somewhere I read, "Killing time isn't murder; killing time is suicide." For some enlivening ideas, see Brad Keeney's (2009) *The Creative Therapist: The Art of Awakening a Session.*

having heart surgery. Mazza and Don Meichenbaum show their spunk when they describe overcoming obstacles in their educational paths. Teresa Robles counsels to follow a path with heart. Several authors refer to the importance of good self-care as well as the support of others—spouses and partners, family, God, Nature, travel, art and poetry, music, and wine are all appreciated!

Being a therapist exposes us to strong emotions—our clients' as well as our own. Living passionately is rich living, although, as Dan Short and Laura Brown caution, we have to be careful not to become overwhelmed or burned out. In her chapter, Lillian Comas-Díaz brings the Spanish term *duende* into the discussion. The term comes originally from Federico Garcia Lorca's (1933/1998) discussion of "black sounds" in music, but can be applied to therapy as well. As Wikipedia (retrieved 22 December 2011) describes it:

> El *duende* is the spirit of evocation. It comes from inside as a physical/ emotional response to music. It is what gives you chills, makes you smile or cry as a bodily reaction to an artistic performance that is particularly expressive.... All love songs must contain *duende*.... The love song must resonate with the susurration of sorrow, the tintinnabulation of grief. The writer [or therapist] who refuses to explore the darker regions of the heart will never be able to write convincingly about the wonder, the magic and the joy of love for just as goodness cannot be trusted unless it has breathed the same air as evil—the enduring metaphor of Christ crucified between two criminals comes to mind here—so within the fabric of the love song, within its melody, its lyric, one must sense an acknowledgment of its capacity for suffering.

Strong stuff!

Lesson: Follow a path with heart—and take care of yourself!

Curiosity and the Willingness to Be Open

I once asked the MRI therapist, John Weakland, what "words of wisdom" he might want to pass on (Hoyt, 1994/2001, p. 31). He hesitated, then offered, "Stay curious."[3] To cite but a few of the preceding chapters, we witness how

---

3 In closing his paper, "Erickson's Essence: A Personal View," Weakland (1994, p. 291) wrote: "In the end, I think the essence of Milton Erickson's work is based on his personal qualities. So I would like to conclude by pointing to three such qualities that I see as fundamental to all he did. This requires going beyond the usual bounds of professional discussion. However, I hope we might follow his example somehow, even though I cannot say how these qualities might be taught to others, not even how he acquired these qualities himself. First, Erickson was and remained a man with a great curiosity about life; he wanted to look at and reflect on everything that came into his view. Second, he had a wide and deep sense of humor, which I see as central for his ability to combine engagement and detachment even in very difficult

Tobey Hiller stays open to her patient, seeing their commonality, or at least their cousinhood "not more than once removed." Eric Greenleaf likes to look forward to what is going to happen. Chris Iveson takes his clients at face value, rather than imposing his judgments. Murray Korngold finally accepts, rather than denying or pushing away, the "anomalous experiences" he keeps encountering. Judy Mazza, inspired by Jay Haley, shifts her theoretical orientation from behaviorism to strategic therapy; Teresa Robles and Karin Schlanger flee psychoanalysis for approaches they find more affirmative and *mas empáticos*. Michele Ritterman looks deeply into a family therapy session in which her patient began to worsen and realizes that symptoms are hypnotically induced trance states—a discovery her mentor, Milton Erickson, encourages her to pursue.

Lesson: Lean into life and stay curious—"not knowing" is the space that precedes discovery.

Hard Workers

All of the authors contained herein love learning and work hard—although they might say the work is "fun" or "energizing." Laura Brown explains "Why I'm not quitting my day job yet." Several travel the world teaching. Carol Erickson says she hopes she has paid her rent on the planet. Judy Mazza tells us that when she no longer finds the work of being a therapist and supervisor interesting and fascinating, it will be time for her to retire. Nick Cummings, in his late 80s and still passionately involved in the healthcare of our nation, says he has "flunked retirement."

Lesson: Embrace work.

Wounded Healer

In Greek mythology, Chiron was the wisest of the Centaurs and the archtype of the Wounded Healer. He was accidentally wounded by one of Hercules' arrows that had been dipped in the blood of the many-headed monster, Hydra. In his search for his own cure, he discovered how to heal others. Jung (1951/1966b; also see Halifax, 1982; Zur, 1994) first introduced the term *wounded healer*. The Wounded Healer understands what the client/patient feels because he or she has gone through the same pain. Thus, in *Letters to a Young Poet*, Rainer Maria Rilke (1904/2004, p. 54) advises: "Do not believe that he who seeks to comfort you lives untroubled among the simple and quiet words that sometimes do you

---

and distressing situations. Finally, and I believe most important of all, a point that needs no documentation: In both his professional and personal life, Milton Erickson was a man of great courage."

good. His life has much difficulty and sadness and remains far behind yours. Were it otherwise he would never have been able to find those words." In popular culture, the tormented doctor and the OCD-ridden detective who star in their respective and eponymous television programs *House M.D.* (Hockley & Gardner, 2010) and *Monk* are examples. In recent literature, the character of Joseph Breuer in Irvin Yalom's (1992) novel, *When Nietzsche Wept*, must confront his own wounds before he can help his patient; another example is the physician in Abraham Verghese's (2010) bestselling medical novel, *Cutting for Stone*, who had to amputate one of his own fingers and thus developed a dexterity that made him more adept at certain surgeries.[4]

In the present volume, a number of authors describe how personal tragedies and misfortunes, as well as a willingness to venture into "dark" places, helped to sensitize them and make them better therapists: Ken Hardy's curiosity about psychology and society are stimulated by his childhood exposure to racism, Terry Soo-Hoo learns martial arts to gain strength against fear, Jack Kornfield goes to Thailand seeking escape from his family-of-origin unhappiness, Lillian Comas-Díaz gets culturally disconnected and temporarily misplaces her soul, Bob Neimeyer becomes interested in psychotherapy and the area of loss and grief after his father ends his own life when Neimeyer is an early adolescent, Laura Brown recounts how disclosing her struggles as a "wounded healer" made her a better teacher.[5] We might also cite here the case of Milton Erickson, who suffered from childhood polio and other significant infirmities. As Jay Haley and Madeleine Richeport-Haley (1993) explain in their fine video documentary, *Milton H. Erickson, M.D.: Explorer in Hypnosis and Therapy*: "Erickson liked to emphasize that his difficulties had a positive effect on his work. An example is pain. He suffered severe pain all his life, based on his polio. Some of the cramps he had were so severe that the muscles pulled away from the ligaments. He used autohypnosis to control that pain when he could. In the process of understanding and working with his own pain, Erickson understood pain better than any other therapist because he had been down that road himself."

---

4 "My intent wasn't to save the world as much as to heal myself. Few doctors will admit this, certainly not the young ones, but subconsciously, in entering the profession, we must believe that ministering to others will heal our woundedness. And it can. But it can also deepen the wound." (Verghese, 2009, p. 7)

5 As Sue Johnson in her chapter and Hoyt (2009, p. 40) both note, the terms *whole, heal, health, hale,* and *holy* all derive from the same old Middle English and Anglo-Saxon words (*hoole, hale*). In a related vein, Grudin (1982, p. 188, emphasis in original) writes: "Happiness (as suggested, for example, by the French word for happy, *heureux*) may well consist primarily of an attitude toward time. Individuals we consider happy commonly seem *complete in the present*: we seem them constantly in their wholeness, attentive, cheerful, open rather than closed to events, integral in the moment rather than distended across time by regret or anxiety."

Lesson: Whatever life gives you, correctly understood, can be used to promote health and happiness.[6]

Significant Figures Aiding Therapist Development

Numerous authors mention someone (or several people) who was very important to them in their development. Sometimes the person was a professional teacher or mentor. Lillian Comas-Díaz and Judy Mazza also appreciate their classmates and professional communities. Milton Erickson figures prominently in several stories, both because of his brilliance (he is kind of a Zeus-like figure, schools of family therapy, hypnotherapy, and strategic interactional therapy seemingly emerging from his forehead) and also partly because of the selection of authors (several of whom trained with him).[7] Some of the authors identify a close family member as a source of inspiration and renewal—Ken Hardy acknowledges his great grandmother; Lillian Comas-Díaz, Nick Cummings, and John Frykman, their grandmothers; Frykman, Joe Goldfield, and Don Meichenbaum, their mothers; Carol Erickson, Frykman, and I cite our respective fathers; Frykman also credits his wife and three children. Jon Carlson's health crisis required him to become temporarily very dependent upon his family and thus discover a different kind of acceptance and gratitude.

There may be a time in our development when we closely identify and model (see Baker, 2003; Goldfried, 2001; Norcross & Guy, 2007; Orlinsky & Ronnestad, 2004; Stovholt & Trotter-Mathison, 2010; Sussman, 1992, 1995), but mature practitioners (and people) eventually move beyond, incorporating aspects and remembering the lessons and inspiration but becoming their own person.[8] This, I think, is what Erickson and Rossi (1979, p. 276) meant when

---

6   I am grateful to my friend, Don Hidalgo of Baton Rouge, Louisiana, for calling my attention to the Biblical Parable of the Talents (*Matthew 25: 14-30*). A *talent* was originally a Greek and Roman unit of weight, primarily used for gold and silver money, although the term has come to mean "an aptitude or skill." Traditionally, the parable is seen as an exhortation to use one's God-given gifts, however one finds them.

   I was touched when my good friend and golf buddy, James Palmer, announced to our Department his fatal illness (a nasty form of cancer) by having a colleague read aloud from an old edition (capitalization and emphasis in original) of *Aesop's Fables*, "An Astrologer and a Traveller": "A certain *Star-gazer* had the Fortune, in the very height of his celestial Observations, to stumble into a Ditch; a sober fellow passing by, gave him a piece of wholesome Counsel. Friend, says he, make a right Use of your present Misfortunes; and pray, for the future, let the Stars go on quietly in their Courses, and do you look a little better to the Ditches" (Aesop, c. 620-560 BCE). James used his remaining time very well, and was an inspiration to all of us who cared for him.

7   I never met Erickson, although in December 2011 I had the privilege of visiting his last home and sitting in his office (see Hoyt & Ritterman, 2012).

8   There was a time when I said, "I just had a crazy thought ..." like Carl Whitaker; lowered my voice to sound like Bob Goulding ("What are you willing to change today?"); and raised my voice to sound like Insoo Berg ("Wow! How did you do that?!") Others (e.g., Rossi,

they said: "To initiate this type of therapy you have to be yourself as a person. You cannot imitate somebody else, but you have to do it your own way."

Lesson: Get inspired and learn a lot, then make it personal and do it your own way.

Cultural Nuance

Terry Soo-Hoo's, Ken Hardy's, and Lillian Comas-Díaz' descriptions of growing up amidst overt racism remind us what obscene cruelty some people must endure—as well as illustrating ways they found strength and fortitude. Michele Ritterman also describes the pathogenic effects of destructive family and social-cultural systems. Coming out of the movie *The Help,* it was easy being self-righteous and indignant toward the oppressors, but I came out also thinking about who I might be oppressing, even if benignly intended or unconscious (e.g., not-too-smart people, old people, people who dress differently than I do or who have accents different than mine, someone who is other—or I want to be Other—than myself).

Much of what has been written in the world of psychotherapy, at least until recently, has largely been based on studies of white Europeans and their descendants, a still largely invisible ethnocentric monoculturism (Sue, 2004). As one critic (Guthrie, 1997) put it in the title of his book, *Even the Rat was White: A Historical View of Psychology!* In addition to the reports by Ken Hardy and Terry Soo-Hoo, Lillian Comas-Díaz (Puerto Rico), Teresa Robles (Mexico), and Karin Schlanger (Argentina) all give us glimpses of culturally diverse ways of seeing and being in the world; as, to some extent, does Chris Iveson from his English perspective. Murray Korngold tells stories of his encounters with healers from Brazil and India. We may all be "much more simply human than otherwise," as Harry Stack Sullivan (1938/1964, p. 34) famously said, but we're not all the same—and don't have to be. It is important to recognize that we may not all mean exactly the same thing when we say "self" or "emotion" or "family" or "therapist-client relationship."

Lesson: We can learn from, not just about, other cultures. There are many ways of being a healthy human. Something that might seem like a valid solution (or problem) to one person may not seem the same way to another.

Whitaker & Haley, 1982; O'Hanlon, 1999) have also commented on similar undigested forms of idealization/modeling, including erstwhile students of Milton Erickson wearing his favorite color (purple) and affecting his speech patterns. This may be a hero-worshipping phase of inspiration some of us go through—but, as they say in Zen, look where the finger is pointing, not at the finger!

Words and Creativity

These people can all *talk* (and write). They've got different styles, different paces and energies—but all are very articulate and can hold forth. "Words were originally magic," as Freud (1915/1961) said, and therapists largely operate in the worlds of words. It pays to learn ways to be clear and communicative, to listen deeply, to be able to capture a listener's ear, and to express oneself. Therapy is a form of conversation, a conversational art. As Michael White (in Hoyt & Combs, 1996/2001, p. 81) said:

> There is much that remains to be said about the language of this work, about how it evokes the images of people's lives that it does.... These images reach back into the history of people's lived experience, privileging certain memories, and facilitate the interpretation of many previously neglected aspects of experience. So the language of the work, of the very questions that we ask, is evocative of images which trigger the reliving of experience, and this contributes very significantly to the generation of alternative story lines.

The authors contained herein are all adept writers and speakers. They are "high verbal." They are skillful with language. They each have their own, compelling way of telling stories, making points, and saying things—they are word merchants *par excellence*. It is a pleasure to hear them.[9]

A number of the authors use poetry and song in their chapters. Art Bohart quotes William Butler Yeats; Laura Brown quotes Leonard Cohen and Cris Williamson; John Frykman quotes his friend, Ric Masten; Joe Goldfield provides us with a rap song he wrote about solution-focused therapy; Ken Hardy evokes Langston Hughes and Sonia Sanchez; Sue Johnson quotes Rumi and Bruce Springsteen; Bob Neimeyer and Michele Ritterman supply their own fine poetry (Ritterman also includes photos of special embroideries she has made); Karin Schlanger quotes Antonio Machado. I quote Mitchell Ginsberg and Walt Whitman in the Introduction. As Kenneth Gergen (2006, p. 166, emphases in original) has written in an essay on "The Poetics of Psychotherapy":

> When we speak of language as poetic we are often referring to its *unsettling capacities*—to the ways in which we are moved, absorbed, or aroused. It is the rare juxtaposition of words and phrases that seems to pierce the veil of the ordinary, and move us into different dimensions of understanding. Second, we speak of language as poetic when it gives *credibility to the*

---

9   Several authors also report that they find inspiration and renewal in nonverbal activities such as martial arts (Laura Brown, aikido; Terry Soo-Hoo, kung-fu and chi kung meditation), dance (Lillian Comas-Díaz, salsa and flamenco), and music (Karin Schlanger); Rubin Battino, John Frykman and Michele Ritterman are also singers.

imaginary—placing wings on whimsy, or bringing fantasy to life. Poetic language takes license to exit the ordinary and invite us into worlds of wishes and wonder. Finally, we speak of the poetic when language brings force *a sense of the aesthetic*—arresting us with its beautiful symmetries, mellifluous harmonies, or enchanting rhythms.

Throughout the book, the authors exemplify good storytelling: always engaging, often educational, occasionally inspirational. Their precise, meticulous use of language can serve as an inspiration to watch how we say things, to choose our words carefully.

Lesson: Endeavor to speak in ways that are vivid and real.

Humor

In archaic times, humor was a moisture or vapor. In old physiology, humor was a fluid or juice that circulated within the body, influencing one's disposition, mood, or state of mind (e.g., *sanguine, choleric, melancholic,* and *phlegmatic*). We now think of humor not in physiological terms, but as a caprice, a whim, a fancy, as something that appeals to the comical or absurdly incongruous. In psychotherapy, having fun can be a lubricant, a balm, a restorative. It can be both the medium and the message. It can be an attitude and an antidote, both where we come from and how we get there. I recall Carl Whitaker (see 1975) saying, "Humor is a way to get around the corner without knocking down the building." Paul Watzlawick (1983) entitled one of his books, *The Situation is Hopeless, but Not Serious.* Dan Greenberg and Suzanne O'Malley (1983) give great tongue-in-cheek relationship advice in their book, *How to Avoid Love and Marriage.* In his autobiography, *Chronicles,* Bob Dylan (2004, p. 20) tell us that his grandmother advised him: "[H]appiness isn't on the road to anything ... happiness is the road."

Humor provides comfort and can strengthen the therapeutic alliance. It can help deconstruct a "stuck" position, addressing how one holds things and shifting frames. With the right tact and timing, it can say "This is serious, but there are other ways to look at this, and some might even give you pleasure rather than all the pain you're currently experiencing." The authors herein take their clients seriously *and* sometimes meet them with a twinkle in their eye.[10] Carol Erickson gives clients directives that will expose the absurdity of

---

10 Jay Haley (e.g., 1969, 1984; Richeport-Haley & Carlson, 2010) was deservedly known, amongst his many admirable attributes, as a master of wit. When I first met him, back in 1992, we were sitting atop the Hyatt-Regency Hotel in Phoenix, at the Fifth International Ericksonian Congress. I had no specific agenda, other than to enjoy the pleasure of his company. Finally, however, an important issue came to my mind. "Jay, may I ask you a question?" "Sure," he replied. I paused, then asked: "What do you feed your twinkle?" He smiled: "Well,

their problem-sustaining "rules," Joe Goldfield tells of rapping with certain teens, Judy Mazza declares, "Who says therapy can't be fun? There was a sense of joy and the realization that we could be playful while learning and helping others." Don Meichenbaum attributes his metacognitive narrative constructive approach to listening to his mother at the dinner table; Nick Cummings laughs gently at himself for leaving the infantry for the paratroopers only to discover that now he would jump out of airplanes and then still have to march 35 miles! (This also led Cummings to Frieda Fromm-Reichmann, and the need to develop brief, effective interventions to help the men he commanded.)[11]

Lesson: When you go into those small rooms to talk people out of their problems and unhappiness, bring your sense of humor with you—holding things lightly, being playful at the right time, and evoking laughter and delight can be salutary for both clients and clinicians.

The Value of Service

As Robert Darnton (2011, p. 23) has written:

> In a famous letter of 1813, Thomas Jefferson compared the spread of ideas to the way people light one candle from another: "He who receives an idea from me, receives instruction himself without lessening mine; as he who lites [*sic*] his taper at mine, receives light without darkening me."

In an *American Psychologist* extensive review on "Lifestyle and Mental Health," Roger Walsh (2011, p. 588) elaborates some possible implications:

> Psychotherapists repeatedly rediscover the healing potentials of altruistic behavior for their patients and themselves. Alfred Adler emphasized the benefits of "social interest," and helping other group members contributes to the effectiveness of group therapy and support groups such as Alcoholics Anonymous (Duncan et al., 2009). Likewise, therapists often report that helping their patients can enhance their own well-being (Yalom, 2002). Wisely perceived, altruism is not self-sacrifice but rather enlightened self-interest (Walsh, 1999). As the Dalai Lama put it, "If you're going to be selfish, be wisely selfish—which means to love and serve others, since love and service to other brings rewards to oneself that

---

you have one, too, don't you?" "Well, yeah … but yours is older—I want to make sure I'm feeding mine the right stuff!" We both laughed. (see Hoyt, 2004, p. 241)

11 "Brevity is the soul of wit" said Shakespeare (*Hamlet*, Act II, Scene 2, line 90). I also recall that in Jeff Zeig's (2011) excellent keynote presentation at the 11th International Congress on Ericksonian Approaches to Hypnosis and Psychotherapy, he delighted the audience by noting that the difference between Heaven and Hell is that in Heaven they tell jokes, whereas in Hell they explain jokes! With this in mind, I'd better not go on too much about the value of humor.

otherwise would be unachievable" (quoted in Hopkins, 2001, p. 150). These benefits of altruism hold major implications for our understanding of health, lifestyle, and therapy. On the basis of their research findings, Brown, Nesse, Vinokur, and Smith (2003) wrote an article titled "Providing Social Support May Be More Beneficial than Receiving It" and concluded that interventions "designed to help people feel supported may need to be redesigned so that the emphasis is on what people do to help others" (p. 326). Other researchers quipped, "If giving weren't free, pharmaceutical companies could herald the discoveries of a stupendous new drug called 'Give Back—instead of Prozac'" (Post & Niemark, 2007, p. 7). Contribution and service to others have long been considered central elements of a life well lived. Now they can also be considered central elements of a healthy life.

Or, as my grandmother may have told me, "It is better to give than to receive." In the chapters that comprise this volume, we again see numerous examples: Laura Brown and Judy Mazza find joy in teaching; Dan Short feels grateful to have met a young man he is psychologically assessing; Eric Greenleaf finds himself in relationships; Carol Erickson says that the mutual sharings and carings "warms my heart," and Jeffrey Kottler acknowledges that "what I do isn't just about helping others, but also fortifying myself"; Joe Goldfield enjoys his client's humor; Don Meichenbaum collects stories of post-traumatic growth and resilience; Nick Cummings builds systems that bring healthcare to people; Brown, Lillian Comas-Díaz, John Frykman, Ken Hardy, Jack Kornfield, Jeffrey Kottler, and Michele Ritterman all mention working for social justice as part of their therapeutic inspiration and passion.

Lesson: What goes around, comes around; giving deeply of oneself feels good and can come back tenfold.

What Is, Is

In golf they say, "You have to play it where it lies" (Hoyt, 2000). The authors display great respect and acceptance as they talk with and about their clients/patients, seeing them as resourceful and "heroic" in the face of sometimes daunting challenges (see Duncan & Miller, 2000). They encourage hope and "believe in" their clients, optimistically seeing them as people with strengths and possibilities. Art Bohart appreciates their courage and creativity. Karin Schlanger "gets off her high horse" and meets her clients "where they are" (including women living very conventional, "non-liberated" lifestyles). Judy Mazza explains how Jay Haley taught her to *speak the client's language* (rather than having the client speak her psychological jargon). Carol Erickson, Joe Goldfield, Chris Iveson, and Michele Ritterman don't doubt their clients, but endeavor to help the clients better utilize their resources. Ken Hardy learns not to pathologize the oppressed. Murray Korngold tells us that until middle age "I was more of a mechanic than I was a gardener." Teresa Robles recounts how she went from being taught that looking at the good side of things was "denial" and "resistance" to learning that "noting the good side of life is called 'positive connotation' and that doing this was indeed a useful tool in therapy." Michael White recommends the same for therapists themselves.

Lesson: We have to meet people where they are and work with what they bring.

The Power of Love

Love goes to places that not even WD-40[12] gets to. Thus, Gerry Jamplosky (1979) named his famous book about attitudinal healing, *Love is Letting Go of Fear*. The Dalai Lama says, "Kindness is my religion." In his chapter, Nick Cummings tells us that Frieda-Fromm Reichmann advised that although anger might produce quicker results in the short-run, love was much more powerful and enduring. Aaron Beck (1989) may have titled his helpful book about the theory and techniques of cognitive-behavioral couple therapy, *Love is Never Enough*, but for most people, life ain't much without it. In 1906, Freud wrote to Jung: "Psychoanalysis is in essence a cure through love" (quoted in Bettleheim, 1982, p. v). Sean Davis (2011, p. 26) reports that when he heard someone ask Jay Haley, "If you could teach students only one thing, what would it be?" Haley said "Love," without hesitation. "I'd teach them to love their clients. Everything else falls into place once a therapist loves their clients." When the well-known existential psychotherapist James Bugental had a stroke that severely damaged his memory, his wife Elizabeth Bugental (2008) and he realized that "Love fills in the blanks."[13]

Throughout this volume, we repeatedly witness examples of love in action—Rubin Battino being present for dying hospice patients, Art Bohart believing in his troubled clients, Sue Johnson's and Laura Brown's openness, Jon Carlson

---

12 WD-40™ is a well-known lubricant and anti-corrosive cleaner famous for getting the "stuck" unstuck.

13 In Jeffrey Kottler and Jon Carlson's (2008) *Their Finest Hour: Master Therapists Share Their Greatest Success Stories*, Kottler observes: "Every single one of these theoreticians is filled with love. They feel intense love for the people who come to them for help....This goes way beyond mere empathy, or concern, or compassion—I really believe that what drives their work is the tremendous caring and love that they feel for other people. Second, almost all the contributors feel intense love for their work as practitioners" (p. 369). Carlson concurs: "The single common factor that stood out to me (as well as to Jeffrey Kottler) was that each expert loves people. They value the human experience and were able to find hope and possibility for the hopeless and impossible.... They consistently supported and attended to their clients, and less so to the facts or presenting (often overwhelming) problems. They saw their roles as freeing the client to become what the client wanted to be and not trying to be gods or goddesses to shape others' futures" (pp. 373–374).

and Jack Kornfield embracing and extolling "loving-kindness," Jeffrey Kottler experiencing deep caring and presence when sitting in front of Albert Ellis during a demonstration interview, a stranger stopping for my father and me in the middle of the night, Ram Dass and Shakti Gawain noting the "natural compassion" that unselfconsciously attends everyday situations, Ken Hardy choosing to be a healer.

Lesson: Love!

The Invitation Revisited and Now Extended to You, Dear Reader

In his chapter, Michael White invites us to embrace the good reasons we went into the business of being therapists, provides some questions to guide us, and strongly argues against psychological analyses that undermine our positive motivation.[14] At the conference panel where all this started—with me as moderator (Hoyt, 2011) and John Frykman, Michele Ritterman, and Eric Greenleaf as speakers (and also, in Shellie's case, singer)—the audience learning objectives were listed as: (a) Identify one source of renewal or inspiration for each speaker, (b) Identify one source of renewal or inspiration for yourself. In the book you hold in hand, our various authors were asked to discuss what fuels their inspiration, passion, and renewal. Here is the invitation again, *now extended to you:*

---

14 This was not to encourage lazy license for an "anything goes" attitude in which the therapist imposes his or her issues on the client-patient. As Ken Hardy notes in his chapter, candid self-interrogation is needed to deconstruct "unacknowledged subjectivity disguised as objectivity." This is consistent with what Michael White (in Hoyt & Combs, 1996/2001, p. 77; also see Davis, 2011; Minuchin, 1992) said: "And, because the impossibility of neutrality means that I cannot avoid being 'for' something, I take the responsibility to distrust what I am for—that is, my ways of life and my ways of thought—and I can do this in many ways." In an interview with Matt Carlson (Hoyt & Carlson, 1997/2000, p. 126), I commented: "I think most therapists have gone into this field for very positive reasons.... I think we have gone into this field because we have basic values—wanting to see the world be a better place, wanting to make things right, trying to help people. We have to resist being undermined in our commitment and our motivation. Having said that, I do think that therapists sometimes are enticed by a certain kind of process. There is a certain kind of intimacy, there are certain status and perhaps financial payoffs for being a therapist, and sometimes there is a need to be needed. I think we have to be honest with ourselves about what our motivations are to make sure we are serving the best reasons rather than others." Interestingly, long ago Freud (1937/1964, pp. 248–249), although emphasizing the potentially pathological and recommending re-analysis "at intervals of five years or so," made a similar recommendation: "[T]he special conditions of analytic work do actually cause the analyst's own defects to interfere with his making a correct assessment of the state of things in his patient and reacting to them in a useful way. It is therefore reasonable to expect of an analyst, as part of his [sic] qualifications, a considerable degree of mental normality and correctness."

I would hope that each reader, in his or her own words, would consider the heart and soul of his or her work, what makes it worth doing, the love and poetics of helping people change, how you renew your hope and energy, etc. Ideas about whatever inspires you and keeps you going strong—family, friends, clients/patients, inspiring teachers, spiritual/religious matters, politics and social justice, "giving back," etc., will be relevant. I am sure that each reader will be moved and encouraged.... Personal stories are welcome in which you, in your own way, tell a revealing tale or recount a compelling incident—more 'Chicken Soup' than scholarly exegesis, so to speak. Why do you do this work? The stories can be dramatic, poignant, humorous, soulful—and touching! Please describe a time in which you were inspired and re-energized in your therapy work, perhaps by something your client/patient said or did, perhaps by some mentor's recalled "words of wisdom," perhaps by something else. How were you moved and rejuvenated? What's love got to do with it? Please include what happened, how you reacted, what sense you make of the experience, how it impacted your work, and what lessons it may have.

So now that you've heard our answers, dear reader, what are yours? What are your stories about inspiration, passion, and renewal? What's love got to do with it?

References

Asch, S.E. (1956). Studies of independence and conformity: A minority of one against a unanimous majority. *Psychological Monographs, 70* (Whole No. 416).

Baker, E.K. (2003). *Caring for Ourselves: A Therapist's Guide to Personal and Professional Well-Being.* Washington, D.C.: APA Books.

Baudelaire, C. (1998). "Au Lecteur" ("To the Reader"). In *Selected Poems from Les Fleur du Mal: A Bilingual Edition* (N.R. Shapiro, Ed.) Chicago: University of Chicago Press. (work originally published 1857)

Beck, A.T. (1989). *Love Is Never Enough: How Couples Can Overcome Misunderstandings, Resolve Conflicts, and Solve Relationship Problems Through Cognitive Therapy.* New York: Harper & Row.

Bettleheim, B. (1982). *Freud and Man's Soul.* New York: Vintage/Random House.

Brown, S.L., Nesse, R.M., Vinokur, A.D., & Smith, D.M. (2003). Providing social support may be more beneficial than receiving it: Results from a prospective study of mortality. *Psychological Science, 14,* 320–327.

Bugental, E. (2008). *Love Fills in the Blanks: Paradoxes of Our Final Years.* San Francisco: Elders Academy Press.

Darnton, R. (2011, November 24). Jefferson's taper: A national digital library. *The New York Review of Books, 58*(18), 23–25.

Davis, S. (2011, November/December). Models or therapists? Power from a common factors perspective. *Family Therapy Magazine, 10*(6), 26–28.

Duncan, B.L., & Miller, S.D. (2000). *The Heroic Client: Doing Client-Directed, Outcome-Oriented Therapy.* San Francisco: Jossey-Bass.

Duncan, B.L., Miller, S.D., Wampold, B.E., & Hubble, M.A. (Eds.). (2009). *The Heart and Soul of Change: Delivering What Works in Therapy* (2nd ed.). Washington, D.C.: American Psychological Association.

Dylan, B. (2004). *Chronicles* (Vol. 1). New York: Simon & Schuster.

Erickson, M.H., & Rossi, E. (1979). *Hypnotherapy: An Exploratory Casebook.* New York: Irvington.

Freud, S. (1961). Introductory lectures on psycho-analysis. In *The Standard Edition of the Complete Psychological Works of Sigmund Freud* (Vols. 15-16, pp. 3–463; J. Strachey, Ed.). London: Hogarth Press. (work originally published 1915)

Freud, S. (1964). Analysis terminable and interminable. In *The Standard Edition of the Complete Psychological Works of Sigmund Freud* (Vol. 23, pp. 209–253; J. Strachey, Ed.). London: Hogarth Press. (work originally published 1937)

Gergen, K.J. (2006). The poetics of psychotherapy. In *Therapeutic Realities: Collaboration, Oppression and Relational Flow* (pp. 165–177). Chagrin Falls, OH: Taos Institute Publications.

Gilligan S. (1997). *The Courage to Love: Principles and Practices of Self-Relations Psychotherapy.* New York: Norton.

Gilligan, S., & Simon, D. (Eds.). (2004). *Walking in Two Worlds: The Relational Self in Theory, Practice, and Community.* Phoenix, AZ: Zeig, Tucker & Theisen.

Goldfried, M. (Ed.). (2001). *How Therapists Change: Personal and Professional Reflections.* Washington, D.C.: APA Books.

Greenberg, D., & O'Malley, S. (1983). *How to Avoid Love and Marriage.* New York: Freundlich Books/Schribner.

Grudin, R. (1982). *Time and the Art of Living.* New York: Ticknor & Fields.

Guthrie, R.V. (1997). *Even the Rat was White: A Historical View of Psychology* (2nd ed.). New York: Harper & Row.

Haley, J. (1969). *The Power Tactics of Jesus Christ and Other Essays.* New York: Avon.

Haley, J. (1984). *Ordeal Therapy: Unusual Ways to Change Behavior.* San Francisco: Jossey-Bass.

Haley, J., & Richeport-Haley, M. (1993). *Milton H. Erickson, M.D.: Explorer in Hypnosis and Therapy* [Videotape/DVD]. New York: Brunner/Mazel.

Halifax, J. (1982). *Shaman: The Wounded Healer.* New York: Crossroad.

Harwood, G. (2001). "Thought is Surrounded by a Halo." In *Selected Poems.* Camberwell, Australia: Penguin Books. (work originally published 1975)

Hockley, L., & Gardner, L. (2010). *House: The Wounded Healer on Television: Jungian and Post-Jungian Reflections.* New York: Routledge.

Hopkins, J. (2001). *Cultivating Compassion: A Buddhist Perspective.* New York: Broadway Books.

Hoyt, M.F. (1994). On the importance of keeping it simple and taking the patient seriously: A conversation with Steve de Shazer and John Weakland. In M.F. Hoyt (Ed.), *Constructive Therapies* (pp. 11–40). New York: Guilford Press. Reprinted in M.F. Hoyt, *Interviews with Brief Therapy Experts* (pp. 1–33). New York: Brunner-Routledge, 2001.

Hoyt, M.F. (2000). A golfer's guide to brief therapy (with footnotes for baseball fans). In *Some Stories Are Better than Others: Doing What Works in Brief Therapy and Managed Care* (pp. 5–15). New York: Brunner/Mazel.

Hoyt, M.F. (2001). Connection: The double-edged gift of presence. *Journal of Clinical Psychology: In Session,* 57(8), 1–8. Reprinted and expanded in M.F. Hoyt, *The Present is a Gift: Mo' Better Stories from the World of Brief Therapy* (pp. 8–17). New York: iUniverse, 2004.

Hoyt, M.F. (2004). *The Present is a Gift: Mo' Better Stories from the World of Brief Therapy.* New York: iUniverse.

Hoyt, M.F. (2009). *Brief Psychotherapies: Principles and Practices.* Phoenix, AZ: Zeig, Tucker & Theisen.

Hoyt, M.F. (Moderator). (2011, December). Topical panel on *Therapist Inspiration and Renewal* (John Frykman, Eric Greenleaf, & Michele Ritterman, speakers). Eleventh International Congress on Ericksonian Approaches to Hypnosis and Psychotherapy. Phoenix, AZ.

Hoyt, M.F., & Carlson, J.M. (1997). Interview: Michael F. Hoyt. *The Family Journal: Counseling and Therapy for Couples and Families,* 5(2), 172–181. Reprinted in M.F. Hoyt (2000), *Some Stories Are Better than Others* (pp. 119–134). Philadelphia: Brunner/Mazel.

Hoyt, M.F., & Combs, G. (1996). On ethics and the spiritualities of the surface: A conversation with Michael White. In M.F. Hoyt (Ed.), *Constructive Therapies* (Vol. 2, pp. 33–59). New York: Guilford Press. Reprinted in M.F. Hoyt, *Interviews with Brief Therapy Experts* (pp. 71–96). New York: Brunner-Routledge, 2001.

294 Michael F. Hoyt

Hoyt, M.F., & Ritterman, M. (2012). Brief therapy in a taxi. *The Milton H. Erickson Foundation Newsletter, 32*(1), 8.

Jamplosky, G. (1979). *Love is Letting Go of Fear.* Berkeley, CA: Ten Speed Publishing/Random House.

Jung, C.G. (1966a). Problems of modern psychotherapy. In *The Collected Works of C.G. Jung* (2nd ed., Vol. 16, pp. 53–75). Princeton, NJ: Bollingen/Princeton University Press. (work originally published 1931)

Jung, C.G. (1966b). Fundamental questions of psychotherapy. In *The Collected Works of C.G. Jung* (2nd ed., Vol. 16, pp. 111–125). Princeton, NJ: Bolligen/Princeton University Press. (work originally published 1951)

Keeney, B. (2009). *The Creative Therapist: The Art of Awakening a Session.* New York: Routledge.

Kottler, J.A. (1993). *On Being a Therapist* (rev. ed.) San Francisco: Jossey-Bass.

Kottler, J.A. (2000). *Doing Good: Passion and Commitment for Helping Others.* New York: Brunner-Routledge.

Kottler, J.A., & Carlson, J. (2008). *Their Finest Hour: Master Therapists Share Their Greatest Success Stories.* Bethel, CT: Crown House Publishing.

Lomas, P. (1973). *True and False Experience: The Human Element in Psychotherapy.* New York: Taplinger.

Lorca, F.G. (1998). Play and theory of the duende. In *In Search of Duende* (C. Maurer, Ed.), New York: New Directions. (work originally published 1933)

Minuchin, S. (1992). The restoried history of family therapy. In J.K. Zeig (Ed.), *The Evolution of Psychotherapy: The Second Conference* (pp. 3–10). New York: Brunner/Mazel.

Norcross, J.C., & Guy, J.D., Jr. (2007). *Leaving It at the Office: A Guide to Psychotherapist Self-Care.* New York: Guilford Press.

O'Hanlon, B. (1999). Not strategic, not systemic: Still clueless after all these years. In *Evolving Possibilities: Selected Papers of Bill O'Hanlon* (S. O'Hanlon & B. Bertolino, Eds.; pp. 45–49). New York: Brunner/Mazel.

Orlinsky, D.E., & Ronnestad, M.H. (2004). *How Psychotherapists Develop: A Study of Therapeutic Work and Professional Growth.* Washington, DC: APA Books.

Post, S., & Niemark, J. (2007). *Why Good Things Happen to Good People: The Exciting New Research that Proves the Link Between Doing Good and Living a Longer, Healthier, Happier Life.* New York: Broadway Books.

Richeport-Haley, M., & Carlson, J. (Eds.). (2010). *Jay Haley Revisited.* New York: Routledge.

Rilke, R.M. (2004). *Letters to a Young Poet* (rev. ed., M.D. Herter Norton, Trans.). New York: Norton. (Letter 8 originally written 1904)

Rossi, E., Whitaker, C.A., & Haley, J. (1982). Creativity: A special interaction hour. In J.K. Zeig (Ed.), *Ericksonian Approaches to Hypnosis and Psychotherapy* (pp. 477–487). New York: Brunner/Mazel.

Short, D. (2010). *Transformational Relationships: Deciphering the Social Matrix in Psychotherapy.* Phoenix, AZ: Zeig, Tucker & Theisen.

Stovholt, T.M., & Trotter-Mathison, M.J. (2010). *The Resilient Practitioner: Burnout Prevention and Self-Care Strategies for Counselors, Therapists, Teachers, and Health Professionals* (2nd ed.). Needham Heights, MA: Allyn & Bacon.

Sue, D.W. (2004). Whiteness and ethnocentric monoculturism: Making the "invisible" visible. *American Psychologist, 59*, 761–769.

Sullivan, H.S. (1964). The data of psychiatry. In *The Fusion of Psychiatry and Social Science* (pp. 32–55). New York: Norton. (work originally published 1938)

Sussman, M.B. (1992). *A Curious Calling: Unconscious Motivations for Practicing Psychotherapy.* Northvale, NJ: Jason Aronson.

Sussman, M.B. (Ed.). (1995). *A Perilous Calling: The Hazards of Psychotherapy Practice.* New York: Wiley.

Szasz, T. (2005, December). Topical panel (M. Munion, Moderator) on *The History of Psychotherapy.* The Evolution of Psychotherapy 5th Conference, Anaheim, CA.

Verghese, A. (2010). *Cutting for Stone: A Novel.* New York: Vintage/Random House.

Walsh, R. (1999). *Essential Spirituality: The Seven Central Practices.* New York: Wiley.

Walsh, R. (2011). Lifestyle and mental health. *American Psychologist, 66*(7), 579–592.

Watzlawick, P. (1983). *The Situation is Hopeless, but Not Serious.* New York: Norton.

Weakland, J.H. (1994). Erickson's essence: A personal view. In J.K. Zeig (Ed.), *Ericksonian Methods: The Essence of the Story* (pp. 287–291). New York: Brunner/Mazel.

Whitaker, C.A. (1975). Psychotherapy of the absurd: With a special emphasis on the psychotherapy of aggression. *Family Process, 14,* 1–16.

Whitaker, C.A. (1989). *Midnight Musings of a Family Therapist* (M.O. Ryan, Ed.). New York: Norton.

Yalom, I.D. (1992). *When Nietzsche Wept: A Novel of Obsession.* New York: Basic Books.

Yalom, I. (2002). *The Gift of Therapy: An Open Letter to a New Generation of Therapists and Their Patients.* New York: HarperCollins.

Zeig, J.K. (2011, December). *Beethoven and Erickson.* Keynote speech, 11th International Congress on Ericksonian Approaches to Hypnosis and Psychotherapy. Phoenix, AZ.

Zur, O. (1994). Psychotherapists and their families: The effect of the practice on the individual and family dynamics. *Psychotherapy in Private Practice, 13*(1), 69–95.